An Old Testament Journey

May We Serve Christ!

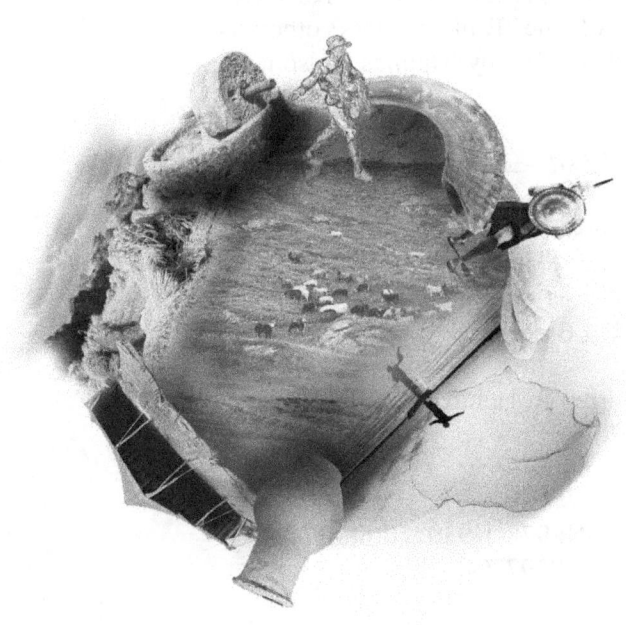

WARREN HENDERSON

All Scripture quotations are from the New King James Version of the Bible, unless otherwise noted. Copyright © 1982 by Thomas Nelson, Inc. Nashville, TN

May We Serve Christ! – An Old Testament Journey

By Warren Henderson
Copyright © 2022

Cover Design: Ben Bredeweg

Published by Warren A. Henderson Publishing
1025 Iron Cap Dr.
Stevensville, MT 59870

Perfect Bound ISBN: 978-1-939770-66-0
eBook ISBN: 978-1-939770-67-7

Copies of *May We Serve Christ! – An Old Testament Journey* are available through various online retailers worldwide. Our website address is: warrenahendersonpublishing.com

Daily Devotions

January 1 – A New Year
Introduction

One day near the end of Christ's earthly pilgrimage, certain Greeks arrived at Jerusalem to observe the Passover feast and to worship God. But their souls were yearning for something beyond religious formality; they asked Philip, *"Sir, we wish to see Jesus"* (John 12:21). *May We See Christ? – An Old Testament Journey* was written to fill the believer's eyes with prophetic allegories, types, and shadows of Christ from the Old Testament. By the light of New Testament truth we are able to appreciate how God the Father previously portrayed His Son in Scripture. Spiritual growth begins when we are in awe of Jesus Christ; otherwise, we will have no appetite for His word or desire to do His good will. The resolve of *May We Serve Christ?* is to better equip believers to trust and obey Christ, and to serve Him as He deems best.

After the Greeks asked Philip "to see Jesus," Philip discussed the matter with Andrew and then both men conveyed the request to the Lord Jesus. The Lord responded to their sincere appeal by saying that He must die soon to be able to share eternal life with them. Those who would receive Him for salvation and then live in obedience to Him would experience the fruitful benefits of His resurrection life. True submission to God's will and faithful service to God are only possible through resurrection power. Because believers are positionally dead to themselves and to the world, each of us has an opportunity to live out what we possess, Christ's life. The lost must see Christ in His Church.

At this moment, each of us is as close to the Lord Jesus Christ as we desire to be. Our patient Savior is always ready to assist anyone genuinely seeking Him and desiring to serve Him in his or her appointed capacity and calling. Through His Word and His Spirit, God aids a true seeker every step of the way into a deeper knowledge of Himself and His purposes. *May We Serve Christ? – An Old Testament Journey* draws practical application from Scripture to convict, to confront, and to encourage us to *"press toward the goal for the prize of the upward call of God in Christ Jesus"* (Phil. 3:14). There is a Savior to know, a work to do, a calling to be fulfilled, and a race to run! As you begin this new year, my prayer is that your daily meditations will draw you into a refreshing and higher experience with our great God and Savior.

January 2 – Perfect Communication
Genesis 1

Our God is a God of perfect communication: *"Let there be light"* (v. 3), *"Let there be a firmament"* (v. 6), and *"Let the waters under the heavens be gathered"* (v. 9), etc. God could have just thought creation into existence, or spoken it into being with one word, but He chose to declare creation order, that we might understand His purposes. Before there was creation, there was communication. God is an articulating God who wants us to comprehend what He reveals to us (Deut. 29:29). We understand, by faith, that creation was spoken into existence (Ps. 33:6-10; Heb. 11:3).

God discloses the first Ten Commandments in Genesis 1. Ten times it is recorded *"And God said...."* All these commands relate to creating or ordering creation, and all ten continue to this day. In contrast to God's faithfulness is man's rebellion against another Ten Commandments given to Israel at Mt. Sinai (Ex. 20). In both cases we see that God is faithful to man, even when man is not faithful to God.

In Genesis 1, God proclaims "it was good" seven times to show that His creative acts perfectly met all His expectations for the purpose of extending an opportunity to mankind to have fellowship with Him. God continues to intimately and perfectly converse with us throughout the remainder of the Old Testament. For example, Psalm 100:3 reads, *"Know that the Lord, He is God; It is He who has made us, and not we ourselves; we are His people and the sheep of His pasture."* God not only wanted Israel to understand that He created them, but that He created them to be His people (His sheep) – He wanted them to appreciate that fact.

This type of intimate communication continues into the New Testament also. As terms like, *"His people"* and *"His sheep"* used in John 21:16 and Revelation 21:3 convey ideas of relationship and fellowship. God desires personal communion with us which is perfectly expressed in the Lord Jesus, God's living Word (John 1:1; 1 Jn. 1:1). "Word" is derived from the Greek word *logos* which means, far more than the act of speaking; it includes the aspirations of the mind also. The Father wants us to know His Son intimately and thereby know Him. He yearns for us to understand His eternal love – a love so infinite that He was not willing to withhold His Son from suffering and dying for us. Christ is God's perfect and intimate expression of truth and love to humanity.

January 3 – Time to Rest
Genesis 2

The key words in Genesis 2:1-3 are "seven" and "sanctified." The number seven is God's number and a fundamental building block throughout Scripture. God speaks of completeness or perfection through the number seven. The word "sanctified" means "set apart" or "holy." The week of creation ended with a day of rest for the Lord. This was not a divine response to weariness, but to satisfaction (Isa. 40:28). Although God did not command mankind to keep the Sabbath at this time, He taught, through example, the principle of resting one day in seven. Later, He would command that the seventh day be "set apart" by the children of Israel (Ex. 20:8-11).

We never read of God resting again in all of Scripture, but to the contrary, God is laboring for the redemption and restoration of man throughout the biblical account until final rest is again achieved in Revelation 21 and 22. The Lord Jesus said, *"My Father has been working until now, and I have been working"* (John 5:17). There are only two Sabbaths that God could truly call a day of rest – the seventh day of creation and the eternal rest after the new creation (i.e., the eternal state, Rev. 21:1-2). Only then may He finally cease from laboring. The Son finished His laboring on earth at Calvary, but in heaven He continues now to make intercession for the Church.

Should a Christian observe the seventh day of the week as a day of rest? God has displayed a pattern in which we should rest one day in seven, yet this is not commanded. Obviously, periodic rest would help remedy physical fatigue and emotional strain. But concerning religious appointment, the Lord Jesus reaffirmed all of the Ten Commandments except "keep the Sabbath day holy." The writer of Hebrews instructs Jewish believers to *"go forth, therefore, to Him outside the camp, bearing His reproach"* (Heb. 13:13, KJV); they were no longer under the law but under a new covenant of grace in Christ (Heb. 13:13). The Lord issued no such command to the Church, as individual believers can worship God anytime and anywhere as believer priests (John 4:23-24). The early Church did not gather on Saturday, but Sunday – the first day of the week – Christ's resurrection day (1 Cor. 16:2; Acts 20:7). The believers then gathered to worship their Savior, not to keep the law. This is why John refers to Sunday as the Lord's Day (Rev. 1:10).

January 4 – The Gift of Work
Genesis 2

  The devil is working fervently to erode the foundational building blocks of a meaningful and healthy society that God decreed in Genesis 1 and 2: What is life? What is the origin of life? What is gender? What is marriage? What is work? Adam was a real man that God fashioned on the sixth day of creation. He is not some fairy tale character or mythological person. The New Testament speaks of Adam as the first created man and as such is the basis for several salvation doctrines. The genealogy of Mary, Christ's mother, is traced back to Adam (Luke 3:23-38). In Romans 5, Paul explains the consequences to humanity because of Adam's sin and then shows how through the obedience of the last Adam (Christ) the damages of disobedience by the first Adam can be repaired (1 Cor. 15). The Lord Jesus spoke of Adam and Eve when addressing the Pharisees about God's plan for marriage in Matthew 19. Those who deny that there was a real Adam, call God a liar and deny the fall of man and the consequent need of a Savior.

  After God created man, He planted a garden and placed man in it. Genesis 2:15 states that Adam had the opportunity to please God by tending and keeping the garden. As this work setting is prior to God cursing the ground in Genesis 3, it is hard to comprehend what exactly Adam's work consisted of. The Hebrew word translated *"to tend"* is *abad*, which means "to serve." Whatever work Adam did do, it was his assigned service and his opportunity to prove his love for his Creator.

  God labored six days and then rested the seventh. He continued to rest until man created work for Him through sin. God will restore His peace to creation, and He will finally rest in the age to come when all wickedness is vanquished and the redeemed of mankind are again with Him in Paradise. Until that time the Church should be laboring diligently. Why? Because man again has the privilege to demonstrate love for the Creator through working the revealed will of God. He in turn labors with us for the cause of righteousness and to affect His own glory (1 Cor. 3:9). *"And whatever you do, do it heartily, as to the Lord and not to men, knowing that from the Lord you will receive the reward of the inheritance; for you serve the Lord Christ"* (Col. 3:23-24). The Lord is worthy of all our best efforts without any reward, and yet, He still shares with us what is His.

January 5 – The First Question
Genesis 3

In Eden, God enjoyed walking with Adam in the cool of the day (perhaps morning and night). This communion was tragically broken on the day man ignored God's only restriction of continued life in Eden. On that sad day man ate from the prohibited tree of the knowledge of good and evil. The cost of savoring the forbidden fruit was immensely high, for our first parents traded a refreshing continuous life with God for a sorrow-filled and brief existence.

There were two notable trees in Eden: the Tree of Life and the Tree of the Knowledge of Good and Evil. As one exercised faith in the partaking of the Tree of Life, rather than the Tree of Death, immortality of the body was maintained. Both trees likely presented low-hanging branches laden with accessible fruit. There was nothing magical in the fruit, but grace was imputed through an operation of faith in God's Word to do what was right instead of what was unlawful.

The first rebel led an angelic revolt against God and now assisted man in his rebellion. Satan side-stepped Adam's authority and directed his assault on the unprotected woman. Fueled by his own jealousy of God and His glory, Satan beguiled her through a barrage of deceptive tactics. His goal was to stir up self-focus and to diminish her perceived need for God. While more high-tech, his core strategies against mankind have not changed since the dreadful day sin intruded into humanity.

Satan begins by casting doubt on what God actually said: *"Has God indeed said, 'You shall not eat of every tree of the garden?'"* (v. 1). The first question in Scripture belongs to Satan; its purpose was not to provoke rational thought but to instill doubt and invoke rebellion. The tactic worked on the woman, who quickly slid from the ground of faith into human reasoning. Satan's question to the woman has a flavor of unfairness: "Could God be good and limit you in such an unfair way?" "Surely a good God would not keep you from all that is good." Man was invited to eat from every tree in the garden, save one. Yet, the serpent beckoned mankind to focus upon the only one off limits. Satan enjoys sowing dissatisfaction. When embraced, dissatisfaction stirs up doubts concerning God's goodness and wisdom. Dear believer, the next time Satan tempts you not to be content, train your eye upon all the blessings in Christ and not what, in your own mind, you lack or deserve.

May We Serve Christ!

January 6 – The Way of Cain
Genesis 4

God blessed the marriage union of Adam and Eve with children. Genesis 4 records the names of two boys that were born to our first parents: Cain and Abel. There were other children also; certainly there were daughters that later became wives for the sons. In the early days of humanity there were no mutant genes in the human DNA so no genetic harm would have resulted from brother-sister marriages.

Scripture does not specifically state that Cain was the first child born, though he may well have been. The Bible records Cain's birth and that of his younger brother Abel because the progression of the narrative is connected with them. These two boys were not born innocent, as their parents had been created, but as sinners with a fallen nature. Eve rejoiced at Cain's birth, but she would soon learn that nothing born of the sinful flesh would continue to please God. Cain in the process of time became a gardener. His younger brother Abel matured and became a shepherd of sheep. There is little doubt that mom and dad explained the horrible events that had tragically transpired in the Garden of Eden to their sons and daughters. Certainly, Adam explained to his children God's means of satisfying their need of clothing by killing and taking the hides of innocent animals, a practice they continued doing to provide clothing for themselves and their family.

Abel was a "keeper of sheep." He took the best sheep of his flock and approached God by offering a burnt sacrifice. God had respect for Abel's offering because it pictured the future means in which He would reconcile mankind to Himself – through the death of His Son the Lord Jesus.

In contrast, Cain was a "tiller of the ground" and brought to God what he had labored for – the fruit from a cursed ground. There is nothing naturally originating from that which is cursed that can please God. The fruit Cain offered to God represented his accomplishments (his good works) and not an innocent substitute to bear judgment in his place – there was no life in the fruit. Cain chose to worship God his way or, as the New Testament puts it, "the way of Cain" – a theology denying the atonement of sin through blood sacrifice. Cain's way denied his guiltiness and his need for a Savior. But even after God pleaded with Cain to approach Him the right way, Cain rejected the way of life. In short, Cain's way is the wide way to hell which many trod down today!

January 7 – Walking With God
Genesis 5

Adam was only 622 years old when Enoch was born. Surely, Adam told his great-great-great-great-grandson, Enoch, how he and his wife walked with God in the cool of the day. Perhaps Enoch, after learning of the intimate fellowship that Adam and God enjoyed in the Garden of Eden, longed for that intimacy too.

Walking with God starts with a desire. Enoch had that desire, and he enjoyed 300 years of closeness with God before God took him home. I like to think that one day God and Enoch were just strolling across a meadow together when God turned to his friend Enoch and said, "I have enjoyed walking with you, Enoch, these last 300 years. Instead of us saying goodbye today, would you like to come home with Me? Then we will always be together." I think Enoch smiled and affirmed his desire, and then in a blink of an eye, he was gone.

What does it mean to walk with God? Firstly, walking with God requires faith. A quick review of Enoch's testimony per Heb. 11:5-6 reveals that he pleased God, for it is impossible to please God without faith in God. Therefore, Enoch had faith in God. He believed what God had revealed to him and trusted God for all that had not been disclosed to him (Rom.1:17).

Secondly, we read in 1 John 1:5-7 that walking with God requires walking in the light of divine truth. A willingness to walk according to revealed truth brings happy fellowship with God and with other saints. If we choose to walk in darkness, we are inviting injury. Believers are to walk not as fools (Eph. 5:15), or as we formerly did in the vanities of our minds (Eph. 5:8), but walk as children of light. Enoch could walk with God because he was in agreement with God about the matter of sin. For *"can two walk together except they be agreed?"* (Amos 3:3). Light has no communion with darkness; thus Enoch walked with God according to divine truth and in moral integrity.

Thirdly, we read these words from the prayer of Jabez in 1 Chron. 4:10: *"that Your hand might be with me."* Like Jabez, Enoch wanted intimacy and close fellowship with God. And wherever there is a man that desires a closer fellowship with God, the Creator will be eager to reveal Himself in new and meaningful ways. By walking with God, Enoch benefitted from God's companionship and protection.

January 8 – When it Comes
Genesis 6

Enoch's conversion seems to be about the time of his son Methuselah's birth. Enoch was 65 years old when Methuselah was born. In a mysterious way, the birth of his son was a prophecy in itself – Methuselah's name means "when it comes." God was telling Enoch that as long as his son lived the world would live, but when his son died, the world would die. How do you think this knowledge affected Enoch's life? He did not know when his son would die, so he had to live in constant anticipation of suddenly being ushered into the presence of God. Likewise, the Church operates today with the anticipation of suddenly being ushered into the presence of Christ: *"Looking for the blessed hope and glorious appearing of our great God and Savior, Jesus Christ"* (Tit. 2:13). The Lord's return may not be immediate, but it is imminent (1 Thess. 4:13-18)!

So, when did Methuselah die? Methuselah was 187 years old when his son Lamech was born, and Lamech was 182 years old when Noah was born. Noah was 600 years old when the flood came (7:6). Hence, Methuselah was 969 years old when the flood came, and Scripture records that he lived 969 years – he died the year the flood occurred.

God was greatly grieved over the wickedness of mankind – the behavior of man had sunk into the miry depths of his depraved heart. So God told a righteous man named Noah that He was pronouncing judgment upon mankind *"for the earth is filled with violence through them* [wicked man]*; and behold, I will destroy them with the earth"* (vv. 13-14). The scope of Calvary is here pre-witnessed – in that, by one act, God could judge all that was wicked and at the same time bestow a marvelous provision of grace on the righteous, for *"Noah found grace in the eyes of the Lord"* (v. 8). Those with a humble heart choosing to obey God's truth receive the undeserved favor of heaven.

The fact that Methuselah lived longer than any other man in the Bible illustrates God's long suffering nature. 2 Peter 3:9 reads, *"The Lord ... is longsuffering toward us, not willing that any should perish but that all should come to repentance."* The Lord was longsuffering because Christ, through Noah, was preaching repentance to the lost (1 Pet. 3:18-20). This preaching lasted until the ark was completed. But eight souls only entered in by faith and were saved from God's wrath.

January 9 – Being Available
Genesis 11

For over 400 years, God suffered a pagan world in silence. Then suddenly the God of glory appeared to a man named Abram. Until Genesis 12, God had been dealing with mankind as a whole, now He would focus His sovereign dealings in the life of one man. Through Abram would come both the written Word of God and the Living Word of life. Despite mankind's overall propensity to rebel, God would bestow mercy again to humanity by making another covenant with a man named Abram and his seed. Through him, God was promising to unconditionally bless all the families of the earth (12:3). The blessing would ultimately come through Christ and would be imparted to all those who would, like Abram, embrace God's revealed truth by faith.

What do we know about Abram? From Joshua 24:2, we learn that those in Abram's family were idol worshipers. He was thus, *"a Syrian ready to perish"* (Deut. 26:5). Stephen informs us that the *"God of Glory"* appeared to Abram in Ur and called Abram to a land He would give him. Why did God pick a man tainted by idol worship for His covenant? God had to choose somebody – He chose Abram (Isa. 51:1-2). God rules over His creation in whatever way He deems to be the best. God made a sovereign choice to bring forth the Messiah through Abram. So, God called Abram to leave his country, to separate from his kindred, and to go forth to inherit a land he had never seen.

Because Abram believed God – God could use him as a fit and faithful example of a pilgrim, elevate his name among men, forge a nation from him, and award him a land of his own. The mystery here lies in the recesses of God's mind, for certainly He foreknew of Abram's faith and proper choice, yet chose him as a vessel of mercy and a tool of righteousness. The choice of Abram to believe God's revealed truth and to reject the social pull of Ur accomplished for him what it does for an individual today when they believe the gospel and reject the wisdom and toxic influence of the world. Namely, it makes him a worshipper of God and a citizen of heaven and, thus, a pilgrim and a stranger on earth as God's witness. Abram's life characterizes that of a Christian who embraces and enjoys the cross but loathes the world. Let us remember, that God "designs," but man is presented a choice in "doing." Let us be trusting, obedient, and available.

May We Serve Christ!

January 10 – Too Much Stuff
Genesis 13

A famine caused Abram to trust in the resources of Egypt (i.e., the world), rather than the Lord's hand. The Lord intervened to deliver Abram and his family from Egypt's grip, but he returned to Canaan only to face another difficulty. Lot had been adversely affected by the trip to Egypt and no longer desired to walk by faith and pursue personal integrity. Besides this, Abram and Lot could no longer dwell together because they were rich in cattle, silver and gold, and they had an abundance of stuff. This is the first mention of "riches" in the Bible. What effect does wealth and too many possessions have on God's people? The result is often strife among the brethren. When brethren strive together, they cease to be a testimony for God.

How are brethren to consider their possessions? The early church held the proper view of "equality" and thus maintained and enjoyed unity. *"Those who believed were of one heart and one soul; neither did anyone say that any of the things he possessed was his own, but they had all things in common"* (Acts 4:32). Paul taught that there should be equality among the brethren: *"For I do not mean that others should be eased and you burdened; but by an equality, that now at this time your abundance may supply their lack, that their abundance also may supply your lack – that there may be equality* (2 Cor. 8:13-14). If a brother is in need and another brother is able to meet that need, he should readily do so. Equality is not communism. Holding all things in equality is not the same as everyone having equal portions. When God's people value God and what He values there is unity, but if their focus is shifted unto temporal things, envy, dissatisfaction, and coveting occur.

Abram and Lot had to separate, and though Abram held the title deed to the land, he waived his rights for the sake of achieving peace and allowed Lot to select his new home in the land. Lot and Abram were dwelling among the Canaanites and Perizzites, and Abram could not endure the idea of there being discord among the brethren in the presence of their enemies. This is why believers are instructed not to take each other to civil court to resolve a quarrel (1 Cor. 6:1-8). The minute matters we bicker about are nothing compared to hindering the spread of the gospel message or publicly defaming our Lord's name. It is better to suffer loss of what is temporal to gain what is eternal.

January 11 – Faith that Counts
Genesis 15

Perhaps Abram was starting to doubt God's promise of an heir as he and Sarai continued to age and yet had no children. This would be the natural tendency of anyone, as a decade had passed since God's initial promise of children. God told Abram to *"Look now toward heaven."* Faith would require Abram to look away from Sarai, his natural abilities, and all that was earthly. When Abram had the proper "up look," God reaffirmed that *"his seed"* would be innumerable.

The fact that Abram attempted to help God accomplish His promise by offering Him Eliezer his servant as an heir, indicates some doubt in Abram's mind concerning what God had previously told him. Eliezer represents man's practical solution to the problem. It was the custom to pass your inheritance on to your chief servant if you had no children. God had a different plan, one that would show His creativity and ability and would leave no room for man to boast. The longer Sarai was barren and went beyond childbearing years the greater the miracle would be.

God's way is not man's way. God's way is perfect (Ps. 18:30) and His ways are past finding out (Rom. 11:33). Hence, mankind's limited understanding of himself and his Creator, offer the very medium in which faith in God must be exercised. True faith is the ability of the soul to reach beyond what can be verified by human senses and to trust in what cannot be proven through reason. We must have faith to please God, *"for without faith it is impossible to please Him"* (Heb. 11:6).

God performed no signs and wonders for Abram. He simply reaffirmed His promise to Abram. That was good enough for him – he simply believed God, who responded by accrediting a standing of righteousness to Abram's account. God wanted no confusion on this matter of salvation, for the words "believe," "counted," and "righteousness" all occur in Scripture for the first time in verse 6: *"He believed in the Lord, and He accounted it to him for righteousness."*

Abram's faith preceded God's imputed righteousness. Yet, God's grace preceded Noah's imputed righteousness. Combining these two truths we have *"For by grace you have been saved through faith, and that not of yourselves; it is the gift of God"* (Eph. 2:8). Both God's means of salvation through grace and man's responsibility to lay hold of this gift by personal faith are clearly presented in Scripture.

January 12 – New Things
Genesis 17

After thirteen years of silence (Gen. 17:25), God again appeared to Abram. The number thirteen is associated with rebellion in the Bible (its first mention is in Gen. 14:4). In this chapter, thirteen relates to Abram's effort to obtain an heir outside of God's will. Therefore, God waited thirteen years to speak with Abram again and when He did, He reminded Abram of His "covenant" thirteen times.

In Genesis 15, Abram's *justification* was witnessed, but in Genesis 17, it is his *sanctification* unto God that is paramount. God was calling Abram to separate from the flesh's desires and ways to be nigh to Him. God appeared and spoke to Abram, *"I am Almighty God; walk before Me and be blameless"* (v. 1). These words should deeply penetrate the heart of everyone professing to know God. Spiritual life would be incomplete if we had salvation without Christ dwelling richly in our hearts by faith (Eph. 3:17). God's command *"Be ye holy for I am holy"* is applied both to those in the Old Testament and in the New (Lev. 11:44; 1 Pet. 1:16). Understanding who God is should cause His children to walk in a way that reflects the holy family resemblance.

Abram, who stumbled in his faith in Genesis 16, was now exhorted to *walk before God* perfectly in Genesis 17. Abram needed a complete walk of faith! God aided Abram in his walk by changing his name; this would remind him who he was in God's sight. His original name meant "exalted father," yet he had lived 86 years without children. His new name, "Abraham," meant "father of multitudes." Abraham's new name may have seemed humorous at the time, but in time, he would father many nations through Ishmael, Isaac, and the sons of Keturah.

Sarai also received a new name, Sarah, meaning "princess," for she would be the mother of kings and nations. The added Hebrew suffix in both Abram's and Sarai's new names has the "hawm" or "raw" sounds, respectively. The only way to properly make the "aw" sound is to exhale a large volume of air through one's open mouth. God would have had to breathe upon His pilgrim family to say their new names. When God breathed on Adam, he became a living being, and when the Lord breathed upon the disciples, they received a new life in the Holy Spirit (John 20:22). When God changed Abram and Sarai's names, He was giving them new identities – a new life in Him – a new beginning.

January 13 – A New Sign
Genesis 17

Besides a new name and a new walk, Abraham would also receive a new sign of the covenant God had made with him. No doubt Abraham was excited to learn that God was going to give him a sign concerning the covenant. However, the sign was not a wonder in the sky or a miracle of healing, it was circumcision. So Abraham, a 99-year-old man, and all the males of his house were circumcised the very day God had commanded it (vv. 26-27). Then, his descendants for thousands of years would continue this symbolic ritual to honor God and to acknowledge His covenant with them. Paul tells us in Romans 4:11 that circumcision was *"a seal of the righteousness of the faith which he had while still uncircumcised."* Circumcision was a "token" of Abraham's righteous standing gained by faith in God's promise.

Why circumcision as a sign? What is the organ of the body that best identifies an individual as a man? Right – that's it. So, by stripping away a piece of foreskin from this organ, God was symbolizing the stripping away of an old identity and the reliance on God for a new one. The act of circumcision in Genesis 17 complements beautifully the name changes given Abram and Sarai. God was about to enact His covenant with them by giving them a son. It was only fitting that they realize their new identities as God's chosen people and as human instruments to bless the entire world. Abraham was already declared justified by God before circumcision was instituted (Rom. 4:11). The "circumcised life" was something Abraham was living before God.

It is the same for the believer today. When individuals humble themselves as sinners before God and confess their need for a Savior, God responds by cleansing and regenerating them (Tit. 3:5), sealing them with the Holy Spirit (Eph. 1:13), and declaring them righteous (Rom. 4:4-5). *"If anyone is in Christ, he is a new creation; old things have passed away; behold, all things have become new"* (2 Cor. 5:17). However, our new identity in Christ demands that we live the "circumcised life," which is the "cutting off" or "putting to death" of the desires and the will of our flesh. Paul summarizes in Romans 2:29 that it is the circumcision of the heart God wants in a believer's life, not just an outward show. A circumcised life is one that acknowledges being dead to self and alive in Christ.

January 14 – Worship for the Lord
Genesis 18

In Genesis 17, God revealed Himself to Abraham as the Almighty God – the only One who can keep promises despite every difficulty. This revelation required Abraham to have full confidence in God and maintain a blameless walk before God. He was to have no confidence in his own flesh. In Genesis 18, we are permitted to witness the privileged communion for those who walk by faith with Almighty God.

Believers today may indulge in the same privileges that Abraham enjoyed in Genesis 18 (e.g., Acts 2:42). Abraham offered worship to the Lord (vv. 1-8), received revelation from the Lord (vv. 9-15), enjoyed fellowship with the Lord (vv. 16-22), and offered intercession before the Lord (vv. 23-33). Those in communion with the Lord may enjoy these same privileges regardless of the age in which they reside.

The Lord appeared again to Abraham near the terebinth trees of Mamre. Though it was the heat of the day, Abraham ran to and bowed himself before his visitors. The Hebrew word for "bow" is *shachah*, which is the usual word for "worship" in the Old Testament. As this is the first occurrence of *shachah* in Scripture, it seems only fitting that the "first mention" of man bowing down and worshipping his Creator be established as appropriate throughout the remainder of the Bible.

Abraham wanted to do whatever he could to "refresh" the Lord; *"Please let a little water be brought, and wash your feet, and rest yourselves under the tree"* (v. 4). Observe that Abraham is the one primarily speaking in verses 1-8. Before Abraham does anything, he proposed what he would like to do and then received the Lord's approval before doing it: *"Do as you have said"* (v. 5). This brief approval is all that the Lord says in verses 1-8. Today, we have Scripture that tells us how the Lord appreciates being worshipped by His people (Luke 22:19-20; 1 Cor. 11:23-34). We do not have to ask Him, but Abraham did not know what the Lord would appreciate, so he did ask. This shows us that true worship must be founded in revealed truth to please God, and no amount of emotionalism or religious fanfare can acceptably replace the behavior that God expects.

Abraham and Sarah set a table for the Lord and His two angels under the shade of the tree. And though the Lord did not need food, He waited for it and ate it to express His appreciation of their worship.

January 15 – Revelation From the Lord
Genesis 18

With the Lord's question in verse 9, *"Where is Sarah your wife?"* the narrative transitions from Abraham worshipping the Lord to Abraham receiving revelation from the Lord. Abraham promptly answered, *"Here, in the tent."* He will not say anything else until verse 23. In the previous section on worship, Abraham did all the talking, except for the Lord's approval of what His servant proposed to do for Him. However, in verses 10-15, God informs Abraham of what He needs to know and therefore Abraham stands silently and listens. As with the "apostles' doctrine" in the Church Age, what matters in life is what God says is important. We also would do well to show reverence for God's Word by listening to it, heeding it, and not adding to it.

The Lord then told Abraham, *"I will certainly return to you according to the time of life, and behold, Sarah your wife shall have a son"* (v. 10). Sarah overheard this conversation and laughed within herself. The Lord overheard Sarah's doubts and asked her why she laughed. The Lord responded to her disbelief with a staggering question to assert one of the greatest expressions of truth in the Bible: *"Is anything too hard for the Lord?"* (v. 14). The obvious the answer is "no" – there is nothing too hard for the Lord. In responding to Sarah's laugh, the Lord affirmed His attributes and His trustworthy character as a covenant-keeping God. No doubt Sarah was stunned by what she had just heard and having joined her husband denied laughing within herself (v. 15). But the Lord again admonished her for doing so. Regardless of the nature of her doubt, Hebrews 11:11 affirms that she was a woman of faith.

Twice in this portion of Scripture the Lord declares, *"I will return to you"* (vv. 10, 14). These words have encouraged God's people through the ages not to lose heart. The night before the Lord Jesus was crucified He comforted His disciples with the same promise, *"I will come again and receive you to Myself"* (John 14:3). The final chapter of Scripture declares three times, *"I come quickly."* For anyone else but the Lord of Glory to make such a promise would be presumptuous. Dear believer, don't lose heart; He is really coming back for you! May we listen to and believe the One who is always faithful and able to do exactly what He says He will do!

January 16 – Communion With the Lord
Genesis 18

After dinner, Abraham walked with his three guests towards Sodom (v. 16). Having received revelation from the Lord in verses 10-15, Abraham now enjoyed communion with the Lord as they walked along together (vv. 16-22). Genesis 18:17 should be an encouragement to all of us who talk to ourselves on occasion, for the Lord said: *"Shall I hide from Abraham what I am doing?"* It is possible that the Lord was talking to the angels with Him, but it seems more likely that He is speaking aloud for Abraham's benefit.

The Lord encourages His servant's heart by informing him that he will be faithful to lead his family in righteousness and justice and be greatly blessed for doing so (v. 19). Righteousness and justice are divine qualities that do not vary. God was informing Abraham that he would not lean on his emotions or the opinions of others to guide his family, but would be faithful to honor the Lord. Notice that Abraham does not say a word as they walk along.

On a human level, we normally think of companionship consisting of mutual communication between two people that enjoy each other's presence. So it may seem strange to us, that the Lord is doing all the talking as He and Abraham walked along together. The prophecy by Zephaniah pertaining to how the Lord will behave towards Israel in the Kingdom Age will help answer this quandary: *"The Lord your God in your midst, the Mighty one, will save; He will rejoice over you with gladness, He will quiet you with His love, He will rejoice over you with singing"* (Zeph. 3:17). Can you imagine the Creator of the universe singing songs of gladness over you and quieting you with His lovely presence? What will it be like to have everything that has ever burdened our soul and caused us sorrow to be instantly gone? Not just Israel, but all the redeemed, will be blessed by the Lord's songs of love and His charming company. There will be nothing to complain about, nothing to petition the Lord about, no guidance to be sought; rather, believers will bask in the pure peace and tranquility of God's presence – now that is profound soul-satisfying fellowship!

All of Genesis 18 speaks of a righteous man's communion with God. This chapter is in striking contrast to God's disposition towards carnal Lot in Genesis 19, for the angels declined his offered hospitality.

January 17 – Intercession Before the Lord
Genesis 18

Besides visibly investigating Sodom's wickedness, the Lord also came to the earth to seek an intercessor for those under condemnation. He found one in Abraham who willingly stood in the gap for Sodom. In verses 1-8, Abraham worked to refresh the heart of his God, then stood in silence to listen to God's Word (vv. 10-15), and then walked quietly along with the Lord while enjoying His fellowship (vv. 16-21). In verses 22-33, the Lord and Abraham were left alone after the angels departed, so Abraham stepped near to the Lord to intercede for Sodom.

This is amazing! The Lord came down from heaven, took human form, waited on a meal He did not need to eat, walked with Abraham in the heat of the day, just so Abraham could take a step or two to intercede for the wicked. The scene illustrates the ease of accessibility the redeemed have to petition the One controlling all human affairs to show mercy to those rejecting His Lordship. Hence, it should be no surprise then that it is Abraham who now does most of speaking.

The man of faith was in touch with the character of his God and bravely pleaded with Him not to slay the righteous with the wicked. The Lord does not reprove Abraham's brashness, but rather granted his request to spare the city if it contained fifty righteous souls. Abraham continued to intercede for Sodom, by obtaining the Lord's promise that He will spare Sodom if there were just ten righteous souls found there.

Abraham started this conversation and Abraham also ended it, *"I will speak but once more"* (v. 32). The Lord does not derive sadistic pleasure from judging the wicked; rather, He desires them to *"turn and live!"* [or repent and be saved]*"* (Ezek. 18:32). Indeed, God's righteous character demands that the wicked be judged. However, through the intercession of His people, God's mercy may delay judgment so that more time for repentance and restoration is permitted. This is why God loves the intercession of the righteous; it permits Him to show mercy without compromising His holy character.

Abraham apparently felt that he had successfully interceded for Sodom. How sorrowful he must have been the next morning to look eastward and see a smoldering landscape. What would have happened if Abraham had continued pleading for Sodom instead of quitting when he thought it was safe? Let us keep interceding for the wayward!

January 18 – Immersed in the World
Genesis 19

Lot met the two angels at the city gate of Sodom. Though the angels had been sent to judge Sodom, their twofold ministry is evident for they also *"minister for them who shall be heirs of salvation"* (Heb. 1:14). Yes, God will judge the world, but He also knows how to deliver the righteous, no matter how carnal, out of it! Peter, speaking of Lot, writes: *"Then the Lord knows how to deliver the godly out of temptations and to reserve the unjust under punishment for the day of judgment"* (2 Pet. 2:9).

Lot was concerned with the visitor's safety and offered to provide them lodging for the night at his home. Initially, they refused. What a rebuke to Lot – the angels preferred to abide in the streets of a perverse city than spending an evening with a righteous man living an indulgent life. The angels certainly had no problem sharing Abraham's hospitality earlier in the day. Abraham's tent stands in sharp contrast to Lot's house.

In previous chapters we have witnessed Lot descending step by step through a sequence of compromises, which now have settled him in spiritual carnality. How did he feel about his spiritual condition and the evil situation that was now his? 2 Peter 2:8 informs us that *Lot "dwelling among them, in seeing and hearing, vexed his righteous soul from day to day with their unlawful deeds."* He was miserable and under constant rebuke from his own conscience. Perhaps Lot thought he could change Sodom. Whatever his thinking was, it was flawed. God's message to His people concerning the world and ungodliness has never changed: *"I have come ... to bring them up from the land"* (Ex. 3:8), *"come to Me"* (Ex. 32:26), and *"separate yourselves"* (Num. 16:21). The Lord said to His disciples, *"I chose you out of the world, therefore the world hates you"* (John 15:19). The world hates godliness, and God hates worldliness in the believer's life (Jas. 4:4).

The believer must counterbalance the call to holy separation with the call of the Great Commission – *"Go therefore and make disciples of all the nations..."* (Matt. 28:19). Where is the symmetry between the Lord's commands to "separate" yourselves and to "go out"? It is being in the world, but not of the world. A ship is designed to operate in water, but when water floods into the ship, it ceases to behave as intended; it sinks. Believers are called to be in the world as a testimony for God, but when the world gets into the Christian's life – you're sunk.

January 19 – Remember Lot's Wife
Genesis 19

The fact that Lot and his family are intoxicated with worldliness is plainly evident throughout Genesis 19. Firstly, Lot was so attached to his existence at Sodom that the angels had to lay hold of him and pry him from Sodom (v. 16). Secondly, even after Lot understood that righteous souls must be separated from ungodly living, he still longed to have a bit of the world in his life. The angel told him to separate and to flee to the mountains for safety, but Lot begged him to allow him to dwell in a "little" city (Zoar) that he die not. This was the very problem: Lot was not willing to die to self and live for God. It is a marvelous testimony of God's grace that the selfish request of carnal Lot saved the inhabitants of Zoar from God's wrath! In the end, Lot, a ruined man, found out that the world offered nothing substantial. Lot felt alone and threatened. Though he had a just position, he was estranged from God, and worse yet, he had been deserted by the world. The world had exacted its price and proven its hatred for all that have been declared righteous. At this realization, Lot is driven by his own fears into further isolation.

Lot learned the hard way what Paul would pen later, *"bad company corrupts good character"* (1 Cor. 15:33; NIV). Satan will never entice the believer with pleasure, glamour, and sensuality without a hook in the bait. There is always a hook! Gobbling up the bait ensures double jeopardy to the child of God – a crushing weight of consequences and a throbbing conscience that haunts the believer day and night. Satan will not leave the child of God alone until he has used every effort to force a believer out of communion with God and into the most terrible extremes of evil.

Thirdly, the angels had commanded that they not look back towards Sodom – they were to make a "clean break" from the world. But, the heart of Lot's wife was still in Sodom, and as God rained down fire and brimstone upon the city, she stole a glance at her old life and instantaneously became a pillar of salt. The Hebrew word translated "looked back" is *nabat* which means "to look intently" or "to regard with pleasure." Christian discipleship requires forsaking the pleasures of the world and following Christ unhindered. Hence, Lot's wife was used as an example by the Lord in Luke 17:32 to warn those listening not to think lightly about His offer of salvation. During His earthy ministry the Lord told His listeners to remember only two people – Himself and Lot's wife.

January 20 – Who's Laughing Now?
Genesis 21

In Genesis 17, God promised Abraham that in a year Sarah would bear him a son. God would keep His promise made 25 years earlier. Though man may fret, God is in no hurry in affecting His plans. Sarah bore Abraham a son in her old age and in accordance with God's ultimate plan. The birth of Abraham's son of promise is a splendid picture of the incarnation of the Son of God. *"When the fullness of the time had come, God sent forth His Son"* (Gal. 4:4). Isaac would be Abraham's heir, but it would be through the One Isaac represented, Christ, that all God's promises to Abraham were made secure.

The Lord told Abraham to name his son Isaac, which means, "he laughs." Isaac's name was appropriate seeing that Abraham had laughed in celebrated amazement at God's promise of a natural son (17:17) and that Sarah had laughed within herself in disbelief (18:12). Perhaps their neighbors were laughing at Abraham's name – "the father of multitudes"? But God had the last laugh – He brought into the world a son from the dead womb of an old woman (Rom. 4:19). How did Sarah respond? *"God has made me laugh, and all that hear will laugh with me"* (v. 6). In Genesis 16, she spoke as though God had failed her, but in Genesis 21, she acknowledges God's grandeur and integrity.

Ishmael represents the "frailty of the flesh," while Isaac portrays the "strength of the Spirit." Paul confirms this analogy in Gal. 4:29. God's miracle solution to a barren couple's problem was not "Ishmael changed;" it was "Isaac born." God demonstrates the same activity in the regeneration of the believer (Tit. 3:5) – God's miracle solution to a barren life is eternal life through rebirth, not a "make over" of the old nature, which is putrid to God. Ishmael was the son of a bondwoman (a slave) – illustrating that we are born slaves to sin with no hope of deliverance. Regeneration, however, implants life – God's divine nature within those who accept His offer of salvation (John 1:12-13). No spiritual rebirth – no spiritual life, no spiritual fruit to God, no heaven to enjoy (John 3:3). The birth of Isaac did not improve Ishmael, but it did bring out the hidden opposition to what is begotten of God. Likewise, the two natures within the believer war with each other. God's begotten children must live by faith according to the new nature and not the flesh – for nothing of the flesh pleases God (Rom. 7:18).

January 21 – Mocking Flesh
Genesis 21

Isaac grew and was weaned, which means Sarah nursed him. Like Isaac, a child of God must have *"the pure milk of the Word"* to grow (1 Pet. 2:2). No milk – no growth. Milk provides calcium for strong bones that provide the structure for the body. Many want to grow in the Lord and be strong for Christ, but they are unwilling to suckle the rudiments of the Word in order to develop a strong faith. So Isaac was nursed, but there came a time when he had grown enough to be weaned. Likewise, the writer of Hebrews exhorts believers to move beyond the foundational truths of the faith to meatier subjects, like Christ's priesthood (Heb. 5:11-12). There should be a natural progression of growth of a new convert from being taught and discipled to being a teacher and a discipler.

Abraham made a great feast on the day that Isaac was weaned. Isaac was probably two or three years old and Ishmael was about sixteen. It was Isaac's special day, and Ishmael, the son of Abraham born of the flesh, mocked little Isaac. In a chapter that symbolizes the incarnation and birth of God's own Son (as pictured in Isaac) that which is of the flesh (Ishmael) can have no preeminence. This is why Isaac's name is mentioned six times, but Ishmael's name never appears in the text, though referred to eighteen times. That which is of the flesh will always mock what is spiritual, but it is only what is spiritual that has God's approval.

Sarah pleaded with her husband to banish Hagar and Ishmael – her Isaac would be Abraham's heir. Though the request grieved Abraham, God endorsed the expulsion, for His promises were centered in Isaac – Abraham's seed. Mother and son were put out into the wilderness with only a meager ration of bread and water. This act seems barbaric, unless we recall that Ishmael represents the frailty of Abraham's flesh and the child of God is to make no provision for the flesh. Fleshly impulses are to be *put to death* (Rom. 13:14) so that Christ can be seen in us (2 Cor. 4:10). The Hebrew word *maveth*, translated "death," first appears in Scripture in verse 16. Though murders and deaths were previously recorded, this is the first reference to the act of dying. Hagar and Ishmael were dying. God had promised Abraham to bless Ishmael, so He would not permit them to die. Their experience however, typifies how believers must put to death fleshly deeds and thoughts (Rom. 8:13; Col. 3:5), in order for Christ to be glorified through all our doings.

May We Serve Christ!

January 22 – Birthright for Bean Soup
Genesis 25

Though Jacob was a schemer, Scripture describes him as a "mild man." The Hebrew word for "mild" is *"tam,"* which means "gentle or undefiled" – Jacob preferred the quiet life at home. His twin brother Esau was a man of the field and a hunter. One day Jacob prepared a pot of bean soup. Esau returned from the field and was famished. Esau declared that he would die soon if he did not get something to eat and asked Jacob for a bowl of his soup. Seeing the opportunity, Jacob swapped Esau a bowl of soup and some bread for Esau's birthright. It was customary for the oldest son to get a family blessing from his father before he died and to acquire a double portion of the inheritance.

Esau was a carnal man governed by his fleshy appetites. Esau despised his birthright, which represented his "spiritual heritage." Hence, the writer of Hebrews declares him to be a "profane" person (Heb. 12:16-17) because he did not value spiritual matters (the blessing) over temporal desires (food). Esau pictures the natural man's propensity to be lured by his own lusts and worldliness – to value things seen and not the promises of God. He is not mindful of the future, but when the future arrives, he is remorseful concerning the consequences of past actions, yet not repentant. The "Esaus" of the world are sorry they get caught, sorry they did not think ahead, sorry they did not get what they wanted, but are not repentant before God. Because they do not know God, they cannot walk by faith; therefore, they are blind concerning spiritual and eternal matters. Our world is full of people like Esau. It is no wonder that God declared, *"Jacob have I loved, but Esau have I hated"* (Rom. 9:13). We understand this statement to be in the "comparative" sense and not an "absolute" declaration, for God loves all men, but hates their behavior (Matt. 10:37; Luke 14:26; 2 Pet. 3:9). Even though Esau's behavior grieved the Lord, He still promised to bless him (Gen. 27:38-40).

It is true that God had pre-selected Jacob for His eternal purpose in time (Rom. 9:12), but He did not force Esau to be faithless and rebellious in character. Nor did He seduce Jacob to value the birthright. The application to the Christian is clear. God has a sovereign plan for our lives; let us be in the center of it! In everything we do or say, we must have this eternal perspective in view and ignore carnal impulses.

January 23 – The Peacemaker
Genesis 26

God greatly prospered Isaac while he was living in Gerar – to the extent that he could not dwell there any longer. Accordingly, Abimelech invited him to leave. The Philistines envied Isaac so much that they filled with dirt the wells his father, Abraham, had dug. This created a hardship on Isaac, who had numerous animals to water, and generated an atmosphere of animosity between Abimelech and Isaac. The narrative indicates that Isaac sought to make peace by redigging two wells of his father's at Beersheba (16:14, 21:25-33) before giving over these wells and moving to the valley of Gerar to dig two new wells. The new wells "Esek," meaning "contention," and "Sitnah," meaning "opposition," were also relinquished to the Gerarites to keep peace. Isaac returned to Beersheba and dug a third new well, which was uncontested, and so finally peace was achieved. What a testimony – *"blessed are the peacemakers for they shall be called the sons of God"* (Matt. 5:9). Isaac differs from his father Abraham and his son Jacob in his meekness; he was not aggressive and never engaged in battle.

It was when Isaac moved back towards Beersheba that his circumstances improved. Beersheba means "the well of the oath." There the Lord met with Isaac and reaffirmed the Abrahamic covenant with him. A refreshed Isaac responded by building an altar to worship God. It was at this location that Isaac found both blessing and the peace of God. Isaac took God's promise of blessing so seriously that he decided to dig a well there also to see if God would bless him – which He did. On the very day Abimelech confirmed a peace treaty with Isaac, Isaac's servants struck water while digging a fourth new well.

Paul exhorts us *"to keep the unity of the Spirit in the bond of peace"* (Eph. 4:3). Only the effectual working of the Holy Spirit can create a bond of peace among believers (literally "making us one in thought and action"). We cannot make peace, but we should endeavor to keep what God has created – it is truly sweet! We destroy unity and peace when we lose the mind of Christ and begin to think individually, as though we were not part of the body of Christ. Isaac absorbed injustice and set aside his rights in order to gain peace with Abimelech and God further blessed Isaac through the ordeal. *"If it is possible, as much as depends on you, live peaceably with all men"* (Rom. 12:18).

January 24 – If . . . Then
Genesis 28

As Bethel is some 60 miles north of Beersheba, the first two or three days of Jacob's trip north passed in silence. Coming to the close of another day, Jacob found a stone that he could use for a pillow and sought to retire for the night. While dreaming, Jacob observed holy angels ascending and descending on a broad and extensive ladder reaching from the earth to heaven with God Himself positioned at the top. In the dream, God spoke to Jacob and reconfirmed the covenant He had made with Abraham and Isaac. The Lord told Jacob that He would be Jacob's companion, guide, and protector during his journey and that He would bring him back into the land that He had promised as an inheritance to his descendants (v. 15). What a comfort to know that God is with His people during the arduous times. Being one with Christ means everything that comes into my life also comes into His; thus His promise: *"I will never leave you nor forsake you"* (Heb. 13:5).

Though Jacob had heard about the Lord all his life, he was ignorant of the Lord's presence – something he acknowledged (v. 16). Yes, Jacob knew facts, but he didn't know the Lord in a personal way yet. Notice, the angels ascended the ladder before they descended on it (v. 12). That means that the angels were already there with Jacob – carrying out God's will when the vision began. Afterwards, Jacob realized that God was with him and took his stone pillow, stood it up on end and anointed it with oil. He now called the place "Bethel," which means "the house of God." However, Jacob would soon learn that there was a vast difference between acknowledging the presence of God and sacrificing your life to Him by faith. Though Jacob was a "supplanter" and ignorant of God's presence, the Lord never speaks harshly to Jacob or of Jacob in all of Scripture. God had chosen Jacob for a sovereign purpose, though Jacob was not yet converted.

Note Jacob's conditional pledge to God: *"If God will be with me ... then the Lord shall be my God"* (vv. 20-21). If God would be with him, then he would believe on Him, trust Him, and give Him a tenth of what he had. Some words just do not belong in the same sentence when talking to God: *"if...then," "never...Lord"* (John 13:8), *"me first"* (Luke 9:59) or *"Lord this shall not happen"* (Matt. 16:22). Our obedience to the Lord cannot be optional, delayed, or negotiated.

January 25 – Praying and Planning
Genesis 32

Jacob's anxiety had been escalating for several days because he believed that he was sandwiched between two threatening militant foes – Esau to the west and Laban to the east. God graciously intervened to rescue Jacob from Laban, but now brother Esau was approaching. If Jacob had recognized God's handiwork in buckling Laban's infuriated heart, he would have retained an enormous peace offering of 580 animals with which he meant to bribe Esau and escape his revenge.

Jacob sent out messengers to find Esau and announce his arrival. The messengers were able to return with a report much sooner than expected, because Esau was already advancing towards them with 400 men. The news of Esau's approach was unnerving, and Jacob became *"greatly afraid and distressed"* (v. 7). So what did Jacob do? Did he pray or cry out to God for help? No, not at first; rather, Jacob chose to meet imminent danger by his own devices instead of resting in the Lord – he sought to manage the situation in his own strength and according to his own intellect. As a precautionary measure to reduce his losses if attacked, he divided his people and livestock into two groups. It was only after Jacob finished all his "busy work" to protect himself that he prayed to God for deliverance. This is Jacob's first recorded prayer, and though a lovely petition asking for God's help based on His covenant promises, it was just a bit late to show his complete trust in the Lord.

It is our tendency to either not fully trust the Lord or to add a short prayer to our own arrangements – hoping for a little divine assistance to make our plans come about. That is what Jacob did: he plans (vv. 7-8), he prays (vv. 9-12), he plans (vv. 13-23), he prays (vv. 24-32) and he plans (33:1-3). Yet, if we really want the Lord's blessing we need to first pray to know His mind and then devise plans according. We mock God if we solicit His counsel and assistance when we have already determined what course of action we will pursue. C. H. Mackintosh writes: "We must be really brought to the end of everything with which self has aught to do; for until then God cannot show Himself. But we can never get to the end of our plans until we have been brought to the end of ourselves."[1] The Lord had resolved the quarrel with Laban – why could Jacob not trust Him to work in Esau's heart also? Unknown to Jacob, that was exactly what God was doing.

January 26 – Brokenness
Genesis 32

On the eve of confronting Esau, Jacob had sent his family over the brook Jabbok while he remained on the other side alone. Ironically, Jabbok means "he will empty." This was a critical point in Jacob's life for he was completely alone with God. To be secluded with God is the only true agency of realizing our frail devices and, more importantly, our depraved hearts. The Lord, incognito, visited Jacob, which he later states (Gen. 35:9). It is worthy of note that the Lord began the wrestling match for the Scripture states, *"a Man wrestled with him* [(Jacob)] *until the breaking of day"* (v. 24). But verse 25 also states, *"he* [(Jacob)] *wrestled with Him* [(the Lord)]." Both the Lord and Jacob desired something from the other. Jacob, nearly 100 years old, wanted a blessing from the Lord. The Lord wanted Jacob yielded before Him. If the Lord has ever wrestled with the reader, it is for the same purpose.

Jacob was agonizing about the enemy when he should have been concentrating on obeying God's instructions. But despite Jacob's misplaced focus, in the end the Lord drew out Jacob's faith at Peniel by first withholding what He intended to impart, and then by bestowing it only after Jacob declared, *"I will not let You go unless You bless me!"* (v. 26). This long wrestling match ended with both the Lord and Jacob getting what each wanted: Jacob was clinging to the Lord and the Lord blessed Jacob. The Lord could have "pinned" Jacob at any time, but He was longsuffering and willing to wrestle with Jacob the whole night to teach him brokenness. Jacob had used his resources to outwit Esau, con his father Isaac, and escape from Laban, but Jacob was about to learn he was no match for the Lord. By divine skill, Jacob was crippled, making wrestling very difficult and painful.

Being disabled, Jacob resorted to the only tactic left, holding on to the Lord with all his might. In the end, the Lord was victorious because Jacob's "will" had been broken and his only recourse was to cling to God. It is at this moment of "self-brokenness" and reliance on the Lord that Jacob received a blessing. The lesson for the Christian is simply this: it is when we yield ourselves and cling only to the Lord that we receive and comprehend God's blessings for us and become a blessing to others. *"The sacrifices of God are a broken spirit, a broken and a contrite heart – these, O God, You will not despise"* (Ps. 51:17).

January 27 – I Have Everything
Genesis 33

The moment had arrived when Jacob would recognize just how useless his plans were and also how unjustified his fears were. The day before Jacob had arranged for a gift of 580 animals, comprising goats, sheep, cattle, camels, and asses to be presented to Esau as a gesture of good. Jacob spent the final moments before encountering Esau staging his wives and children at various intervals in front of him. We fault Jacob here because the shepherd selfishly used his sheep to buffer himself from potential jeopardy. The Lord declared that the good shepherd will risk all, even his own life, to deliver his sheep from harm (John 10:10-13). Being a good shepherd of one's children today is hard work! It takes courage to rebuff the peer pressure exerted on one's children by others, the secular dictates of a Christ-less educational system, and the badgering of other parents as to what is best for our children. So exhibit courage, raise the crook when needed, fling the stone from the sling if threatened, and fend off devouring foes; your children's future prosperity and spiritual vitality are at stake.

Within moments of meeting Esau, Jacob's apprehensions were transformed to jubilee. Instead of a hotheaded brother seeking his "double portion," a warmhearted Esau embraced him. Esau must have been stunned to see how much Jacob had increased in posterity and prosperity in only 20 years. The gift from Jacob to Esau was enormous. But Esau did not want it – he had "enough" already (v. 9). But Jacob insisted that Esau receive it *"because God has dealt graciously with me, and because I have enough"* (v. 11). Esau then begrudgingly received the gift. The Hebrew word for "enough" in verse 9 is *rab*, which means "abundant" and is often translated "much." The Hebrew word used to speak of Jacob's "enough" is *kol*, which means "all" or "the whole" and, by implication, "everything."

Esau had much, but in Jacob's own mind, he had everything; he had Almighty God for his full resource. Yes, Jacob had a bent to rely on his own "doings," but now he understood that, despite himself, God was the One who was really in control of his life and the source of every good thing. David writes: *"Oh, how great is Your goodness, which You have laid up for those who fear You, which You have prepared for those who trust in You in the presence of the sons of men!"* (Ps. 31:19).

January 28 – Trading Idols for God
Genesis 35

Jacob had lived near Shechem for approximately ten years. It was now time for him to ascend from the low moral ground of Shechem to the dwelling place of the Most High God. So, God again called Jacob to return to Bethel (vv. 1-2) and to build an altar there unto Him. God's decree, though not directly mentioning idols, sufficed to admonish Jacob for his tolerance of foreign gods in his house. Jacob knew these strange gods were among him, but now his conscience was prodded about the matter. He immediately sought to sanctify his household and to purge these images from his family's presence. Why were there idols in Jacob's house in the first place? Although Jacob had experienced conversion, certain members of his family and some of his servants were still embracing false gods (e.g., Rachel stole her father's images before leaving Haran.). We applaud Jacob for abruptly gathering his house together, instructing his family from God's very words, and then calling them to sweep the household clean of any false gods.

Jacob's family readily responded to his instructions, and *"So they gave Jacob all the foreign gods which were in their hands, and the earrings which were in their ears; and Jacob hid them under the terebinth tree which was by Shechem"* (v. 4). Jacob quickly got rid of this evil paraphernalia and buried it all under a tree. The fact that Jacob did not melt them down and try to reuse the metal for other practical or legal uses is admirable. He realized that God's people must *"Abstain from all appearance of evil"* (1 Thess. 5:22; KJV). This, in principle, is good counsel for new converts that may be tempted to sell tokens of the old life (magazines, music, movies, etc.), which ought to be destroyed instead of being made available to stumble others.

Why did Jacob's family give him their earrings? Earrings were frequently used in the manufacturing of idols or to support other immoral idolatrous practices (Ex. 32:2-4; Hos. 2:13). Thus, not only was Jacob ridding his family of their idols, but he was also ensuring that they did not have a provision to create new ones. What wisdom! Think of how Christian homes today would be transformed for God if all believing fathers purged everything that displaced love for the Lord from their family's presence, then ensured that no new toy, activity, relationship, or job would diminish their affection for the Savior.

January 29 – Forgetting
Genesis 41

Now, it was Pharaoh's turn to dream dreams, and similar to the experience of the butler and baker two years earlier, he was greatly bewildered by two series of mental images. Not only did Pharaoh not know the meaning of his dreams, but none of his wise men could interpret the dreams either. Then, the butler remembered Joseph and how he had told him the correct interpretation of his dream while in prison. After Pharaoh learned of Joseph, he was summoned from prison for the purpose of interpreting Pharaoh's dreams.

After informing him that Jehovah had revealed the meaning of Pharaoh's dreams to him, Joseph also suggested a wise course of action to escape the terrible forthcoming famine. Joseph was then exalted to the second position of authority over the whole kingdom (v. 40). He received an exalted name from Pharaoh, "Zaphnath-Paaneah," which meant "the revealer of secrets." When his chariot passed through the streets of Egypt, a herald passed before his chariot shouting, *"Bow the knee!"* (v. 43). In seed form, Joseph's exaltation foreshadows that of Christ. Proportionately to the low extent that the Lord was humbled as a servant unto death, He was exalted in heaven by His Father after His resurrection. In a future day, He will be recognized by all as Lord of lords and King of kings (Phil. 2:9-11).

We read of "forgetting" twice in this chapter. First, the butler forgot about Joseph for two years after he was released from prison. Then, Joseph, after he was released from prison and exalted in Egypt, was able to forget the thirteen years of being a slave and a prisoner. Joseph was thirty years old when he was exalted in Egypt (v. 46, 37:2). Afterwards, Pharaoh gave Joseph a wife and a new name. Likewise, the Father will give His Son, the Lord Jesus, a bride in heaven (the Church – Eph. 5:27) and a name above all other names. Joseph did not receive his bride while a servant or a prisoner but in the dignity of royal status.

How do we know that Joseph was able to forget the past? He named his first son "Manasseh," which means "forgetting." He understood God's control of his life and knew that all that had happened to him was for his good and allowed God to greatly bless others. He, therefore, named his second son "Ephraim," which means "fruitfulness." May each of us experience such a testimony of God's grace (Rom. 8:28).

January 30 – All These Things are Against Me
Genesis 42-45

The severe famine continued in the land into the second year. In the course of time, Jacob's family, servants and animals devoured the grain they had secured in Egypt. Simeon was imprisoned in Egypt until Joseph's brothers returned with their youngest brother Benjamin to validate their testimony and prove that they were not spies. Finally, the inevitable day that had been tormenting Jacob's soul arrived. He knew his family needed to eat, and Egypt was the only place where grain could be found. Judah reminded his father that they could not return to Egypt without Benjamin – a fact Jacob was painfully aware of: *"You have bereaved me: Joseph is no more, Simeon is no more, and you want to take Benjamin. All these things are against me"* (Gen. 42:36).

To encourage his father in the matter, Judah pledged his own life as a guarantee that he would return Benjamin to his father once their business in Egypt was completed (Gen. 43). Jacob had only one choice – to trust God with the life of his youngest son. So, he sent Benjamin with his other nine sons back to Egypt with money and gifts to the austere Egyptian leader who had dealt so harshly with his family.

The brethren arrived in Egypt and bowed themselves before Joseph. His brothers were refreshed by Joseph's hospitality and then experienced one final test to prove that they were changed men (Gen. 44). After witnessing Judah's resolve to take condemned Benjamin's place, Joseph reveals himself to his brothers and tells them to come near to him (Gen. 45:4). They were terrified, but Joseph consoled them: *"Do not therefore be grieved or angry with yourselves because you sold me here ... God sent me before you to preserve a posterity for you in the earth, and to save your lives by a great deliverance. So now it was not you who sent me here, but God"* (Gen. 45:5-8).

It is our natural tendency to suffer from tunnel vision when events in our lives do not meet our expectations. Like Jacob, we get so focused on our narrow sliver of time, that we forget that God is weaving our circumstances into his sovereign tapestry of blessing to humanity. All that Jacob perceived was against him was actually God's means of saving his family from starvation. God is good and does good! We can trust him to work all things for good, though hardships are inevitable in the unfolding of His purposes, as the events of Calvary demonstrate.

January 31 – Dead in the World
Genesis 50

The closing chapter of Genesis contains one of the most elaborate funeral processions and burials in the Bible. This chapter symbolizes the completion of God's great plan to restore and bless the only creation to bear His image – man. The embalming of Jacob's body took forty days. All of Egypt mourned with Joseph over the death of his beloved father for seventy days, then an enormous funeral procession carried Jacob's body back to Hebron for burial. They mourned seven more days after arriving at the cave of Machpelah, and then they buried Jacob and returned to Egypt. The multitude that came out of Egypt to bury Jacob was so great and the lamenting so strong for Jacob that even the inhabitants of Canaan were disturbed. They renamed the place "Abelmizraim," which means "mourning of the Egyptians."

Joseph's brothers again feared that Joseph would recompense them for selling him into slavery. Herein Joseph's serene faith in God's plan is again expressed. He understood that the life-preserving blessings for the many were only possible through the ill experiences of one man – himself. Before Joseph himself died, he beseeched his brethren to not abandon his bones in Egypt when God brought them again into Canaan. The children of Israel kept this promise years later when they exited Egypt (Ex. 13:19), and Joseph was finally laid to rest in Shechem in the land given to his two sons (Josh. 24:32).

The last verse of Genesis is the key to this chapter: *"So Joseph died ... and they embalmed him, and he was put in a coffin in Egypt."* Although God has shown how He will bring about His plan of redemption, this verse calls our attention back to the fact that man is spiritually dead in the world – "in a coffin in Egypt." The key words in this chapter are "mourning," "weeping" and "lamentation" (seven times). These words capture the anguish of God over the fallen spiritual condition of man. Man was created to bring Him pleasure and fellowship, but His Holiness precludes close fellowship with a rebellious and self-willed race. Genesis has shown that God is in control, and is longsuffering to bring about His purposes and is faithful to His promises! *"The Lord is not slack concerning His promise, as some count slackness, but is longsuffering toward us, not willing that any should perish but that all should come to repentance"* (2 Pet. 3:9).

February 1 – Strangership
Exodus 2

There are forty years of silence between the events of Exodus 1 and Exodus 2; Moses was now a grown man (v. 11). He has had a privileged upbringing in the house of Pharaoh. Moses enjoyed social status, the riches of Egypt, higher education, and all the things that made life easy, but his people, the Hebrews, were suffering under the brutality of Egyptian rule; how long could he sit still and do nothing?

One day Moses witnessed an isolated Egyptian smiting a Hebrew slave. After ensuring there were no witnesses, he slew the Egyptian and buried his body in the sand. But he found out the next day while trying to end the squabble between two Hebrews slaves that the matter was known. Although God had chosen Moses to deliver Israel out of Egypt, Moses was going about it the wrong way. Yet, the writer of Hebrews commends Moses for being willing to forsake great riches and high status to suffer *the reproach of Christ* in the world (Heb. 11:26). Though Moses didn't suffer because of his testimony for God, he did honor God by foreshadowing Christ's suffering by identifying with God's people. Somehow Moses understood that there was a day of reckoning with God, and he determined that it would be better for him to identify with God's people and forsake the splendor of Egypt rather than to be associated with a system of rule that brutalized God's people.

In verse 11, God's people are identified as "Hebrews," which means "the passenger." Abram is called a Hebrew in Genesis 14, a term that beautifully encapsulates his pilgrimage and his strangership in a world estranged from God. Likewise, "Hebrew" signified the calling of Abram's descendants to be delivered out of Egypt and into God's presence. To be a Hebrew meant that you were a stranger in the world; thus, Egypt could never be the resting place for God's people.

Moses lived in the wilderness of Midian for forty years after escaping Pharaoh's vengeance. During this wilderness journey he too felt a stranger in the world. Though Egyptians despised shepherds, Moses was content to marry Zipporah, the daughter of Jethro (Reuel) and become a shepherd of his flocks. He named his first son Gershom, which means "a stranger." The man of high Egyptian status was now a humble stranger in the world. May every believer feel his or her strangership in the same way – we are just passing through.

February 2 – Come to Go
Exodus 3

God called to Moses by name as he neared the burning bush and commanded him: *"Do not draw near this place. Take your sandals off your feet, for the place where you stand is holy ground"* (v. 5). Moses obeyed. God then revealed Himself to Moses, His plan to deliver His people from Egypt, and that He was summoning Moses to be their deliverer. After introducing Himself to Moses, the Lord made known His resolve: *"I have **come down** to deliver them out of the hand of the Egyptians"* (v. 8). God had come to earth to speak to him and the only acceptable response for Moses was to come near. Moses had to be willing to *come to God* before he would be willing to *go for God*. This explains his objection about going to Egypt; without knowing the Lord, such a venture would be impossible. Notice that God did not tell Moses to "go" to Egypt until he had first "come" to God, otherwise there would be no "going." Moses needed to personally know God before he would be effective in co-laboring with Him in service. God's invitation to humanity to "come" always precedes His commissioning to "go." Service for God without personal knowledge of Him cannot be based in truth or motivated by love, and thus, is meaningless for eternity.

What was Moses' response to God's command, *"**Come now**, therefore, and I will send you to Pharaoh"* (v. 10). He replied, *"Who am I that **I should go** to Pharaoh"* (v. 11)? Moses had a two-fold identity crisis: first, he was unsure of who he was and, second, he didn't know who God was. The Lord then answers these questions and Moses learns that doing God's will did not depend on who he was, but rather on who God is. God's answer to Moses' "Who am I" objection was *"Certainly I will be with you"* (v. 12). When called by God to action, Moses initially focused on his own inabilities, rather than trusting in God's capabilities. We will find satisfaction in life by accepting and fulfilling our divine calling; preoccupation with our abilities, inadequacies, or personal interests is time-consuming and only hinders our availability to be used by God. Accordingly, each of the personal inadequacies Moses identified as an excuse as to why he was not fit to be the deliverer only served to highlight the very reasons God had selected him for the task. God desires to use the weak and the foolish, *"that no flesh should glory in His presence"* (1 Cor. 1:26-29).

February 3 – The First Objection
Exodus 4

In presenting his objections, Moses was not protesting going to Egypt; he had already agreed to go. Rather, his doubts center in his own inabilities to adequately do God's bidding. The Lord already knew all about Moses' strengths and weaknesses and that His grace would overcome both, especially his strengths. As Oswald Chambers notes, "Unguarded strength is double weakness."[2] As the great I AM, the command to go should have been sufficient to settle Moses' quandaries, yet God graciously answered each of his objections.

The first objection Moses voiced was that the Jews would not believe that he had been commissioned by God and therefore, they would ignore his message. God responded to this objection by personally involving Moses in the working of two miracles. Moses would have used his hands earlier to remove his shoes, and in so doing he must have put aside his shepherding rod. Apparently, after removing his shoes he picked the rod up again and continued to hold it while talking with I AM. The Lord began with an easy question, *"What do you have in your hand?"* Moses answers correctly, *"a rod."* The Lord then instructed Moses to cast the rod to the ground, which he did. The familiar rod became a threatening serpent and Moses fled from it. God then instructed Moses to pick up the safe end of the serpent, its tail. Moses obeyed and after grasping the serpent it became his shepherding rod again. A rod speaks of *power* in Scripture (Rev. 12:5). Egyptian power had become satanic in nature, as pictured by the serpent (Gen. 3), and God was going to reclaim that power through Moses. Moses' shepherding rod had now become the "rod of God" (v. 20).

God then instructs Moses to put his hand into his bosom. God never told Moses to pull it out, but Moses did and found it leprous. Moses was told to put his leprous hand again into his bosom. When he removed his hand the second time it was found to be normal. Leprosy, an incurable disease at this time, pictures sin in Scripture. A child of God cannot righteously serve the Lord with leprosy (sin) in his or her bosom (heart). Sin in our flesh must be supernaturally put to death *"because they that are in the flesh cannot please God"* (Rom. 8:8). One cannot rightly exercise the power of God without being under His moral authority and possessing a pure heart that beats for Him.

February 4 – The Second Objection
Exodus 4

Moses' next objection was that he was not an eloquent speaker, but was in fact, slow in speech. How could he possibly be the best man to face off against Pharaoh? The comment was an affront to the Creator who had fashioned Moses as a unique vessel to serve Him as He deemed best. God answered Moses' objection, *"I will be with your mouth and teach you what you shall say"* (v. 12). Moses did not need to be anxious about the matter; he was to repeat to Pharaoh only what God told him to say. Moses spoke as if everything depended upon his persuasive speech before Pharaoh, rather than God's handiwork.

The Lord Jesus extended similar counsel to His disciples. He was preparing His disciples for their arduous task of apostleship, a commission which would commence shortly after He had returned to heaven: *"Now when they bring you to the synagogues and magistrates and authorities, do not worry about how or what you should answer, or what you should say. For the Holy Spirit will teach you in that very hour what you ought to say"* (Luke 12:11-12). Christ promised that all those who were brought into hardship because of their testimony for Him would be issued special enlightenment from the Holy Spirit in order to answer questions and accusations with the wisdom of God. Believers would do well to remember this today when engaged in evangelism – we don't talk lost souls into "getting saved." Christians are merely facilitators of God's Word; we say no more than what God has commissioned us to speak; only the Holy Spirit can save souls.

Consider the Lord's response to a lawyer who was testing Him concerning how someone could inherit the kingdom of heaven. The Lord answered the lawyer's question with two of His own: *"What is written in the law?"* and *"What is your reading of it?"* (Luke 10:26). The Lord Jesus caused the man to personally consider what the Word of God stated about the matter of salvation. An individual cannot repent and receive Christ as Savior without first understanding God's Word (Rom. 10:17). Moses was to learn that it would not be his fanciful words or eloquent speeches that would pry the Jews from Pharaoh's clutches. He was to convey to Pharaoh only the words that God put in his mouth. God's power would be shown to Egypt through His word.

February 5 – The Third Objection
Exodus 4

Sensing the overwhelming nature of what he was being asked to do, Moses pleads, *"O my Lord, please send by the hand of whomever else You may send"* (Ex. 4:13). This self-centered frankness angered God, but His wrath was tempered by mercy and His foreknowledge had already provided the solution – Aaron, who even then was already en route to Moses. God's gracious response to Moses' lack of faith resulted in a sign with which to enrich his faith. The coming of Aaron at this timely juncture demonstrated to Moses God's wisdom and control. God did not choose to send someone else to Egypt, nor did He give Moses a persuasive tongue, but He did transfer some of the honor offered to a hesitant Moses to a willing Aaron.

The Lord Jesus told the Church at Philadelphia, *"Behold, I am coming quickly! Hold fast what you have, that no one may take your crown"* (Rev. 3:11). His reward, which He bestows at His Judgment Seat, will be with Him when He comes to the clouds to snatch away His Church from the earth (1 Thess. 4:13-18; Rev. 22:12). In light of the Lord's imminent return, the saints at Philadelphia were to be attentive and faithful, lest they lose their reward (crown); this would allow someone else to earn it. This is what happened to Moses: God had given him a service opportunity, but he complained and wavered, so the Lord transferred part of the prospect, and the accompanying honor, to Aaron. God has a work to do and it will be done by those who are willing to serve Him, and God shall reward them accordingly.

Because Moses balked, fluent Aaron was brought into the work as Moses' spokesman; later, he would become God's high priest. God would speak to Moses and he would convey God's Words to Aaron who then would speak to the people. Moses was to be the deliverer and Aaron was to be his helper. Ministry can be grueling without a co-laborer and the enlistment of Aaron in the work seemed to quell Moses' apprehensions. Moses' faith in Jehovah was but in infancy; it would be refined and developed in the coming years, but presently Moses received more consolation in having along a feeble mortal like himself than in the abiding presence of his God. Let us not rely on what is visibly tangible, but rather on the vast capabilities of our great God.

Daily Devotions

February 6 – Lessons on the Way
Exodus 4

While Moses was en route to Egypt, God personally met with His servant; Moses would learn three important truths from this encounter. Previously, God had informed Moses that at first Pharaoh would not let the Hebrews go; only after He had worked mighty wonders would their release be obtained. The Lord now explained to Moses that there would be times that He would harden Pharaoh's heart in order to accomplish His sovereign plan in Egypt. There would be times that God would harden Pharaoh's heart to accomplish a particular purpose, but at other times, Pharaoh would harden his own heart against the Lord. Pharaoh had a free choice to bow to Jehovah or to continue revering the gods of Egypt, but in the matter of delivering the Jews, all of Pharaoh's decisions would ultimately be used to glorify God (Rom. 9:21-22).

The second revelation to Moses pertained to God's relationship with the nation of Israel. He had adopted them (Rom. 9:4) and they were as a firstborn son to Him. This adoption was not an adoption of individuals, as it is with believers in the Church Age (Rom. 8:15-16), but of a nation. Through His covenant with Abraham, Israel had been singled out from among the nations as a special object of God's favor; hence, God considered the nation His son (Jer. 31:9).

The third truth that Moses would learn was that delayed obedience was still disobedience. As a continuing sign of God's covenant with Abraham, his descendants were to circumcise their males. Moses had apparently obeyed this command with Gershom, but not with Eliezer, likely a newborn. Moses did not want to have an altercation with his wife Zipporah who opposed the rite. The Lord was ready to slay His chosen deliverer, if the act was not immediately carried out. As the head of the home, Moses was responsible to God for his family, and until things were right with God in his own house, there could be no God-honoring ministry outside the home. A fuming Zipporah was forced to circumcise her son in order to save her husband's life. Circumcision spoke of God's covenant plan for Israel and, as she was not a Hebrew, she did not recognize the symbolic significance of the act. Yet the Lord was satisfied with her action and released or healed Moses. To be used mightily in Egypt, Moses must fully obey the Lord!

February 7 – Suffering in the Will of God
Exodus 5

The two days following Moses' encounter with Pharaoh were oppressive ones for the Hebrews; they fell behind on their brick quotas and the Hebrew foremen were beaten for the delinquency in production. When these men complained to Pharaoh about the logistics of making bricks without straw, Pharaoh repeated his earlier statement, accusing the Hebrews of just being lazy. If they had leisure to dream about venturing into the desert to have a feast and to worship their God, they obviously had too much time on their hands. No relief was granted and Israel was now suffering more at the hands of the Egyptians than before Moses had arrived to deliver them. Yet the more hopeless Israel's situation was in Egypt, the greater the opportunity for Egypt, and indeed the world, to know Jehovah's great power (Ex. 9:16).

Returning from Pharaoh, the Hebrew foremen confronted Moses and Aaron about their amplified misery: *"You have made us abhorrent in the sight of Pharaoh and in the sight of his servants, to put a sword in their hand to kill us"* (v. 21). Moses apparently gave no response to their complaint; he knew that it was true. A distraught Moses petitioned the Lord: *"Lord, why have You treated Your people badly?" "Why have You sent me?"* He informed the Lord, as if He needed the information, *"It has been worse for Your people since I have confronted Pharaoh in Your name and they have not been released"* (v. 23).

A prophet is a mouthpiece God uses to warn, to rebuke, and to proclaim judgment on individuals, groups, and nations. God's spokesmen often drank from their own ministries (e.g., Elijah, Ezekiel, and Jeremiah). Moses, too, suffered for doing the will of God and, like the prophets that would follow him, he suffered with his people in the will of God. Should those who do the will of God expect suffering? The Lord Jesus told His disciples the night before He was crucified that because the world hated Him, the world would also hate and persecute them for identifying with Him (John 15:18-19). This profound truth is put by Paul in this simple way: *"Yes, and all who desire to live godly in Christ Jesus will suffer persecution"* (2 Tim. 3:12). This was the example that Christ left for us to follow – suffering patiently in the will of God is a powerful witness to the lost of what is real (1 Pet. 2:20-22).

Daily Devotions

February 8 – Worship in the Land
Exodus 8

The plague of swarms was announced a day in advance and was initiated as Moses and Aaron decreed. Pharaoh summoned Moses and Aaron in order to present a counter-offer to their demand that the entire nation leave Egypt to sacrifice to Jehovah: *"Go, sacrifice to your God in the land"* (Ex. 8:25). The rebel king offered a compromise to Moses; the Hebrews could go and sacrifice, but within the borders of Egypt.

Paul instructs believers not to be ignorant of Satan's devices (2 Cor. 2:11). Satan blinds (2 Cor. 4:4), beguiles (2 Cor. 11:3), and buffets (2 Cor. 12:7) humanity to cause us to ignore what God has revealed; we should be wise to his ways. In the "no straw for bricks" scheme the devil sought to keep the Hebrews so busy that they would have no time to think about their God. This strategy is effective today in keeping believers from serving Christ. Now Pharaoh sought to keep God's people in Egypt (i.e., in the world under a God-hating influence).

Moses declines Pharaoh's offer for several reasons. Firstly, it was not what God had commanded. It is not the dictates of a religious system or a secular movement which regulates the believer's worship and service, but the authority of God's Word. Moses would not compromise God's command on this matter and neither should the Church – the Bible is the Church's worship manual and the Holy Spirit its Leader. Secondly, sacrificing animals which the Egyptians thought represented deities would likely result in harm to the unarmed Hebrews. Thirdly, and most importantly, if they remained in Egypt, they would have to sacrifice to Jehovah the very objects of abomination, the animals which the Egyptians worshipped as gods. Worship influenced by paganism would be an affront to the God of the Hebrews. Consequently, Pharaoh's attempt to hoodwink the Israelites to worship their God in Egypt failed.

Satan uses this same tactic today to convince the saved that it is acceptable to worship God in a doctrinally corrupt church. As foretold in Scripture, in the latter days of the Church Age, Satan will reside comfortably in various branches of Christendom (Matt. 13:32). Paul states that there will be apostasy in the professing Church just prior to the appearing of the Antichrist (2 Thess. 2:3-4). Such are our days!

February 9 – Worship near the Land
Exodus 8

After Moses rejected Pharaoh's concession of worshipping Jehovah in Egypt, the king offered a second compromise in verse 28: *"I will let you go, that you may sacrifice to the Lord your God in the wilderness; only you shall not go very far away."* When Satan cannot control the Lord's people from his stronghold in the world, he will settle for a "border position." Instead of blatant corruption, he is content to negatively influence believers and to dilute the certainty of truth in their minds. But the aftermath is still the same from God's perspective; following that which is not wholly true cannot please the Lord. Rather, God promises to judge all those who suppress the truth (any part of it) to engage in unrighteousness (Rom. 1:18, 25).

Pharaoh would have allowed the Hebrews to leave Egypt to worship, but he wanted them close enough that he could still influence their relationship with Jehovah. He knew that if the people did "not go very far" it was not much different than for them to remain in Egypt. A week or two in a bland and arid wilderness and the fleshpots, garlic, leaks, and onions of Egypt would be calling the Hebrews back to Egypt. This satanic device highlights the critical need for a healthy separation from the world in the believer's life. The reason for resigning the world is to have Christ and Him alone – no border position is permissible. Spiritually speaking, God's people are not only to be out of Egypt, but as far as possible from its interfering tentacles.

At Calvary, Christ died and passed out of this world. Three days later His body was raised from the grave. The Lord Jesus was then highly exalted by His Father to the right hand of majesty on high (Heb. 1:3). This is why God demanded that the Jews leave Egypt to worship Him. The world crucified His Son, and thus Christ is no longer in the world – to enjoy spiritual life with Him we must come along to where He is by faith. Believers are privileged to sit at His table and to receive from Him and commune with Him there (1 Cor. 10:16-21). It is offensive to the Lord Jesus to desert Him to party with demons in the world; it provokes His jealous zeal for us (1 Cor. 19:21-22). The Jews had been invited to Jehovah's table in the wilderness; it was a private affair, and no solicitations from Egypt would be allowed.

Daily Devotions

February 10 – Leave Your Children in the Land
Exodus 10

Moses and Aaron departed from Pharaoh's presence after issuing him an ultimatum: Let the Israelites leave or locusts would decimate Egypt the following day. Pharaoh's servants pleaded with Pharaoh to let the Hebrews go since Egypt lay in ruins. Pharaoh summoned Moses and Aaron to present his own terms for their departure – they could go, but their children (vv. 9, 24) must stay behind. Pharaoh seemed to know that if all the slaves received liberty to worship Jehovah in the wilderness they would not return to Egypt. He was right; Moses had never mentioned the possibility of returning to Egypt after worshipping the Lord in the wilderness.

Pharaoh thought to control the Israelites by holding their children (and likely the mothers of young children too) captive, thereby forcing the men to return to Egypt after their wilderness adventure. Moses already knew the will of God on the matter and immediately rejected Pharaoh's compromise. The Hebrews had no intention of seeking one thing for themselves, namely the Promised Land, and something different for their children; the entire Jewish nation would depart from Egypt with all their goods and livestock. Receiving no assurance that the Hebrews would return to Egypt, Pharaoh refused to free the Israelites, and Moses and Aaron were driven out of Pharaoh's presence.

Given the desperate nature of the situation, a compromise by Moses may have led to the slaughter of the Hebrew women and children after the men had departed. Because Moses did not say anything more or less than what God put in his mouth all Egypt would see Jehovah's power without negative consequences for the Jews. Pharaoh's proposed compromise demonstrates yet another technique of Satan to conquer God's people. Overcome, the enemy concedes the older generation and is content to entangle, ensnare, and corrupt the next generation.

Parents have a God-given responsibility to train up their children for the One who gave them, for *"He seeks godly offspring"* (Mal. 2:15). If children are permitted to dabble in a God-hating system of thinking, a lack of appetite for spiritual things will be the consequence. How can Christian parents make an allowance for worldliness in the home and still proclaim they are raising their children for the Lord?

May We Serve Christ!

February 11 – Leave Your Resources in the Land
Exodus 10

God told Moses to stretch his hand towards heaven to begin the plague of darkness that could be felt throughout Egypt, but not in Goshen. The lack of sunlight for three days meant that Jehovah was stronger than one of Egypt's chief deities – *Re* (or *Ra*), the sun god.

Pharaoh again called Moses to him in order to present another compromise: *"Go, serve the Lord; only let your flocks and your herds be kept back. Let your little ones also go with you"* (v. 24). This compromise demonstrates yet another technique of Satan to conquer God's people. Firstly, the enemy sought to keep the Hebrews *busy in the land* so that they would have no time for their God. Secondly, he agreed to permit the Jews to worship Jehovah, but only *in the land*; thus, their sacrifices would be abominable. Thirdly, he would have allowed the Israelites to have communion with their God, but only *near the land* (a border position) so that he could still entice and influence them. Fourthly, the enemy conceded the older generation and was content to keep *part of them in the land*; he would then focus on entangling, ensnaring, and corrupting the next generation. In sheer desperation, Pharaoh offered a final compromise – all the Jews could leave Egypt, but *their flocks and herds must stay in the land*. If Pharaoh could not force the Israelites to sacrifice in Egypt, he would yet have a partial victory if he could send them out of the land with no sacrifices for Jehovah. No doubt Pharaoh was thinking about replenishing the Egyptian livestock slaughtered by pestilence and hailstones. But beyond that, Satan desired to rob the Hebrews of their resources to worship God and also to sustain themselves in the wilderness.

Not knowing in advance which animals would be needed to offer sacrifices to Jehovah, Moses told Pharaoh that all of their livestock must go with them. God's plan for delivering His people from Egypt included equipping them with abundant resources to adequately worship Him in the wilderness; consequently, the Jews would take with them not only their own livestock, but also the spoils of Egypt as they departed. Likewise, the Lord equips believers today with all the resources they need to worship Him. Let us be careful not to confer to Egypt what we know has been entrusted to us to honor the Lord.

February 12 – Get the Leaven Out
Exodus 12

The seven-day feast of Unleavened Bread directly followed the feast of Passover. These feasts were to be kept annually as a memorial to God's incredible feat of delivering the Jews from Egypt. Only unleavened bread was eaten on the night of the Passover, but a further restriction was observed during the following seven days of the feast of Unleavened Bread; there was not to be any leaven in any of the Jewish homes. Leaven, in Scripture, speaks of sin, corruption, or evil doctrine (Matt. 13:33; 1 Cor. 5:8). Though the Israelites were immersed in a pagan culture, its filth and corruption should not be in their homes. Though they were in the world, they were not to be of the world. In a later tradition, Jewish parents actually hid leaven in their homes so that their children could search it out and sweep it out of the house before the feast of Unleavened Bread commenced.

Did sweeping of the leaven out of the house merit salvation? No, the Israelites did not sweep out the leaven in order to be saved from the final plague, only applied lamb's blood would save them from that judgment. In years to come, they would put leaven out of their homes, not to be saved, but because they had been saved. If a Jew wanted to continue to enjoy fellowship with God's people (i.e. to remain a part of the general assembly), the leaven had to go. Leaven in the home degrades our fellowship with God and with His people – it must be swept clean.

Something of the world can be ignorantly introduced into our homes and, by its very availability, ensure chaos the moment we walk in the flesh and not by faith. Often what lays dormant for a time will, in due season, solicit the flesh to manifest itself. These worldly influences are like spiritual land mines, which can lay hidden and dormant for a time, but with one missed step of faith the child of God becomes a casualty of his or her own carnal appetite. Just as the Jews symbolized spiritual sanctification by sweeping all the leaven from their homes during the feast of Unleavened Bread, believers should take great care to remove anything from their homes that might entice the flesh to sin. The Christian home should be a safe haven which encourages spiritual growth not a minefield of secular temptations. If the leaven is not there to begin with, it will never pull us under its power.

February 13 – Sanctified What Is God's
Exodus 13

By the substitutional death of a lamb, the firstborn of man and beast among the Hebrews had been spared death in Egypt. The destroyer passed by each home that had lamb's blood on its doorway. Since God had purchased the lives of the firstborn, He now claimed special ownership of them. They were to be sanctified, or literally "dedicated," to Him. The Hebrew word *qadash* translated "sanctify" in verse 2 means "to dedicate." Later, this firstborn group would be exchanged for the tribe of Levi – soul for soul through substitutional sacrifices and redemption money (Num. 3:40-51). As a result of this exchange, the entire tribe of Levi would be consecrated to serve the Lord and to affect worship in the tabernacle/temple on behalf of the nation.

While the outcome of redemption was still fresh in the Hebrews' minds, Moses reiterated God's command concerning the keeping of the feasts of Passover and of Unleavened Bread. Moses added an additional instruction to the seven-day feast of Unleavened Bread: *"no leavened bread shall be seen among you"* (v. 7). Not only was leaven a symbol of sin that was to be removed from their homes, the Jews were not to look on it either. This illustrates a safeguard for avoiding sin in our own lives – don't look at or listen to anything that would stimulate the flesh to desire what was beyond God's will.

To remind Israel of God's ongoing work of sanctification in them the yearly feast of Unleavened Bread and the perpetual redemption of the firstborn were instituted. The firstborn (man or beast) was God's portion among the nation, and it had to be substitutionally purchased by a lamb. In this way, the firstborn were not put to death as a sacrifice to God, but rather were redeemed by a substitute sacrifice which then allowed them to live as God's purchased possession upon the earth. In other words, their consecration to God demanded that they "set apart" their first fruits to God. The Hebrew word *abar* translated "set apart" in verse 11 implies the act of "passing along." Because of their sanctification, the Jews were enabled to *pass along* acceptable service and worship to God. In the same way today, the Lord desires believer-priests *to dedicate* themselves in holiness to Him and then pass along living sacrifices in response to their redemption through Christ's blood.

February 14 – No Short-cuts In Growing Faith
Exodus 13

The Israelites had arrived safely at Succoth and now were continuing on to Etham, which was located on the edge of the wilderness. One of the most awe-inspiring expressions in Scripture is found in verse 18: *"but God."* Found forty-two times in the Bible, "but God" normally identifies an incredible feat of God's grace in response to man's desperate need for it. In verse 18 the expression speaks of God's providential means of preparing the Israelites for Canaan. *"The way to the land of the Philistines"* was a quicker route to Canaan from Egypt, but God knew if He took His people by that way they would not be ready for battle when they arrived at Canaan. The Jews were unprepared for this hardship and Jehovah knew the tendency of their flesh would be to circumvent the challenge and head back to Egypt.

The same is true today for the Christian. In matters that concern spiritual maturity and growing faith, there are no short-cuts in a believer's life. Wilderness experiences, tests, and trials are necessary to produce a battle-hardened soldier of the cross. Initially, a new Christian enjoys learning for the first time of God's love and grace towards them; yet, the hard road is still ahead. During the next several months, the excitement wanes as the new convert endures insults and demeaning statements from lost family members and friends. The natural tendency of the flesh when confronted with spiritual opposition is to retreat – there is nothing in the flesh that wants to engage in such a battle, nor does the flesh have any wherewithal to fight it. But the spiritual man presses forward, enters the fray, and is victorious in Christ: *"For whatever is born of God overcomes the world. And this is the victory that has overcome the world – our faith"* (1 Jn. 5:4).

God was putting His people through boot-camp to ready them for conflict in Canaan. Without the wilderness training, they would not be able to seize their God-given possession in the Promised Land. Likewise, through properly using one's spiritual armor, personal victory over the enemy is not only possible, but is expected. With each new victory the believer becomes more aware of all their *"spiritual blessings in heavenly places in Christ"* (Eph. 1:3). So let us be diligent to enter into the victory which Christ has already won.

February 15 – Go Forward
Exodus 13

Pharaoh and his army were what the Israelites feared most. To strengthen their faith in Him, God would overcome their enemy as His people looked on. The situation was bleak; they were boxed in against the sea, but it is in such times that man becomes the most willing to recognize God's intervention. The Israelites were not to fight; rather, they were given two commands to obey: *"Do not be afraid, stand still and see the salvation of the Lord"* (v. 13), and *"Go forward"* (v. 15).

They were not to fear, for this was God's battle (v. 14), not theirs; they had no strength to fight it anyway. The Israelites were to *stand still.* Willingly standing still in the midst of terrifying circumstances demonstrates faith, a spiritual quality that prompts God's consideration in every situation. If the Israelites had spent their time fortifying their weak position, they might miss seeing God's spectacular handiwork. In Egypt, the Israelites had been sheltered from God's wrath by blood; now God would, by His power alone, bring them through the place of death (the Red Sea). These two monumental events relate in type to Christ's judgment on the cross leading to His death and the burial of His body in the grave. Positionally speaking, the believer died with Christ at Calvary and was buried with Him in His garden tomb. The souls redeemed by lamb's blood in Egypt would be brought through the place of death in the Red Sea to enjoy life with Jehovah on the other side. These events symbolize the total victory that Christ would gain over Satan in the future through His death, burial, and resurrection.

The Israelites were completely helpless; they could do nothing but trust the Lord to save them. At God's command, Moses stretched out the rod of God over the sea. This resulted in a strong East wind which not only parted the waters of the sea, but which also provided a dry land bridge through it. Besides providing an escape for His people through the midst of the sea, the Lord illuminated every step taken in faith by the pillar of fire. Because they obeyed the Lord and went forward, the Israelites were kept from harm and their enemy was wiped out when the sea returned on them. May believers today likewise storm the gates of hell with the gospel of Jesus Christ. In Christ, nothing can be lost, but much can be gained by going forward in faith.

Daily Devotions

February 16 – The Redeemed Sing
Exodus 15

Exodus 15 records the first occurrence of singing in the Bible as well as the lyrics of Scripture's first song. Euphoria swept through the Israelite ranks as they marched further into the wilderness under the shadow of Jehovah's cloud. They had escaped death twice in recent days, and by the most unlikely means: blood and water. Death in Egypt at the hands of the destroyer had been averted by lamb's blood, and death in the wilderness by Pharaoh's army had been circumvented by water. Jehovah had used unpretentious things to manifest His salvation to His people: a rod (a symbol of His authority), water (which represented death), and applied blood (the ransoming payment). Through these agents, Jehovah had delivered His people and toppled the mightiest power on earth.

God's redemption for His people was now complete; they had been purchased by blood in Egypt and had been powerfully delivered from Egypt through the sea. Presently, the Church waits for the culmination of its redemption in Christ, that is, to be instantaneously caught up with Him into heaven in glorified bodies. The Church has already been ransomed by blood, but the fullness of that redemption will not be realized until the Church is raptured to heaven. In that event, the same phenomenal power which defeated the power of hell at Christ's resurrection will be exercised to resurrect believers from Satan's domain – the world. Paul wanted the Christians at Corinth to understand this important truth, saying, *"Who delivered us from so great a death, and does deliver us; in whom we trust that He will still deliver us"* (2 Cor. 1:10).

Positionally speaking, the believer has already died with Christ, but, practically speaking, the believer will be delivered through death at the rapture to be with Christ forevermore. Just as the Israelites were brought through the place of death in the Red Sea, every child of God will ultimately experience the power of God and will be brought through death and will then receive an incorruptible and immortal body (1 Cor. 15:51-52). The Israelites, understanding their great deliverance from death, were prompted to sing to God. This is a fitting response for all God's redeemed throughout every age!

February 17 – Destined for Trouble
Exodus 15

Moses led Israel from the Red Sea into the wilderness of Shur where for three days they did not find any water (v. 22). Israel would learn that every time God's cloud guided them into adversity, His grace would overcome it. When water was finally located at Marah, it was determined to be too bitter for human consumption and Israel murmured against Moses. Their steady complaining was more than Moses could bear, so he cried out to the Lord for a solution and the Lord provided one: *"the Lord showed him a tree. When he cast it into the waters, the waters were made sweet"* (v. 25). Once the tree was cast into Marah's water, its bitter taste was replaced with sweetness. Not only was the water made fit for human consumption, but it produced a sense of satisfaction and enjoyment in all those that drank from it. Consequently, the Lord is introduced in verse 26 has *Yahweh-Rapha*, "The Lord Who Heals." In type, the tree that was cast into the water by faith represents the healing of the human soul made possible through the cross of Christ alone. Christ's cross not only removed the bitterness from our pre-Christ life experiences, but it also transformed our lives into a satisfying and meaningful existence.

Many of our failures in life can be attributed to having the wrong view of what a wilderness experience is all about. If new converts would realize that they are destined for disappointments, hardships, and persecution because of their identification with Christ, then every provision of God's grace in the wilderness would be answered with joyful praise. But if the new believer starts out on his or her wilderness journey expecting ease and rest in the world, the relentless hardships to follow will be overwhelming (this is the outcome of prosperity gospel preaching). The mental starting-point then, for all believers, is Marah, which means bitterness. By expecting bitterness in life, God's supplied grace to overcome each difficulty will just seem all the more *sweet*.

Every devoted Christian is destined for trouble, but not for despair (2 Tim. 3:12). Dear believer, do not expect anything less and you will not be disappointed. Prepare your mind for the hardships ahead, so that you are not disheartened by unmet expectations or overcome by despair or self-pity when those forecasted storms of life arrive (1 Pet. 1:13).

Daily Devotions

February 18 – Why Do We Complain?
Exodus 16

Just as the tree at Marah ended the murmuring of God's people, the cross of Christ should bring an end to dissatisfaction in life. Practically speaking, how can a believer be joyfully content in a life immersed with uncertainties, trials, and suffering? It is only possible by adopting a thankful mind frame. Paul exhorted the believers at Thessalonica to *"in everything give thanks; for this is the will of God in Christ Jesus for you"* (1 Thess. 5:18). A sovereign God has us right where He wants us in every situation to extend the most benefit to us, to others, and to affect His glory. Does a critical spirit strangle your mind from thinking positively? A thankful and critical mind frame cannot exist together.

Thanksgiving and contentment are closely related. Paul informed those at Philippi that he had learned to be content whether he had much or little because his joy and strength were in the Lord; his circumstances could not rob him of these blessings (Phil. 4:11-13). The most common cause of sin seems to be dissatisfaction, with selfishness and pride trailing close behind. When we are not content with what we have, we murmur against God. Murmuring is half-uttered complaints that God fully hears anyway. It results from looking downward into carnal desires and secular philosophies and backwards, as we compare where we are to where we were previously and our expectations are not met. Why did the Israelites complain the entire time they were in the Sinai Peninsula? (Exodus 16 contains the most references to grumbling in the entire Bible.) It was because they were always comparing what they presently had with that which they once had in Egypt – in slavery!

Looking backwards to that which once was and comparing it to our wanton desires leads to complaining. The spiritual response to life's difficulties is to look up and appreciate the awesome character and attributes of our great God and then look forward with expectation as to how He might honor Himself by resolving our hardship. This is why Christians are to give thanks "for all things" (Eph. 5:20); God is for us and we can trust him with the big picture. We will find this mindset much easier to obtain if we do not permit worldly perspectives or past attainments to dominate how we evaluate our present circumstances; rather let us look up and forward with joyful expectation.

February 19 – No Lack and No Hoarding
Exodus 16

Whether one gathered little manna or much on a particular day, the outcome was still an omer (i.e., six English pints) for each person. If there was not a supernatural supply of manna, how would it be possible to explain Israel's survival during those 40 years of wandering in the wilderness? God's daily provision of manna would teach the Israelites to rely on Jehovah each and every day for their nutritional needs.

Manna was a daily provision which could not be hoarded; it was always collected fresh. Similarly, each day the believer must draw a fresh portion from God's Word for that day. Some will labor longer and harder for their portion, just as some of the Israelite men labored more than others to collect manna for their families, but yet none lacked any provision from God. But why do some work harder than others for their daily portion? If our hearts are right with the Lord, gathering new manna each morning will be a refreshing experience; it will be an activity that is longed for and then appreciated throughout the day. A believer should so relish his or her time with the Lord that he or she would never think of facing the toils of the day without first strengthening the inner man with the joy of the Lord: *"Do not sorrow, for the joy of the Lord is your strength"* (Neh. 8:10).

While teaching His own disciples how to pray, the Lord Jesus emphasized the need for divine dependency with the words, *"Give us this day our daily bread"* (Matt. 6:11). He then informed them that there was no need to worry about daily staples; these would be provided by God if they first sought to do His will in their lives (Matt. 6:25-34). For those of us who live within the affluent western culture, the idea of trusting the Lord for our daily bread is a mostly untested concept. Little of our abundance is needed to supply our actual daily necessities and even less of it is used to feed and clothe the poor. Rather, our vast wealth is used to insulate ourselves against any conceivable mishap, to collect stuff we really don't need, and to indulge or pamper our flesh with creature comforts that last only a moment and waste valuable time. May we learn what Moses did when he turned his back on the riches of Egypt: God was his full sufficiency. Consider the adage: "Use it up, wear it out, make it do, do without."[3]

February 20 – Working Too Hard?
Exodus 18

Moses had been divinely appointed to lead the Israelites and to be God's mouthpiece to His people. As Jethro witnessed the arduous nature of his son-in-law's workday, he felt that Moses was undertaking too much. In his estimation, there were too many people for one man to effectively teach, advise, and judge; anyone trying to do so would *"wear away"* (v. 18, KJV). Jethro genuinely feared for Moses' health and suggested that his son-in-law appoint some assistants.

After listening to Jethro's counsel, Moses appointed various helpers among the people without consulting the Lord (vv. 25-26). Shortly after this, he complained to God about his overwhelming leadership responsibilities (Num. 11:14-15). Furthermore, Moses expressed his doubts that God could supply meat for the entire nation in a wilderness. The Lord responded to Moses' complaints by removing some of his so-called "burden" (and its honor) and to rebuke him (Num. 11:16-17).

The spiritual correlation between doubting the goodness of God and having a diminished capacity to serve Him is thus apparent. God had chosen Moses to be Israel's deliverer and had given him the Holy Spirit to enable Moses to prosper in his calling. Moses' service was a testimony of God's abundant power, which was a tremendous privilege extended to Moses. As long as Moses trusted in the Lord instead of his own abilities, every difficulty he would face would be amply met with divine grace. Moses had given ear to a different one, an earthly and familiar voice; Jethro's well-meaning advice prompted Moses' flesh to respond in an earthly way, one that was not under the Spirit's control.

Instead of following God's Word and His Spirit, new thoughts and ideas infiltrated Moses' thinking. Unexpectedly, he was awakened to the overwhelming nature of his calling. The work had not changed and he still had God's Spirit upon him; nothing had changed but Moses' attitude – he had a new perspective, an earthly vantage point of his ministry.

Any of us can fall prey to the subtle suggestion of a sincere and well-meaning person, especially when he or she is a loved-one. The right thing to do is to humbly wait at our assigned posts and fully rely on the Lord in the execution of our duties until new marching orders are received from our divine Captain relocating us to a strategic position.

May We Serve Christ!

February 21 – Transgression for All
Exodus 19

The events on Mount Sinai mark a new era in divine revelation. Until this time, God had on rare occasions revealed His will to individuals in the form of a charge or a call; now, He spelled out His code of ethics in intricate detail. In this respect, the Jews had an advantage over all other nations. Yet privilege and responsibility are yoked together, meaning that the Jews had greater accountability to God than the other nations did. Obedience would be rewarded, but disobedience against God's Law would be reckoned as transgression against God: *"The law brings about wrath; for where there is no law there is no transgression"* (Rom. 4:15) and, *"For until the law sin was in the world, but sin is not imputed when there is no law"* (Rom. 5:13).

All of mankind was condemned in Adam and through Adam all humanity received a fallen nature, which opposes God (Rom. 5:12). Sin, therefore, has continued in the world, but from the time of Adam until the time of the Law it was not imputed as transgression. This does not mean that human sin during this time did not offend God – all sin offends God – but rather that sin was not regarded as transgression.

During this interim (and presently), the human conscience experientially proved to one's own soul that he or she had an imbedded code of ethics which could not be perfectly obeyed (Rom. 2:15). Internal feelings of guilt meant that sin had been committed. Now that God's Law had been specifically revealed, ignorance would no longer be an excuse; sin would be accounted as transgression against God.

To illustrate this point, consider this example. Until a highway has a posted speed limit, a patrol officer has no authority to pull you over and write you a citation for speeding – you have broken no law. However, this does not mean that you have not been driving excessively fast, for one's conscience bears witness of what appropriate conduct is. But once the law is decreed (posted), a legal responsibility to obey it is realized. If an individual drives responsibly he or she is able to maintain the privilege of driving, but if he or she doesn't, fines and loss of privilege normally result. The Jews now had no excuse for continuing in sin; they knew exactly what was expected of them and the consequences for not obeying God's moral demands upon them.

Daily Devotions

February 22 – God Introduces Himself
Exodus 19

After Moses had personally conveyed to God the Israelites' pledge to fully obey all that God would command of them, the Lord told His servant to sanctify the people, for in three days He would descend upon the mount and would speak to him again in the hearing of the people. The Israelites were about to personally meet Jehovah and hear His voice, though He Himself would be engulfed by a dark cloud on the mount. The Lord instructed Moses to impose a strict boundary about the mountain's base; any person or beast that trespassed upon the mount should be put to death. This was a precautionary measure to keep the people from casually approaching God, and thus, being consumed by His presence.

In preparation for this meeting with God the Jews were to wash their clothes, and husbands and wives were to abstain from sexual relationships. This restriction punctuated the solemn nature of the upcoming event and the need for complete devotion while preparing to meet Jehovah (1 Cor. 7:5, 32-33). Though they saw displays of Jehovah's presence each day, such familiarity should never lead to a lackadaisical attitude about approaching a holy God, *"a consuming fire"* (Heb. 12:29).

When the day came for the nation of Israel to meet the Lord, a long blast of a trumpet signaled Moses to lead the people to the base of the mount. The mount quaked exceedingly, it burned like an overheated furnace, and thick billows of smoke ascended up from it into heaven. From the thick darkness, a deafening voice which increased in volume uttered words as if blasted from a trumpet. So overwhelmed were the people by what they heard, felt, and saw, that they *"begged that the word should not be spoken to them anymore"* (Heb. 12:19) and *"they moved and stood afar off"* from the mountain (Ex. 20:18).

So mighty was the scene that day that even God's deliverer, Moses, said, *"I am exceedingly afraid and trembling"* (Heb. 12:21). This day would never be forgotten in Israel, some 1,500 years later the writer of Hebrews referred to this event to epitomize the holy nature of God (Heb. 12:18-21). Though the Israelites had cleansed themselves the best they could they immediately felt unclean in Jehovah's holy presence. This was the purpose of the Mount Sinai experience and they fearfully retreated and *"stood afar off"* (v. 18). In any era, the first step of salvation is to realize that God is holy and we are not!

May We Serve Christ!

February 23 – Bear One Another's Burdens
Exodus 21

Hebrew history shows that there were two main reasons Jews would become slaves to other Jews: they could sell themselves into slavery in order to pay off a debt (such as a bride's dowry or an economic hardship) or they could be forced into slavery as a result of a punitive judgment (e.g. recompense for a crime committed). In any case, God did not desire His people to be forced to serve others as slaves, but rather, to be a liberated people who would freely serve Him. Consequently, no Jew was to be held in slavery against his or her will for more than six years, no matter what situation caused the servitude.

For the Christian, both the legislation on slavery and the ill-treatment of women is loathsome, but as F. B. Hole reminds us, the Law was not God's best for man, the best was yet to come:

> We may remark that under the law things were permitted that should not be tolerated by Christians today. That this was so is shown by the Lord's own words (Matt. 19:7-8). We must ever bear in mind that, "the law made nothing perfect" (Heb. 7:19), since it set forth the minimum of God's demands, so that all, who in any way or at any time fell short of it, came under the sentence of death. The maximum of all God's thoughts and desires are realized and set forth in Christ.[4]

God instituted slavery regulations to protect His people from abusing each other in future generations; however, His desire for them was that they assist one another in economic hardships, not take advantage of each other: *"If one of your brethren becomes poor, and falls into poverty among you, then you shall help him, like a stranger or a sojourner, that he may live with you. Take no usury or interest from him; but fear your God, that your brother may live with you"* (Lev. 25:35-37).

Though Christians are not under the Law, this regulation highlights what God deems appropriate conduct for His people throughout all ages, that is, to rally around and help each other during times of distress: *"Bear one another's burdens, and so fulfill the law of Christ"* (Gal. 6:2). Indeed, this was the practice of the early Church (Acts 4:32-35, 6:1; 1 Tim. 5:3-5).

February 24 – I Will Not Go Out Free!
Exodus 21

After six years of service, or at the fifty-year Jubilee if it occurred prior to the six year tenure (Lev. 25:39-42), a Hebrew slave was to be released, unless the slave desired to remain with his master for life. If this was the slave's choice he was taken to a doorpost, his ear was placed next to the wood, and the master pushed or pounded an awl through the slave's ear. The resulting hole marked him as a bondservant for life. In the Epistles, Paul often applied this phrase to express his own love for the Lord Jesus Christ. The only reason a man would become a perpetual bondservant would be to express love for his master, or perhaps, if had been given a wife while in slavery, love for his family (for his family would not be released if he chose to go free).

As love for the master is mentioned first, it seems to be the primary reason a slave would be willing to enter into a life-long commitment to his master. Certainly, the exceptional care of the master for his slave had already been experienced, for what slave would willingly enter into a lifetime commitment of brutality. The slave had two options at the conclusion of his time of binding service: he could *"go out free and pay nothing"* (v. 2), or he could tell his master, *"I will not go out free"* (v. 5). If he chose the first option he was to be set free; he was at liberty to live his life however he chose to do so, but he departed empty-handed. Likewise, since his association with his master was severed, there would be no future assistance or benefits received from him either. If the slave chose the latter option, he would be committing himself for the remainder of his life to serve his master and he would also enjoy all the blessings of that association.

Commitment entails being given over to a cause without reservation; such was the pledge of a slave to his master, and such should be the pledge of every child of God to his or her Master. Only after a believer has consciously made such a determination will he or she have the unwavering obedience and devotion of a true disciple of Christ (Luke 9:23-25). What you do for eternity the world cannot destroy, nor can anyone steal (Matt. 6:19-20). What is desperately needed in the Church today is for believers to look heavenward and tell the Master: "I will not go out free for nothing!"

February 25 – Thrones and Altars
Exodus 24

Scripture often presents seemingly contrasting subjects in tandem to draw out their deeper spiritual meaning. Such is the topical pairing of the *throne* and the *altar*. In Exodus 21 and 24 Mount Sinai is God's majestic throne, His glorious habitation before His people, though not intimately among them. Gazing upon God's throne-mountain, the Israelites witnessed His awesome nature and received His righteous Law (Ex. 21). Their response to God's holiness was to fear and to stand afar off – this is the proper response of sinful man to God's throne. The chapter then closes with God's provision for His people to worship Him – an altar upon which to present burnt offering and peace offerings (Ex. 21:24). The altar did not allow the people to come intimately near Jehovah, but it did allow them to worship Him from a safe distance.

Moses had verbally reviewed God's Law with the people and had also communicated their verbal acceptance of it in Exodus 21; now God would formally ratify and record the covenant with them. In Exodus 24, Moses built an altar at the foot of Sinai per the instructions provided in Exodus 21. This altar was for all the people since it had twelve pillars (stones), one for each tribe. Young men acted as priests, as Aaron and his sons had not yet been appointed to the priesthood.

The book of Hebrews furnishes a few details that were not recorded in Exodus. Moses *"took the blood of calves and goats, with water, scarlet wool, hyssop, and sprinkled both the book itself and all the people"* (Heb. 9:19). Not only the altar and the people, but also the book of the Law he had written was purified by blood – blood was the basis for the covenant of the Law.

After the people were sprinkled with blood, Moses, Aaron, Nadab and Abihu, and the seventy elders of Israel (representing all the people) ascended part way up the mountain to see God. They not only saw the base of God's sapphire throne, but ate and drank before the Lord! Earlier, the people fled from God's presence when they witnessed His grandeur in a smoking and quaking mountain, but now they were permitted to come as close as possible to Him and enjoy fellowship before Him. We, by Christ's shed blood, can now come boldly into the throne room of heaven whenever we desire to worship or seek grace from the same awesome God!

Daily Devotions

February 26 – Watching and Waiting
Exodus 32

In receiving the Law, Moses had been alone with God for forty days on the mount. Below Mount Sinai, the children of Israel had become anxious about Moses' welfare, and apparently presumed him dead. Rather than waiting any longer for information about Moses' wellbeing, the people coerced Aaron into creating a golden image of Jehovah for them to worship. The One who had brought them out of Egypt was now epitomized as a golden calf. The event exposes the utterly depraved nature of the human heart; left to himself, man will always turn aside from the path of righteousness and go his own way.

God was furious over the Israelites' offense and instructed Moses to immediately return to camp. Joshua, who had been faithfully waiting part of the way up the mount for Moses' descent was completely separate from the depravity of the Israelites. In fact, he was not even aware of it and suggested to Moses that the camp was under attack. But Moses, who already knew of the Israelites' debauchery, told Joshua that the noise he heard had nothing to do with victory or defeat, but was *"the sound of singing."* In Exodus 17, Joshua pictured Christ among His people as he led them to victory over the Amalekites, but now, Joshua is seen apart from Israelites. Christ cannot have fellowship with or victorious power among His people while they are in sin.

Moses had instructed all of the seventy elders to wait upon the lower part of the mountain until he returned after his meeting with God (Ex. 24:14). Perhaps some waited a day or two, perhaps others a week; in any case, only Joshua remained until the coming of Moses. In so doing, Joshua was kept undefiled by the sin of the people below.

Likewise, the Lord Jesus exhorted His disciples to faithfully watch, wait, and be ready for His coming (Matt. 24:42-44). John understood the purifying benefit of living each day as if the Lord could return for the Church at any time (1 Jn. 3:2-3). If Israel's leadership had been expecting fresh revelation from God through Moses, they would have remained on the mount and the opportunity to create a golden calf would have been avoided.

Likewise, believers living with the hope of the imminent return of Christ are prompted to live purely before God. Anything or anyone that draws away our heart's affection for Him is nonetheless a golden calf.

February 27 – God Judges Sin
Exodus 32

The children of Israel had broken their covenant with God; if Moses had brought the Law of God into the camp at that moment, swift judgment would have been executed. Therefore, in breaking the tablets, Moses anger served the people in that it presented to them the possibility of repentance and restoration with God.

No system had yet been established to atone for the sins of the people, and no one can stand against God's justice for sin unless God's grace presents a means of righteous pardon. This is why the blood of an innocent substitute was required upon the Mercy Seat on the Ark of the Covenant. The ark contained God's Law, which offered the only means of escaping His righteous wrath. The Mercy Seat was the only place on earth where God's righteousness and His grace cooperated as one for man's good.

Moses, who as an intercessor had pleaded that his people not be destroyed, now took on the role of judge, executing punishment upon them so that they might be made to feel the bitterness of their sin. He burnt the golden calf, ground it into powder, scattered it over the camp's drinking water, and then made the people drink it. This was a humiliating end to their supposed "god" that brought them out of Egypt; however, it was only the beginning of God's disciplinary judgment on His people. Their *relationship* with God was sealed by God's covenant with Abraham, but their *fellowship* with God would depend upon their obedience to His laws.

This distinction is upheld in the New Testament. Believers must understand the difference between relationship and fellowship or they will misunderstand the reason for God's disciplinary judgments. Relationships are established through acts (e.g. marriage, birth, and adoption), but fellowship between these parties is contingent on proper behavior.

Offenses limit fellowship in a relationship, but the opposite can never be true – fellowship cannot exist without relationship. Today, one becomes a member of God's family by spiritual birth (John 1:12-13) and this relationship is eternally secure. However, God cannot have fellowship with His erring children (1 Jn. 1:6). Instead, He proves His love to them by chastening them in order to restore them (Heb. 12:6).

February 28 – "I Will Give You Rest"
Exodus 33

Moses enjoyed full fellowship with God. When they met together, Jehovah spoke to Moses *"face to face, as a man speaks to his friend"* (v. 11). This is not a literal statement, for no one in his or her natural state can look upon God's face and live (v. 20); rather, it is a figurative expression used to convey blessed intimacy. As Moses demonstrated, one of the great privileges of being in intimate fellowship with God is the opportunity to intercede on behalf of the wayward. But first, Moses petitioned the Lord on his own behalf:

> *See, You say to me, "Bring up this people." But You have not let me know whom You will send with me. Yet You have said, "I know you by name, and you have also found grace in My sight." Now therefore, I pray, if I have found grace in Your sight, show me now Your way, that I may know You and that I may find grace in Your sight. And consider that this nation is Your people* (Ex. 33:12-13).

God had commissioned Moses to lead the people, but if God were not with them, it didn't matter where they went. So, while in the spirit of prayer, he reverently reminded God what He had previously promised to do. Though God had told Moses that He would send His Angel (pre-incarnate Christ) before him, Moses had limited knowledge of "God's way" in the matter. This sincere prayer of Moses was offered on the sole basis that God personally knew him by name (i.e. that Moses belonged to God) and that he had found grace in God's sight.

The answer to Moses' prayer is brief, but tremendously consoling: *"My Presence will go with you, and I will give you rest"* (v. 14). God's response was a solace to Moses' soul, for he knew that he could do nothing apart from Jehovah and that there was no reason for the nation to exist apart from its connection with Him.

Moses' reason for living and his strength for living came from the abiding presence of Jehovah. This was "God's way," and would be sufficient for the desolate path ahead. This is true for every Christian also; the indwelling presence of the Holy Spirit enables the believer to overcome difficulties and to commune with God. The Lord's presence bestows us rest too!

February 29 – "Show Me Your Glory"
Exodus 33

Next, Moses offered intercession for the people, saying, *"Consider that this nation is Your people"* (v. 13). His intercession for the Israelites was successful; the Lord responded, *"I will also do this thing that you have spoken; for you have found grace in My sight, and I know you by name"* (v. 17). The Israelites will be restored to Jehovah; they will again be His people, and will again be put under the covenant of the Law, the same covenant they broke (Ex. 34; Jer. 31:32).

By this act, God demonstrated that though the Law revealed sin and condemned the sinner, His overall plan of salvation included the opportunity of receiving grace, but since this would be obtained by Christ's work at Calvary this truth was broadly concealed until after Christ's resurrection (1 Cor. 2:7-8). Moses was elated over the demonstration of God's mercy in forgiving and restoring the Israelites to Himself.

The Lord then responded to Moses' prayer to see His glory with a warning: *"You cannot see My face; for no man shall see Me, and live"* (v. 20). Since no human in his or her natural state can look on the fullness of God's glory and live, the Lord told Moses that He would tuck him into a cleft of a rock and allowed Moses to view His "afterglow" as He passed by. In this fashion, Moses could appreciate as much of the Lord as possible without being harmed.

Moses was extended a great privilege, but in the Church Age, the humblest Christian is brought nearer to beholding the glory of God by viewing Christ through Scripture than Moses was when he was in the cleft of the rock. Paul, speaking of the transforming power of God's Word, puts it this way: *"But we all, with unveiled face, beholding as in a mirror the glory of the Lord, are being transformed into the same image from glory to glory, just as by the Spirit of the Lord"* (2 Cor. 3:18). As we peer into the Holy Page, the Spirit of God shows us the glory of Christ in God; to the extent that we desire to behold His glory, we are changed into the same image. Every believer should long to see Christ's glorious appearing; but while waiting for that day, may each of us earnestly beseech the Lord, as Moses did, *"Please, show me Your glory."* The more we see of Him – the more we become like Him.

Daily Devotions

March 1 – Gifts from Willing Hearts
Exodus 35

After again reminding them to sanctify the Sabbath day, Moses announced that a collection would be taken for the Lord for the purpose of constructing the tabernacle and its furnishings. The following items were to be collected: precious metals, gems, olive oil, and various fabrics and skins. Three important points are noteworthy at this juncture.

First, though Moses mentioned the tabernacle and its various furnishings, he did not tell them what the tabernacle was for, though he knew that the collected resources would be used to construct and equip God's dwelling place among them.

Second, giving was not compulsory; only those who wanted to give were to contribute. Moses declared, *"Take from among you an offering to the Lord. Whoever is of a willing heart, let him bring it as an offering to the Lord"* (Ex. 35:5).

Third, an invitation to construct the articles of the tabernacle was offered, but only those who were willing and wise-hearted could participate. The people, still rejoicing in their pardon, gave generously to the Lord, even though they did not completely understand what the collection was for. An opportunity to show their appreciation for Jehovah had been offered, and the people quickly took advantage of it.

The people's response to Moses' call to contribute and to labor was overwhelming. Two aspects of their giving are stressed: First, that they were willing to donate their possessions, skills, and time to the construction of the tabernacle, and second, that *everyone* was involved in the activity. The contributions and the labor needed to construct the tabernacle, its furnishings, and the priestly attire were given by the entire assembly – everyone chose to be involved with the work! How wonderful a scene this is – God's people jointly giving of themselves for the work of the Lord, not knowing the end result, but yet willing and obedient to what they understand is required of them.

If brethren today could recapture this enthusiasm, the Church would be transformed into a vibrant, living testimony for Christ. Giving to the Lord brings joy to the heart, and laboring together with like-minded believers for the cause of Christ builds unity, strengthens the Body of Christ, and accomplishes what individual efforts could never do.

March 2 – Work from Wise Hearts
Exodus 35

Willing hearts contributed resources to the work of the tabernacle; and wise hearts offered time, skills, and energy to accomplish the work. The phrase "wisehearted" is employed several times in this chapter to describe the people who constructed the tabernacle and its furnishings. The construction of the tabernacle involved sewing, weaving, forging, carving, pounding, cutting, forming, polishing, etc.; the Israelites were a ready workforce.

However, the natural abilities of the people were not sufficient to accomplish the work of the Lord; it required individuals that were filled, gifted, and controlled by the Holy Spirit. Bezalel, the son of Uri, the grandson of Hur, and Oholiab, the son of Ahisamach of the tribe of Dan, were specifically named as the individuals whom the Lord had prepared with wisdom, knowledge, and workmanship to lead and achieve *all* of the tasks related to the construction project. Apparently, these men were to lead the effort, guiding others who had also been given wisdom in various aspects of the work (Ex. 36:1-2).

This chapter foreshadows several New Testament truths concerning the work of the members within of the body of Christ. First, note that giving to the work of the Lord was done by all the Israelites. Years later, Paul would exhort the Church at Corinth, *"On the first day of the week **let each one of you** lay something aside, storing up as he may prosper"* (1 Cor. 16:2). All believers are to willingly and regularly give to the work of the Lord, as they have been prospered by God.

Second, everyone was given an opportunity to serve God and everyone was to fulfill their assigned ministry. The Lord Jesus gave individuals, such as evangelists and teachers, as gifts to the Church for a reason: *"for the equipping of the saints **for the work of ministry**, for the edifying of the body of Christ"* (Eph. 4:12). Every believer has a work to engage in, which in turn, blesses the entire body of Christ.

Third, the Holy Spirit gifts, equips, and enables God's people to serve the Lord in a way that would not be naturally possible. As believers correctly use their spiritual gifts, they equip others in the body to minister as well. This edifies the Church and enables individuals to reach their full potential in Christ and His purpose for their lives.

March 3 – Be Holy and Come Near
Leviticus 1

In Exodus, God's covenant people had been redeemed by the blood of the Passover lamb and delivered from both bondage and Egypt. The book of Leviticus then reveals two central truths concerning Jehovah's new beginning with His people: they were permitted to come near to worship Him through blood atonement and they must be a holy people, for their God is holy. To this end, the book can be divided into two thematic sections: The Way to Approach God (chps. 1-16), and The Walk of Holiness Before God (chps. 17-27).

The first Hebrew word of the Leviticus text, *qara'*, which means "to call out" (1:1), introduces us to the theme of the book. Jehovah is calling His people to come near to Him, but they must be cleansed from defilement to do so – they must be holy. The key verse is Leviticus 20:26: *"You shall be holy to Me, for I the Lord am holy, and have separated you from the peoples, that you should be Mine."* Leviticus shows us that holiness has two main components: our separation from sin and our commitment to God's glory. God is holy and He wants His people to come near Him in holiness but only by His means of purification. The writer of Hebrews confirms this same reality today:

> *Let us have grace, by which we may serve God acceptably with reverence and godly fear. For our God is a consuming fire* (Heb. 12:28-29).

> *Let us therefore come boldly to the throne of grace, that we may obtain mercy and find grace to help in time of need* (Heb. 4:16).

> *Brethren, having boldness to enter the Holiest by the blood of Jesus, by a new and living way which He consecrated for us ... let us draw near with a true heart in full assurance of faith, having our hearts sprinkled from an evil conscience and our bodies washed with pure water* (Heb. 10:19-23)

God invites believers in the Church Age to come near Him, but only as redeemed and cleansed by the blood of the Lord Jesus Christ; this is what is symbolized by the various offerings in Leviticus.

March 4 – Skin for the Priest
Leviticus 7

The Old Testament is full of portraits of God's substitutionary sacrifice of His Son for the sinner and the imputation of divine righteousness to his or her account. Christ is the believer's righteousness, in both the practical and positional sense of the word (1 Cor. 1:30; 2 Cor. 5:21). When the offerer put his hand on the head of his sacrifice, he was identifying himself with it and so was God. This identification is further extended to the offering priest who received the skin of the animal offered in a burnt sacrifice.

The priest would likely fashion coverings for himself with the skin, such as shoes or clothes. While the priest was in the tabernacle, his priestly service required him to be clothed with priestly garments. However, during his routine apart from the tabernacle, his clothing derived from the skins would be a constant reminder of the offering previously sacrificed. When observed by others, it would be the burnt offering sacrifice (the priest's covering) that would be noticed, not the priest himself.

What is the application for the believer today? *"Put on the Lord Jesus Christ, and make no provision for the flesh, to fulfill its lusts* (Rom. 13:14). The position of righteousness we have in Christ should cause us to "shine out" Christ practically during daily priestly service to Him. In our day to day life, others should not see us, but the "sacrifice" – the Lord Jesus. The inherent beauty of the bride of Christ in Revelation 19:7-9 is the glory of Christ seen in the bride. Not only does she have a position of righteousness, but the works of righteousness Christ has done through her are spectacular.

When God looks at a believer, He sees the perfection of Christ. Thus, in Christ, there is nothing for the believer to fear, except to disappoint the One for whom he or she is to live. John put the matter this way: *"There is no fear in love; but perfect love casts out fear, because fear involves torment. But he who fears has not been made perfect in love. We love Him because He first loved us"* (1 Jn. 4:18-19). Just as the burnt offering was voluntary in Moses' day, so is our service to Christ today. Having understood our complete acceptance in Christ and our opportunity to declare His righteousness in word and deed, may we all wear the skin of His sacrifice with honor.

March 5 – Strange Fire
Leviticus 10

This is one of the most sorrowful portions of Scripture. Jehovah had selected Aaron and his four sons, Nadab, Abihu, Eleazar, and Ithamar to officially minister in the tabernacle on behalf of Israel. But shortly after their consecration, before the Israelites moved northward from Mount Sinai, Nadab and Abihu, Aaron's oldest two sons, were fatally judged for intruding into God's presence with "strange fire" (vv. 1-5).

What a contrast to the scene which had just concluded! At the initiation of the Aaronic priesthood all was done *"as the Lord commanded,"* and the result was the glory of God appeared to the entire nation. In Leviticus 10, something is done *"which He had not commanded,"* and the result was prompt, irrevocable judgment. Hardly had the last echoes of exaltation faded away before the entire camp was shocked by grief at the cost of presumptuous worship. The newly installed priests had failed to properly execute their high office and holy vindication was swift and final.

Having kindled their own censors of incense, the two sons brought them into the tabernacle to offer worship to the Lord. The Lord had not yet given instructions as to how the holy incense was to be kindled and presented before Him (Lev. 16:12-13). The reference to "strange fire" may speak of fire that did not come from the Bronze Altar, which is where atonement for sin was accomplished and thus pictures God's ultimate judgment of human sin at Calvary. To approach God on any other basis than through Christ's propitiation would be intensely insulting to God.

One way this is done today is when people tell God they can earn their way to heaven through good church attendance, water baptism, giving to the poor, etc. instead of trusting in Christ's finished work alone. Like many today, Nadab and Abihu had good intentions, but they were intruding on the things of God without having the mind of God. Their actions angered the Lord and fire came out from the Lord and the two lads died. Their judgment was just for their offense; hence Aaron was not permitted to grieve for his sons.

Moses reminded Aaron of Jehovah's decree: *"By those who come near Me, I must be regarded as holy; and before all the people I must be glorified"* (v. 3). May we never forget this important truth.

May We Serve Christ!

March 6 – Diagnosis of Leprosy
Leviticus 13

The atonement associated with childbirth in Leviticus 12 called our attention to the inherited sinful *nature* within all newborns. Leviticus 13 speaks of the visible outbreak of that nature in sinful *activity*, as represented in the disease of leprosy. Leprosy, as a type, focuses on the corrupting and defiling power of the sin within, rather than its guilt or the fallen nature itself. Leprosy speaks, not of what we are in Adam, but rather of who we prove we are by our lives. Like sin, leprosy exists within an individual long before it works its way outward and becomes evident to observers. Hansen's disease has an incubation period of about 3-5 years. In reality, all lepers were lepers long before they became aware of their symptoms. Likewise, a man does not become a sinner because he stole his neighbor's belongings. We are all born into sin, and sooner or later the worst of us comes to light (Rom. 5:12).

Leviticus 13 identifies two main types of leprosy that infected people: leprosy of the flesh and leprosy of the head. Spiritually speaking, these relate to two classes of deadly sins. Leprosy of the flesh refers to fleshly lusts and includes gluttony, drunkenness, fornication, lasciviousness, etc. Leprosy of the head speaks of lusting in the mind which results in pride, unbelief, arrogance, envy, humanism, etc. There are two biblical examples of proud individuals whom God smote with leprosy.

The first was Miriam, the sister of Moses, who with Aaron spoke against their brother, God's chosen leader for the people (Num. 12:1-4). As Aaron was the high priest, he was spared judgment as that would have cut off the nation from Jehovah, but Miriam was a leper for seven days before the Lord healed her through Moses' intercession. Because Jewish women were well-covered in public and her leprosy was visible, it was likely her face and head that were infected.

Besides Miriam, King Uzziah was also struck with facial leprosy because of his pride. He brought a censer into the temple to offer worship to Jehovah. This was an intrusion on the priesthood which God had strictly forbidden. May we all recall that: *"A man's pride will bring him low, but the humble in spirit will retain honor"* (Prov. 29:23) and *"By pride comes nothing but strife"* (Prov. 13:10). Let us bestow on the Lord the honor He deserves instead of trying to retain it for ourselves.

March 7 – Honor Your Father and Mother
Leviticus 19

The diversity of subjects addressed in this chapter illustrates that the matter of practical holiness is to extend into every aspect of our lives. The Jews were to learn that holiness is not merely correct behavior, but it extends to one's attitude: loving what God deems good and hating what He calls evil. Israel was to stand with God (and against themselves) on every point of the Law, and to do so with tenacity.

Moses commenced this set of warnings by affirming that children are to honor and obey their parents and that the Sabbath day was to be kept holy. Ultimately, the reverence for both commandments will be taught and observed in the home. If parents do not teach their children to respect God-ordained authority, they will, as adults, have little regard for law and order. Those who do not respect authority go their own way in life and suffer the harsh reality of an insubordinate spirit.

Paul also quotes the fifth of the Ten Commandments in his epistle to the Ephesians and notes the promise associated with it: *Children, obey your parents in the Lord, for this is right. "Honor your father and mother," which is the first commandment with promise: "that it may be well with you and you may live long on the earth"* (Eph. 6:1-3).

A child not corrected would be socially miserable and a nuisance to society. His sinful ways and rebellious manner would probably lead him into an early grave. However, a child who practices obedience is much more likely to live a happy and prosperous life. The Greek word translated "children" in Ephesians 6:1 is *teknon,* which means "that which is derived of another" (i.e., children are derived from their parents). Age is not implied, meaning that the application of the word is not limited to small children. A different word, *paidion,* is used to speak of small children. Hence, children should always respect and honor their parents regardless of how old they are.

Yet when children marry and have children of their own, they become accountable to do what is God-honoring and best for their own family. The stipulative phrase, *"in the Lord,"* implies children are to serve their parents as unto the Lord in matters of righteousness, but not in matters of sin (e.g. Korah's sons refused to follow their father into rebellion against God).

March 8 – Condemned Behavior
Leviticus 20

This chapter levies harsh penalties for many of the prohibitions listed in Leviticus 18 and 19. Once guilt had been established, the appropriate penalty for the crime was to be executed immediately. As Solomon notes, when justice is not swiftly enacted on the guilty, the idea of "free sin" gains a grip in the carnal nature of man: *"Because the sentence against an evil work is not executed speedily, therefore the heart of the sons of men is fully set in them to do evil"* (Eccl. 8:11). If people begin to think they will escape punishment for their crimes, they will sin more. When this ideology gains ground, the tenuous moral foundation of our society will speedily crumble away.

Twice in this chapter, which pronounces judgment on sexual perversions and religious sins, God exhorts His people to holiness (vv. 7-8, 22-26). God had chosen the Jews to be a distinct people living among the nations and, thus, the Jews were not to follow the world's pattern of life. Even what the Jews touched and ate marked them as a peculiar people. They were to be holy people because their God was, and is, holy.

The exhortations to godly living and the severe consequences for failing to do so contained in this section of Leviticus prove to us that there is no deception, no secret sin, no immoral act, no impurity of any kind that is compatible with God's character: *"God is light, and in Him is no darkness at all"* (1 Jn. 1:5). The Lord will not, in fact cannot, have any part in our sin (1 Jn. 1:6-7). If we want to enjoy communion with a holy God, we must choose the lighted pathway of holiness to reverently venture into the wonders of His presence.

Thus, the child of God is to constantly discern between what is holy and what is evil, between what is wise and what is foolish. That which is holy and wise should be obeyed, and that which is evil and foolish should be shunned. God's will for the believer is that he or she should refrain from doing sin, and that he or she should indeed practice a sin-free life altogether (1 Jn. 2:1). However, on this side of glory, sinless perfection is a pursuit, not a reality – thank God our salvation is not based on our doings, but upon His grace in Christ. Let us all pursue holiness, for in holiness we find not the inability to sin, but the ability not to sin.

Daily Devotions

March 9 – Don't Blaspheme
Leviticus 24

We read the account of two men striving together, and that one of the two men, a son of a Hebrew woman and Egyptian man, blasphemed the name of Jehovah. The blasphemer was put into prison until Moses consulted the Lord on the matter. There was no ambiguity about Jehovah's ruling: *"Whoever curses his God shall bear his sin. And whoever blasphemes the name of the Lord shall surely be put to death"* (vv. 15-16). Jehovah's name is holy and anyone cursing the almighty God, deserved death. The accused man was removed from the camp and the entire congregation immediately stoned the blasphemer. God was to be reverenced in the land, and not even "strangers" were to blaspheme the name of Israel's God.

This sin of blasphemy relates to violating God's commandment: *"You shall not take the name of the Lord your God in vain, for the Lord will not hold him guiltless who takes His name in vain"* (Ex. 20:7). Accordingly, God Himself is blasphemed when dishonor is affixed to His name. This can be accomplished in two ways, either by exalting what is ordinary to a high and holy status, or by reckoning what is lofty and divine, such as God's name, as of common value. The sin of blasphemy involves showing disdain or a lack of reverence for God or for what He deems as sacred (Matt. 26:65), or attributing divine features to something or someone other than God (Mark 14:64). The psalmist reminds us that only fools blaspheme God's name (Ps. 74:18)!

Believers should be careful not to desecration God's *"holy and awesome"* name (Ps. 111:9)! You may be thinking to yourself, "I do respect God's name!" However, this reflects a human understanding of blasphemy, not a biblical one. In actuality, we often unconsciously demean God's name. For example, how often have you heard someone say, "Holy ------"? This is a form of blasphemy – taking what is high and holy and associating it with something low and earthly.

Besides evil speech, various behaviors result in disdain on the Lord's name: teaching false doctrine (1 Tim. 6:3-4), swearing falsely (Lev. 19:12; Matt. 5:3; Jas. 5:12), stealing (Prov. 30:9; Eph. 4:28), demoting the character of God (Matt. 26:74), and having an impudent heart (Matt. 23:16-22; Col. 1:18). May we all learn not to blaspheme (1 Tim. 1:20)!

March 10 – Caring for the Poor
Leviticus 25

Laws governing the land are contained in this chapter. Commandments pertaining to the Sabbatical year and the year of Jubilee are stated, as well as instructions governing the redemption of both land and people sold because of economic hardship.

The Jews were to be a hospitable people, especially to their destitute brethren. Favoritism was discouraged; their homes were to be open not just to esteemed visitors but also to each other. God had been gracious in deeding them the Promised Land; likewise, they were to be generous in assisting their poor brethren.

Although the Jews were not forbidden to exact interest from foreigners (Deut. 23:20), there was to be no charging of interest to worsen the plight of their fellow countrymen (vv. 36-37). Moses exhorted his brethren: *"You shall not oppress one another, but you shall fear your God; for I am the Lord your God"* (Lev. 25:17). Besides our care for fellow believers in need, David and Solomon remind us to also attend to the needs of the poor:

> *Blessed is he who considers the poor; the Lord will deliver him in time of trouble* (Ps. 41:1).

> *He who has pity on the poor lends to the Lord, and He will pay back what he has given* (Prov. 19:17).

> *He who gives to the poor will not lack, but he who hides his eyes will have many curses* (Prov. 28:27).

The Lord rewards those who attend to the needy. In the Church Age, through the power of the Holy Spirit, believers are able to fulfill God's fuller intention of the Law – to demonstrate divine love for each other (Rom. 13:10). One kept the Law by not stealing, but to fulfill the Law goes beyond this to selflessly giving to another. Therefore, Paul exhorts believers not only to care for each other and the poor, but also to extend compassion to those who oppose us. If they are hungry and thirsty, we are to provide them food and drink (Rom. 12:20). He explains that such kindhearted acts *"overcome evil by doing good"* (Rom. 12:21). Such conduct is a tangible and lasting testimony of Christ in our communities.

March 11 – Blessing or Chastening
Leviticus 26

The message of this chapter is reminiscent of the scene which occurred at Marah a few months earlier. The Lord spoke of His statutes and commandments for the first time after transforming the bitter waters at Marah into satisfying, life-sustaining drink (Ex. 15). The principle Moses conveyed to the people was a simple one: obedience would be rewarded with God's blessing, but disobedience would be met with severe judgment. Moses reiterates the idea by identifying six forms of blessing for obedience and five means of retribution for disobedience in this chapter.

The irresistible love of God can only be experienced by answering His invitation to know Him through His revealed Word. Our understanding of God's plan and our commitment to live it out will be directly proportional to the extent that we have known and experienced Him. The Lord Jesus said, *"He who has My commandments and keeps them, it is he who loves Me. And he who loves Me will be loved by My Father, and I will love him and manifest Myself to him"* (John 14:21). Continued submission to divine truth is the pathway to intimately experiencing and knowing God in deepening degrees.

In order to walk with the Lord, we must be in agreement with Him on the matter of sin. For, *"can two walk together except they be agreed?"* (Amos 3:3). Surely, light has no communion with darkness; thus, may each of us walk with God according to divine truth and in moral integrity (1 Jn. 1:5-7). This is what Jehovah wanted for the Israelites, and it is what the Lord Jesus wants for His Church today.

Our choice is the same one Moses set before his countrymen in this chapter; will we, as children of God, receive His divine care (i.e., we practically enjoy the blessings we have in Christ) or the rod of His parental reproof? The apostles warn us: *"Be you therefore followers of God, as dear children"* (Eph. 5:1); *"as obedient children, not fashioning yourselves according to the former lusts in your ignorance"* (1 Pet. 1:14); *"for whom the Lord loves He chastens"* (Heb. 12:6). Compliance prompts God's blessing, and defiance, His chastening hand. The Lord's faithfulness to chasten and His balanced approach in doing so fully exhibit that He knows how to deal with human rebellion.

March 12 – True Warriors Numbered
Numbers 1

The book of Numbers commences thirteen months after Israel's departure from Egypt. The Jewish nation had been encamped before Mount Sinai for about a year when Jehovah instructed Moses and Aaron to number the army. Every male who was a true Israelite was officially counted as a member of a specific tribe and validated as being a part of the Jewish nation. Men of each tribe were to gather under their leader's banner.

The total number of non-Levite men who were twenty years of age or older was 603,550 (v. 46). This meant that the population of the Jewish nation was likely between two and three million people. The official census now would legitimize the number of warriors in Israel's army. This ensured that no one of "the mixed multitude" (i.e., those who were not God's people) could represent Jehovah before the nations, especially in warfare. Only those formally validated as God's people could engage His enemies.

In ordering the camp, Jehovah designated **warrior**s (non-Levites), **workers** who were put in charge of the sanctuary (Levites, less the priests), and **worshipers** who would offer sacrifices and offerings on behalf of the entire Jewish nation (Aaron and his sons). Similarly, in the Church Age, only those who have become *"sons of God through faith in Christ Jesus"* (Gal. 3:26; 1 Jn. 3:2) can be led into victorious warfare: *"For as many as are led by the Spirit of God, these are sons of God"* (Rom. 8:14). Only a true child of God can put on the whole armor of God, wield the sword of the Spirit (the Word of God), and pray in the Spirit (Eph. 6:11-18). Believers today do not trace their spiritual pedigree to men, but directly to Jesus Christ who was raised up from the dead and ascended into glory.

Caleb would be a great example of warring for the Lord and in His strength even at the age of eighty-five (Josh. 14). Indeed, no one retires from the Lord's army until the Lord Jesus, the Head of the Church, releases His soldiers. Then, the shield of faith, the sword of the Spirit, and the helmet of salvation will suddenly fall to the ground and the discharged believer will be in the dear Savior's presence forever (2 Cor. 5:8). May all those who stand in faith under His banner be faithful warriors, workers, and worshipers.

March 13 – Uncleanness, Restitution, and Jealousy
Numbers 5

Moses provides instruction on how to deal with uncleanness, offering restitution for offenses and resolving jealousy. The long of these sections deals with a jealous husband who suspects the unfaithfulness of his wife, but has no proof of the matter (vv. 11-31). This section naturally affronts our modern sense of justice as there was no provision for a jealous wife who suspected the unfaithfulness of her husband. Yet we must remember that, under the Law, the punishment for proven adultery was death, for both sinning parties. The focus of this section, then, is to highlight the need for God's people to quickly address inner thoughts which would hinder them from serving the Lord.

To alleviate this jealous condition, a husband who suspected his wife's infidelity could bring her and a prescribed offering to the tabernacle. The wife was then to be brought before the Lord at the Bronze Altar where she would affirm her innocence and the righteous demands of the Law concerning adultery were recorded on a scroll. Once the ink dried, it was scraped off and added (with dust from the floor of the tabernacle) to holy water in the earthen vessel.

After placing her grain offering on the Altar, the priest gave the wife the holy water to drink. There was nothing magical about this concoction, but the sheer terror of the ceremony was designed to cause the guilty conscience to convulse. If nothing happened to her, the wife would be proclaimed innocent that she *"may conceive children"* (v. 28). If the wife was guilty, her abdomen would swell. This likely meant that she would be sterile and thus be cursed among her people.

If our hearts be not true to Christ, we will not be able to stand the searching power of His Word, which exposes the true nature of all things (Heb. 4:12). But if truth resides in our inner man, the more we are searched and tried, the more we are blessed. An innocent woman had nothing to fear, but rather would be rewarded by God for her purity. She could stand before the Lord confident of His blessing. Jehovah is a jealous God, and in His presence, Israel must ever be conscious of their holiness.

In the Church Age, we too must remember that the Lord is likewise jealous of our affections and our care of His saints. May our love for Him not be sidetracked by carnal emotions and unbecoming suspicions.

March 14 – Murmuring Again
Numbers 11

Fourteen months after being delivered from slavery in Egypt, and about a year after arriving at Mount Sinai, the Israelites were finally on their way to the Promised Land. They traveled three days before the cloud stopped to mark their new campsite. However, the tent pegs were barely pounded in the ground before the people's murmuring and complaining were heard by the Lord. The three-day march was physically exhausting and as we all know, the worst part of us just oozes out when we get fatigued. Sadly, the people became contemptuous and doubted God's goodness towards them.

Months earlier fire from the Lord devoured Nadab and Abihu, the two oldest sons of Aaron who had offered strange fire and incense to the Lord (Lev. 16:2). God is holy, and man can approach Him only in the way He deems as holy; two of Aaron's sons ignored God's revealed way. Now the complainers, living as far from God as possible (on the fringes of the camp), were burnt by God's fire.

We learn from these two instances that to live apart from God is death and to approach Him in our own way also results in death, or separation, *"for the wages of sin is death"* (Rom. 6:23). To experience His goodness we must approach Him through Christ's finished work alone and then remain near Him in purity and through confession of sin (1 Jn. 1:9). God wants us to come near, but the only option is to do so in practical holiness and through His holy Way – the Lord Jesus Christ.

Coming out of Egypt, the Israelites did not have the Law, and therefore they were not punished for their earlier complaining. But now they were under its judicial authority and the Lord would teach them about the consequences of sin and not revering Him. However, God's judgments are tempered with mercy in that God's anger had to be "aroused" or "kindled" before it produced righteous indignation. Not only is God slow to be angry, but once provoked to anger, it must fully develop before action is taken. The murmuring of the people greatly displeased the Lord, which aroused His anger and His chastening hand. Yet Moses cried out to the Lord on behalf of those being judged and God's indignation was stayed. Murmuring is offensive to our sovereign God who controls every aspect of our lives; this is why we are exhorted to do *"all things without complaining"* (Phil. 2:14).

March 15 – The Mixed Multitude
Numbers 11

The smoke rising from smoldering bodies had barely been extinguished when "the mixed multitude" among the Israelites began to lust after the staples of Egypt. Their lusting stirred up others in the camp to complain against the Lord also. They lamented, *"Why did we ever come up out of Egypt?"* (v. 20). Who was this "mixed multitude?" The supernatural feats of Jehovah in Egypt had inspired many Egyptians to depart with the Jews. Why did these pagans leave their homes, their people, and their way of life to venture into a desert with their liberated slave population? Perhaps it was because Egypt had been decimated by plagues and there was nothing left to live for in Egypt.

This troublesome group of foreigners is referred to as "rabble" (v. 4 NASV). They complained against Jehovah despite His goodness to them in the wilderness (because they were with the Israelites), and they stirred up the Jews to voice dissatisfaction also. The carnal man longs to feed on the things of the world and this mixed multitude lusted for the fancies of Egypt; they were not humbled by Jehovah's magnificent presence or satisfied with His simple provisions.

The mixed multitude caused the Israelites to crave what God had determined was not necessary for their diet and to loathe what He had provided to sustain them. He had given them manna, but they still had the taste of the world in their mouths. They craved the flesh pots, the fish from the Nile, and fresh vegetables they had enjoyed in Egypt.

Murmuring and complaining must be replaced by thanksgiving and contentment (Phil. 4:11-13). Paul instructed Timothy, *"Now godliness with contentment is great gain ... having food and clothing, with these we shall be content"* (1 Tim. 6:6-8). Sadly, some are neither content nor thankful for what God has provided (1 Tim. 6:10). They coveted money and erred from the faith.

If God wanted us to have more than what we have, He would have bestowed it upon us. Being thankful defeats dissatisfaction. The children of Israel were being led by God into consecutive wilderness experiences – this was for the purpose of testing and perfecting them. His provision of bread from heaven (manna) was all they needed to be sustained through it. Likewise our good God has provided us everything we need to daily serve Him.

March 16 – Canaan
Numbers 13

The Israelites arrived at Kadesh-Barnea in the far northern portion of the Wilderness of Paran (v. 26). The Lord commanded Moses to *"send men to spy out the land of Canaan, which I am giving to the children of Israel; from each tribe of their fathers you shall send a man, everyone a leader among them"* (vv. 1-2). The names of the men selected from each tribe to spy out Canaan are noted in verses 3-15.

What did Canaan mean to Israel? What does Canaan represent to us in type? Some hymns liken physical death to crossing the Jordan River and the land of Canaan to heaven, but this is not correct. Redemption brought the Israelites out of Egypt, through the Red Sea, and into the wilderness as a nation, but when each one passed through the Jordan, they experienced death, practically and individually. Jordan is not the sign of natural death, because afterwards Israel met with fighting. For those in Christ, passing through the death of the Jordan, spiritually speaking, is necessary to live victoriously for Christ in Canaan.

Canaan represents all of the believer's inheritance in Christ who is seated in heavenly places (Eph. 1:3; Heb. 1:3). In Christ, believers will find an infinite treasury of spiritual resources which enable them to powerfully represent the Lord while on earth, but these provisions must first be possessed to do so. Certainly, there are future aspects of our inheritance in Christ that believers will enjoy after glorification (i.e., ruling and reigning with Christ in His coming kingdom). Yet, Canaan does not represent what we will enjoy with Christ later, but rather the benefits of possessing much of our inheritance in Christ now.

In summary, the Canaan rest for Israel illustrates the spiritual rest we have in Christ when we, by faith, submit to His Word (Heb. 4:11-12). Salvation rest is experienced when we respond in faith to Christ's kind invitation (Matt. 11:28); through His gospel message we obtain peace with God (Rom. 5:1). As we learn of Him and yield to His will, we enjoy the peace of God (Phil. 4:6-8).

By faith we enter into God's salvation rest (Heb. 4:3), and, by continuing in faith and obedience, His rest enters into us. When faithful believers depart from their mortal bodies, they depart from Canaan rather than enter it. Their fighting days will be behind them and they will be with Christ in heaven (2 Cor. 5:8).

March 17 – The Blue Tassel
Numbers 15

Not only were foreigners living among the Jews to honor Jehovah, the Jews living in the Promised Land were to be a testimony to foreigners. Besides honoring Jehovah's Law, the Jews were to add a blue tassel or cord to the fringes of their garments. John J. Stubbs explains the addition to their attire:

> Fringes or tassels were to be placed on the four wings or corners of their garments (Deut. 22:12). "The ordinary outer Jewish garment was a quadrangular piece of cloth like a modern plaid, to the corners of which, in conformity with this command, a tassel was attached. Each tassel had a conspicuous thread of deep blue, this color being doubtless symbolic of the heavenly origin of the commandments of which it was to serve as a memento." The Jew regarded the tassels on the borders of the garment with much sanctity.[5]

The blue tassel would publicly identify themselves as Jehovah-worshipers and would also serve to remind them of their covenant with Him. They must remain holy before the Lord! Blue, the heavenly color, represented where God's covenant came to them from – heaven. Likewise, Paul exhorts believers today to be a heavenly-minded people (Col. 3:1-3). Regrettably, the Pharisees in Christ's day had enlarged the borders of their garments and set aside this specific commandment of God's Law (Matt. 23:5). When human traditions replace God's edicts, it is not superior spirituality that is demonstrated, but vain piety.

Likewise, we should remember that while evangelical methods and the particulars of church meetings may change over time, we should never set aside God's order for the Church for what seems more profitable or spiritual to us. We are creatures of rote, so let us guard against making our worship a mindless activity, but rather let our worship be a fresh declaration of love and thankfulness to God.

Today, believers are not required to wear a blue tassel as a part of their attire to identify them as Christ-ones. Yet, we are to carry in us the sweet fragrance of Christ wherever we go (2 Cor. 2:15). By living out His life, others can breathe Him in, appreciate His goodness, and be drawn to His presence just as we were.

March 18 – Rebellion Against God's Leaders
Numbers 16

The flames of revolt that blazed up in Numbers 14 had been extinguished by the Lord, but smoldering resentment still lingered, resulting in a fresh flare up of rebellion. Many desired a captain to lead them into their inheritance in Canaan. The people were revolting against God's leaders and His ruling against them at Kadesh-Barnea.

Because Korah was closely related to Moses and Aaron (they had the same grandfather, Kohath), he felt slighted by his God-given role in caring for the Tabernacle. Dathan and Abiram, Reubenites, also joined Korah's conspiracy. These rebels desired to reassert the firstborn leadership rights of the tribe of Reuben against Moses and to replace the priesthood of Aaron and his sons. In all, Korah, Dathan, Abiram, and 250 men of renown rose up to defy God's prescribed order and leaders. Their rebellion cost them their lives, some were consumed by fire from the Lord and others were swallowed alive by the earth.

Moses reminded Korah of the privileged role in the tabernacle that God had assigned him as a Kohathite and warned him not to rebel against it by seeking the priesthood. Korah used the truth of *sonship* (i.e., all God's people are sanctified and thus equal) to argue against God's order of *headship*. God made us, redeemed us, called us, and equipped us to serve Him the way He determines best – end of story.

It is a terrible blunder to suppose that all believers in the body of Christ are called to positions of prominence or that we can select our role within His Body. Rather, Christ alone is to have preeminence in the Church – He is the head! Furthermore, every believer's role in the Body is appointed by Him (Eph. 2:10, 4:11) and all must adhere to His order for the Church (1 Cor. 14:33-34).

Korah was called into Levitical ministry, but not to the Levitical priesthood. Korah did not want to minister in his calling, but sought what he could not be, a priest. While today all believers are ministers to Christ (1 Pet. 4:10) and believer-priests to God (Rev. 1:6), there is but one Great High Priest, who is the mediator between God and man – the Lord Jesus Christ (1 Tim. 2:5; Heb. 4:14). Woe to those who intrude on His priestly office and assume a position before men that is not theirs. Such pomposity will surely result in God's condemnation.

March 19 – Responding to Disrespect
Numbers 20

The Israelites returned to Kadesh in the first month of the fortieth year since their Egyptian exodus. Miriam died and was buried at Kadesh. Thirty-nine years earlier the Kadesh oasis had an abundance of water; however, that was not the case now, which prompted the people to bitterly complain to Moses and Aaron. We have not heard such strife against God's leaders since Korah's revolt in Numbers 16.

Numbers is a book about testing and refining. At their first arrival at Kadesh, the Lord tested the Israelites to expose their unbelief, but the purpose now is to cause them to further value the priesthood, which God had established to administer grace to them. For thirty-nine years, God's faithfulness has been demonstrated. Moses will later tell his countrymen that they *"lacked nothing"* during their wilderness wanderings (Deut. 2:7).

Apparently, this was the Israelites' first test in a long time and it quickly revealed a need that they could not provide for themselves. But instead of seeking the Lord's help through the priesthood, they chose to complain. How often the Lord's people today commit this same error despite knowing God's past faithfulness. As the narrative affirms, doubting God's goodness troubles our souls and leads us into contention with others, especially God's appointed leaders.

The people's statements against Moses and Aaron were hurtful for several reasons. First, they were rejecting their leaders after their thirty-nine years of faithful service. Second, the complainers were of the new generation and they had observed firsthand the consequences of doubting God's faithfulness. Third, Moses and Aaron were quite elderly at this time and deserved the respect of the younger people, not their disdain.

Although offended by the people's accusations, they wisely did not respond because they did not know the mind of God on the matter. This demonstrates the wisdom Scripture often associates with the hoary crown (Prov. 16:31). Moses and Aaron went to the tabernacle to seek the word of the Lord. Although the two brothers failed to honor the Lord by executing what they were told to do; their example of being slow to anger and seeking divine wisdom before responding to wayward sheep is praiseworthy.

May We Serve Christ!

March 20 – Moses and Aaron Err
Numbers 20

The glory of God appeared to Moses and Aaron at the Tabernacle. There was an urgent need for water, so the Lord told Moses: *Take the rod; you and your brother Aaron gather the congregation together. Speak to the rock before their eyes, and it will yield its water; thus you shall bring water for them out of the rock, and give drink to the congregation and their animals* (vv. 7-8). These instructions were patently clear.

Moses took the rod, a symbol of God's authority, and he and Aaron led the people to a particular rock. The rod that Moses carried was not his own rod, but Aaron's fruitful rod that had been residing in the most holy place for thirty-eight years. Regrettably, what Moses said to the people was not what God had told him to say: *"Hear now, you rebels! Must we bring water for you out of this rock?"* (v. 10). Then we read that *"Moses lifted his hand and struck the rock twice with his rod; and water came out abundantly, and the congregation and their animals drank"* (v. 11). Since Moses was speaking for God and had a symbol of God's authority in his hand, the Lord brought water from the rock despite Moses' disobedience.

Although the life-threatening situation for the Israelites was instantly alleviated, the consequence of disobedience for their leaders was not. The Lord spoke to Moses and Aaron: *"Because you did not believe Me, to hallow Me in the eyes of the children of Israel, therefore you shall not bring this assembly into the land which I have given them"* (v. 12). Nothing more was said. Israel's prominent leaders did not argue with the Lord about their punishment; rather they accepted it as just punishment for their pride. This is a good example to follow.

We might think that God was too harsh with Moses and Aaron. Does not years of faithfulness count much more in God's estimation than one mistake about striking a rock instead of speaking to it? The Lord would still reward Moses and Aaron for their faithfulness, but their disobedience and pride, especially while representing the Lord, had to be sternly reprimanded. When God assigns responsibility to His servants, they also are under greater accountability (e.g., Luke 12:48; Jas. 3:1). Although Moses and Aaron received a measure of mercy in this matter, they were punished for their indiscretion.

March 21 – The Doctrine of Balaam
Numbers 25

In Numbers 22, Balak, the king of Moab, had become alarmed at both the military feats of the Israelites and had solicited help of a well-known prophet named Balaam from Pethor to come and curse the Israelites. Balaam's name means "confuser of the people" which describes the effect of his doctrine on the Israelites in this chapter.

Balaam's true character and spiritual disposition are revealed in the New Testament by Peter, Jude, and John. Peter refers to the *"way of Balaam"* as an indictment against the false teachers of his day who pursued the *"wages of unrighteousness"* (2 Pet. 2:15). Like covetous Balaam, these false teachers were attempting to represent God for financial profit. While God did choose to speak through Balaam to Balak, he was nonetheless an impure vessel in God's hands. Peter highlights the true character of Balaam as like other false teachers who use religion as a cover for their self-seeking. The outcome of their teaching is all the same – to lead God's people into sin and away from Him, instead of drawing them nearer to Him (Num. 31:16; 2 Pet. 2:14).

Jude speaks of *"the error of Balaam,"* which wrongly assumed that God had to judicially curse His people on the basis of their spiritual and moral failure. Balaam understood neither God's merciful character, nor His means of righteously judging sin through a substitution. Finally, John records the last mention of Balaam's name in Scripture, when Christ refers to *"the doctrine of Balaam"* in his letter to the church at Pergamos (Rev. 2:14). The Israelites were God's people and Balaam knew that any curses he levied on them would be meaningless, so Balaam instructed Balak to seduce the Israelites to commit idolatry and immorality with the daughters of Moab, so that God would be forced to punish them.

While *"the way of Balaam"* speaks of his corrupt motives and *"the error of Balaam"* his wrong assessment of God's character and ways, *"the doctrine of Balaam"* refers to the willful teachings to purposely cause the corruption of God's people. Of course the Lord hates every bit of it, so Balaam, a corrupt false prophet who did not know the true God, eventually reaped what he had sowed and perished among the very people whom he sought to assist. Let us be careful to avoid the dangerous pitfall of the doctrines of Balaam!

May We Serve Christ!

March 22 – The Daughters of Zelophehad
Numbers 27

Zelophehad was from the tribe of Manasseh. He had died with the older generation in the wilderness, but had taken no part in the rebellion of Korah. He had five daughters, but no sons (Num. 26:33). Claiming the promises of God for their own, the daughters of Zelophehad came to the tabernacle to appeal to Moses, Eleazar, and Israel's leaders.

In faith the daughters of Zelophehad prized what had not yet been secured in Canaan, their possession in the Promised Land. Their testimony stands in sharp contrast to the unbelief and corruption of their countrymen in recent history. They did not want their father's name to be forgotten, nor did they want to live in Israel's inheritance without having a part in it. Laws of inheritance previously delivered by Moses did not address their situation, so Moses took the matter to the Lord for a ruling and the gracious God of heaven sided with the daughters of Zelophehad.

The Lord said, *"the daughters of Zelophehad speak what is right."* When God's people speak unprejudiced words of faith, they always speak right in God's estimation. God is obliged to honor such requests fostered in genuine confidence in Him. Indeed, God's own heart is refreshed when we count His promises as good as done and choose to earnestly wait for the blessed outcome of our faith.

The book of Joshua records that when the land was being divided among the tribes, these women of faith received a portion for their inheritance (Josh. 17:5-6). This text upholds the authority of Joshua and Eleazar, who were speaking for the Lord in the matter of allotment, and also the corporate authority of the tribe in conferring grace to the family of Zelophehad.

The daughters of Zelophehad were rewarded for their faith which was rooted in God's revealed truth, but in such a way to also ensure tribal interests were safeguarded. We see this same pattern in the New Testament, as individuals are given to the Church by Christ for its edification, rather than for mere personal benefit (Eph. 4:11-12). May the Lord's people always act in truth-based faith for the good of others. The believer's spiritual blessings in heavenly places in Christ (Eph. 1:3) are not for self-focused doings, but for selfless Christ-exalting ministry, which, of course, will benefit the serving believer also.

March 23 – Vows
Numbers 30

While the necessity of vows is not imposed in Scripture, if anyone did make a vow to the Lord, it was binding unless disallowed straightaway by male headship. For this reason, vows were not to be made impulsively (Prov. 20:25). Moses first instructed the men: *"If a man makes a vow to the Lord, or swears an oath to bind himself by some agreement, he shall not break his word"* (vv. 1-2). It was much better not to vow at all than to do so and not honor it. Associating God's name with a falsehood would be insulting to Him.

Vows in the Old Testament might be to abstain from something (Ps. 132:2-5), or to promise things or services to the Lord (Lev. 27). For example, a Jew might propose to offer the Lord a peace offering in recognition of some favor He granted to the offerer (Lev. 7:16). Such offerings ministered to the offering priest and enriched the communion and fellowship of the saints before the Lord.

The fulfillment of such vows then became the substance of things prompting common joy among God's people; thus David wrote, *"I will pay my vows before them that fear Him"* (Ps. 22:25). And Psalm 116:14 reads, *"I will pay my vows to the Lord now in the presence of all His people."* As the Church is not under Law, how may we apply this principle now?

First, the Lord Jesus forbids us from making vows today (Matt. 5:33-37), as we cannot promise what we may do in the future. James warns, *"Instead you ought to say, 'If the Lord wills, we shall live and do this or that'"* (Jas. 4:15). While a vow may be viewed as a legitimate expression of one's devotion to God, it would be better to express one's aspiration to serve God in prayer and through pursuing a consecrated life, rather than committing to some particular vow which may not be within one's control.

Second, the idea of a free-will gift to the Lord (but not through a pledge) to benefit the fellowship and communion of God's people is commendable. May each of us view our fellow brethren in our local assembly with such high esteem that we are prompted to give to the Lord in order to enhance the body-life and to bless others. This is really the idea of the Jewish peace offering that was often vowed – enjoying the Lord while together in His presence.

March 24 – A Long Journey, but Lacking Nothing
Deuteronomy 2

Moses quickly passes over thirty-eight years of wilderness wandering to pick up Israel's history shortly after the death of Aaron and after turning back south to avoid confrontation with Edom. Israel had sought passage through Edom and Moab on the King's Highway (even offering to pay for food and water required while passing through), but was denied. Circumventing Edom added many miles to their trip, but was necessary because the Lord had commanded Israel not to meddle with or harass the Edomites, the Moabites, or the Ammonites. These people groups were distant kin through Esau and Lot, respectively; therefore, the Lord would not permit Israel to inherit the land He had given them.

So to avoid bloodshed, the Israelites skirted both Edom and Moab. Moses led the Israelites around Edom's western, southern, and eastern borders and then Moab's eastern border through the Zered Valley to arrive at Moab's northern boundary at the Arnon River. It was after suffering this extra hardship of journeying through arid and rough terrain, but prior to engaging the Amorites, that Moses reminds his countrymen that they had lacked nothing during the last forty years.

Before they became inundated with the plunder of the Amorites, Moses reminds them that it was only because of the Lord's faithfulness to them during their wandering years that they would be able to enjoy the spoils of victory as they approached Canaan. Arriving in the plains of Moab, the Israelites discovered that the Amorites had pushed the Moabites south and the Ammonites eastward from their homelands between the Arnon and Jabbok Rivers. There was no prohibition against attacking the Amorites; they were a wicked people and not kin.

After crossing the Arnon, the Lord declared: *"This day I will begin to put the dread and fear of you upon the nations under the whole heaven, who shall hear the report of you, and shall tremble and be in anguish because of you"* (v. 25). Then, Moses recorded how the Israelites had vanquished the Amorites as they moved northward through Moab. The Lord was rewarding and building the reputation of His own people because they had chosen to trust Him. The Lord delights to show Himself strong in those who will rest in Him.

Daily Devotions

March 25 – The Greatest Commandment
Deuteronomy 6

The Lord desired two things primarily from His people in the land that He was giving them – in fear to revere Him alone as God and to observe His commandments. By doing so they would have God's blessing in the land and would enjoy a full and long life. As already observed in Numbers, rebels and law-breakers often suffer short lives. But those who are respectful and obedient to God's authority, generally, live happier and longer than those who do not!

Who would not relish a life marked by longevity and plenty? Hence, the Jews developed a tradition of reciting morning and evening verses 4-9 as a daily prayer called the *Shema Yisrael*, or "Hear, Israel" as drawn from verse 1. It has been a longstanding Jewish custom for parents to end the day by reciting this prayer to their children.

The first two of the Ten Commandments relate to the subject of recognizing God as Creator and not worshiping creation. Moses further explained how one obeys the first commandment: *"You shall have no other gods before Me"* (Deut. 5:6). One must believe in the one true God and give Him first place in your life: *"The Lord our God, the Lord is one! You shall love the Lord your God with all your heart, with all your soul, and with all your strength"* (vv. 4-5).

The second part of the command required Israel to be fully devoted to Jehovah, the one true God. During the final days of the Lord's earthly ministry, a lawyer tested Him with a question: *"Teacher, which is the great commandment in the law?"* (Matt. 22:36). The Lord responded to this question by quoting Moses' words here: *"You shall love the Lord your God with all your heart, with all your soul, and with all your mind.' This is the first and great commandment"* (Matt. 22:37-38). Notice that the Lord added *"and with all your mind"* to the Greek Scriptures.

The New Testament puts much emphasis on strengthening, shaping, girding, and renewing the believer's mind in order to properly live for Christ. Besides having sound minds, the Lord desires His people to have devoted hearts. When it comes to having no other god besides the Creator, it means that He has first place in our life, our thinking, our allegiance, and our affections – and there are to be no close seconds concerning our love for God (Matt. 10:37).

March 26 – Do Not Forget Me
Deuteronomy 6

What would be the chief reasons Israel would willfully neglect teaching the younger generation God's Law? Moses warned against two – first, prosperity and second, idolatry. In the arms of affluence God's people tend to forget to cling to the Lord. When we are distressed or in need, we most eagerly call out to God for help, but how often do we neglect appreciating Him when we are full.

For this reason, Moses solemnly warned his countrymen not to forget the Lord after they were settled in the Promised Land and enjoying its abundance: *"when you have eaten and are full – then beware, lest you forget the Lord who brought you out of the land of Egypt, from the house of bondage* (vv. 11-12). The profusion in Canaan would be in sharp contrast to their tenure as oppressed slaves in Egypt and their modest existence in the wilderness for forty years. They were about to inherit cities and homes that they did not build, wells for water that they did not dig, farmland which they did not clear, vineyards and olive groves that they did not plant. No doubt this would all be exhilarating.

Our carnal nature craves the easy lifestyle, pampering, and receiving whatever we desire. However, there is no cruise-control when living for the Lord; the child of God must beware of anything or anyone that would rob their affections for the Lord. Jehovah is jealous over His people. He would not tolerate His people having displaced affections, especially in relation to them embracing false gods (as shown by Israel swearing in their names); *"You shall fear the Lord your God and serve Him"* (v. 13).

After just witnessing the Lord's annihilation of the Amorites and Midianites, Moses' threat in verse 15 likely carried more weight: *"For the Lord your God is a jealous God among you, lest the anger of the Lord your God be aroused against you and destroy you from the face of the earth."* But how could God make an unconditional covenant with Abraham, while also threatening the nation of Israel with extinction? The answer is that the basis for God's covenant with Abraham (Gen. 12:1-3) was unconditional grace, while the covenant at Horeb with Abraham's descendants was conditional – blessing for obedience. God Himself has always been the greatest threat to Israel's prosperity.

March 27 – Remember the Lord – Your God
Deuteronomy 8

The expression, *"the Lord your God,"* occurs 25 times in Deuteronomy 8 and 9. Moses is emphasizing not only the uniqueness of Israel's God, but that He has chosen Israel from among the nations to have an exclusive relationship with Him. If the Israelites wanted the Lord's blessing in Canaan, they had to keep *"every commandment"* they had received (v. 1). No one could pick and choose what part of the Law they would obey. All that God commanded was required of them.

Moses then explained that God was using various wilderness experiences to test them: *"And you shall remember that the Lord your God led you all the way these forty years in the wilderness, to humble you and test you, to know what was in your heart, whether you would keep His commandments or not"* (v. 2). How refreshing it is to look back over the course we have traveled as pilgrims to see the faithful, wise hand of God. The Lord has carefully managed thousands of turns, tests, sorrows, failures, and successes to get us to where we are today.

Indeed, God had led His people through subsequent wilderness experiences to test them. Obviously, God already knew what was in their hearts and what they would do, but they did not know what they would do until tested. We never know how we will respond until we are challenged by a trial. A wilderness experience then reveals where we are spiritually – either strong in the Lord, or, deficient in faith, needing refining and growth.

Such were God's dealings with Israel during their forty-year wilderness experience. Each time God's cloud had guided the Israelites into adversity, His grace had been sufficient to overcome it. The number forty is used in Scripture to represent *probation* and *testing*, which explains its frequent occurrence.

Despite all their failings, God had been completely faithful to them – He had proven His love repeatedly. Besides refining them morally and spiritually, He had provided food and water for them, and even their garments and sandals had not worn out. All they possessed had come from the Lord; there was nothing to boast about. Paul writes: *"What do you have that you did not receive? Now if you did indeed receive it, why do you boast as if you had not received it?"*

March 28 – Beware of Self-Confidence
Deuteronomy 9

In the previous chapter, Moses warned the Israelites not to forget the Lord when they were living prosperously in Canaan. In this chapter, he warns the people three times not to attribute their achievements in Canaan to their own self-righteousness. God would give them the land because of His covenant with their forefathers and to punish the wicked inhabitants of the land.

Thirty-nine years earlier the Israelites were shocked by the Canaan reconnaissance report delivered by the twelve spies. Moses did not want the people to be dismayed again by the immensity of the task before them. It was important that they neither underestimate Canaan's military strength nor be paralyzed with fear because of it. From a tactical standpoint, Canaan's fortifications, vast armies, and giants could not be overcome by sheer determination. The Israelites needed to realize that it was impossible to conquer Canaan on their own. The only solution was for the Lord their God to go before them as a consuming fire to wipe out the enemy.

Ten of the spies Moses sent into Canaan were terrified by the size of the Anakim. Instead of stirring up trust in the Lord to invade Canaan, these men caused their countrymen to doubt God's ability to overcome the inhabitants of the land: *"Who can stand before the descendants of Anak?"* (v. 2). Moses wanted the Israelites to know the answer to this question: "We can, when Jehovah fights for us!" Without the Lord, the Jews were helpless, but with the Lord even the giants would fall before them. This meant that any victories in Canaan were the Lord's and that all boasting should then be in Him. The Israelites were not to think too highly of themselves or their accomplishments – they did not deserve God's favor and they could do nothing in Canaan without Him!

Paul applies this principle to the ministry of believers in the Church Age: *"So then neither he who plants is anything, nor he who waters, but God who gives the increase"* (1 Cor. 3:7). It is natural for us to boast of our accomplishments, but this is not profitable for eternity. May we remember the lesson that the Israelites came to appreciate: if the Lord is not in the work, we are wasting our time and our resources! Conversely, when we are in the will and strength of God, we *"can do all things through Christ"* (Phil. 4:13).

March 29 – God Is Worthy of Your Love
Deuteronomy 11

In this chapter, Moses again underscores the inseparable connection between devoted love and willing obedience. Moses poses two reasons Israel should continue to love the Lord. First, His past faithfulness and mighty deeds on their behalf prove He is worthy of their piety. Second, they could not conquer Canaan and flourish there unless they were loyal to Jehovah. Verse 1 poses a concise preface: *"Therefore you shall love the Lord your God, and keep His charge, His statutes, His judgments, and His commandments always."* Israel would be wise to show their love for Jehovah by obeying His Law.

Moses addresses the generation who had witnessed Israel's miraculous exodus from Egypt and experienced God's superb care in the wilderness. The older generation was now gone, and many in the middle generation had also perished in the wilderness because of insurrection. Parents who had seen the wonders of the past and had survived and benefitted from the Lord's chastening in the wilderness are reminded of the importance of teaching their children what they had learned. Parents should set a good example of compliance also.

Israel's entire history in Egypt and their forty-year wilderness journey were God's training program to reveal His majesty to His people and to refine them morally and spiritually. They had witnessed God's wrath on Egypt, the opening of the Red Sea, and many life-sustaining miracles. Additionally, they had been taught, corrected, rebuked, and punished throughout their desert wanderings. The purpose of their past school days was to cause them to revere and to love God. What better heritage could they pass down to their children!

Additionally, Moses declared that Israel's days in Canaan would be prolonged only if they obeyed all of Jehovah's commandments. They would *"be strong"* only if they kept *"every commandment"* (v. 8). Such unreserved obedience would be possible only if motivated by love – inward affection would be outwardly displayed through willing submission to God.

Moses promised that God would sustain them in Canaan, a fertile and well-watered land, if they remained loyal to Him. Moses' message to Israel is still valid today: the Church would be wise to show their love for Christ by obeying His Word too (John 14:15).

March 30 – Walking After the Lord
Deuteronomy 13

Having affirmed the one sanctuary law and a strict prohibition against paganism, Moses turns his attention to three corrupting influences that would tempt God's people into spiritual infidelity. These are false prophets, corrupt relatives, and anarchists promoting wholesale abandonment of Jehovah (vv. 1-18).

Paul warned the elders at Ephesus that false teachers would secretly come among them as wolves to devour the flock (Acts 28:15-17). Similarly, Moses warns the Israelites that false prophets and dreamers of dreams would come among them with signs and fanciful messages to deceive them. God would permit this to happen in order to test their love for Him and their allegiance to His Law: *"You shall walk after the Lord your God and fear Him, and keep His commandments and obey His voice; you shall serve Him and hold fast to Him"* (v. 4).

Notice that the Israelites were to "walk after the Lord." After Abraham doubted and stumbled in his faith in Genesis 16, God admonished him to *walk before God* perfectly in Genesis 17. A walk "before" God can only be accomplished by walking in faith. In this chapter the Israelites were exhorted to *walk after God*. We also know that previously Enoch and Noah *walked with God*. In the Church Age, those receiving Christ are *to walk in Him* (Col. 2:6). Arthur Pink provides the following observation concerning these various phrases:

> To walk *before* is suggestive of a child running ahead and playing in the presence of his father, conscious of his perfect *security* because he is just behind. To walk *after* becomes a servant following his master. To walk *with* indicates fellowship and friendship. To walk *in* denotes union. We might summarize these varied aspects of the believer's walk as intimated by the four different prepositions thus: we walk **before** God as *children*; we walk **after** Him as *servant*s; we walk **with** Him as His *friends*; we walk **in** Him as *members of His body*.[6]

Moses is highlighting Israel's total resolution to obey and serve the Lord – they must "walk after the Lord." In the Church Age we must do the same, but we have the greater privilege of walking in the Lord for we are one with Him forever!

March 31 – Spotting False Prophets
Deuteronomy 13

Moses then provides the criteria for spotting future false prophets who would test Israel's faithfulness. It is noteworthy that Moses did not deny that these supposed messengers of God would be able to work wonderful signs and may be able to correctly predict some events. Yet, such things did not validate the origin of the message; for this reason, Moses gave the people a standard for determining the authenticity of a prophet's message.

First, a miracle did not prove truth, as Satan is capable of accomplishing supernatural feats, as witnessed in Moses' confrontation with Pharaoh and his magicians in Egypt. Second, a false prophet would be identified if his message was contrary to a revelation already given by someone verified to be a true prophet of Jehovah, like Moses. Third, whatever a true prophet of God says would happen, will always happen (Deut. 18:22; Jer. 28:9). Fourth, a true prophet of God will always lead His people into repentance and humility before God, never away from the Lord.

This is why Moses prescribed such a stern punishment for false prophets: *"But that prophet or that dreamer of dreams shall be put to death, because he has spoken in order to turn you away from the Lord"* (v. 5). False prophets may for a time feign humility and morality (Matt. 7:15), but they are inherently self-exalting (i.e., they compete for God's honor) and self-gratifying (often secretly immoral, 2 Pet. 2:10, 14).

Such individuals will eventually lead the Lord's people away from Him, so those individuals were to be exposed and slain in the Old Testament, and rejected and avoided in the New Testament. Like Moses, Peter warns believers in the Church Age of false prophets and also predicts their doom (2 Pet. 2:13).

In responding to His disciples' question about things to come, the Lord Jesus confirmed that in the latter days of the Church Age many false doctrines would be spread. Besides mass deception, many would come claiming to be the Christ (Matt. 24:5). With the coming of the Lord nigh, His warning two thousand years ago, *"Take heed that no one deceives you"* (Matt. 24:4), could never be more critical to obey. "No one" means well-meaning preachers (and authors) too.

April 1 – God Over Personal Relationships
Deuteronomy 13

Moses anticipated the most tragic and heartbreaking of circumstances which might lead some Israelites to forsake Jehovah for false gods – the influence of loved ones. Moses painstakingly included a variety of close relationships, so that everyone would understand that there were no loopholes in his decree: *If your brother, the son of your mother, your son or your daughter, the wife of your bosom, or your friend who is as your own soul, secretly entices you, saying, "Let us go and serve other gods"* (v. 6). Moses commanded that if any Jew enticed another friend or family member to forsake the Lord for false gods, they were to be rejected and put to death. In fact, the one who had been solicited to do evil was to cast the first stone (vv. 9-10). This decree applied to everyone, no matter what social status they might have – Israel was to be completely free of idolatry, even if it meant the death of erring loved ones.

Although today false teachers are to be rejected and avoided rather than stoned, we find the same high level of devotion expected from God's people. The Lord Jesus said, *"If anyone comes to Me and does not hate his father and mother, wife and children, brothers and sisters, yes, and his own life also, he cannot be My disciple"* (Luke 14:26).

From the parallel account in Matthew 10:37, we understand that the word for "hate" expresses a comparison: our love for the Lord should be so great that any natural affection would, comparatively, seem like hate. The Lord was weary of shallow followers; He wanted true disciples. He desired quality in consecration, not a large quantity of half-hearted patriots. When it comes to misplaced affections and devotions, there is no middle ground with the Lord. This was the critical point Moses was trying to get across to his countrymen.

The Lord expects our love for Him to be so astounding that by comparison our affections for anyone else would seem like hate! To love anyone or anything more than the Lord is idolatry. This truth is conveyed in the decree of stoning a loved one who attempted to solicit family members away from the Lord. Although today we are under grace, it is profitable for us to appreciate God's desire for His people of all ages to be totally committed to Him and to love Him above all else.

April 2 – Tithing
Deuteronomy 14

The tithe to the Lord was previously commanded in Leviticus 27:30-31 and Numbers 18:21-32. However, it was necessary for Moses to modify certain procedures now that Israel was about to enter the Promised Land and would soon be required to worship at the central sanctuary.

The firstfruits of the harvest were to be waved before the Lord as an offering of thankfulness to the One who had granted the increase. The Lord laid claim to one-tenth of their entire harvest; this would be His provision for sustaining the Levites and their ministry. Likewise, one-tenth of the clean animals and the firstborn of their herds and flocks were also His. Leviticus 27 demanded that every tenth animal that passed under the shepherd's rod was the Lord's. The selected animals would provide the Levites with meat and would also be used in Levitical sacrifices. Additionally, Moses spoke of a second tithe to be given to the Lord every three years. This may have been in addition to the annual tithe, but was more likely a substitute for the first in that the second tithe required feasting locally and not at the central sanctuary.

The Jewish tithing requirements were also abolished in the New Testament. However, the congregational joy and fellowship around the Lord pictured in the tithe feast lives on in New Testament Church practice. Under the Law, God demanded the tithe. But in the age of grace each believer is required to regularly and proportionately give back to the Lord as God has prospered him or her (1 Cor. 16:2).

In the Church Age, God makes no demands as to the specific amount we are to give back to Him; rather, we are permitted to evaluate our situation, and to freely express our love and appreciation to Him through giving: *"So let each one give as he purposes in his heart, not grudgingly or of necessity; for God loves a cheerful giver"* (2 Cor. 9:7). God has wonderfully shown us that true giving commences with selfless sacrifice (John 3:16). The Lord Jesus affirmed *"to whom little is forgiven, the same loves little"* (Luke 7:47)! The portion that we return of what we have received from the Lord directly reflects how much we believe we have been forgiven and how much we love Him. Those who have been forgiven much, give much, because they love much!

April 3 – Do Not Muzzle the Ox
Deuteronomy 25

Moses then stressed the fair and kind treatment of beasts of burden: *"You shall not muzzle an ox while it treads out the grain"* (v. 4). An ox that was serving its master by trampling stalks of grain on the threshing floor in preparation for winnowing should be permitted to eat some of the stalks. Paul later refers to this verse to show that those laboring for the kingdom of God were likewise worthy of financial support from those who had benefitted from their preaching (1 Cor. 9:9).

The New Testament indicates that Church workers were employed by the Lord, not by local churches. Serving the Lord is not a career to be chosen, but a heavenly calling to be fulfilled! God enables the worker's ministry and is responsible for supporting them financially (Phil. 4:10-19; Col. 4:17). As He most often accomplishes this through His people, Paul emphasizes that those who had been spiritually blessed by ministry had a "duty" to support those who blessed them (Rom. 15:27). Examples of not muzzling the laboring ox in principle would include the support of:

- The evangelist (1 Cor. 9:14).
- A teaching elder (1 Tim. 5:17-18).
- A teacher in general (Gal. 6:6).
- A commended worker (1 Cor. 9:4).

Gaius provides a good pattern to follow in the care of the Lord's servants. He extended hospitality to itinerant church workers and then did not send them away empty-handed (3 John 5-8; also see Tit. 3:14). At times workers may need to engage in secular employment for financial reasons (Acts 18:3), but nowhere in Scripture do we see them making public appeals for their own financial support.

Commended workers serve the Lord (Acts 14:26), and thus the Lord wants His people to freely and amply provide for them in His name. This arrangement permits His workers to do His bidding and for the Lord to endorse their efforts by attending to their daily needs. Workers doing God's work God's way will never need to worry about God's support.

April 4 – Eradicate the Amalekites
Deuteronomy 25

Amalek was the grandson of profane Esau, *"who for one morsel of food sold his birthright"* (Heb. 12:16). Consequently, both Esau and Amalek picture lusting flesh which continues to war against God's people. The Amalekites attacked the straggling Israelites who were weak and weary after leaving Egypt. This is often when the flesh gains a victory over God's people: just after a major victory when they are exhausted.

We see this was the case for Joshua, who acted in the flesh in advancing against Ai after the great victory at Jericho (Josh. 7). Because Joshua did not seek the Lord's counsel, he was unaware that there was sin in the camp which hindered Jehovah from going into battle with them. As a result, thirty-six Jewish soldiers died. Achan's sin against the Lord was then revealed and he and all that was his were publicly judged for it.

After the children of Israel had experienced separation and cleansing from that which had defiled them, they were ready to be used as Jehovah's agency against Ai and Bethel. This time they would not advance in human wisdom and in their own strength, but in faith and in accordance with Jehovah's plan and with His power. Joshua 8 records their whimsical victory over Ai and Bethel without any Jewish casualties. Human reasoning and fleshly vigor were to have no part in God's operation – death to all Amalekites!

The Lord desires that the same pattern be followed in the Church Age. Until an individual experiences regeneration and receives the Holy Spirit, the flesh nature is uncontrollable (Rom. 8:2-4). Even after regeneration, a child of God cannot righteously serve the Lord with sin in his or her heart. Sins in our flesh must supernaturally be put to death *"because they that are in the flesh cannot please God"* (Rom. 8:8). One cannot rightly exercise the power of God without being under His moral authority (Luke 7:6-9). Accordingly, once the Israelites had secured Canaan, they were to relentlessly and ruthlessly war against the Amalekites until there was no remembrance of them under heaven (v. 19). In type, carnal appetites must be brought under the control of the Holy Spirit and thus be eliminated from the work of God. What the flesh controls robs honor from the Lord and harms His people!

April 5 – The Basket of Firstfruits
Deuteronomy 26

Leaving the Laws of Responsibility, this chapter paints a more cheerful scene which anticipates Israel's entrance into their own land. This chapter speaks of priestly service in conjunction with the Jews worshipping Jehovah. Every family was to offer a basket of firstfruits from the bounty of their first harvest in the land.

Levitical Law already required the Jews to present the firstfruits of the barley harvest at the Feast of Firstfruits, which was celebrated on the sixteenth day of the first month (Lev. 23:9-14). The firstfruits of the wheat harvest were also presented to the Lord at The Feast of Pentecost, which followed fifty days later. At the Feast of Firstfruits, a priest was to wave a barley sheaf before the Lord as an acknowledgement that He was the Lord of the entire harvest. This grain was for the priests who continually served in the temple. The Jews were not allowed to partake of the harvest until these offerings had been presented before the Lord.

After settling in Canaan, the Jews were to arrange a sample of all their first year's produce in a basket and bring it to the central sanctuary with their tithe. With basket in hand, the offerer was to acknowledge before a priest, *"I declare today to the Lord your God that I have come to the country which the Lord swore to our fathers to give us"* (v. 3). This assertion recognized the Lord's faithfulness in bringing Israel out of Egypt and settling His people in the land He had promised them. The priest then set the basket before the Bronze Altar.

Israel's profession at the time of their firstfruits presentation is noteworthy. The Israelites did not say, "I am coming" or "I hope to come" or "I am longing to come," but "I have come" into the land. Their baskets of firstfruits would be offered to the Lord because they *were* in the land of promise and possessed it. One must truly be saved and know they are saved to honor the Lord with spiritual fruitfulness (1 Jn. 4:18-19). The fruit of the Spirit accompanies salvation – salvation is not obtained by mimicking what only the Holy Spirit can produce from within. The whole idea of "firstfruits" is that there has been a new blessing and spiritual understanding in the believer's soul that had not been previously experienced – this is what is to be brought before the Lord in a spirit of worship and praise.

April 6 – Invasion, Siege, and Dispersion
Deuteronomy 28

Moses sternly warned the Israelites not to force God to evict them from their land through disobedience. To do so would cause God to scatter them among the nations that worship false gods. There they would be compelled to serve idols and would suffer unending days and nights of torment and anguish of soul. Moses then summarizes their plight: *"Your life shall hang in doubt before you; you shall fear day and night, and have no assurance of life"* (v. 66). Some surviving Jews will be shipped back to Egypt (their original place of bondage); slavery will be their only option to escape starvation. Yet, because of their feeble physical condition, no one will want to buy them (i.e., buyers considered them to be a poor investment; they were not worth the food required to sustain them for work, v. 68).

While this chapter is long and grueling to read, apparently it was not blunt enough when reviewing Israel's long, sad history of chastening. God did exactly what He said He would do if His people erred from the Law and abandoned Him. While none of these stated chastisements pertain to the Church, it behooves believers today to consider these as an indication of God's hatred of rebellion and misplaced devotion. If the Lord so severely judged His covenant people for their willful idolatry and wickedness, why would He not hesitate to chasten those committing the same offenses who are but mere second benefactors of the New Covenant confirmed with Israel (Heb. 8:8)?

In fact, this is the essence of Paul's warning to the Christians at Rome (Rom. 11:21-22). In Paul's olive tree analogy of Romans 11, the Abrahamic covenant is the root of the tree through which all nations of the earth shall be blessed (Gen. 12:3). The olive tree represents the Lord Jesus Christ, through whom all the blessings of God flow from the root to the branches.

If the Church is to be restored to a testimony of power and vibrancy, she must repent, return to the Lord, and obey His Word (John 15:5). Without abiding in Christ, the Church is powerless and nothing more than dried up branches clattering in the secular winds of humanism. Sadly, this is a depiction which describes Christendom today. Let us have no part in it! The days are evil; may God enable the true Church to hold fast to Christ and His Word.

April 7 – The Renewed Covenant
Deuteronomy 29

In this chapter, Moses begins his address by mentioning the wonderful feats accomplished by God both in Egypt to secure their release and during the past forty years. But though Israel had seen many signs and wonders with their eyes, they did not really perceive the full ramifications of what God had accomplished on their behalf: *"Yet the Lord has not given you a heart to perceive and eyes to see and ears to hear, to this very day"* (v. 4). This was not to say that their rebelliousness resulted from their ignorance of God's accomplishments, but rather that their disobedience sprang from a mind that could not understand the ways of God and His purposes.

For example, in the wilderness, they had been completely sustained by God for forty years. He provided them shade from the hot sun during the day, preserved their clothing and shoes from wearing out, and sustained them with the humble diet. He did not provide them what they desired – grain to grind for bread and wine to drink. All this was to teach the nation that joyful sufficiency was in the Lord, not in satisfying the sinful impulses of lusting flesh.

Furthermore, when His people fully relied on the Lord and not on themselves, they were invincible, as shown in victory over the Amorites, which provided an inheritance for two and a half tribes in the Plains of Moab.

Moses' point in verse 5 is that without divine enlightenment, God's people will remain ignorant of His wondrous ways and judgments. But just because they do not understand what God is accomplishing before them, they are not released from obeying what they do know to be true.

Paul also affirms that without God's help we would never understand the mysteries associated with our salvation (1 Cor. 2:10-12). Without God's Word and the Holy Spirit to enable us to understand what God has revealed, we too would be ignorant of what is important to God. This is why the lost cannot come to Christ without the Holy Spirit's convicting work on their conscience (John 16:7-9), nor can the believer grow in knowledge and grace without His teaching ministry (John 14:26, 16:12-13). So, while the Israelites did not understand all that God was doing (as it had not been revealed to them, v. 29), they were still accountable to obey what God had revealed – and so are we!

April 8 – A New Heart and Renewed Favor
Deuteronomy 30

At Christ's second advent, the purified Jewish nation will receive the Holy Spirit and receive Jesus Christ as their Messiah (Joel 2:28-29; Zech. 12:10). That is when verse 6 will be fulfilled: *"And the Lord your God will circumcise your heart and the heart of your descendants, to love the Lord your God with all your heart and with all your soul, that you may live."* The Old Covenant had no provision of mercy by which to reinstate Israel after failure, but through the Lord Jesus Christ's work at Calvary, God instituted a New Covenant with His covenant people that could (Jer. 31:31-32).

Jeremiah says that this would be an everlasting covenant resulting in eternal blessing to the Jews (Jer. 32:40). This promise is understood to be literal, for God will erect an eternal city where the Jewish remnant will dwell (Isa. 52:1). The prophet Ezekiel refers to the New Covenant as a *"Covenant of Peace"* with the Jewish nation (Ezek. 34:25). Isaiah proclaimed that through this covenant, *"Israel shall be saved in the Lord with an everlasting salvation"* (Isa. 45:17). Not only was the New Covenant needed to restore Israel to God, but to also secure them forever in blessings promised to Abraham.

For example those who oppose Israel will be punished by God and those who favor Israel will be blessed by Him, just as was promised Abraham long ago: *"I will bless those who bless you, and I will curse him who curses you; and in you all the families of the earth shall be blessed"* (Gen. 12:3). Those nations who troubled His covenant people in the past will be recompensed for their evil and no authority on earth will be permitted to harass them during the Kingdom Age.

Once Israel is finally restored to God at the end of the Tribulation Period, the Holy Spirit will ensure that they never leave Him again for false gods; instead, they will continue in His Law. As a nation, they will receive the Holy Spirit, and He will circumcise their heart. That is, He will remove what is carnal and unwanted, so the heart of the nation beats only for God. Moses told his brethren that only then would they be able to follow the Lord their God with all their heart and with all their soul. The prophets Ezekiel and Joel refer to this as "a new heart" by spiritual regeneration (Ezek. 36:23-28; Joel 2:27-29).

April 9 – Life or Death?
Deuteronomy 30

In anticipation of possible excuses for neglecting the Law, Moses reminded the congregation that the Law was not confusing or beyond their grasp to understand. Paul acknowledges that God's righteousness and means of blessing had been first revealed to Israel in the Mosaic Law. However, He had now revealed His righteousness and means of salvation in a superior way – in Jesus Christ. *"But now the righteousness of God apart from the law is revealed, being witnessed by the Law and the Prophets, even the righteousness of God, through faith in Jesus Christ, to all and on all who believe"* (Rom. 3:21-22). Christ sealed the New Covenant with Israel with His own blood to accomplish what the first covenant could not (Heb. 8:8).

Later in Paul's epistle to the Romans, he quotes Moses to show that God's plan of salvation through Christ can also be easily understood and is attainable (Rom. 10:6-9). God reveals Himself in many ways: in creation, through the human conscience, in His written Word, through miracles, and expressly in His Son, Jesus Christ. There is plenty of revelation near all men to lead them into truth, if they will trust it. The lost do not have to explore the heights of heaven or depths of hell to find truth. What God wants them to appropriate by faith has been revealed. Likewise, what has been rejected will govern their ultimate punishment. This was the same point Moses was making in his life-or-death appeal in this chapter.

The climax of Moses' forty-year ministry is this appeal to his countrymen to "love," to "obey," and to "cling" to the Lord. Moses wanted them to make a choice at that very moment which would guide Israel into life for generations to come. God is Israel's life; apart from Him is death (separation from life). Moses was not talking about positional justification at this juncture. Israel had been redeemed by the blood of a lamb and justified by faith at the first Passover in Egypt. Moses was speaking of a consecrated way of life which maintains fellowship and communion with God.

Hence, the biblical standard of sanctification is summarized in Romans 6:23: *"For the wages of sin is death, but the gift of God is eternal life in Christ Jesus our Lord."* Disobedience causes separation; obedience results in divine fellowship.

April 10 – I Will Be With You
Deuteronomy 31

A few weeks prior to this address, the Lord had told Moses that it was time for him to be gathered to his people (Num. 27:13). When it was time for his departure, Moses was to climb the mountain range of Abarim so that he could behold a vista of the Promised Land to the west before he died; the specific summit was Nebo (32:49). The Lord reminded Moses that he could not enter the Promised Land because of his failure to obey Him and to honor Him before the people a few months earlier at Kadesh. Numbers 27 also records Moses' request that the Lord appoint a strong shepherd to guide Israel – that man was Joshua, who was then publicly recognized as Israel's new leader.

Moses had enjoyed robust vitality in his autumn years (Deut. 34:7), but now, at 120 years of age, he did not have the strength to lead Israel into battle. The Lord would not permit His servant to suffer the rigors of extended warfare; it was time for him to depart. But Moses reminded his countrymen that though he would not be crossing the Jordan with them, God would go before them.

Under Joshua's leadership they would vanquish their enemies as in the plains of Moab and secure Canaan; that is, if they would be faithful to do to the Canaanites as commanded. Moses then charges them, *"Be strong and of good courage, do not fear nor be afraid of them; for the Lord your God, He is the one who goes with you. He will not leave you nor forsake you"* (v. 6). Then Moses called Joshua forward, before the entire nation, and gave him a similar charge.

The Lord had been with Moses for forty years; He now extended to Joshua the same promise He had made to Moses (Ex. 3:12): *"I will be with you. I will not leave you nor forsake you"* (Josh. 1:5). The Lord promised Jacob, *"Return to the land of your fathers and to your family, and I will be with you"* (Gen. 31:3). Whether the child of God is commanded "to come," "to go," or "to return," the same solace of peace is enjoyed – the communion of God's presence.

Living for Christ in a sin-cursed world is challenging, but the believer's calling in Christ is not burdensome because he or she is yoked with the Lord (Matt. 11:28-30). It is through this vital connection that we learn that every victory is the Lord's victory and that without Him we can do nothing!

April 11 – A Closing Song
Deuteronomy 32

Moses may have written other songs, but three are preserved in Scripture. Exodus 15 records the wonderful deliverance of Israel from Pharaoh's army at the Red Sea. Then there is the historical record of God's faithfulness throughout Israel's history in Psalm 90. It is noteworthy that Moses begins the final message of his ministry with a song and ends it with a blessing (Deut. 33).

The song of this chapter was to assist Israel in the future to make sense of why they were suffering disaster and calamity in the Promised Land – namely for apostasy. Moses had already confirmed that in that day, this song would *"testify against them as a witness"* (Deut. 31:21). Yet, Moses' song also anticipated God's grace being lavished on Israel in a future day.

The song commences with a congregational call to listen and then a prompt to acclaim praise to Israel's just, faithful, and upright God. He is the God of truth and all His ways are perfect, unlike the Israelites who are foolish and perverse and whose ways are corrupt. The song then reviews Israel's history from the time of their bondage in Egypt, through their wilderness wanderings, to their establishment in the Promised Land. The Song then becomes prophetic in nature: Israel's future ingratitude and gross idolatry against their Father and Creator are foretold, as are the severe judgments they will suffer for their sin. Then the song offers hope to Israel; God will avenge His people against their enemies.

The song then concludes on a joyful note. Despite Israel's past failures and God's just chastening, there is a day coming when righteousness will be restored to the land, Israel will be cleansed of all defilement, and Gentiles and Jews will rejoice together in what God has accomplished. This longed-for utopia will occur in the Millennial Kingdom under Christ's rule. He is the only One who can *"provide atonement for His land and His people"* (v. 43). Only Christ can reconcile both Jew and Gentile to God (Col. 1:20-22) and only after Israel's restoration will both Jew and Gentile rejoice together in God's presence. But this blessed reality of the Kingdom Age cannot occur until "the fullness of the Gentiles" (i.e., the Church Age; Rom. 11:25) and "the times of the Gentiles" (Gentile oppression) have concluded.

April 12 – Moses, My Servant
Joshua 1

Joshua commences his book by recounting the Lord's message to him shortly after the death of Moses: *"Moses My servant is dead. Now therefore, arise, go over this Jordan, you and all this people, to the land which I am giving to them – the children of Israel"* (v. 2). Moses had resolutely guided the Israelites for forty years in the wilderness, during which time he expounded God's Law to them, and brought them safely to the brink of the Jordan River. It was here that the life and the ministry of Moses conclude. Moses died after being permitted to view Canaan from Mount Nebo (Deut. 32:49), and the Lord then buried him in the land of Moab, near Beth-peor (Deut. 34:6).

Moses, a man empowered by the Holy Spirit, exhibited steadfast faithfulness throughout his life, yet he grew in faith as well. When Jehovah first summoned Moses to deliver His people from bondage and from Egypt, Moses rejected the idea. He argued that the Israelites would not believe that he was from God, that the Egyptians would not release their slaves, and that he was not an eloquent speaker. Yet, after a small demonstration of God's power, Moses surrendered to God's calling for His life. He went to Egypt, confronted Pharaoh, instigated devastating plagues, and freed the Israelites and brought them to Sinai.

The New Testament attributes a special honor to Moses' service to the Lord. The Greek word *therapon*, translated as "servant" in Hebrews 3:5, is used to describe the type of servant Moses was. *Therapon* is not the typical word used in the New Testament to describe a servant or a slave; in fact, it is only used in connection with Moses. This word speaks of a servant who is motivated by devotion for his superior. At first, Moses was hesitant to accept the call of God for his life, but when he did, he did so of his own free will because he loved the Lord.

At the burning bush, Moses' faith was but in its infancy, but over the strenuous years that followed, his faith in and devotion to Jehovah steadily grew. Joshua refers to him as "the servant of the Lord" sixteen times. While living, Moses was spoken of as a servant once (Ex. 14:31), but after his death he is repeatedly refered to as "the servant of the Lord" (Deut. 34:5); he finished well. Moses was not a perfect man, but his life was characterized by faithfulness; may we follow his example.

April 13 – Be Strong and Very Courageous
Joshua 1

After acknowledging the faithfulness of Moses, the Lord puts Joshua in charge of leading His people into the Promised Land. The Lord promised Joshua that if he obeyed His command and led His people into Canaan to obtain their inheritance, no one would be able to withstand him. The Lord had stood with Moses for forty years in the wilderness, and now He was extending to Joshua the same promise He made to Moses at the burning bush: *"I will be with you. I will not leave you nor forsake you"* (v. 5). If Joshua merely knew what God wanted him do for Him without His presence and facilitating power he would be powerless before his enemies.

Though God had made the right path known, it should never be concluded that this path is therefore easy or comfortable to follow. The opposite is true, for the moment God opens His way before His people, the enemy will ruthlessly attempt to hinder their progress. This is why Moses challenged Joshua to *"Be strong and of good courage, do not fear nor be afraid of them; for the Lord your God, He is the One who goes with you. He will not leave you nor forsake you"* (Deut. 31:6). Moses had experienced God's faithfulness and abiding presence and encouraged Joshua to do the same.

Hence, the foremost thing impressed on Joshua at this point is *"to be strong and very courageous"* (v. 7). That is to say, when God's will is apprehended by His people, they must also have divine strength and courage to do it, otherwise they will be overcome by the enemy. After affirming His abiding presence, the Lord exhorted Joshua three times with the words: *"Be strong and of good courage"* (vv. 6, 7, 9). These three calls were meant to energize Joshua to action.

The context in which the first is found relates to fulfilling his divine calling by leading the Israelites into Canaan to obtain their possession. The second resounds the timeless biblical principle that obedience to God's Word ensures success in God's plan. Finally, the Lord promised His abiding presence if Joshua would step forward in faith. Likewise, if believers are to further the cause of Christ in this wicked world, they must be faithful to their calling, be obedient to God's Word, and with the knowledge of God's abiding presence aggressively engage the enemy with confidence.

Daily Devotions

April 14 – The New Commander
Joshua 1

Jehovah had used Moses to redeem the Jews and deliver them from bondage and from Egypt, but He would use Joshua to seize their inheritance in the Promised Land. Joshua's years of serving Moses not only prepared him for his own ministry of leading the Israelites, but also pointed to it. Even before Joshua's confirmation in Numbers 27, we see indications of his future ministry during the years he served Moses. Joshua first appears in Scripture as a young man leading the attack against the Amalekites (Ex. 17). The scene is glorious: Moses, on the mount, holding up the rod of God over the battlefield, pictures Christ's intercessory power for His people from the throne of grace in heaven. But while Moses intercedes above, Joshua wields the sword victoriously below. This sight portrays Christ's unrestrained power in the believer's life as he or she uses the Word of God (the sword of truth, Heb. 4:12) and fully relies on the strength of the Holy Spirit.

Next, Joshua is seen at the base of Mt. Sinai waiting for Moses to descend with the Word of God; he stood apart from the idolatrous clamor within the camp of Israel (Ex. 32:17). Likewise, in behavior the Lord Jesus was separate from sinners and longed only to do God's will (John 5:30).

Joshua would again demonstrate faithfulness when, months after leaving Mt. Sinai behind, he was one of the twelve spies sent into Canaan on a reconnaissance mission. They brought back a pledge of the land's fruit which was their promised inheritance. Ten of the spies doubted God's faithfulness, but Joshua and Caleb, resolutely withstood them. Afterwards, much of Joshua's ministry was centered in confronting those who would deny God's faithfulness to His promises.

The above events were a foretaste of Joshua's later ministry; he had been chosen by God to subdue the nations of Canaan and then divide their land for an inheritance for His people. As is often the case before one comes into the fullness of his or her divine calling, Joshua's accomplishments cast their shadow beforehand. He was a man of courage, tenacity, conviction, and holiness – a proven leader among his peers. In God's plan, the young Joshua of the wilderness had forty years of preparatory training before becoming the victorious Joshua of the Promised Land. Spiritual growth and faithfulness walk together.

April 15 – The Symbolism of Canaan Revisited
Joshua 1

As previously mentioned, some have likened physical death to crossing the Jordan and the land of Canaan to heaven, but this is not correct. Redemption brought the Israelites out of Egypt, through the Red Sea, and into the wilderness as a nation, but when each one passed through the Jordan they experienced death, practically and individually.

William MacDonald explains why Canaan does not represent heaven: "There was conflict in Canaan, whereas there is no conflict in heaven. Actually the land of Canaan pictures our present spiritual inheritance. It is ours, but we must possess it by obeying the Word, claiming the promises, and fighting the good fight of faith."[7] Canaan represents all of the believer's inheritance in Christ who is seated in heavenly places (Eph. 1:3).

In Christ, believers will find an infinite treasury of spiritual resources which enable them to powerfully represent the Lord while on earth, but these provisions must first be possessed to do so. Certainly, there are future aspects of our inheritance in Christ that believers will enjoy after glorification, such as, ruling and reigning with Christ once He returns to establish His kingdom (2 Tim. 2:12; Rev. 21:7). Yet, the book of Joshua closely aligns with the book of Ephesians to consider the benefit of possessing as much of our inheritance in Christ now, rather than what will come in Him later.

The Canaan rest for Israel illustrates the spiritual rest we have in Christ when we, by faith, submit to His Word (Heb. 4:11-12). Salvation rest is experienced when we respond in faith to Christ's gospel message; in so doing we obtain peace with God (Rom. 5:1). As we learn of Him and yield to His will (as expressed in His Word), we enjoy the peace of God (Phil. 4:6-8). By faith we enter into God's salvation rest (Heb. 4:3); and by continuing in faith and obedience His rest enters into us. In a coming day we will rest in His presence forever.

For the Israelites, the long journey across the desert had come to an end. In the wilderness God had set a table before them and nurtured them, but it was now time to cross the Jordan under a new leader and to seize and enjoy a land flowing with milk and honey. Likewise, although we sojourn on earth, we are to lay hold of the heavenly blessings in Christ and thus possess our "Canaan" here and now.

Daily Devotions

April 16 – The Two and a Half Tribes
Joshua 1

As Israel's new leader, it was necessary for Joshua to remind the tribes of Reuben, Gad, and the half-tribe of Manasseh that though they had received their requested inheritance east of the Jordan River, they must fulfill their promise to Moses and fight alongside their brethren so that the remaining tribes might obtain their inheritance. Only once they had finished conquering Canaan could they return to their homes. While it is true that the Eastern Plateau was within the overall boundaries God had bestowed to Abraham and his descendants, it was God's design for them to first possess the heart of that land and secure the one place in all the earth where Jehovah had chosen to place His name – Jerusalem.

Canaan formed a land-bridge with three continents and therefore was the perfect location for Jehovah to dwell among His people and to be a beacon of light to the nations. Sadly, the two and a half tribes were more interested in the welfare of their cattle than establishing His name in the land (Num. 32:19). With this said, the response of the two and half-tribes to Joshua's charge was favorable; they had not forgotten their pledge to Moses and intended to honor it. In fact, Joshua placed them at the head of the column – they would be the first into Canaan.

Israel in the wilderness pictures the believer who is weak and immature, who still struggles with sin – his heart is divided between the Lord and Egypt (the world). The Jews who died in the wilderness picture the carnal-minded Christian (they continue to long for Egypt). The two and one half tribes picture the believer who loves the Lord and fellow believers, but have not fully given themselves over to Him because of their love for worldly things. The faithful who crossed the Jordan and settled in the Canaan picture those few believers who enter into the fullness of fellowship with the risen Savior and enjoy the blessings which that fellowship ensures.

On the other side, the Israelites would experience the power of God in a practical way as they obeyed the Lord's command to possess the Promised Land by driving out their enemies who dwelt there. It is the same for believers today, although we sojourn on earth, we are to lay hold of the heavenly blessings in Christ and thus possess our "Canaan" here and now.

April 17 – Crossing the Jordan
Joshua 3

God had promised to work a *wonder* to magnify Joshua and motivate the Israelites to enter into Canaan and to seize their possession. The priests were to carry the Ark of the Covenant to the brink of the Jordan. After they stepped into the river, God would pile up the waters at the city Adam and permit His people to cross over on dry ground. When this occurred, the Jews were to portage the dry riverbed while the priests stood holding the Ark of the Covenant in the channel that remained. After everyone was safely on the other side, the priests would then carry the Ark up the western bank of the Jordan River and the water would return as before. Not only did the Lord accomplish this feat; He did it during the spring rainy season when the Jordan was out of its banks.

As each person came to the brink of the Jordan and by faith stepped down its banks, the Ark would have become fully visible. It is indeed sobering to ponder the scene before us, for with the eye of faith we understand that the Ark, held in serene stillness below the level of the ground, represents the Lord Jesus Christ's body in the grave. Yet, He is the bridge from death to life and the multitudes passing by (i.e., through Him) enter into Canaan (i.e., the heavenly places). The Ark going into, within, and coming out of the river pictures the death, burial, and resurrection of Christ. All crossing the Jordan joined that experience.

In the Jordan, the believer died with Christ (He being our representative), and thus passing through death with Him we are brought into resurrection life on the other side. Accordingly, believers today, like the Israelites before us, stand as trophies of the victory achieved over the raging waters of death.

To save us, Christ had to go into death because that is where we were (i.e., we were all dead in trespasses and sins). After His death, Christ then had to come out of death in order to grant us eternal life and confer to us the ability to live for God (2 Cor. 5:14-15). *"Even when we were dead in trespasses, made us alive together with Christ (by grace you have been saved), and raised us up together, and made us sit together in the heavenly places in Christ Jesus"* (Eph. 2:5-6). Christ died to enter into and rescue us from death that we might live for Him now and with Him forevermore.

Daily Devotions

April 18 – Remember Me
Joshua 4

Joshua describes two signs or memorials in this chapter that are inseparable in meaning. One of the memorials would be erected later that evening at the location of the Israelite campsite (vv. 3, 8). After all the people had crossed the dry riverbed, representatives from each tribe (who had been waiting to cross the river) walked to where the priests were standing, chose a stone, placed it on his shoulder, and carried it up out of the Jordan. The other memorial, also constructed of twelve stones from where the priests were standing, was set up at that site by Joshua himself. The latter memorial would be covered over by water when Jehovah returned the floodwaters. The former memorial would testify to future generations as to how Jehovah had miraculously ushered His people safely into Canaan.

The stack of twelve stones at Gilgal would serve as a constant reminder to God's covenant people of their deliverance. The stone monument at the entrance of Canaan would serve to recall the magnificent feat God had performed to bring His people into the Promised Land. This memorial reminds us of the life of Christ which is to be lived out in victorious conflict to secure God's blessings for us.

The twelve stones set up in the riverbed by Joshua also have special significance for believers today, for they remind us of death itself and the One who took our place in death – the death we deserved. Once these stones were covered with water again, the monument would be gone from view, except through the eyes of faith. Thus, we are to continue to remember by faith the value of Christ's death.

Paul expounds that this is one of the purposes of the Lord's Supper: *"For as often as you eat this bread and drink this cup, you proclaim the Lord's death till He comes"* (1 Cor. 11:26). The Lord Jesus instituted this feast on the night before His crucifixion with the command: *"Do this in remembrance of Me"* (Luke 22:19). It is good for God's people in any dispensation to recall to mind the goodness of God, especially through the means He has deemed most appropriate to revere Him. God's Word does not give the Church any yearly feasts to commemorate any aspect of the Lord's birth, life, death, or resurrection; rather, the Church was to regularly memorialize the Lord Jesus by keeping the Lord's Supper.

April 19 – The Necessity of Circumcision
Joshua 5

The news of Israel's miraculous crossing of the Jordan and their encampment at Gilgal was demoralizing to the Amorites and Canaanites. Who could possibly stand against Israel's God? Yet, Joshua understood that Jehovah would only be with His people in battle if they were obedient to Him, so he quickly set about the task of circumcising the males born during the forty-year wilderness sojourn.

During the wandering years, the Jews did not obey the circumcision commandment that was first given to Abraham in Genesis 17, and then formally ratified by the Law of Moses at Sinai (Lev. 12:3). Jewish unbelief had kept them from inheriting the Promised Land almost thirty-nine years earlier. During the disciplinary years that followed, much of the operations of God's covenant with them were suspended. In the wilderness, the Jews did not maintain their appointed sign of separation, but nonetheless God ensured their separation by isolating them from pagan influences during their chastisement.

With the older generation gone, it was time for the younger new nation to exercise faith in Jehovah; the seal of God's covenant with them (circumcision) would be demanded. Expediency was also required, for the Passover was only four days away and the Law prohibited any uncircumcised male from eating it (Ex. 12:44, 48). Hence, Joshua sharpens knives and ensured that all males within the Jewish encampment were circumcised. This meant that Israel had no army to protect them if attacked; their trust was in Jehovah alone.

While circumcision marked the Jews as God's covenant people, Paul explains that circumcision had a deeper spiritual meaning which the Jews did not perceive: *"For he is not a Jew who is one outwardly, nor is circumcision that which is outward in the flesh; but he is a Jew who is one inwardly; and circumcision is that of the heart, in the Spirit"* (Rom. 2:28-29). In type, circumcision speaks of a life that has no confidence or glory in the flesh (Phil. 3:3). This is why the circumcision was to be done with *"sharp knives"*; only the sharp sword of the Spirit, the Word of God, can bring about spiritual circumcision in believers.

All Christians have been positionally circumcised in Christ (Col. 2:11), and they are to manifest this inner spiritual reality daily.

Daily Devotions

April 20 – Jericho: Victory Over the World
Joshua 6

By faith the Israelites had entered the land, but now found themselves encamped between Jericho, which checked their advance, and the Jordan which blocked their retreat. This was a grave situation strategically, but they knew that they must wait for instructions before proceeding. The Lord revealed His battle plan for the fall of Jericho to Joshua. From a human perspective, the revealed strategy seemed foolish; Jehovah would not be including any man-made weapons of war or orthodox military strategy into His battle plan. Rather, the Jewish soldiers were to walk silently around the city for six consecutive days, and on the seventh day they were to circumnavigate it seven times; when they heard the trumpet sound everyone was to shout, the walls would come tumbling down, and every man was to go straight into the city from the position he found himself.

Not only the men of war were going to journey around Jericho a total of thirteen times, but seven priests blowing trumpets were to follow the men of war; the Ark of the Covenant (as carried by priests) would follow the seven priests, and there was also to be a rear guard. The priests were to be blasting their *showphars*; these were the trumpets of gladness – a demeanor of joy and enthusiasm was to mark the Israelites as they walked around the walls of Jericho; they were to anticipate their forthcoming triumph. Likewise, Christians today should be marked by a spirit of joyful expectation as they faithfully serve Christ and wait for His coming and their glorification.

God's plan was executed flawlessly and Israel conquered Jericho; only Rahab and her family, who were displaying the scarlet cord from her window, were spared. Jericho pictures the world and its influences. Worldliness is any sphere in which the Lord Jesus is excluded.

The Lord told His disciples that the world loves its own, hence, they would be hated by the world because the world hates Him (John 15:18-19). It is impossible to love the Lord as we should and also adore a satanic system which openly rejects Him: *"Friendship with the world is enmity with God* (Jas. 4:4). Worldliness is the love of passing things which have no eternal value. Worldliness opposes God, and God hates it. Whatever is born of God is destined to overcome the world! (1 Jn. 5:4).

May We Serve Christ!

April 21 – Achan's Sin and End
Joshua 7

Joshua 6 records that the Hebrews *"utterly destroyed all that was within the city"* (v. 21) and that apart from the precious metals they *"burned the city with fire, and all that was in it"* (v. 24). Why did Jehovah command that Jericho be completely obliterated? Jericho was the initial city the Israelites would confront and thus a representative of the entire land, which was thoroughly pagan. Thus, Jericho became a symbol of the world, a society apart from Jehovah, and He didn't want His people to have any part of it.

Accordingly, not only were Jericho's inhabitants to be wiped out, but all the spoil of the city was to be destroyed (animals, money, clothing, household goods, etc.). Only the gold, silver, bronze, and iron were to be gathered and stored in the Lord's treasury until refining fires could remake the metals into something useful for the Lord. Jericho was the first-fruits of their conquest, and the first–fruits always belong to the Lord alone.

Although the battle was a success, we learn in this chapter that not all the spoil was destroyed. A man named Achan covertly kept two hundred shekels of silver, a wedge of gold, and a Babylonian garment. The gold and silver was the Lord's and the garment should have been burned. His secret sin would tragically affect the entire nation (36 men died in the first battle with Ai), just as worldliness in believers affects the Church negatively today. The Israelites, especially Achan, would learn the consequences of valuing the trifles of Jericho, which God deemed "accursed," because they were to be devoted to Him, over His inexhaustible provisions. The Hebrew *cherem* is translated "accursed" and means "dedicated to be utterly destroyed." The *cherem* things were the Lord's and were destined for the fire (to be burned or refined).

The Lord promised that He would not be with Joshua in battle until the guilty was discovered and judged, and the accursed things removed from the presence of His people. The penalty for the offense was to be severe; not only the accursed things, but also the offender and all that pertained to him were to be burned. Achan, by stealing the accursed things became accursed himself. His unchecked lusting destroyed him, his family, and all that was his. This narrative is a good reminder to us that sin destroys and corrupts secretly from the inside.

April 22 – Ai: Victory Over the Flesh
Joshua 7

Joshua did not know about Achan's sin, or that they would not have the Lord's help in attacking the next two cities to the west, Bethel and Ai. Joshua had obeyed the Lord's instruction and led Israel into an astounding victory at Jericho. Yet, Joshua did not seek counsel from the Lord, nor did the Lord provide any, before the next battle. This should have been a warning sign that something was wrong.

Joshua sent spies to do some reconnaissance work. The spies brought back a good report and suggested that because Bethel and Ai were smaller cities than Jericho, only 2,000 or 3,000 soldiers should be sent to take the cities. In their estimation, the opposition *"were few"* and did not require the attention of the entire army. Yet, the basis for the spies' conclusion was flawed, for Jericho had not been overthrown by the Israelites; they merely finished off those who survived the ensuing catastrophe. It had been the Lord who had knocked the walls down.

God's people still suffer from such mistaken reasoning today; the pride of victory has caused the abasement of many fine Christians. We boast of the number of our converts, our ministry statistics, the size of our congregations…do we really believe that the Spirit of God is energizing the work? For God to exalt Himself through our service, we must co-labor with Him in purest humility. He will honor those who do so, but chasten those who rob Him of His rightful glory.

Joshua heeded the scouts' counsel and committed 3,000 troops for the battle without consulting the Lord. The Israelites were guilty of overestimating their own strength and underestimating the power of their enemy and they were soundly defeated. Thirty-six Hebrews died in the failed attempt to seize Ai. Ai represents the corrupt wisdom and weak power of the flesh. What God says about the flesh is all negative.

In the flesh there is *"no good thing"* (Rom. 7:18). The flesh profits *"nothing"* (John 6:63). A Christian is to put *"no confidence"* in the flesh (Phil. 3:3). He is to make *"no provision"* for the flesh (Rom. 13:14). A person who lives in and for the flesh is destined for failure and sorrow. To be victorious soldiers for Christ we must adopt a *no sin* and *no self-estimation* mentality in warfare. Joshua 8 records Israel's victory over Ai; the battle was fought God's way and in His strength.

May We Serve Christ!

April 23 – The Devil's Deceptive Gibeonites
Joshua 9

The Gibeonites, who lived about twenty miles southwest of the Israelite encampment, did not want to join one of the larger confederations mobilizing to war against the Israelites. They knew the God of Moses had granted the Israelites the land of Canaan and that they were to destroy all the inhabitants. The Gibeonites believed this was true and were in fear for their lives, but they did not want to leave their homeland either. This is where their actions contrast with the faith of Rahab who, also fearing for her life, openly declared her faith to the spies and then chose to fully identify with Jehovah and His people; she was therefore brought into the commonwealth of Israel. The Gibeonites only wanted to be spared from death. They had no desire to worship Jehovah, to submit to His will, or to identify with the Israelites and receive Jehovah's blessings promised to them.

The Gibeonites' dilemma was resolved by contriving a cunning plan to trick the Israelites into forging a peace treaty with them. The Israelites would be required to honor a covenant established in Jehovah's name, even if fostered in deceit. The plan was to portray themselves as a group of ambassadors who had traveled from a faraway country after learning about Jehovah's astonishing feats in Egypt and against the Amorites.

After arriving at the Hebrew camp, this phony envoy would express their respect for Jehovah and their desire to live in peace with His people. To strengthen the ruse by giving the appearance of having undergone a long journey, the Gibeonites loaded their donkeys with worn-out sacks and patched-up wine skins; they also wore ragged clothes and scruffy shoes. They carried a portion of dry, moldy bread to deceive the Israelites into thinking their supplies were nearly depleted.

This is a classic evil strategy used often by the devil (e.g., against Eve in Eden): the mixing of truth and deception to create a bold solicitation to confuse and to stumble the hearer. The Israelites, who believed the Gibeonites, would soon learn that whenever Satan presents a half-truth, there is only one half that he wants you to act on, and it's the wrong half. Believers are not commanded to confront Satan directly, but rather to rest in revealed truth by faith and resist him – submitting to God means ignoring the devil's ploys (Jas. 4:7).

Daily Devotions

April 24 – Gideon: Victory Over the Devil
Joshua 9

Jericho and Ai had miraculously fallen by the hands of the Israelites as empowered by their God Jehovah. Obviously, the enemy would not be able to overcome the Jews by direct assault or by hiding within fortifications, but what if the Canaanites could establish a friendly agreement to coexist in peace; would not this thwart God's agenda? This is the satanic tactic of unnatural unions, which has often been used to hinder God's work. This is why Paul warned the Corinthians not to be yoked with non-believers (2 Cor. 6:14-16). What true communion can a child of God and a child of the devil have with each other? None!

It was three days before the Gibeonite deception was discovered. The people wanted to destroy the Hivites, but were not permitted to do so because of the covenant their leaders had sworn in Jehovah's name. The Israelites complained against their leaders for disobeying God's command to remove the inhabitants from the land. They had learned at Ai, that disobedience has an expensive price tag. Yet, Joshua knew that Jehovah was not a lying God and thereby was compelled to honor his agreement with the Hivities, no matter how wrong it was.

Accordingly, the Hivites would remain in the land unharmed, but only as slaves. This allowance was against Moses' command (Deut. 12:28-30), but Joshua and the elders chose not to right a wrong with another wrong, but to submit themselves to Jehovah and suffer the consequences for one rash mistake, rather than two. This was a decision that God honored, for years later Saul's family would be punished for the king's attempt to eliminate the Gibeonites (2 Sam. 21).

Fearing that other people groups would defect to Israel, the king of Jerusalem, Adoni-zedek, solicited four other southern kings to bring their armies north to teach the Gibeonites a lesson. Gibeon sent an urgent message to Gilgal, and Joshua, compelled to honor the treaty marched his men all night. The Hebrews arrived at Gibeon at dawn and through divine enablement, extended daylight, and hailstorms they completely wiped out the major armies in southern Canaan.

This victory is a good reminder that our failures are not final; God wants us to learn from our mistakes, rise up in grace, and confront the enemy in His power. Then, we too will be in awe of God's answer to our past failures.

April 25 – Three Enemies to Be Conquered
Joshua 10

Three different enemies of the believer have been introduced to us in typological form in the book of Joshua thus far: the world (Jericho), the flesh (Ai), and the devil (Gibeon). Those who have been born again overcome the world by faith as they submit to God's Word: *"For whatever is born of God overcomes the world. And this is the victory that has overcome the world – our faith"* (1 Jn. 5:4). By faith we hold to the truth and reject God-denying secular philosophies and human traditions, rather than be ruined by them (Col. 2:8).

A different strategy is needed to overcome the flesh. Victory over the flesh is achieved by identifying with Christ in His death and in His life (Rom. 6:1-10). Then, we must choose not to strengthen the flesh nature by engaging in its deeds (Col. 3:5), but rather by the power of the Holy Spirit mortifying desires outside of God's will for us (Rom. 8:13). This strengthens the inner man to resist temptation in the future.

The third enemy, the devil, is not to be directly confronted, but resisted by submitting to God in faith (Jas. 4:7). There is no need for believers to fear or flee the devil; if they continue resisting him in truth, he will be the one to depart. Believers are to be knowledgeable of his tactics so that he does not gain an advantage over them through ignorance (2 Cor. 2:11). Paul further warned the Corinthians that Satan often transforms himself into an angel of light and his servants into ministers of righteousness because he knows it is easier to deceive God's people than it is to deter them from a purpose (2 Cor. 11:14-15).

Satan rarely presents outright lies; rather, he depends upon a series of blurred deceptions to gain his footing and to wreak havoc within the Church. If the devil can deceive the believer into compromising even a small portion of the truth, be sure that he will return to accomplish the same objective again and again. He may wait a bit until we become comfortable in our complacency, but he will always come back! Let us stand fast in the light of divine revelation and not be moved into the darkness by the enemy's trickery.

May God give us grace to *slay* the deeds of the flesh, to *submit* by faith to the truth and not be moved from it, and to *stand* fast in the faith to resist evil!

Daily Devotions

April 26 – The Rest of Conquest
Joshua 11-12

The northern campaign of Canaan, including the battle at Hazor where the Israelites were greatly outnumbered, is recorded in Joshua 11. A roster of the kings and armies conquered throughout Canaan are listed in Joshua 12. The region was in turmoil for seven years, meaning that a number of battles occurred without an explicit biblical reference. Moreover, the Anakim, the giants who terrified most of the spies sent into Canaan some 45 years earlier, had been vanquished. The Israelites had learned that without the Lord they were helpless, but with Him even the giants could not stand against them.

Joshua supplies this summary: *"So Joshua took the whole land ... and Joshua gave it as an inheritance to Israel .... Then the land rested from war"* (11:23). Yet, this statement seems to contradict what the Lord said to Joshua later: *"there remains very much land yet to be possessed"* (13:1). Joshua did destroy the cities, however, many Canaanites hid in caverns and caves in the vicinity and then return to their homes after the Israelites had passed. Though conquered, the inhabitants were not completely removed. So, while it was true that there were pockets of resistance remaining in Canaan (13:2-6), the Lord decreed that the land had been sufficiently conquered to be divided among His people as an inheritance. Jehovah had promised to help each tribe drive out the remaining inhabitants from their possession, if they would go on with Him to do so; this posed a new test of their faith.

Now the entire nation could enjoy the same restful quality of life gained through faithful conquest that Joshua said the two and a half tribes who settled in the Eastern Plateau had obtained previously (1:13, 15). By faith the Israelites had obediently entered the land and engaged in conquest to possess the land. The rest they now enjoyed was only realized because they had seized their inheritance through active warfare.

"The land rested from war," but a resting heart does not mean it has rest from difficulties, but rather we choose to tranquilly abide with the Lord through them. Through each successive trial we have a higher experience with Christ and we learn of Him (His mind, His will, His character, etc.). Though believers are first possessed by Christ through grace, it is also by grace that we possess more of Him.

April 27 – Give Me This Mountain
Joshua 14

Having designated the land allotments east of the Jordan to the two and a half tribes, Joshua turned his attention to dividing and proportioning the land within Canaan to the remaining tribes. Prior to the first lot being cast, the veteran Caleb stepped forward to assert his claim. Moses had promised him 45 years earlier that the region he spied out would be his inheritance, this included the fortification of Hebron, where the powerful Anakim (the giants) resided (Deut. 1:36; 9:2).

Moses rewarded Caleb for being a faithful scout in Canaan and for withstanding the rebel spies at Kadesh Barnea. Caleb's devotion to the Lord never waned, a fact he asserted before Joshua: *"I wholly followed the Lord my God"* (v. 8). Despite years of blistering desert heat and numerous battles, the Lord had preserved Caleb; he was now 85 years of age, but despite his age, he remained strong in the Lord. He now wanted his promised inheritance. He knew that if the Lord would continue to be with him and would secure Hebron for his possession.

Caleb is a great example to us in our present day of weakness and complacency. His character upholds the finest virtues to be found in soldiers of the cross today: one who is sold out for the Lord and yet mistrusts oneself. He exhibited unabated divine strength because he lacked self-confidence. His humility and continued dependence on God were unrelenting. Caleb understood that his dependence on the Lord infused him with divine power; thus, it did not matter to him that his possession was a fortification occupied by giants.

Joshua was moved by his friend's address and responded by blessing him and granting his request. Hebron was Caleb's possession, and in the power of the Lord he subdued the giants and restored to the city its proper name; Hebron (15:13-14).

Caleb's fortitude demonstrates how God's people in any dispensation are able to overcome their adversaries and adversities: *"Not by might nor by power, but by My Spirit, says the Lord of Hosts"* (Zech. 4:6). May we, like Caleb, experience ongoing personal revival by wholly following and depending on the Lord God. Then we too, will be strong in the Lord and live in the enjoyment of heavenly things as we patiently engage in earthly conflict.

April 28 – You Have Blessed Me... Bless Me Again
Joshua 15

Having blessed Caleb and confirmed his inheritance, Joshua initiated the allotment process for the nine and a half tribes determined to settle in Canaan. The lots were cast and the tribe of Judah was chosen first. Joshua 15 describes the land endowed to Judah. Judah was the largest tribe and would therefore receive a greater portion of land. Although composing some fertile sections, especially in the western coastal plain, much of this southern region was barren hill county.

Hebron was located within Judah's portion and Caleb not only took the city from the Anakim, but with the help of his courageous nephew Othniel, he captured Debir also. Caleb had promised that whoever was victorious at Debir would have his daughter Achsah's hand in marriage, so Othniel (later a judge in Israel; Judg. 3:8-11) became Caleb's son-in-law. Caleb bestowed Achsah and Othniel with an arid region of land south of Hebron for their own inheritance, but after their marriage, Achsah asked her father Caleb for the springs near this land also, which Caleb granted her.

While the inheritance of all believers is in Christ in heavenly places, each believer must labor to possess what divine providence agrees to confer. In this chapter, we learn that the Lord desires us to ask Him for our portion that we might obtain abundant grace (Matt. 7:7-9; Mark 11:24; John 16:23-24).

Achsah had been bestowed a superb gift of land as a wedding present, but the significance of that possession was increased because she gained the nearby springs also. She received more inheritance because she requested it of her father Caleb. Likewise, our heavenly Father is aware of our needs and is able to grant to us all that we lack and all that would enhance our service for Him. Accordingly, may we not forget to respectfully and earnestly plead with Him, "You have given me" ... "give me also."

It is worthy to note that because Caleb trusted his God and engaged the enemy in His strength, he was victorious and, as a result, increased his inheritance. The land allotments were to pass down from generation to generation within the same tribe. In other words, an individual or clan could not increase their inheritance by buying or stealing from their brethren, but only by engaging and defeating the enemy.

April 29 – It Is Not Enough
Joshua 16-17

Because Joseph had preserved the young Hebrew nation from starvation and was the firstborn of Rachel, he would receive a double portion of the Promised Land. Hence, his sons, Ephraim and Manasseh, both became the heads of their respective tribes. Each received a sizeable portion in Canaan and the Transjordan when it was divided. However, some within the tribes of Ephraim and Manasseh complained to Joshua that the rugged forest land was not sufficient for them: *"Why have you given us only one lot and one share to inherit, since we are a great people"* (17:14) ... *"The mountain country is not enough for us"* (17:16). They reasoned that because they were *"a great people"* and had only received one portion for Ephraim and the half tribe of Manasseh, they deserved more land for their possession.

But their allotment justly portioned with their population. Instead of granting them more land, Joshua turned their statement around and admonished them. Because they were a powerful tribe, they should be able to drive out the Canaanites and clear the woodlands – then they would gain more land in which to settle.

The children of Joseph countered this charge by reminding Joshua that the Canaanites who remained in the land had iron chariots, and that much of the hill country was forested and untillable. Joshua upheld his decision, telling Ephraim and Manasseh something to the effect of: you will not be receiving any more by lot; there is plenty of land for you to possess, but you will have to work to obtain it – *"get up"* and *"cut down"* (17:18).

It is our nature to want "freebies," but the spiritual believer will better appreciate what is accomplished though perseverance than what is gained without it. Co-laboring with God in His program and with His power is a great privilege and produces lasting results for which we can glorify Him. Regrettably, instead of the swinging the ax and wielding the sword to secure their possession, those in Ephraim and Manasseh thought it better to tolerate and profit by the Canaanites who resided within their borders. What seems to be the path of least resistance at first becomes the arduous way later; in time, both tribes would suffer harsh consequences for their defiance. May we do our best and show diligence in our duties to the Lord, lest we regret not doing so later.

April 30 – It Is Too Much
Joshua 19

Simeon and Levi were men of violence, referring to the time they slaughtered the Shechemites (Gen. 34:25-29) to avenge their sister Dinah's defilement. Because of their cruelty, Jacob had said they would be divided and scattered in Israel (Gen. 49:5-7). By the time of the second census of the children of Israel, the tribes of Simeon and Levi are recorded as the smallest two (Num. 26:12-14, 62); hence, Simeon now received a smaller portion of land for an inheritance. The Levites would live in forty-eight cities; the Lord and not land was to be their inheritance (Josh. 21).

As Judah had a vast region of territory, which was more than they needed to settle their tribe, Simeon was given seventeen of their towns with the associated villages for a possession. This tribe would later be mostly absorbed into Judah and lose their distinction. In fact, some from Simeon would later migrate northward and re-settle in Ephraim and Manasseh after the kingdom split following Solomon's death (2 Chron. 34:6). Thus, the Southern Kingdom was essentially composed of the tribe of Judah alone, as the tribe of Benjamin had been nearly eliminated by civil war.

Judah received a portion of land that was *"too much for them"* (v. 9). However, in God's plan He would bestow the weaker tribe of Simeon an inheritance within Judah's territory. Without Simeon's presence and assistance, the region would have been too vast for Judah to settle, maintain, and protect. However, the cooperative spirit that developed among these two tribes in driving out and conquering the remaining inhabitants is one of the encouraging highlights of the book of Judges (Judg. 1).

In some instances, God grants us a greater portion than what we are capable of inheriting alone, that we might learn to grow in grace by working with others for the cause of Christ. Believers have different spiritual gifts, ministry callings, talents, and developed maturity in Christ. Each of us have differing capacities to receive and retain resurrection power as a spiritual possession. This means that we can accomplish much more working together in unity, than we ever could by individual efforts. We need each other; otherwise the work to be accomplished will seem overwhelming.

May 1 – It Became Too Little
Joshua 19

Jacob had seen that Dan, whose name means "judge," was going to be as treacherous as a snake by the roadside instead of being righteous and providing justice to Israel. The least desirable portion fell to Dan. Their tribal margins are not described because they were bounded by the already-detailed borders of Ephraim and Manasseh to the north, Benjamin to the east, and Judah to the south.

Later, after losing part of their territory to the Amorites, many from this tribe abandoned their God-given inheritance and moved north of Naphtali. They conquered and burned the city of Leshem (Laish), settled in that region, and rebuilt the city, calling it "Dan" (Judg. 18:27-29). They would also be the first tribe in Canaan proper to engage in flagrant idolatry (Judg. 18:30).

The tribe of Dan had determined that their portion was *"too little for them"* (v. 47). Initially, it was not so, but in time the Amorites took over much of their position. While the best response would have been to drive out the inhabitants within their designated possession, as God had commanded them to do, they did move north to conquer Leshem and claimed it as their new possession. Like the Transjordan (the home of the two and a half tribes), Leshem was within the vast region of land promised to Abraham centuries earlier. God's permissive will ensures that His grace is available to us, even when we willfully stray from His best plan for our lives. God permits us to choose what we do, but He chooses the consequences of what we do.

There are consequences of choosing the *permissible* instead of the *good*, or choosing the *good* rather than the *best*, but our heavenly Father is capable of bestowing blessing as He chastens, corrects, and redirects. As the writer of Hebrews affirms, this parental discipline is an affirmation of God's love for us (Heb. 12:6).

The Lord may bestow to us what we request to teach us a valuable lesson as He did with the nation of Israel after they demanded a king. It was not what He wanted for His people, but His people needed to learn this fact through experiencing the consequences of lusting for what was outside the will of God. May we choose to stay in the center of God's will and receive His best for us, so that we can return what is our best back to Him!

May 2 – Joshua's Portion
Joshua 19

Only after Joshua had finished dividing the entire region among the tribes did he request and receive his inheritance. His spirit of humility contrasts with the "me-first" mentality that many church leaders regrettably exhibit today. Caleb (Josh. 14) and now Joshua were specifically rewarded for their past faithfulness at Kadesh-barnea. Joshua did not ask his brethren for a prime piece of real estate, nor did they offer one to him; rather, he requested Timnath-serah for his possession. Timnath-serah was a city situated in the rugged and barren hill country of northern Ephraim about eleven miles southwest of Shiloh. This proposal was readily agreed to by the entire nation.

What determines our portion of blessing (given possession) from the Lord? The pattern first shown to us in Joshua 14 when Caleb received his inheritance is again duplicated with the giving of Joshua's portion. Our possession is obtained by *conquest*, in accordance with *providence*, is bestowed in grace as *requested*, and is in proportion to how we will use what God has given us to bless others. Joshua labored with his countrymen to drive out the inhabitants from his possession. His portion, the city of Timnath-serah, was by providence: *"according to the word of the Lord"* and he received the very inheritance that he had asked for (v. 50). Lastly, Joshua received his possession in accordance to his *capacity* to retain it and use it to bless others.

Like Joshua's forefather Abraham when he parted from Lot, he was pleased to inherit the lesser position and the greater work associated with it, in order to gain an even better inheritance in God's kingdom (Gen. 13:9-18). Hence, Joshua endeavored to build up the city and live among his tribal brethren until the end of his days. Joshua had no thoughts of retiring, though he certainly deserved a break after years of faithful and arduous service.

Instead of relaxing, he chose to improve the quality of life for others in his autumn years. Whether as general or administrator, his tenacious yet unpretentious character in serving others and the Lord is to be admired. His years of moral and spiritual grooming increased his capacity to receive and retain a greater portion from the Lord. He blessed others with his received possession while at the same time preserving God's rest. May the Lord do the same for us!

May 3 – The Altar of Misunderstanding
Joshua 22

Having faithfully fulfilled their commitment to secure Canaan for their brethren, Joshua released the two and a half tribes to return to their homes on the eastern side of the Jordan. He also exhorted them to obey the Law if they wanted to keep their inheritance. As they traveled eastward from Shiloh and approached the fords of the Jordan a sudden anxiety of future isolation and abandonment overcame them. They thought in years to come the Jordan might become a barrier to national fellowship. Their solution was to construct a lasting memorial that would stand as a testimony of their commitment to follow the Lord and obey His Law. It was *"a great, impressive altar"* erected on the edge of Canaan's frontier. But it was not intended for sacrifices.

Unfortunately, as the altar was not directed by God, the nine and a half tribes west of the Jordan immediately misunderstood its purpose and assumed the worst – their brethren had become apostates. These tribes assembled at Shiloh with every intention of correcting the matter, even if it meant civil war. Thankfully, cooler heads prevailed and a delegation that included Phinehas and ten men of renown from each tribe west of the Jordan were sent to investigate and through dialogue know the truth of the matter without bloodshed.

Indeed, building the altar was a mistake. The Transjordanian tribes soon learned that promoting spiritual unity among God's people through a humanized means results in division. The unscriptural altar gave every appearance of denying unity, not fostering it.

Regrettably, many Christians today are erecting similar altars in the attempt to procure visible uniformity. It is a flawed notion to think that common creeds, declarations, and traditions will somehow bind believers together more strongly than the Body of Christ which God created. In the end, these have the opposite effect and draw away Christians from the true gravitation point in the Church – Christ. The unity of the Church is preserved by the power of the Holy Spirit as Christians pursue a better understanding of Scripture; it is not upheld by fabricated "altars of witness" (Eph. 4:3, 13-15). If division is necessary, let it be for upholding the truth in love and not the result of stumbling over some contrived religious mandate, such as the Altar of Witness.

May 4 – Choose You This Day
Joshua 24

Joshua commenced his final address to the nation by reminding them that Abraham and his family were previously pagans in Mesopotamia. Joshua continued on from Abraham through the course of Israel's history to show all God's dealings with Israel were forged in His grace. There is no mention of human strength or wisdom in the process of placing the nation in the Promised Land.

After noting their origin in faithful Abraham, and that they had been recipients of God's abundant grace, Joshua charged the people to follow Abraham's example and obey the Lord. Joshua's initial remarks concerning Abraham would undergird his entire message.

First, Abraham maintained the proper disposition concerning the land promised to, but not yet possessed by, him. He continued to trust God with the timetable while he waited for God's promise to be realized. During this interim he was determined to be a stranger and a pilgrim in the land. Likewise, if the Israelites wanted Jehovah's blessing, they would need to follow Abraham's example of faith and sanctification.

Second, Abraham's example was emphasized in this message. The location in which the God of Glory confirmed His covenant with Abraham was the very place the Israelites now stood – Shechem (Gen. 12:6). Historically speaking, Shechem, at the crossroads of central Palestine, has been a place of decision. Now, at the very location where Abraham had been rewarded for his faithfulness in leaving idolatry, Joshua charged the nation of Israel to do the same: "Choose for yourselves this day whom you will serve!" Then and now, God does not tolerate misplaced affections; He must have first place always.

The people thundered back that they were not serving other gods. Sensing their insincerity, Joshua rebuked them two more times to put away their gods and to incline their heart to the Lord. To this the people replied, *"The Lord our God we will serve, and His voice we will obey!"* The Jews had consented to the same at Sinai and had failed; now at Shechem they affirmed their fidelity, and again they would fail. Whether people seek to justify or to sanctify themselves through self-effort, the result is the same – failure. We may have good intentions, but it is only when we draw near to God that we get to experience Him.

May 5 – Idolatry Ensures Slavery
Judges 2

God allowed a contingency of Canaanites to remain in the land after the main conquest under Joshua's leadership was complete in order to "test" the resolve of His people. Would they obey His decree to rid the land of the remaining pagans? God would keep His promise to Abraham to build up a nation in His name. Yet, God is able to accomplish His word and still test each generation in the corridors of time leading to culmination of His covenant. Each generation will either have His blessing or judgment depending upon their obedience.

Unfortunately, after Joshua died, the Levites apparently quit instructing the people and parents became apathetic in teaching God's Law to their children. As a result, the Jews comfortably dwelt alongside the Canaanites, Hittites, Amorites, Perizzites, and Hivites. In time, their complacency led to compromise and they disobeyed God's command forbidding intermarriage with the heathen of the land.

The Jews' comfort, complacency, and compromise then resulted in carnality – and the next generation forsook the Lord and embraced the false gods of the land. John would later remind the Church of this hazard: impurity and immorality are strongly connected with idolatry; therefore, *"keep yourselves from idols"* (1 Jn. 5:19, 21). What controls the affection of one's heart will determine his or her conduct.

The opening pages of Judges present a principle which is paramount in Scripture: Separation from evil is essential, and nothing can be maintained for God except on that basis. God's people dwelt among the Canaanites instead of driving them out of their inheritance and in time developed social connections with them. The longer such relations with the world remain, the less God's people think about their separation inwardly, and eventually they do outwardly what God hates.

The aftermath of Joshua's death illustrates the fallacy of depending upon any spiritual influence outside the family to maintain your family's spiritual welfare. How did God respond to His people's departure from Him to embrace other gods? God seized the role of the parent in order to teach the new generation about Himself through the disciplinary rod of military invasion and conquest. He loves His people too much to leave them void of truth and the benefit of His presence.

May 6 – A Feeble Weapon?
Judges 3

The third judge of Israel, Shamgar, and his doing are conveyed to us in one verse: *"After him was Shamgar the son of Anath, who killed six hundred men of the Philistines with an ox goad; and he also delivered Israel"* (v. 31). Some commentators refer to Shamgar as a "minor judge," and others do not consider him a judge at all. However, C. T. Lacey reminds us to be careful in undermining the value of another's ministry in the kingdom of God:

> It is as well that the assessment of a believer's service does not rest in the distorted and ill-formed opinions of men, but in the righteous estimate of the Lord! Whatever unjustified conclusions men might have reached in relation to Shamgar, the record of Scripture remains, *"he also delivered Israel"* (v. 31). His achievements for the Lord have an abiding message of encouragement for all servants of the Lord.[3]

How long the Lord used Shamgar to oversee His people after conquering the Philistines in the far west is not known, nor do we know what region he resided over as judge. What is revealed is that one man empowered by the Spirit of God used an ox goad (a sharp metal-tipped stick about 8 or 10 feet long), an instrument used to herd animals, to defeat six hundred Philistine soldiers. Whether he used this crude weapon to fight all six hundred Philistines at once or during the period of his judgeship is unknown. Let us remember that the Lord often uses what is deemed feeble to confound the might and intelligence of men (1 Cor. 1:26-30). God was teaching His people not to rely on their physical strength to conquer their enemies, but rather His.

It makes no sense to use an ox goad to fight men armed with shields, spears, and swords, yet that was what God used to accomplish the spectacular. This would serve to keep His people humble and to incite fear in their enemies. The Israelites would repeatedly learn in the era of the judges that the land was a gift from God that had been received by faith and must be maintained in faith; it could not be conquered through human effort.

As believers in the Church Age, we too must realize that all our engagements with the enemy are the Lord's battles. We have no strength against the devil, other than in the Lord.

May 7 – A Wise Woman
Judges 4

Israel again did evil in the sight of the Lord after Ehud died. God responded by permitting the Canaanite nations to unify and come to power under the leadership of Jabin. The Canaanites oppressed God's people for twenty years. Because they possessed sophisticated weapons of warfare, i.e., iron chariots, the Israelites saw no possibility of overcoming their oppressors except through supernatural deliverance – thus they cried out to the Lord.

Apparently, there was no man in all of Israel with the faith to step forward and be used of God to remedy the situation. Yet, there was a woman of faith, Deborah, who was grieved over the humiliating condition of God's people. Deborah was not the choice vessel for the task at hand, but she was available and willing and God therefore used her in such a way to deliver His people and also rebuke the men of Israel for their shallow confidence in Him.

The Lord did not often use a woman to express His mind to His people, but sporadically did so in times of spiritual declension, often to awaken men of their lack of spiritual fortitude. Scripture records, *"Deborah, a prophetess, the wife of Lapidoth judged Israel at that time"* (v. 4). Deborah was not a presumptuous woman, but she also understood God's ways when His people were in a desperate way. Deborah's entire ministry was centered at home, both in caring for her family and in helping her people, who came to her for counsel. One day Deborah summoned Barak, to come to her; she had a message from the Lord for him. Deborah informed Barak that he was to deploy 10,000 troops from Zebulun and Naphtali at Mount Tabor and that God would deliver Jabin's army into his hands at the River Kishon.

Barak cringed at this decree, so he requested Deborah's presence with him or he would not go. To request her presence as a condition for obeying God's command revealed that his full reliance was not in the Lord, plus his request would pull Deborah from her place of ministry. Deborah agreed to go with Barak, but she also confirmed that because his confidence was not in the Lord alone, he would not receive the full honor in the victory. Barak's faith was in its infancy, and required someone to come alongside him to urge him on in his calling. Perhaps you know someone like Deborah that encouraged you in the same way.

Daily Devotions

May 8 – A Brave Woman
Judges 4

Sisera had forded the Kishon River in Jezreel Valley and then moved southeasterly to gather his Canaanite forces near Megiddo. After learning that Barak had gathered his troops at Tabor, Sisera moved his army, including 900 iron chariots northwesterly towards Tabor. The Canaanite army again forded the Kishon River and assembled in the Plain of Esdraelon; they knew better than to engage the Jewish army positioned on Tabor. Deborah confirmed God's will to Barak: *"Up! For this is the day in which the Lord has delivered Sisera into your hand. Has not the Lord gone out before you?"* (v. 14). Barak obeys the word of the Lord and leads a surprise attack against the Canaanites. This bold assault made no sense; indeed the Canaanites were not expecting the Jews to attack them. So, Barak and his ten thousand ill-equipped infantry bravely departed the safe haven of their rocky fortress and charged down Tabor to assault a much larger and better equipped Canaanite army. On flat ground, the iron chariots were the most lethal weapon of war at that time. But the Jews had an advantage that the Canaanites were unaware of – Jehovah God!

Deborah told Barak that the Lord was fighting in advance of the Jewish army. How did Jehovah go out before them? The Kishon River was known for its swift current and also to be enclosed by a wide marshy area which was dangerous to cross. A sudden and unseasonable downpour caught the Canaanite army by surprise (5:21). Perhaps their chariots became stuck in the bogs and then the soldiers were swept away and drowned by a flashflood when they attempted to escape westward while re-crossing the river. Barak and his 10,000 men pursued the fleeing Canaanites and they were soon joined by men from Ephraim and Manasseh (5:14). The Canaanites were routed, but it was Jael, the wife of Heber the Kenite, who would fulfill Deborah's prophecy and vanquish Sisera. Jael provided the fleeing captain refreshments and made him rest in her tent. Then, when he was asleep, she drove a stake through his temples into the ground.

Because Barak balked at God's command, the Lord bestowed honor to a brave woman who did not hesitate to be used when afforded the opportunity to be used. God uses and honors those with willing and obedient hearts, but those who hesitate to serve Him, lose His honor!

May 9 – A Call to Serve
Judges 6

The story of Gideon is more fascinating than any of the previous judges, in the respect that we are permitted to observe his personal experiences relating to his calling. Of particular interest is how his thinking was conformed to Jehovah's will. His growth in leadership is remarkable, first leading his father's house against idolatry, then an entire city, and finally much of the Jewish nation.

Gideon, the son of Joash, was secretly threshing wheat for his people at a winepress in Ophrah to avoid being discovered by the Midianites. This was an unusual scene; wheat was normally threshed in an open area on the top of a hill, not in the lower confines of a vineyard. Although being inconspicuous, this was still a bold move by just the kind of man that Jehovah was looking for.

The Angel of the Lord interrupts Gideon's threshing by his sudden appearance and declaration: *"The Lord is with you, you mighty man of valor!"* (v. 12). Gideon does not seem to be surprised by the abrupt incursion into his secluded workplace or by the profound accolade; rather, he responds with immediate intercession on behalf of God's people. The Lord is delighted when those in fellowship with Him stand in the gap and intercede for those who are not or for those in dire need. The Lord responds to Gideon's prayer by commissioning him as the next judge of Israel; Israel was to be delivered from the Midianites.

Gideon was surprised by this statement and attempted to negate his calling by telling his honorable visitor something that he apparently did not know: he was of the smallest tribe, Manasseh, and the least in his father's house. In the presence of this heavenly representative, Gideon was conscious of his own littleness in a way that he never had been before. He felt insignificant; he had no social clout and no inherent power or authority to accomplish such a feat. Yet, Scripture repeatedly demonstrates to us that this is exactly the type of person that the Lord uses to manifest His awesome power (1 Cor. 1:26-30).

Contrite Gideon was concerned for his countrymen. If he obeyed the Lord and moved forward in humble faith, he would be able to save the Jews from their oppressors, for God promised to be with him. Although Gideon was hesitant at first, he did step forward in faith against incredible opposition; may we have the audacity to do the same.

May 10 – Those Called Must Worship
Judges 6

Was this impromptu meeting a dream or had Jehovah really called him to deliver Israel from the Midianites? Gideon seems unsure, and therefore asks for a sign to validate the discussion. Gideon does not yet seem to realize that he is speaking with the Lord, not merely a prophet. He addresses the messenger as *Adown*, meaning "Master." It is not until the sign is witnessed that Gideon realizes that his visitor is a heavenly messenger – *"the Angel of the Lord."*

Gideon sought to refresh his visitor and gains permission to prepare a meal for his guest, who has agreed to wait for it under an oak tree. Gideon quickly prepares a kid and unleavened bread. Clearly, such a sacrifice during abject poverty and need was very costly. Gideon placed the cooked meat, freshly baked bread, with a pot of broth in a basket and brought it to God's messenger, who tells him to place the meat and bread on a rock, and to pour out the broth.

God accepts those offerings and sacrifices which rightly portray various aspects of His Son's character and sacrifice. The Angel of the Lord then touched the meat and the unleavened bread with the end of his staff and fire promptly came out from the rock and consumed all. The life of an innocent victim, the unleavened quality of a sinless life, and the foundation rock of truth are all accurate presentations of Christ in Scripture. Hence, Gideon's sacrifice was accepted, despite his ignorance concerning the broth. Having completed His message, the divine messenger then vanished from sight.

At that moment, Gideon realized that his visitor was "the Angel [Messenger] of the Lord" and is arrested with fear; he surmises that such an intimate encounter with God must result in his imminent death. But the Lord consoles His chosen deliverer, *"Peace be with you; do not fear, you shall not die"* (v. 23). Despite all the spiritual chaos and human sorrow, the One who perfectly controls all things could extend peace to the one that was fearful and doubtful of the future.

Gideon's reaction to the Lord's presence and words of assurance should be our response also – he worshiped. Genuine faith is fostered in awe, appreciation, and trust; without such qualities our service for the Lord will fail miserably and nothing will be gained for eternity.

May 11 – Too Many for God
Judges 7

Thirty-two thousand Jewish volunteers gather to Gideon at the spring of Harod east of Mount Gilboa. The Midianite force of 132,000 was in the Jezreel Valley at the Hill of Moreh situated about five miles directly north of their position. The Lord informed Gideon that too many had assembled for Him to vanquish the Midianites; otherwise Israel would be lifted up in pride. The solution was to tell all who were afraid to return to their homes, and 22,000 men did just that.

But Gideon's army must be further downsized to ensure that everyone knew it was the Lord giving Israel the victory. The solution was to have the remaining 10,000 men venture down to the spring and be observed while they drank its water. This is a good reminder that the Lord often tests His people in the ordinary activities of life to determine their availability for service. The 300 men drinking from their hands became Gideon's new army (they were now outnumbered 450 to 1).

From the northern slope of Gilboa, Gideon saw an innumerable host of Midianites, Amalekites, and Arabs before him. The Lord told Gideon that if he was afraid to sneak down to the enemy's camp and he would be strengthened. Gideon and Purah do so and were encouraged after overhearing one soldier interpreting another's dream which foretold of Gideon's victory over them. Gideon then worshiped God.

He then told his men that Jehovah was going to deliver the Midianites into their hands. He divided his troops into three separate groups of 100 men. Each man was to carry a trumpet and a torch; the torches were to be hidden in earthen jars which were to be broken on command so that all the burning lamps would shine out at once. Around midnight, the alarm was sounded and suddenly 300 trumpets were blown and 300 torches lit up the countryside surrounding the enemy's camp. The Jews stood still, but yelled out their assigned battle cry: *"A sword for the Lord and for Gideon!"*

Divinely stimulated chaos swept through the enemy's camp, and as each band of soldiers ascended Moreh to discern what was happening they met others doing the same and in the confusion and darkness slaughtered each other. When the Lord's servants have nothing to lose and everything to gain for the excellence of Christ, then similar wonderful feats can be accomplished for Him today.

Daily Devotions

May 12 – Driven By Lust
Judges 14

The Philistines occupied the coastal plain directly west of the Judean foothills. During the era of the Judges, the Philistines repeatedly attempted to expand their dominion by invading Jewish territory. The narrative of Judges 14 and 15 centers in the unfortunate marriage between Samson and a Philistine woman. This marriage represents the unacceptable and unnatural relationship between God's covenant people and the Philistines at this time. Samson first saw the unnamed woman in Timnah and then promptly requested that his parents mediate a betrothal agreement on his behalf. This matter grieved Manoah and his wife and they attempted to sway Samson to choose a Jewish maiden for a wife, rather than a woman who worshipped false gods. The Mosaic Law prohibited Jewish men from marrying foreign women, because the union would introduce heathen influences among God's people (Ex. 34:16). The children of these mixed marriages, usually did not learn the Hebrew language and became little pagans (Neh. 13:24).

Likewise, in the Church Age, believers are forbidden to marry nonbelievers, as such a relationship would also negatively influence the child of God (1 Cor. 7:39; 2 Cor. 6:14). What true spiritual harmony can a child of God and a child of the devil enjoy in such a union?

Samson's determination was neither rational, nor spiritual, but rather the result of sensual lusting; *"I have seen a woman in Timnah."* There is nothing in the text to suggest that Samson even talked to this foreign damsel or her family; rather he observed her and wanted her – *"Get her for me."* Samson was requesting that his parents conduct the necessary negotiation, and pay the requested dowry to the parents of the bride.

Morally speaking, Samson was not separate from sinners or the influences of the world – he was not a true Nazirite. Samson, as a Nazirite, should reflect the type of testimony that the Church is to also have in the world as a consecrated people empowered by the Holy Spirit and in communion with God. By divine power Samson did much to honor the Lord and assist His people, despite the moral weakness. The prominent feature of Samson's judgeship was his incredible strength, not his integrity. In time, his failed morality resulted in his loss of power. May we learn from his failure, lest we suffer the same.

May 13 – Self-righteous Presumption
Judges 20

Four hundred thousand battle-ready men from the land of Israel, including the Transjordan region, journeyed to Mizpah to learn the meaning of the gruesome message they had received. The phrase *"before the Lord"* implies that the tabernacle was likely located nearby, perhaps at Bethel. Representatives from the eleven tribes listened as the Levite man recounted the wicked deeds that the vile men of Benjamin in Gibeah had done, as recorded in Judges 19. To ensure the entire nation was aware of this lewd behavior, he had cut his concubine into pieces and distributed her remains throughout Israel.

The events of this chapter indicate that we are more likely to be provoked by what offends moral decency than by something that deprives God of His proper reverence and service. While the natural conscience can reckon the former as unethical, without genuine love for the Lord we will not feel the true weight of the latter offense. Such was the appalling spiritual state of Israel at this time; not the nation's idolatry, but the lewd behavior of Benjamin caused "outrage in Israel."

To hopefully avoid a civil war, ten men from the eleven tribes were sent to Benjamin to ask that the guilty parties be turned over to them. Rather than purging the evil, the tribe of Benjamin mustered up 26,000 sword-wielding men and 700 stone-slingers to assist the 700 fighters at Gibeah. Not only was the army at Gibeah outnumbered fifteen to one, when the fighting began they left the safety of their fortifications to confront the larger army of Israel in open combat.

Israel did consult the Lord, but they asked Him the wrong question. Being already determined to go to war, they asked which tribe should lead the attack; God's answer was Judah. They should have inquired of the Lord how to best handle the situation. In the initial confrontation, Israel suffered 22,000 causalities.

The next day, the army of the eleven tribes put themselves in battle array again, which presupposed that God wanted them to engage in warfare. Some leaders, weeping before the Lord (probably at Bethel), asked if they should fight Benjamin. This question showed that Israel was deepening its dependence on the Lord, but as of yet, they were still not examining the integrity of their own hearts; they were rather all about judging others for their waywardness.

Daily Devotions

May 14 – Self-judgment Before Judging Others
Judges 20

The answer to Israel's question to the Lord, should they attack Benjamin again, was affirmative, but there was no promise of victory and sadly, another 18,000 soldiers died in the second engagement. The nation had neglected proper worship of God as decreed by the Mosaic Law. It took the deaths of 40,000 men to realize that though they were attempting to cleanse the land of blood, they had lost sight of a more important matter – their love, respect, and awe for Jehovah. The nation rightly hated the immorality in Benjamin, but had wrongly approached Jehovah in the matter and therefore did not have His endorsement in judging the sin, though indeed it needed to be dealt with.

Believers cannot properly deal with a sinning brother or sister unless they are first humbly before the Lord in innocence, have pure motives, and are dedicated to obeying His Word. Only through this type of attitude can the work of rebuke and restoration be effectively accomplished: *"Brethren, if a man is overtaken in any trespass, you who are spiritual restore such a one in a spirit of gentleness, considering yourself lest you also be tempted"* (Gal. 6:1). Paul reminds us that we are all of like passions, and if it were not for the grace of God, each of us would be capable of doing the most vile works of unrighteousness. Realizing that should keep us broken before the Lord.

After the second defeat, the *entire* nation traveled to the house of the Lord. While fasting with a spirit of brokenness, the people remained before the Lord all day. Priests offered proper sacrifices to the Lord. The Lord then affirmed the right action and the result – go to battle and victory will be achieved and it was; Benjamin's army was wiped out.

With the main Benjamite army destroyed, the remaining cities of their tribal region were easily captured and destroyed by fire. Jehovah had not endorsed this latter slaughter, but the eleven tribes discerned that Benjamin's refusal to turn over a few guilty culprits of a hideous crime showed that the entire tribe was morally depraved. Regrettably, the entire tribe of Benjamin was wiped out, except for the 600 men securely garrisoned in the rock cliffs of Rimmon. These survivors lived in the safety at Rimmon for four months, until they received terms of peace by the nation (21:13-14). These men would later receive wives to preserve the tribe that was nearly no more through self-righteous folly.

May We Serve Christ!

May 15 – Christ – Our Kinsman-redeemer
Ruth 1-4

Spiritual corruption and idolatry became rampant among the Jews during the era of the Judges. This angered the Lord, who repeatedly punished His people by military invasion. After an era of oppression, the Jews would repent and cry out to the Lord for deliverance. On these occasions the Lord raised up judges to remove the oppressors from the land and to guide the nation in righteous conduct. Amidst this long and gloomy backdrop of failure and chastening, a bright ray of redemptive hope is conveyed in the lovely story of Ruth, a young Moabite widow who is sacrificially devoted to her mother-in-law, Naomi, also a widow.

From a typological sense the story of Ruth pictures the fulfillment of all God promises in connection with Israel, on the ground of sovereign grace, after the nation (portrayed in Naomi) had lost all claims to God's blessing because of moral and spiritual failure (as witnessed in Judges). Judges displays the ever increasing depravity of Israel, despite divine chastening and intervention, which ultimately leaves God's people in a thick hue of spiritual deadness. Thankfully, the activities of God's grace are not overcome by human failure; this leaves us with a wonderful scene of joy as the book concludes.

Naomi, representing the chastened nation of Israel, is a backsliding believer, who returns to the Lord after experiencing the consequences of departing from God's will. She departed Judah "full," but willingly "returns" (a key word in Ruth) "empty," after God stripped everything away by disciplinary action. Having been emptied of all self-ambition and self-fortitude, she again experiences God's blessing in her life.

Through her connection with Naomi, Ruth steps forward in faith to reject the deep-seated pagan heritage of her own people to become a Jehovah worshipper. After approaching a potential kinsman-redeemer, Boaz, and requesting to be redeemed, she receives his pledge to do so. Later, she will experience the redeeming love of Boaz through marriage and be not only brought into the commonwealth of Israel, but also the genealogy of Christ.

In Boaz, Ruth's kinsman-redeemer, we see the Lord Jesus typified as the future Savior, who is both willing and able to redeem all who desire to be saved by Him. Grace originated in the heart of God and centers in the Lord Jesus. He is our Kinsman-redeemer too!

Daily Devotions

May 16 – Willing to Sacrifice What Was Most Desired
1 Samuel 1

First Samuel records the name of Israel's fifteenth and final judge, Samuel. Samuel's father was Elkanah, a Levite by birth, who resided in the town of Ramah. Elkanah had two wives, Hannah, who was barren, and Peninnah, who had at least four children. Because the Jews considered children as evidence of God's favor (Ps. 127:3), barren women were often scorned in addition to being childless. Elkanah likely took Peninnah as a second wife because Hannah was barren.

At this time, the tabernacle was at Shiloh, about fifteen miles north of Ramah. The high priest at Shiloh was Eli; he judged Israel for about forty years (4:18). Elkanah was a religious man who annually visited Shiloh to offer a sacrifice. At Shiloh, Elkanah's family enjoyed a fellowship feast. Even though Elkanah gave Hannah a double portion of the meat, but being *in bitterness of soul* she would not be comforted, nor did she eat or drink wine at the feast. Her rival, Peninnah, had made her life miserable by continually ridiculing her barren condition.

After the family finished feasting, Hannah quietly departed and made her way to the entrance of the tabernacle. With eyes swollen with tears, she prayed inaudibly to the Lord of Hosts to remove her affliction and then vowed that if He did that she would dedicate her firstborn son to Him as a Nazirite. Eli, who had been secretly observing her, rebuked her for being drunk. Eli, who was far from the Lord, mistook the activity of the Spirit of God for the activity of the flesh, when in fact she was in anguish of soul! Poor Hannah, not only had she suffered years of barrenness and jeering from her rival, but now she was misjudged by the chief spiritual leader of her people. Hannah countered Eli's charge by saying she was of sorrowful spirit and petitioning the Lord. Eli told her that the Lord would grant her request.

Clearly, Hannah understood better than Eli that the spiritual need of the nation for godly leadership could be met only in one who was a Nazirite – a leader fully devoted to the Lord. She was willing to be the vessel used of the Lord to provide such "a male child." It took years to come to this decision – to give up what she most wanted for what was most needed by God to bless others. The Lord granted her request and she dedicated her son, Samuel, to the Lord as vowed. Samuel became Israel's final judge; he led the people with wise integrity his entire life.

May 17 – Complacency to Be Judged
1 Samuel 2

After hearing of the evil deeds of his sons (even their immorality with women at the entrance of the tabernacle), the elderly Eli warned Hophni and Phinehas to cease from their corruption. He told them that they were causing God's people to sin and that there was no one who could make intercession for priests who engaged in such conduct. But Eli's sons ignored their father's toothless warning.

Though objecting to their wickedness, Hophni and Phinehas knew their father would not act against them, hence, Eli condoned their sin. God, however, was determined to execute Eli's sons for their crimes against Him, since Eli would not judge them. Eli, as high priest, was accountable to the Lord and should have at least put his sons out of the priesthood, but he did not, so God would judge him also.

The Lord sent an unnamed prophet to Eli to foretell God's judgment of Eli's household. The prophet reminded Eli the great privilege that God had extended to Aaron's descendants who were to be priests before Him. God rewarded their service by providing food for them from the Altar, His table. Yet, Eli had permitted his sons to violate God's law for the offerings and to demean their importance. Eli had made God's sacrifices a thing of contempt; he had not punished his sons, and he had gorged himself and become fat on the best that Israel had brought to His altar.

The prophet told Eli, that his behavior was an abomination to God; therefore, God was going to cut off Eli's arm, meaning he would have no male descendants to continue his name. Not only would Eli's sons die, but if they had sons, they also would perish.

The prophet then told Eli that both his sons would die on the same day. The Lord promised to render to Eli's household what was deserved for the dishonor caused to His name. Spiritual complacency eventually leads to carnality and judgment: *"Do not be deceived, God is not mocked; for whatever a man sows, that he will also reap"* (Gal. 6:7). Although the Lord promised to bring Eli's house to an end, He would not terminate the priesthood totally. Instead the Lord would raise up to Himself a faithful priest. This prophecy was fulfilled when Solomon took the priesthood from Abiathar, and assigned it to faithful Zadok, a descendant of Eleazar through Phinehas (1 Kgs. 2:27-35).

Daily Devotions

May 18 – The Call of Samuel
1 Samuel 3

The Jewish historian Josephus suggests that Samuel was twelve years of age when this incident occurred. Although there is no scriptural evidence that Samuel was twelve, his activities in this chapter suggest that he is not a small boy, but an able lad. The fact that Samuel was responsible for opening the doors of the tabernacle each morning, that God determined he was mature enough to be His prophet, and that Eli put him under an oath seem to validate this conclusion. *"Samuel ministered to the Lord before Eli"* (v. 1). He was not merely Eli's boy-servant, but was in training for his life's ministry among God's people.

The narrative begins as a nearly-blind Eli and young Samuel were sleeping in the wee hours before dawn. Apparently, at this time, it was acceptable not to trim lamps on the lampstand in the tabernacle. The Lord calls to Samuel, but Samuel mistakenly believes that his elderly mentor has summoned him. Samuel hurries to where Eli was sleeping and replies, *"Here I am, for you called me."* A startled Eli replied, *"I did not call; lie down again,"* which Samuel did (v. 5).

The Lord called Samuel two more times and again the lad, thinking that Eli had beckoned him, aroused the slumbering priest. On the third occasion, Eli perceived that the Lord may be calling the boy, so he instructed Samuel: *"Go, lie down; and it shall be, if He calls you, that you must say, 'Speak, Lord, for Your servant hears'"* (vv. 7-8).

Samuel returned to his bed and waited. Then, *"the Lord came and stood"* by Samuel before calling his name, *"Samuel! Samuel!"* In the dark, Samuel was probably able to see the form of a person, but regardless, he answered, *"Speak, for Your servant hears"* – he knew it was the Lord. Samuel had been a faithful servant at the tabernacle since his early childhood, but *"Samuel did not yet know the Lord, nor was the word of the Lord yet revealed to him."*

Like Samuel, we cannot have an effective ministry, until we first personally know the Lord, and then know and yield to God's revealed Word. Until we learn to rest in the Lord and His Word, we too are just running back and forth aimlessly in ministry. A true servant of God knows and loves the Lord, and is determined to abide in His Word (John 8:31). This is why young Samuel is not long without a message from the Lord.

May 19 – Time for Revival
1 Samuel 7

After the Ark of the Covenant had been in Kirjath-Jearim for 20 years, Samuel senses the time for revival has come. He flatly rebukes his countrymen's idolatry, and then challenges them to prove their loyalty to Jehovah by ridding themselves of their images. He poses two paramount truths: First, the lost cannot be delivered without first becoming aware that their sin grieves the Lord.

Second, the Lord will not tolerate a divided heart in those who worship Him; they must *"serve the Lord only."* The Lord warned His disciples that having more than one master would keep them from living for Him (Matt. 6:24). Divided allegiance is not possible, for a slave can be devoted to only one master. The Lord states that there can be no middle ground; He is either the believer's first love or He is not the believer's Master at all.

The people responded by putting away their idols. After observing this step of consecration, Samuel summoned the nation to Mizpah so that he might pray for them there. Much of the nation came to Mizpah to fast and to weep before the Lord to confess their sins. They also drew water and poured it out on the ground symbolizing their utter unworthiness before the Lord. Water on the ground is completely lost.

This gesture confirmed that a real work of God was taking place in His people. Their confession of sin together with this symbol indicated that they no longer had confidence in a lifeless form (i.e., the Ark; 1 Sam. 4), but rather in His means of restoring them (the atoning blood of a lamb), which Samuel offers on their behalf. It is when God's people humble themselves in His presence and rely solely on the blood of His Lamb, the Lord Jesus Christ, that *"He who is able to do exceedingly abundantly above all that we ask or think"* (Eph. 3:20) – does so!

The Philistines were alarmed by this mass assembly and assumed that Israel was preparing for battle, so they gathered their own forces to preempt Israel's supposed attack. God accepted Samuel's burnt offering and heard his prayers for Israel. In response, the Lord "thundered" on the Philistines to confuse them and Israel then pursued and smote their stunned attackers all the way to Beth Car. The Jews were not prepared for battle, but the Lord was ready to fight for His revived people. When the Lord fights for you – victory is assured!

Daily Devotions

May 20 – Appointing Unfit Judges
1 Samuel 8

Samuel had two sons, likely in their mid-twenties, whom he could have appointed as judges in Beersheba over Israel. But sadly, Samuel's sons, Joel and Abijah, did not possess the integrity of their father in upholding their duties; rather, they sought *"dishonest gain, took bribes, and perverted justice"* (v. 3). Apparently, Samuel's many years of itinerant ministry came at a personal cost to his family. His family situation is a warning to all God's servants not to neglect their primary responsibility to honor the Lord in their homes. Spouses should not be neglected and children should be nurtured in the admonition of the Lord, lest God's Word be blasphemed by onlookers (Tit. 2:5).

Samuel's only mistake recorded in Scripture was stepping ahead of the Lord in appointing his sons as judges over Israel. Their duplicitous behavior prompted the elders to visit Samuel at his home in Ramah. Their message was painfully blunt: *"Look, you are old, and your sons do not walk in your ways. Now make us a king to judge us like all the nations"* (v. 5). Although the years had not yet diminished Samuel's ability to judge Israel, the elders knew that he was almost fifty years of age, the appointed time for priests to retire from the rigors of their office (Num. 8:25). Scripture does not record any sign of senility or decay in Samuel's faculties even to the very end of his full and eventful life. For example, in about twenty-five years from now he will rebuke Saul for his folly and will hew Agag into pieces with a sword.

If Samuel had not appointed his sons as judges, the elders would probably not have confronted him at this time. Because he had relinquished some of his judicial responsibility to unfit men, these leaders assumed that Samuel would be retiring soon. Certainly, no one wants to suffer injustice at the hands of perverse judges, but the elders' excuse really revealed a deeper problem – their dissatisfaction with God's administration over them.

Realistically, it is doubtful Samuel's sons would be more prone to take bribes than ordinary Gentile judges would be, meaning that the complaint enabled the deeper issue to surface – a desire to be like the Gentile nations. The motivation of the request was not to pursue greater holiness with God, but for greater freedom to pursue personal gratification and political vanity.

May 21 – Israel Demands a King
1 Samuel 8

The fact that the elders had rejected Samuel's sons, and even called him "old," did not upset Samuel, but he was greatly displeased that they wanted a king to judge them. Their request was a flat rejection of God's form of government, which Samuel knew must result in stern discipline. It seems evident that Samuel also felt slighted by the request because the Lord consoled him over the offense.

Samuel then sought guidance from the Lord, who promptly answered his request. The Lord told Samuel not to take the offense personally; Israel was rejecting Him, not His prophet, as their ruler. The Lord consoled Samuel by telling him that He too had felt dejected by Israel's previous idolatry. Now Israel was rejecting Him as their King. Could He not oversee Israel better than any human ruler?

The Lord also desired that His people remain unique among the nations and consecrated to His holy purposes. Obviously, none of this caught the Lord by surprise. Moses had foretold centuries earlier that Israel would eventually want a king, instead of the Lord, to rule over them. Moses also warned his countrymen of the dangers of anointing a king. In God's plan of redemption, He always intended to anoint a righteous king to rule over Israel – David – who typified a descendant of his who would be the King of kings and would rule over the earth in righteousness. Recall that God had previously promised Abraham and Sarah that some of their descendants would be kings (Gen. 17:16).

The Lord told Samuel to forewarn the people of the cost of choosing a human king to rule them. Samuel told the people that a king would demand many of their sons, daughters, and servants to create an army, to make weapons, to till and to reap his fields, and to cook and to bake for him. Samuel sarcastically warned the people not to complain if they were oppressed by a tyrannical monarch in the future; God would not heed their prayers.

Despite the stern warning, the people would not relent; they wanted to have a visible ruler, like the nations. So, God, in his judicial anger (Hos. 13:11), gave Saul to be Israel's king in order to teach them the repercussions of rejecting Him. Praise God for His providential care of His people, but woe to those who needlessly choose to stir up His indignation to be taught a lesson.

May 22 – The Power of a Good Testimony
1 Samuel 12

While Israel was gathered at Gilgal, Samuel seizes the opportunity to address those he has faithfully served. He began by asserting that he had appointed them a king as requested. This meant that Samuel would no longer bear the weight of leading the nation. Regrettably, the unfolding chapters prove that whenever a natural man (like Saul) leads, there will always need to be a diligent prophet alongside. When God's shepherds are complacent and carnal, they must be rebuked by the One who placed them in authority (e.g., Ezek. 34:1-10; 1 Tim. 5:20).

As this would be Samuel's final address to the nation, he calls on his audience to listen to him. The man of God then spreads out his entire life before them. He speaks of his childhood when he obeyed God's calling for his life to be a prophet. Samuel lived a faithful and blameless life, which permitted God to wonderfully bless His people and to honor Himself. He then says, *"my sons are with you."* Samuel cannot commend his sons, for they were not upright men. Rather, his contempt for their behavior further contrasted and emphasized his own veracity.

Samuel then challenges them to witness against him if covetousness, self-interest or injustice had ever clouded his judgments. If wrongs had been committed, this was their opportunity to have them righted, if indeed there were any. Only a righteous man walking in holiness could throw out such a taunt to every Jew in the commonwealth of Israel and before the king. Samuel was such a man. His only blemish was rearing sons who were not as upright as himself.

The people admitted that he had been an honest judge and a selfless leader. He had neither defrauded, nor oppressed them in any way. Having heard from their own mouths a full exoneration of his character, Samuel uses the opportunity to uphold God's honor, rather than upbraid them for their ingratitude for his lifetime of selfless service. The faithful prophet wanted his countrymen to glean an important principle from their history and from their recent victory over Nahash in how to live for God. They must obey the Lord and learn to wait on Him for all their needs, rather than ignoring His Law and trusting in themselves. The people heed Samuel's message because he lived it himself – he shows us the power of a good testimony.

May 23 – A Sudden Storm
1 Samuel 12

Samuel continued his discourse before Israel with a solemn rebuke: To ask for a king was not only a rejection of God's authority over them, but it ultimately put blame on God because things were not better than they were. Samuel then comes to the main point: you desired a king and God has set him over you as requested – here he is; now obey the Lord, or having a king over you will avail you nothing.

To prove his assertion, Samuel called on the Lord to immediately send a thunderstorm. Because it rarely rained during the late-spring wheat harvest, they would know that such an impromptu storm was from the Lord. The Lord honored Samuel's prayer. The immediate torrential rain and pounding thunder caused the people *"to greatly fear the Lord and Samuel"* (v. 18). The people then begged Samuel: *"Pray for your servants to the Lord your God, that we may not die; for we have added to all our sins the evil of asking a king for ourselves"* (v. 19).

Two things are noted in their petition to Samuel. First, that the people did not beg Saul to pray for them, but rather the man they knew had God's ear. When the human conscience is exercised, as in this situation, the guilty seek the prayers of those whom they know intimately know God. The ornamental prayers of non-believers, no matter how influential they are, count for nothing. Saul, being a man of the flesh, could pray only if in duress. In fact, Scripture never records Saul praying to the Lord even once in his forty-year reign as king. In contrast, godly kings like David and Hezekiah were moved to pray often for the people and then relied on the Lord for deliverance. Obedience and dependence always characterize those engaged in effective praying. Saul lacked both qualities.

Second, they requested that Samuel pray to *"the Lord your* [his] *God,"* not "their God." This acknowledges that the prophet enjoyed a special communion and privilege with the Lord that they did not. This highlights that willing, holy consecration to the Lord places the believer on a higher plane of experiencing God than carnality can ever obtain. In any dispensation, a holy walk is characterized by spiritual power and joyful fellowship with God. Effective praying requires a genuine pursuit of God in righteousness and humility.

May 24 – A Prayer of Intercession
1 Samuel 12

Samuel's response to Israel's request for prayer is one that all truly repentant, forgiven, and God-seeking believers should heed:

> *Do not fear. You have done all this wickedness; yet do not turn aside from following the Lord, but serve the Lord with all your heart. And do not turn aside; for then you would go after empty things which cannot profit or deliver, for they are nothing* (vv. 20-21).

The Lord loved His covenant people despite all their past unfaithfulness. They were His people and, though He must chasten them for their wickedness, He could not forsake them. They could not change their past, but their future could be bright and blessed if they remained devoted to the Lord. Samuel promised to faithfully pray that they would cling to the Lord and to teach them *"the good and the right way"* to tread before Him (v. 23).

Indeed, Samuel was quite willing to pray for them; he even felt that it would be sin not to pray for them. Samuel epitomizes what James would later write: *The effective, fervent prayer of a righteous man avails much* (Jas. 5:16). In this chapter Samuel has been shown to be a man of integrity, in tune with God's heart, and burdened for his countrymen to wholly follow the Lord. Because he was a righteous man and knew the will of God, he had great confidence that his prayers would be answered. *"Now this is the confidence that we have in Him, that if we ask anything according to His will, He hears us* (1 Jn. 5:14). Believers today can have this same assurance in the Lord.

We probably will not call down a thunderstorm as a sign to God's wayward people to consider, but we should be willing to pray that God will do whatever it takes to show the Church her sin and complacency.

Like Samuel, we should also consider it a sin not to pray for other believers to know the truth, and then to fearfully and to faithfully walk in it: *"fear the Lord, and serve Him in truth with all your heart; for consider what great things He has done for you"* (v. 24). If the Church fervently focused on these two aspects of prayer, might we also see a revival of God's people today, as Samuel did at Gilgal?

May 25 – Fear the Lord Only
1 Samuel 12

Samuel closes his address with a final warning: fear the Lord only, serve Him in truth with all your heart, and do not forget all the great things He has done for you; if you return to wickedness, He will sweep you and your king away in judgment. The Lord's people often forget God's past faithfulness and *"the great things He has done"* when distressed. Yet, we are indebted to the Lord's goodness and must serve Him with gratitude at all times: *"In everything give thanks; for this is the will of God in Christ Jesus for you"* (1 Thess. 5:18).

Samuel mentions the word "fear" three times in this chapter and comes full circle in instructing the people how to behave: *"Fear the Lord"* (v. 14), *"Do not fear"* (v. 20), and *"Only fear the Lord"* (v. 24). After the thunderstorm, the people feared God and Samuel, but the prophet, being zealous for the Lord's glory, corrects them – they should "only fear the Lord." They were to fully honor their holy and righteous God above all else. It was He who had promised to severely chasten them if they departed from Him and His Law. They should fear His chastisement, but if they revered God as they should, then they did not need to be anxious about His wrath upon them.

Jehovah is not an angry God poised to instantly crush those who stray from righteousness. Rather, He is a longsuffering, merciful, gracious, loving God who is slow to anger and quick to forgive. The more we know of God, the more we will reverently fear Him and appreciate Him, but there is no reason for His children walking with Him to fear anything else but Him.

From God's perspective, any fear other than towards Him, indicates faithlessness. That is why believers are to *"be anxious for nothing, but in everything by prayer and supplication, with thanksgiving, let your requests be made known to God; and the peace of God, which surpasses all understanding, will guard your hearts and minds through Christ Jesus"* (Phil. 4:6-7).

Indeed, the enemy can harass believers during their lives, and if permitted by God, end their natural lives, but the devil has no hold on the hereafter and does not possess eternal life. Believers should not be distracted by needless worry, such as whether they are heaven-bound or not (John 5:24). May we fear the Lord and experience His full love.

May 26 – The Pressure of Circumstances
1 Samuel 13

About 20 years had passed since Samuel's final address (1 Sam. 12). While Samuel governed Israel, the Philistines withdrew from the land, but under Saul's inactive rule, raiding parties had ensured that the Jews did not have weapons to retaliate against them. Finally, Saul sounded the shofar to summon men to serve as soldiers in a standing army: 2,000 soldiers were stationed at Michmash with Saul and 1,000 soldiers remained with Jonathan at Gibeah; the king sent the rest home.

Apparently, Saul directed Jonathan's attack on the Philistine garrison at Geba, as he attributed Jonathan's victory to himself. However, his attack became a rallying cry throughout Philistia, raising an enormous army to avenge the insult. Why Saul wanted to provoke a much larger and better-equipped army to move against Israel at this time is unknown (only he and Jonathan had swords). As agreed previously during times of distress, Saul blew the trumpet to summon the Jews throughout the land to Gilgal within seven days.

Many Hebrews did respond to the summons. But when it was learned how outnumbered they were, some soldiers began deserting Saul's ranks. Even the loyal soldiers who remained with Saul at Gilgal *"followed him trembling."* This was an agonizing situation for Saul, who had to wait seven days for Samuel to arrive to offer sacrifices to the Lord. Feeling the pressure of time lest he lose any more men, Saul decided he could wait no longer for Samuel (he waited seven days, just not seven full days). The king either intruded on the priesthood himself by sacrificing a burnt offering or he may have ordered the priests to do it, but regardless he still acted contrary to the prophet's command.

As in Jonathan's assault, the self-sufficient king acted without the counsel and blessing of God's prophet. Flesh is impulsive and impatient; its stops where faith begins – when all natural solutions are gone! The sacrifice had hardly been laid on the altar when Samuel arrived and rebuked Saul; as punishment for his sin, he would have no lasting dynasty.

May we learn from Saul's mistake and not let intimidating circumstances prompt us to act outside of God's will. It is easy to be impulsive and do the wrong thing, but genuine faith rests in the Lord, obeys His Word and waits for His solution to our problems.

May 27 – The Pressure of Time
1 Samuel 14

Saul and his 600 men join Jonathan at Gibeah. The Philistines had gathered an enormous army at Michmash (about five miles northeast of Gibeah and only three miles northeast of Saul's position). Inactivity was unacceptable to Jonathan, who was ready, if the Lord be with him, to walk boldly to the enemy's stronghold and challenge them in hand-to-hand combat. Jonathan places the lives of his armorbearer and himself in the hands of God and apart from Saul's direct control. His armorbearer was of the same mind. Their challenge was accepted and the Philistines invited the two Jews to come up into their fortification. Having received God's endorsement of his plan, Jonathan told his armorbearer, *"Come up after me, for the Lord has delivered them into the hand of Israel"* (v. 12). Clearly, this bold assault was not for personal fame; rather, Jonathan identifies with his countrymen; he longs for the entire nation to prevail through his efforts.

The two men climbed up Bozez to engage in combat. Jonathan defeated Philistine after Philistine and his armorbearer finished off those Jonathan had wounded. In all, twenty enemy soldiers fell in the conflict. The Lord used Jonathan's victory and a well-timed earthquake to create panic in the Philistines who broke ranks and began fleeing. One of Saul's watchmen observed the enemy's disorder and reported it to Saul. Saul did a quick roll call of his troops and found that Jonathan and his armorbearer were missing. A priest from Shiloh named Ahijah was with Saul and the king asked him to seek counsel from the Lord.

But, seeing that the opportunity to advance against the fleeing Philistines would soon be lost, Saul told Ahijah *"withdraw your hand."* This either meant to cease building an altar for sacrifice (that usually preceded the use of the Urim and Thummim), or that he was to lower his hands that were lifted in prayer. Saul knew what had to be done; he did not need to wait for the Lord to confirm it. His motivation: to avenge himself on his enemies. He did not view the Philistines as the Lord's enemy. His thoughts were not towards God, but rather toward the pursuit of selfish gain and vain praise.

If we allow the pressure of time to keep us from knowing the Lord's mind before we act, we likewise are pursuing selfish gain. As we will shall soon see, the outcome of such decisions results in misery.

May 28 – The Price Tag of Human Traditions
1 Samuel 14

Jews from the surrounding countryside joined Saul and Jonathan in pursuing and slaughtering the Philistines who first retreated northwestward towards Beth Aven and then later southwestward into the Aijalon Valley. Regrettably, though God miraculously saved Israel that day (through Jonathan's boldness), Saul diminished God's blessing to Israel by uttering a rash oath: *"Cursed is the man who eats any food until evening, before I have taken vengeance on my enemies"* (v. 24). Saul placed a curse on any man who ate anything before evening so he could more fully avenge himself of his enemies.

However, the hasty vow was not well thought out for the soldiers deserved and required sustenance while they were vigorously laboring in battle (Deut. 25:4). The motivation for his vow was not to benefit his men or to extol the Lord; he wanted to vindicate himself on *his* enemies to preserve *his* own honor in Israel.

Conversely, Jonathan honors the Lord and adopts a noble view of oneness with his countrymen: *"the Lord has delivered them into the hand of Israel"* (v. 12). In contrast, we see the carnal man working to benefit himself in God's name and the man of faith seeking to benefit others for the glory of God.

While cutting through the forests of Ephraim, wild beehives saturated with honey were found on the ground, perhaps shaken from the trees by the earthquake. Jonathan, who had not heard his father's charge, tasted some of the honey and was immediately refreshed. Afterwards, he was informed of his father's curse. Jonathan understood that his father's selfish curse had actually limited Israel's slaughter among the Philistines. If Saul had permitted his famished men to eat properly as they pursued the Philistines, they would have had more strength to achieve an even greater victory.

Saul's edict expired at the end of the day and the Jewish soldiers were so hungry that they quickly slaughtered captured animals and ate the meat with its blood, which was forbidden (Lev. 17:10-14). Even carnal Saul was shocked by his men's behavior, *"Look, the people are sinning against the Lord by eating with the blood!"* (v. 33). This scene illustrates what we know to be true today: man-made traditions eventually lead God's people into sin and a loss of God's blessing!

May We Serve Christ!

May 29 – The Insanity of Egocentric Leadership
1 Samuel 14

Seeing his men eating blood even alarmed the carnal king. He commanded that a large stone be rolled to him so that animals could be properly slaughtered and bled out. This was done and portions of the animals were offered to the Lord on an altar that Saul had built to atone for the offense. This was the first altar Saul had erected to the Lord. It was built in haste in reaction to his soldiers' sin, not for the purpose of worship or in response to his own sin.

With his men fed, Saul suggested that they go down after the Philistines by night, and plunder and slaughter them until the morning light, lest they lose the opportunity to do so. The men were agreeable to this, but the priest (probably Ahijah) thought it would be good first to seek counsel from the Lord. This was not Saul's idea, but he agreed to the suggestion and asked the Lord: *"Shall I go down after the Philistines? Will You deliver them into the hand of Israel?"* (v. 37). Since Ahijah was wearing the priestly ephod, God's mind could be discerned through the Urim and the Thummim. But the Lord did not answer Saul's questions.

Saul rightly assumed that the silence meant that there was sin in the camp; someone had defied his oath. Although Saul's decree was follish, God honored his authority as the one who ruled Israel and had invoked His name. Some knew what Jonathan had innocently done, but since Saul threatened to kill the perpetrator, even if it was his own son, everyone kept silent. Nobody wanted the king to kill their valiant hero in a foolish rage. But the priest, either by casting the lot or by the Urim and Thummim identified Jonathan as the guilty party. Jonathan does not accuse his father of erring, nor does he defend himself, but rather he acknowledges what he did and what he deserves as a consequence.

Saul was infuriated that his own son would defy his command. The Lord had put His finger upon the utter folly of Saul's oath and everyone knew it. Will the king realize the absurdity of his vow and confess it as such? No! Instead, without consulting the Lord, Saul instantly passed sentence on his own son to save face – Jonathan must die. Thankfully, the people rescued Jonathan; the sanity of the people overruled their king's folly. The enemy was not pursued; everyone returned to their homes; the greater victory was forfeited because of Saul's imprudence.

May 30 – Gloating Flesh
1 Samuel 15

The strength of Saul's kingdom is at its apex; the Philistines to the west and the Ammonites to the east have been vanquished. Saul has bolstered his army with the sturdiest men in Israel. The time is now come for the Lord to settle a four-century-old score with the Amalekites. These nomadic raiders were never fully punished for their unprovoked attack on the weary Israelites coming from Egypt to Sinai. For the first time since the Canaan Conquest, Israel has a sizable army and the Lord desired to honor His word spoken through Moses. The Amalekites were to be attacked and nothing was to be spared!

After receiving his divine marching orders, Saul led Israel's army of 210,000 soldiers south against the Amalekites. This scene shows us that the flesh (pictured in Saul) will pretend to act on God's behalf if it can gain something in the process. Yet, Paul affirms that God will not tolerate such mock piety: *"He who glories, let him glory in the Lord"* (1 Cor. 1:31). Sadly, Saul, a man of the flesh, will use God's favor to exalt himself and to diminish God's glory in the eyes of others.

After the Kenites departed, Saul attacked the Amalekites' capital city and successfully smote Amalekites from Havilah all the way to Shur. But Saul spared Agag, their king. The writer also identifies other Amalekites who survived Saul's assault (30:1-17; 2 Sam 8.12). Saul brought the Amalekite king and the best of Amalekite livestock back into Israel. Saul did not spare Agag because he was compassionate, but for personal glory.

Previously, Saul was willing to kill his own son for unknowingly defying his foolish command to fast. Later, Saul will have the entire priestly community of Nob slaughtered for innocently aiding David's escape. Saul was not a man marked by mercy or decency. He kept Agag alive for one reason – to gloat over his accomplishment.

Saul, acting in the flesh against another who, like him, represented the flesh, failed God's test. If Saul had been right with God, he would have executed God's justice swiftly and fully. A believer consecrated to God understands that the flesh must be given no provision in one's life; otherwise one's lusts become further inflamed (Rom. 13:14). Amalek was the first obstacle to the redeemed coming into God's presence at Sinai and today it still attempts to keep us from communion with God.

May 31 – Must Be Put to Death
1 Samuel 15

The flesh measures success differently than God does. Saul thought he had performed his task spectacularly and so, while en route to Gilgal, he stopped to erect a monument at Carmel (southeast of Hebron) to celebrate his achievement. Despite his egotistical efforts to exalt himself before others he was about to learn that partial obedience is disobedience and disobedience always has consequences.

Ironically, the Lord will use what Saul failed in as a rod of chastening against him. For sparing the Amalekite king – Saul would lose his kingdom, and for sparing an Amalekite – an Amalekite would later claim to have slain him (2 Sam. 1:1-10). The repercussions of Saul's sin would again be felt six centuries later. Esther 3 introduces us to Haman, who persuaded King Xerxes to approve a law that would exterminate Jews throughout the Persian Empire. He was an Agagite, a royal descendant of Hammedatha of the Amalekites. Because Saul failed to obey God's command to wipe out the Amalekites, they lived on to war against God's covenant people centuries later.

Believers today must desire to be controlled by the Holy Spirit, and not by their lusting flesh (the Amalekite within) – only then are the deeds of the flesh mortified and fellowship with God maintained: *"If by the Spirit you put to death the deeds of the body, you will live"* (Rom. 8:13). Positionally speaking, co-crucifixion took place at the cross and became effectual for believers at their conversion (Rom. 6:6). Believers are to be on active duty to mortify the deeds of the flesh. If your flesh nature raises its ugly head – you are to inflict a mortal blow against it. The only way to deal with lusting flesh is to put it to death; no pity, no mercy, and no procrastination.

Death and dying are not pleasant topics of conversation. There is a certain finality associated with death that our flesh loathes, because it ceases to function. But from God's standpoint, as Paul reminds the Galatians, Christians have already died positionally with Christ, and should therefore live out this truth (Gal. 5:24). The purpose of crucifixion was to end a life, though death would occur sometime after the victim was crucified. Accordingly, the cross ensures that as time moves on, there will be less of the believer's flesh and more of Christ apparent in his life.

June 1 – A Blame-shifting King
1 Samuel 15

After being deeply moved by the severity of the Lord's statement against Saul, Samuel wept before the Lord in intercessory prayer all night. Early the next morning the faithful prophet began his heartbreaking journey to rebuke Israel's king, who was back in Gilgal.

Saul was not expecting Samuel and the suddenness of his arrival probably signaled trouble for him. Saul pretentiously greeted Samuel with an air of religious piety: *"Blessed are you of the Lord! I have performed the commandment of the Lord"* (v. 13). Instead of patiently waiting to hear whether the Lord had a message for him, Saul hastens to justify his action, but Samuel will have nothing to do with this pitiable attempt to gloss over his sin. With Saul's hollow words still ringing in Samuel's ears, the prophet hears a more convincing testimony – the bleating of sheep and the lowing of oxen. Samuel wasted no time in addressing the king's disobedience.

Seeing that there was no means of refuting the evidence against him, Saul then shifts from being the guilty defendant to the scornful accuser: *"the people spared the best of the sheep and the oxen, to sacrifice to the Lord your God"* (v. 15). Even if this were true, Saul is the king and bears the responsibility for the actions of those under his authority. Samuel promptly rejects Saul's attempt to deflect guilt: *"Be quiet! And I will tell you what the Lord said to me last night"* (v. 16).

Samuel then reminds Saul of his former insignificance and that he was indebted to God for his present high status. Next, the prophet reviews the command given to Saul and then indicts him: *"Why then did you not obey the voice of the Lord? Why did you swoop down on the spoil, and do evil in the sight of the Lord?"* (v. 19). Saul tries to duck under the prophetic blow by justifying his sin. In effect Saul says, "I did obey the Lord, but I kept Agag as a prisoner to testify of our victory and permitted the people to spare the best animals for a higher cause – to honor the Lord through sacrifices."

This is the most dreadful condition a person can reach – to be so controlled by the flesh that sin can be justified no matter the cost. When God withdraws from those who reject His word, the worst carnality within them comes out (Rom. 1:18-32). Obedience, not blame-shifting, is the true test of our loyalty!

May We Serve Christ!

June 2 – Seven Things Better Than Sacrifice
1 Samuel 15

So far, Samuel has been unsuccessful in reaching Saul's conscience through probing questions. Saul initially lied about what he had done, then blamed the people for his failure, and then tried to justify his sin by smug religiosity. But there was nothing valuable enough that Saul could place on the altar to compensate for his rebellion.

The prophet now sentences the king. Because Saul thought that sacrifice was greater than obedience, an irreversible curse from heaven fell upon him: the kingdom had been given to a better man than Saul. There was nothing more valuable to God than devoted obedience! What God values trumps what we think He should want more! Sacrifices offered to God which ignore His expressed will are but self-willed forms of idolatry.

Interestingly, the Bible reveals seven things that God values more than burnt offerings: obedience to His Word, a broken heart (Ps. 51:17), genuine praise and thanksgiving (Ps. 69:30-31), the knowledge of God (Hos. 6:6), walking humbly with God in justice, love and mercy (Micah 6:8), loving God with your whole heart (Mark 12:33), and doing the will of God (Heb. 10:9-10). These are the things that please the Lord and cause His face to shine on His people in every age.

Previously, Samuel had told Saul that he would have no lasting royal dynasty. Now God's messenger informs the king that God had fully rejected him. If Saul had just humbly admitted his sin instead of justifying it and had pleaded for mercy, God would have shown some kindness to Saul. But it was not to be. As God's anointed, he would be permitted to sit on a phantom throne until his death, but God already had another in mind to replace him – a young man named David.

Many sought Christ after hearing the appealing Great Supper parable of Luke 14. Yet, the Lord did not desire a throng of followers, but rather disciples who would learn of Him and be committed to Him. Our Lord later affirmed in John 14:15 that a true disciple demonstrates love for Him by willingly obeying His Word: *"If you love Me, keep My commandments."* Is there any greater way to show the Lord you love Him than by doing what He says to do? Samuel declared, *"to obey* [God] *is better than sacrifice"* (v. 22). Obedience can be forced, but submission is a heart issue, a matter of the will.

June 3 – Yet Honor Me Now
1 Samuel 15

Samuel's words expressing God's judgment against him overwhelmed Saul who finally admitted his sin, but yet he still wanted Samuel to return with him to worship the Lord. If Saul had uttered those words in all honesty when Samuel first arrived at Gilgal, the outcome of his failure may have been different, though Saul, a man of the flesh, was never destined to sit on Israel's throne for long. Saul not only admits his guilt, but then explains why he disobeyed the Lord – because he feared the people. What kind of king fears the people he rules more than the God who rules him? What kind of king worships a God that he fears less than his people? The answer is a carnal man who does not truly know or fear God. Saul's conscience is briefly awakened, but his admission was not one of sincere repentance, for he still wanted to maintain a favorable public opinion: Samuel was still for him.

Saul's request that Samuel offer sacrifices for him and that they worship the Lord together indicates Saul's refusal to accept God's judgment against him. Thus, the prophet says, *"I will not return with you, for you have rejected the word of the Lord, and the Lord has rejected you from being king over Israel"* (v. 26). There was nothing more to say. The prophet was prepared to let Saul go his own way and fall prey to his own devices. However, when Samuel turned to depart, the desperate king seized the prophet's robe and tore it.

Saul further compounds his sin by again rejecting God's Word, so Samuel uses his torn garment to utter one last prophecy against Saul – the kingdom has been torn from you. Saul responds with this plea: *"I have sinned; yet honor me now, please ... before Israel, and return with me, that I may worship the Lord your God"* (v. 30). Saul accepts the judgment against him, but still desires Samuel to accompany him to worship the Lord, so that he will retain the honor of the people.

Samuel obliges Saul's request because his office deserved respect, although he could not honor the man in that office. So Samuel did not depart from the king, but neither did he worship the Lord with Saul – *"Saul worshiped the Lord."* What a laughable sight, the carnal man that has been rejected is publicly revering Samuel's God; yet Samuel and the Lord are absent. Many are doing the same thing today (Matt. 7:21-23).

June 4 – The Flesh at Its Worst
1 Samuel 15

Saul's behavior in this chapter highlights the unproductive rudiments of the fallen nature in all of us:

- The flesh justifies incomplete obedience (vv. 8-9).
- The flesh boasts itself against the truth (v. 13).
- The flesh defends itself when confronted (v. 20).
- The flesh fears man more than God (v. 24).
- The flesh values the honor of man more than God's (v. 30).
- The flesh has two ends, gratification or mortification (v. 33).

We should also consider and learn from the consequences of Saul's recent carnal decisions. We should not forsake the truth to alleviate difficult circumstances (1 Sam. 13). We should not permit the pressure of time to cause us to act before we know God's mind (1 Sam. 14). We should not fear man more than God (1 Sam 15). As previously mentioned, both Saul and the Amalekites are types of the flesh. Saul represents the flesh's best attempts to puff up self through religious fanfare. The Amalekites reflect its outright rebellion against God, His people, and His plans and inheritance for them (Ex. 17:7-8). Hence, it was impossible for Saul to do what only the Holy Spirit could accomplish – the execution of Agag (i.e., mortification of the flesh).

Saul, a man of the flesh, could never mortify another form of the flesh represented in the chief Amalekite. Only a servant of God empowered by the Spirit of God can overcome the impulses of the flesh and land the death blow (Rom. 8:1-13). Samuel is such a man. Those under the Spirit's control never hesitate to mortify the flesh (Rom. 13:14).

So before Samuel, God's appointed judge in Israel, departs from Gilgal, he renders judgment against Agag. Samuel took a sword and hacked Agag in pieces after affirming his sentencing: *"As your sword has made women childless, so shall your mother be childless among women"* (v. 33). Likewise, it is *"the sword of the Spirit, which is the Word of God"* (Eph. 6:17) which defeats the impulses of our flesh that are outside God's will. Full submission to God's Word provides no opportunity for the flesh to escape its deadly blow. Samuel's actions declare God's hatred for the carnal impulses lurking within all of us.

Daily Devotions

June 5 – A Man After God's Own Heart
1 Samuel 16

The Lord tells Samuel to anoint him as king over Israel, yet David is only about thirteen or fourteen years old at this time. Against the dark backdrop of Saul's carnal leadership appears a young man who is honorable, brave, and tender-spirited and who loves the Lord above all else. David's fitness for leading was gained through his unobserved conflicts while caring for his sheep before he ever contemplated ruling Israel. David had a heart for God and His people, which Saul did not; that alone would make him a better king than Saul ever could be.

David is the main author of Psalms and many of his poems were composed during distressing circumstances. A greater understanding of these arduous experiences in the unfolding chapters will enable us to better appreciate how David lived a blessed life amidst them. After David, around the age of fifteen, slew Goliath, he dwelt in Saul's palace at Gibeah for about seven years (17:45-18:2). From the age of twenty-two to thirty, David was either on the run from King Saul or was dwelling among the Philistines in Ziklag (27:7).

During his years of fleeing from Saul, David wrote several psalms, ten of which address this crisis directly; the likely order of these poems would be: 7, 59, 56, 34, 52, 63, 54, 18, 57, and 142. In all, Saul made fourteen recorded attempts on David's life.

Regrettably, while dwelling at Ziklag, David lapsed spiritually and engaged in gruesome covert raids on villages; there is no evidence that David composed any psalms during this time. At the age of thirty (after Saul's death) David began to reign over Judah in Hebron. Seven years later he captured Jerusalem from the Jebusites and was subsequently anointed king over all the tribes of Israel (2 Sam. 5:1-3). He ruled over God's people for a total of forty years before dying at the age of seventy (2 Sam. 5:4).

It is evident from David's writings that the man after God's own heart (13:14) frequently suffered a broken heart. He was often despised, plotted against, slandered, and persecuted for doing God's will. Many sought to kill David; yet, through each difficulty, he found the Lord to be a faithful Refuge of peace and a mighty Fortress of protection. David proves that those who suffer patiently with the Lord in righteousness know more about God's true nature than those who do not.

June 6 – Out of Step With God
1 Samuel 16

The Lord admonishes Samuel for continuing to mourn for Saul because He had rejected Saul from reigning over Israel (v. 1). As many years had passed since their last exchange, it was not likely that Samuel was grieving for Saul personally, but rather for the man on whom all the hopes of Israel rested at that time. God's rejection of Israel's king could mean only shame and sorrow for the nation he ruled over. So the Lord's next words concerning Israel's new king must have encouraged Samuel's doleful heart. This meant that Israel's shame would not continue for much longer.

Dear believer, there is a valuable lesson for us to glean from Samuel's disposition. It is quite possible for a faithful servant of God to be emotionally out of sorts because his or her thoughts are not aligned with God's mind. Note the ways that Samuel demonstrates that he is out of step with God in this chapter: First, he mourned for the king that God had flatly rejected. Second, he hesitated to go to Bethlehem to anoint Israel's new king after being told to. Third, Samuel approved of Eliab based on sight, but God reminded his prophet that integrity and devotion in a man was what He valued.

The solution to Samuel's melancholy demeanor was to enter into the thoughts of God, advocates C. H. Mackintosh: "Communion with God will ever lead us to acquiesce in His ways. Sentimentalism may weep over fallen greatness, but faith grasps the great truth that God's unerring counsel shall stand, and He will do all His pleasure."[8]

Indeed, human sorrow will ever flow until the human heart finds tranquility in the immense resources of our most blessed, sovereign God. The Lord offered Samuel the solution to his apprehension – he was to align his mind with God's thoughts. This would require him to fill a horn with oil and to journey to Bethlehem to anoint one of Jesse's sons as Israel's new king. The Lord then announced, *"For I have provided Myself a king."*

Hannah had asked for Samuel, and the people had demanded Saul, but David was God's own provision of grace for Israel. The progressive expressions in Scripture of God's joy in exalting David to the throne of Israel are quite lovely and picture the future day when God will place His own Son over all principalities and powers.

Daily Devotions

June 7 – A Troubled Saul
1 Samuel 16

The Holy Spirit had already departed from the rejected king, but He came upon David powerfully. The absence of light is darkness (Isa. 45:7); the absence of God's abiding presence permits the darkness of the human mind to be harassed and controlled by demonic forces. This is what is meant by the reference to *"a distressing spirit from the Lord"* that was troubling Saul (vv. 15-16). Saul may have been suffering from some form of mental illness, meaning his agitation would be further heightened when harassed by satanic forces. With the absence of the Holy Spirit, demonic foes would have been permitted to attack Saul through possession, oppression, and obsession.

Possession occurs when an unbeliever is indwelt by a demon, or demons. These demons gain direct control of the body and the mind, much the same way commandos would forcibly gain control over a weak military installation. A believer cannot be indwelt by demons (they cannot reside with the Holy Spirit; 1 Cor. 6:19), but demonic oppression inflicted on a vulnerable or carnal believer may indeed lead to behavior that seems much like that of a possessed individual.

Oppression, in respect to believers, refers to the external influences that try the patience of our faith. Satan not only afflicted Paul's body (2 Cor. 12:7), but hindered him from visiting believers at Thessalonica also (1 Thess. 2:18). Christ came to deliver the oppressed (Acts 10:38).

Obsession is the direct injection of evil thoughts into the human mind. Paul acknowledges that there is a *"spirit that is now at work in the sons of disobedience"* (Eph. 2:2). The enemy may plant tempting thoughts so he can establish a stronghold in the flesh, or he may observe a self-erected stronghold in the heart, such as bitterness, and seek to stir up unforgiving thoughts. These injected thoughts then cause anxiety, distress, and depression in our minds.

Ananias is an excellent example of satanic obsession targeting the mind. Apparently, a stronghold of greed and envy existed in the heart of this believer and he became susceptible to attack (Acts 5:3). Holy living, renewing the mind, and the power of prayer bring victory over such demonic attacks. Unfortunately, Saul was not holy, his thoughts were self-focused, and the Lord did not heed his prayers because he had been rejected.

June 8 – Jealousy and Envy
1 Samuel 18

Saul decided that David should reside with him in Gibeah and not return to Bethlehem. Seeing that David behaved wisely on whatever errand he sent him, Saul set him over some of his men of war. Saul probably hoped that David, being a young man and an untrained warrior, would fail in leading veteran soldiers or better yet, fall in battle. However, it was not to be. David conducted himself favorably before everyone. In time, Saul's soldiers, the people, and even Saul's servants all accepted and approved of David's leadership in Saul's court. David went in and out among the people in a manner suggestive of a true selfless shepherd, and they all cherished him for it.

However, David's troubles began soon after he returned home from slaughtering the Philistines one particular day. (Two or three years have passed since David first relocated to Gibeah.) Women danced joyfully in the king's presence with musical instruments while singing: *"Saul has slain his thousands and David his ten thousands"* (vv. 6-7). The lyrics infuriated Saul, for David had won the hearts of the people, and the only thing remaining for him to take would be the kingdom. Saul observed David with suspicion and apprehension thereafter.

The next day, Saul's jealousy got the best of him. David is softly playing his harp and singing praises to God in order to ease the king's turmoil and violent raving. The king can take no more. Controlled by unchecked jealousy and seeing a nearby spear, he picked it up and tried to pin David to the wall with it. Thankfully, David escaped without injury, even after a second effort by Saul with the spear.

In the next chapter, Saul will stick a spear in the wall in an attempt to kill David (19:10). Clearly, Saul's jealousy is swelling with time and will eventually lead him into a murderous fit and obsession that will usher him into his grave. *"Jealousy as cruel as the grave; its flames are flames of fire, a most vehement flame"* (Song 8:6).

Believers must learn to quickly extinguish such blazing passions lest carnal savagery be permitted to rage in our own hearts also. We must be controlled by the Spirit of God, not by passion. Our anger is to have a present righteous purpose in our doings or be doused; otherwise it will lead us into sin and we too will behave like ludicrous Saul.

June 9 – A Man of Few Words
1 Samuel 19

The soul of his son Jonathan quickly bonded with David and a deep admiration developed between the two men, Jonathan being David's senior by twelve to fifteen years. Jonathan watched David descend into the valley to face a giant and return again with the spoils of victory. David had earned his esteem and devotion. This deep friendship was so strong that *"Jonathan and David made a covenant, because he [Jonathan] loved him [David] as his own soul"* (18:3). As a sign of his loyalty to David, Jonathan gave David the robe he was wearing, his armor, sword, bow, and belt. Jonathan's surrender of his royal robe, which marked him as heir to the throne of Israel, was a poetic way for Jonathan to lay his own claims to honor and glory at David's feet. He knew it was God's plan for David, not himself, to be Israel's next king!

In contrast, Saul did not want David to be Israel's next king and commanded his servants and Jonathan to slay David, if given the opportunity. Jonathan informed his younger friend of his father's plot against him and volunteered to intercede on his behalf. Jonathan did so and reminded his father about David's triumphs in the king's name against the Philistines, that David had behaved wisely before everyone, and that he had not sinned against the king. Hence, there was no just reason to execute David; he was innocent before God and the king, who had also rejoiced in David's feats.

Jonathan's intercession for David is one of his longest discourses in Scripture. He was a man of few words, but when he did speak, his speech was marked by grace and truth. Such were the words of the Lord Jesus (John 1:14), who set the perfect example of communication that all believers should aspire to (Col. 4:6).

The king heeded his son's words and swore, *"As the Lord lives, he shall not be killed"* (v. 6). Sometimes a prudent presentation of the truth may convict a person's conscience to take a particular moral action but without repentance of their evil intentions. This was the situation with Saul; he did not fully act on the truth with a sincere heart, therefore, there was not long-lasting benefit of his confession. Jonathan informed David of his father's vow of goodwill and then brought him to the king. David then played music in the king's presence as he had previously done.

June 10 – Failure in Gath
1 Samuel 21

After receiving bread and Goliath's sword from the priests at Nob, David fled to the Philistine-controlled town of Gath. About seven years had passed since Goliath's defeat, so perhaps David thought that he might not be easily recognized. Nonetheless, David had gained much notoriety among his enemy and his presence did not go unnoticed. He was seized and immediately taken to Achish, the king of Gath.

Apparently, Achish sought to profit from an alliance with a skilled warrior, who, like them, was Saul's enemy too. But being in Achish's clutches provoked stark fear in David's heart. Fear, not faith, led David to Gath, so we should not be surprised that the inclinations of the flesh are ruling his behavior.

David reasoned that the king would not make sport of a madman, so he acted like he was an insane fool. He even scrawled on the doors of the gate while permitting his saliva to run down his beard. The man of God who in faith charged a giant in battle, the anointed king of Israel, now lowers himself to the unworthy strategy of faking insanity to preserve his life, but he does so at the cost of his integrity.

Achish was offended by the display or at least seemed to be. He likely knew that David was faking the whole thing, but did not want his servants to be aware of it lest they hurt David and forfeit any possible future alliance with him. The king therefore told his servants to remove the lunatic David from his home. David was promptly released from custody and retreated to the cave of Adullam in Israel.

David wrote Psalms 34 and 56 to express what he had learned from his failure at Gath. In Psalm 56, David acknowledged that he was surrounded by his enemies and those loyal to him were just a few, but then he cried out to the Lord for mercy (Ps. 56:1-2). At first David acknowledges his fear, saying, *"Whenever I am afraid, I will trust in You"* (Ps. 56:3), but after a season of prayer he affirms: *"In God I have put my trust; I will not be afraid. What can man do to me?"* (Ps. 56:11). Notice how David flipped the order of his fear and his trust in these two verses to encourage his own heart. This illustrates the transforming effect prayer has on the believer's thinking, that is, when real faith in a sovereign God is exercised in ominous situations.

June 11 – The Rescuer Is Rescued
1 Samuel 23

After learning that the Philistines were robbing the threshing floors of Keilah, David was moved to do something, but wisely sought the Lord's counsel first. *"Shall I go and attack these Philistines?"* (v. 2). The Lord's answer was, *"Go and attack the Philistines, and save Keilah"* (v. 3). While speaking to the Lord, David humbly refers to himself three times as "Your servant." Before acting on the Lord's behalf, it is wise to seek His mind with a spirit of meekness and submission; we too should want only what the Lord wants.

David's men, already on the run from Saul, were not as eager to confront an enemy that was not seeking them, especially a much larger one like the Philistines. He does not ignore the reservations of his men, but rather, seeks the Lord's counsel a second time to be sure of His direction. Again the Lord confirmed what David was to do, but gave the added promise that He would ensure a complete victory.

Seeing that this was the Lord's battle, David obeyed and led his men against the Philistines, who were soundly defeated and despoiled of their livestock. It did not take long for news of David's rescue of Keilah to reach the ears of Saul. The deranged and rejected king actually believed that God was showing kindness to him by entrapping David in a walled town so that he could be captured.

Saul quickly assembled a sizeable complement of men to besiege Keilah and capture David. Yet David understood that Saul would not rest until he was dead, so he inquires of the Lord (through Abiathar) as to whether Saul will come after him and if the men of Keilah will betray him? The answer is "yes" to both questions. Having discerned the mind of the Lord, David immediately left Keilah with his men and Saul halted his advance on Keilah after learning that David had escaped.

David's response to his difficult circumstance was quite different than Saul's reaction to his trouble in 1 Samuel 13. Saul compromised the truth, but David waited on the Lord to ensure he knew the truth before acting. The believer should never compromise the truth to alleviate their unwanted circumstances. The consequence of not having God with us in our trials will always be more costly than if we had continued in faith doing what we know He wants us to do.

June 12 – Resting In God's Sovereignty
1 Samuel 24

Saul was informed that David had gone to the Wilderness of En Gedi. The king chose 3,000 choice soldiers to pursue David and his men. The area that David was thought to be hiding in was a labyrinth of rocky crags, ravines, and caves known as *"the Rocks of the Wild Goats."* Saul paused his search for David at En Gedi to enter one of its many caves to relieve himself; he was unaware that David and his men were hiding in the recesses of the same cave.

David's men believed that God had rewarded David's faithfulness by delivering his enemy into his hand. However, that was not David's sense of the situation. Rather than smiting Saul, David quietly snuck up behind Saul and cut off part of his royal robe and then retreated. The anointed king of Israel knew better than to strike down God's anointed; even cutting Saul's robe bothered David's conscience, but he needed irrefutable evidence that he meant Saul no harm.

David's comrades were hoping their long ordeal would soon be over with one thrust of David's sword. But David restrained his men and explained that God would remove those He placed into authority in His timing, and that he had received no divine command to strike God's anointed down. Only a man of principle who feared the Lord more than the wicked king would behave in such a way, and David was such a man. Our carnal nature seeks revenge at the slightest provocation, but true faith waits on God to resolve the matter.

After finishing his business, the king exited the cave and went his way. David then humbly and respectfully revealed himself to Saul and presented his evidence which proved he intended no harm to the king. Being innocent of wrongdoing, David was willing to let the Lord execute justice against Saul on his behalf. Even if Saul did continue to pursue David, he was assured that the Lord would deliver him out of the king's hand.

During his speech to Saul, David appeals twice to the Lord to act as Judge. How much less contention would there be in the Church today if believers permitted the all-knowing and all-powerful Lord to judge all the injustices, false gossip, and slander amongst us? In actuality, He will judge all such things completely and He will do a much better job than we ever could.

Daily Devotions

June 13 – Abigail's Wise Discretion
1 Samuel 25

Nabal was a wealthy man living in Maon. He was a harsh and evil man, but his young wife Abigail was beautiful and wise. Nabal was busy shearing his sheep, which was accompanied by a festive time of feasting. Hearing that Nabal was shearing his sheep, David sent ten men to petition Nabal for food. David and his men had been living peaceably among Nabal's shepherds and had not taken anything from Nabal. Rather, they had protected his flocks and servants from bandits and predators. David now asked for provisions as a courtesy.

But instead of rewarding David for his generosity, Nabal upbraided David, suggesting that he was a rebel servant that was setting a bad example. Nabal did not even fear David's skilled militia just over the ridge. He valued a few provisions more than his own life and the lives of those in his household. After hearing of Nabal's churlish response, an enraged David assembled 400 armed men to take vengeance on Nabal.

One of Nabal's shepherds informed Abigail about the situation, confirmed their favorable experience with David, and warned her of imminent peril. After hearing this report, Abigail quickly prepared a large quantity of foodstuffs to take to David, which she hoped would avert his wrath. Some fault Abigail for usurping her husband's authority, but Scripture rather applauds her behavior – she was attempting to save her husband's life by jeopardizing her own. Subordinates are to respect the authority God places over them as unto Him, unless that authority opposes His expressed will (Acts 5:29).

Thankfully, she reached David before he found Nabal. She asks David to accept her offering of provisions and to judge her for her husband's sin, for he was of weak character and naturally foolish. This meant Nabal was no threat to David. Abigail then praised David's righteous character and affirmed that Jehovah would place him on the throne and reward him with a long-lasting dynasty. Every point of her self-effacing address touched David's heart. It was evil for him to avenge himself on one so foolish; rather, he should be fighting *"the battles of the Lord"* (v. 28). Abigail had caused David to look beyond the *present* petty offense to his *future* grandeur in Israel. May we too overlook what is petty in comparison to our glorious future in Christ.

June 14 – Separation Before Restoration
1 Samuel 29

The day finally came in which David's identification with the Philistines posed an inescapable predicament for him. He was with the Philistines and they were preparing to war with Israel. How could David withdraw from the confrontation after deceiving Achish about his enterprises and his sympathies? Furthermore, how could he fight against Saul, whose life he had spared twice because he was God's anointed? How could he lift up a sword against his beloved Jonathan?

David was learning that it was easier to set off down the wrong pathway than to forsake it later and suffer the consequences of one's folly. Clearly, David was in a bad way, but thankfully the Lord had not abandoned him. God was going to intervene to ensure that David would not fight against His covenant people but also to chasten David in such a way that his faith and his way would be restored.

At Aphek the ranks of the Philistine soldiers were reviewed by their princes. It was soon discovered that Achish had a band of renegade Hebrews as his rear guard and the Philistine commanders resented their presence and demanded that Achish remove them from their ranks. Although Achish vouched for David the decision was final (Achish did not know that David had been secretly raiding his Philistine allies); the Philistines could not risk being sandwiched between Hebrews lines.

Achish orders David to return to Ziklag. Clearly, the Lord had intervened to deliver David out of his terrible predicament; yet, David chose to dispute the decision probably as a deceptive tactic to appear loyal to Achish. Thankfully, the Lord had used the disdain of the Philistine lords to redirect His servant's steps.

Later, David would realize that God's providential care spared him the humiliation and shame which would have been attached to his name if he had gone into battle with the Philistines. He would write: *"The steps of a good man are ordered by the Lord and He delights in his way. Though he fall, he shall not be utterly cast down; for the Lord upholds him with His hand"* (Ps. 37:23-24). But at this juncture, David is self-willed; he is not delighting in the path that God has chosen for him. He must learn that deliverance from trouble is not the same as restoration to God; he must, therefore, come under God's chastening rod for disobedience.

June 15 – Chastening Before Restoration
1 Samuel 30

The news that the Philistines had gathered their armies to attack Israel in the north prompted the Amalekites in the far south to raid unguarded southern Philistia. It took David and his men three days to travel from Aphek to Ziklag. When they arrived, they found that Ziklag had been burned and all the people had been taken away. As the ground was not littered with bodies this meant that their wives and children had been enslaved and not killed. This offered a glimmer of hope to David's weary men, although they blamed David for their calamity and spoke of stoning him. David was responsible; he should have left soldiers to guard their loved ones. Living sixteen months among the Philistines and away from the Lord had taken its toll on David's men.

David knew his God, and realized that the entire situation was too well crafted to have happened by chance. Having recognized the hand of God, a contrite David *"strengthened himself in the Lord his God"*. The fact that the Amalekites had struck shortly after David had impudently gone to fight with the Philistines, but not a single person belonging to David was killed, demonstrated God's control of the entire situation, especially since David had slaughtered every man, woman, and child of the Amalekites during his raids.

God was causing David to face his sin and to learn again the joy of pursuing the heart of God. We will be the happiest when we yearn for what God wants, and detest what He hates; thus, may we *not despise the chastening of the Lord*!

God was judging His servant, but He was doing so in measure to bring about David's restoration, not his crushing, and David realized it. Jehovah would not permit the Amalekites to harm what was His servant's, nor would he allow David and his men to resolve the situation on their terms or with their resources. The Lord had wrung out of them every ounce of human energy so that they would have no choice but to turn to Him and advance with Him against the enemy. David knew to Whom to turn for comfort and help in his dire crisis. So while David's men further disheartened each other, David chose to permit God's grace to work in his own heart; he thus remained calm and optimistic. God's grace is magnified in man's failures, and the more keenly our ruin is felt, the more we appreciate God's grace.

May We Serve Christ!

June 16 – The Rewards of Restoration
1 Samuel 30

This scene at Ziklag confirms that Abiathar and the priest's ephod were with David and his company while accompanying Achish, otherwise the Amalekites would have confiscated both at Ziklag. Because the Lord was not consulted, it suggests that David knew what he was doing was wrong, but for whatever reason, he did it anyway. Although the situation is dire and every moment that passes means that loved ones are being carried further away, David pauses (for the first time in sixteen months) to seek the mind of the Lord. He realizes that his past folly has created his present distress and he is determined to look beyond the smoldering ruins and faithless friends to obtain the blessing of His God.

David shows his loyalty to Jehovah by seeking and waiting for God's counsel even when the answer was blatantly obvious. Because he did, the Lord promised that all that was lost would be recovered! A life pleasing to God does not merely seek to do what He approves, or permits, but rather what will best honor God's name.

The young commander and his 600 weary and emotionally distraught men then pursued hard after the Amalekites. Fifteen miles from Ziklag, David had to leave 200 of his exhausted men at the Brook Besor, they could go no further. A sick Egyptian slave left behind to die by the Amalekites is assisted by the Hebrews and in return for his freedom agrees to show them where the Amalekites are encamped. The Hebrews found their enemy in a sprawling celebration because of the great spoil they had taken from the Philistines and from Judah. Clearly, they were not anticipating a counterstrike from anyone.

David and his men rested briefly and then attacked the Amalekites from dusk until the following evening the next day; they slaughtered the drunken Amalekites, except four hundred young men who escaped on camels. Just as the Lord had said, David recovered all that the Amalekites had taken, including his two wives; nothing was lacking. Moreover a great spoil of sheep, cattle, ornaments, jewels, weapons, money, clothing, camels, and donkeys was seized. David learned a valuable lesson at Ziklag – a child of faith must trust in the Lord's character and promises even if all appears to be bleak and ominous, especially if the difficulty is one resulting from personal sin.

June 17 – The Right Thing the Wrong Way
2 Samuel 6

Now that David had been recognized by all the tribes as Israel's king, his first order of business was to bring the Ark of *"the Lord of Hosts"* from Abinadab's home (its resting place for about 70 years) to the City of David. David selected 30,000 choice men to accompany him on the ten-mile journey to "Baale Judah" and then to return with the Ark.

It was carried out of Abinadab's home and put on a new cart. David should have known God's restrictions concerning how His Ark was to be transported (on the shoulders of the Kohathites; Num. 4:15). But instead, he permits those serving God to adopt the ways of the world in the matter (i.e., to repeat the method the Philistines used to return the Ark to Israel years earlier). The Philistines were not judged for their actions, because they were not Jehovah's covenant people and did not know better, but Israel had no excuse.

Two sons of Abinadab, Uzzah and Ahio, guided the cart; Uzzah was on the cart and Ahio was leading the oxen. When the cart came to Nachon's threshing floor, the oxen stumbled, and Uzzah put out his hand to hold the Ark steady. Apparently, he felt the Ark needed to be safeguarded, as if God were not sufficient to protect what is His. But his casual act of touching what was most holy to God only underscored the fact that Israel was dishonoring the Lord by what they were doing.

Uzzah's act aroused the Lord's anger and he was immediately struck dead. The matter greatly displeased David who had desired to revere God by bringing His Ark to Jerusalem. David did not understand why God had acted against him and feared moving the Ark any further lest more people die. The procession dispersed and the Ark was taken into the house of Obed-Edom the Gittite.

The king's error was not his zeal, however, but his lack of reverence for God's sacred things for which He is jealous. David wanted to reestablish proper worship of Jehovah at a central sanctuary in Israel. Sadly, David was doing what the Lord wanted, but the wrong way; then, he ceased to do what he was supposed to do because God objected to the way it was being done. Clearly, believers must discern both the *what* and the *how* in serving the Lord. What is done must be in obedience to Him, and how it is done must reflect His character.

May We Serve Christ!

June 18 – David Brings the Ark to Jerusalem
2 Samuel 6

The king was informed that the Lord had blessed Obed-Edom because the Ark resided in his home. This showed David that the Lord appreciated Obed-Edom's care of the Ark and that God did not oppose the relocation of the Ark. The king was reminded that standing aloof from the Ark (which represents God's presence among His people) caused the loss of His blessing, but approaching God in reverential respect and holiness prompted God's goodness.

Believers today must understand the same concept: to stand apart from God is death (spiritual separation) and to come into His presence wrongly causes the same. It is only by being sanctified in Christ, with sins cleansed by His blood, that we can enter God's presence with joy and have confidence of His acceptance.

David again led the nation to fetch the Ark, but this time the Ark was appropriately carried by the Levites. The priests were presenting burnt offerings of oxen and fattened sheep about every six paces along the route the Ark traveled. Exactly what distance this represents is unknown. It is ironic that on their first attempt, they had a new cart (picturing their disobedience), but no sacrifices (they did not worship), but on their second attempt, they had no cart, but offered their complete obedience and many sacrifices to the Lord. As we will see, the people's genuine adoration for God forged in obedience was the difference between failure and success – the same is true today!

Not only did the priests present many burnt offerings on makeshift altars as the Ark journeyed along, but also the king leading the procession was busy honoring the Lord as well: *"David danced before the Lord with all his might; and David was wearing a linen ephod"* (v. 14). The people were ecstatic over the sight; all Israel shouted and the trumpets blasted their exuberant approval.

The psalmist tells us that it is most appropriate for God's people to be cheerful in spirit and joyful in praise before Him (Ps. 149:2-4). The Ark was placed in the tabernacle that David had erected and when all the burnt and peace offerings were concluded, David blessed the people and sent them home. But he did not send them away empty-handed. Each person received bread, a piece of meat and a cake of raisins.

June 19 – David's Unchecked Lusting
2 Samuel 11

The Ammonites were still secure in their capital city of Rabbah (2 Sam. 10). Their punishment for insulting David's ambassadors and instigating a Syrian attack on Israel was still unsettled. With the winter months over, it was time to put Rabbah in siege, but this was a time-consuming venture, so the king tasked Joab with the effort. David, now likely in his late-forties chose to remain in Jerusalem instead of going to war. David suffers a mid-life crisis, so to speak, which will have severe and lingering ramifications for his family and the nation.

The king spent a leisurely afternoon in his bed. David arose from his afternoon siesta sometime after three o'clock and then strolled out on the flat roof of his house to view the city. The king saw a beautiful woman bathing and inquired about her. It would have been unfitting for a woman of the Ancient East to bathe in an open court so that anyone could see her from a rooftop. Because of her lack of feminine modesty, someone did see her – the king. Proverbs 7 teaches us that the sexual sin of the woman is *to lure* and of the man is *to follow*.

Whether Bathsheba was merely indiscrete or flaunting herself is unknown. Regardless, the lion's share of guilt falls squarely on the one God put into authority and who was to represent God's character in executing his royal office, David. A lusting David inquires about the woman he has seen bathing. He learns that her name is Bathsheba, and that she is the wife of Uriah the Hittite, one of his soldiers. This meant that David could not marry the woman. It was likely that a few days had passed since the initial lustful impulse, but the king chose not to extinguish his cravings which he knew were against God's will.

If David had been at Rabbah fighting the Lord's battle, then his eye would have never rested on the object which the devil hoped to entice him with. This is a good reminder for us to be vigilant in what we should be doing, so that we have no time to do what we ought not to be doing. If our hearts are filled with Christ, there will be no room for what does not have His approval. It is only when Satan prompts us to desire something apart from Christ that he can succeed in drawing us after his things. Satisfaction in Christ is the best defense against sin and keeping busy in His work is a proven means of avoiding sin's opportunities.

June 20 – David's Great Sin
2 Samuel 11

The king sent messengers to bring Bathsheba to him. Regrettably, David had sexual relations with Uriah's wife. Afterwards Bathsheba purified herself (bathed, per Lev. 15:18) and returned home in the evening. Ironically, she ignored God's command against adultery and so was punishable by death (for she did not cry out for help), but yet observed the ceremonial aspects of the Law because she desired to be clean before the Lord! But in God's sight, neither of them was *clean*. They were defiled by gross sin for which there was no Levitical offering by which one could be reconciled to God. A few weeks later Bathsheba informed David that she was pregnant with his child.

Being the granddaughter of David's counselor Ahithophel (23:34) and being childless (i.e., she likely had not been married long) meant that Bathsheba was likely some thirty years younger than the king. Her younger age, and the king's status as a great man, may explain why she consented to the adulterous rendezvous. Although a chaste married woman, perhaps she thought that yielding to such a renowned king would not be a sin. Yet David knew what he was doing was wrong and God would hold him accountable for abusing His authority.

David's folly and sin abound in this chapter. First, he neglected the business of suppressing the Lord's enemies as he had been personally tasked to do (5:2). Second, the king did not consult the Lord as to who should lead the troops against Ammon. Third, he became slothful – something we have not previously witnessed in David. Fourth, he is guilty of a wandering eye and lusting for what displeases God. Fifth, he used his power to lead a subordinate into sin. Sixth, he committed adultery. Seventh, instead of admitting his sin, he tried to cover it up. Eighth, he had Bathsheba's husband, one of his valiant servants, murdered. Ninth, the king made Joab an accomplice to the murder of Uriah. Tenth, other faithful soldiers died with Uriah in David's cover-up scheme. Eleventh, David used his position to steal what was not his; David took what belong to Uriah, Bathsheba (Matt. 1:6). Twelfth, David carried on as if God had not noticed what he had done or would not act against him! David shows us that neglecting what is important to God eventually leads to the rejection of His Word also.

Daily Devotions

June 21 – Miserable for a Year
2 Samuel 12

God sent the prophet Nathan to confront David over his adultery with Bathsheba and the murder of her husband to conceal it. David, like our first parents after they ate the forbidden fruit, tried to hide from God. This meant that Nathan's sudden arrival at the palace was unsolicited, unannounced, and probably unwelcomed. Might there be more Nathan-like believers in the Church today who will not ignore those believers spiritually suffocating in sin. It takes real courage to lovingly rebuke those we love despite their social or religious rank. May we stand in the light of God's truth and *"have no fellowship with the unfruitful works of darkness, but rather expose them"* (Eph. 5:11).

Nathan loved David and in obedience to God's command sought to restore David by confronting him over his sin. The prophet spoke in a parable, and spiritually despondent David had no clue that he was the actual perpetrator in the story. Nathan told the king about a wealthy man who seized a poor man's only ewe lamb, which he greatly treasured, in order to serve a meal to an unexpected visitor. David was enraged over the tale. Although the king was himself under the heavy yoke of sin, David quickly judged the lesser offense of another by saying the wealthy man deserved death.

The prophet used this story to express God's anger over David's sin. David had abused the power of the throne which God had given him; thus, stern judgment would be forthcoming. David's anger aroused by Nathan's story was just, but hypocritical. David upheld the Law's fourfold-restitution for stealing, but also demanded the death of the guilty party; yet, under the Law, the consequences for David's more grievous sin was the death penalty. David was enraged at the injustice done to the poor man, yet he had committed a much worse offense and had remained unrepentant for about a year. It demonstrates how easy it is for sin to cloud rational thinking.

When we are not in communion with God, our anger has the greatest opportunity to be provoked and to result in ungodly behavior. Unknowingly, David had pronounced his own sentence – he deserved death! It is at this moment that we, in our mind's eye, see the brave prophet raising his finger and pointing it at David to voice God's indictment: "You are the man!"

May We Serve Christ!

June 22 – Confession and Repentance
2 Samuel 12

The prophet's rebuke is carefully crafted. He first acknowledges the goodness of God to David before identifying David's crimes against God: *"I anointed you ... I delivered you ... I gave you ... and gave you ... I also would have given you much more!"* (vv. 8-9). The indictment contrasts God's manifold blessings with the unreasonableness of David's wicked behavior: *"Why have you despised the commandment of the Lord, to do evil in His sight?"* (v. 9). The prophet then reveals the sordid details of David's covert and abhorrent crimes – nothing had escaped the attention of David's omniscient God.

In David's wretched spiritual state he was numb to his accountability for his own sin, even after Nathan aroused his sense of justice with the parable of the stolen lamb. Yet, when Nathan indicted David, *"You are the man"* the hidden sin was traced to its source and David instantly became a conscience-smitten, broken-hearted sinner before a holy God. All was revealed, there could be no more hiding and David confessed his sin against God.

Nathan's rebuke of David should remind us that, though others may not know our secret sins, God knows and we know all about them. *"Be sure your sin will find you out"* (Num. 32:23). Nathan also told David the cost of his sin, *"the sword shall never depart from your house"* ... *"I have raised up adversity against you"* ... *"I will take your wives"* from you and another will publicly defile them. We wonder what went through David's mind after hearing that his children would be a grief to him, his enemies would oppress him, and that another man would sexually assault his wives to shame him? He must have realized that a few moments of wanton pleasure was not worth the grave and enduring consequences to himself and his household. No doubt he wondered why he had preferred his sin over joyful fellowship with God.

As David affirmed to Nathan, the Law demanded that four lambs be given in restitution for a stolen lamb that had been killed (Ex. 22:1-2). David had stolen what was not his and had then killed Uriah, and God would exact from him the life of four of his own sons for that crime: Bathsheba's newborn son, Amnon, Absalom, and Adonijah. Sin always has a hidden price tag; it costs far more than we expect and has consequences that last a lot longer than we ever anticipated.

Daily Devotions

June 23 – Restoration with God – June 23
2 Samuel 12

When a child of God humbly and honestly confesses his or her sin, God is then able to put it away for good (1 Jn. 1:9). Indeed, Nathan avowed that the Lord had chosen to pass over David's sin, in that he would not die for his offenses. But then the prophet adds a painful "however." Because David's transgression had caused God's enemies to blaspheme Jehovah's name, Bathsheba's newborn son would die. After delivering God's message, the faithful prophet left the palace.

We wonder why the Lord permitted David to remain in his sin an entire year before sending Nathan to censure him. The answer is partly revealed in Psalm 32, for David informs us that he was miserable during this time (Ps. 31:9-10). Clearly, the Lord had been using David's wounded conscience and the lack of communion with Himself to break His servant. Our private sins are no secret to us or to the Lord and will be a burden to our souls until rightly dealt with. As foretold, David did receive unmerited forgiveness and was restored to God. He pens Psalms 32 and 51 to report the outcome of God's chastening.

In Psalm 31, although David did not know how God could forgive him, David knew by faith that his transgressions were forgiven (Ps. 32:1-2). David recalls the time he was silent in his sin and under God's heavy hand: he groaned deep in his bones day and night; he grew old and his vitality dried up as crops in a long summer's drought (Ps. 32:3-4). The way out of this pitiful spiritual condition was to confess his sin and ask for forgiveness (Ps. 32:5).

Given the outcome of his experience, David counsels others not to linger in denying their sin, but to get right with the Lord while He may be found, rather than being overwhelmed by the mighty waters (i.e., correction by calamity; Ps. 32:6). Having confessed his sin, David appreciated the Lord as his Hiding Place – God is a Refuge to those who trust in Him (Ps. 32:7).

Although under the Law the punishment of adultery and murder demanded David's death, God's righteousness would be upheld in executing judgment: he would lose four sons! Because of His covenant with David, God spared his life, but God's justice cost David dearly and his household never knew peace afterwards. No doubt as David looked back over his life, he greatly regretted his unchecked lusting.

May We Serve Christ!

June 24 – A Giant Falls
2 Samuel 21

These Philistine battles occurred just after the fall of Rabbah and the defeat of the Ammonites (1 Chron. 20:4-8). This would mean David was likely in his early fifties. The king led his men into battle again against the Philistines. David fought against a giant named Ishbi-Benob, who had a bronze spear weighing three hundred shekels and a new sword, who desired to kill David.

Seeing that David had become weary and was in trouble, Abishai rescued the king and killed the giant. While at times Abishai was rash, he did not exhibit the depraved tendencies of his brother Joab. Abishai's courage and loyalty to his king here are admirable, and confirms why his name is listed among David's mighty men. Age had affected David more than he realized.

His men were determined not to permit their king to return to the battlefield in the future, *"lest you quench the lamp of Israel"* (v. 17). They knew that David was God's anointed and represented His favor on the nation; if David died in battle, the nation would lose hope of God's blessings. Based on Romans 8:37 and James 4:6-8, Matthew Henry suggests an application for us to consider from David's example:

> David fainted, but he did not flee; though his strength failed him, he bravely kept his ground, and then God sent him help in the time of need, which, though brought him by his junior and inferior, he thankfully accepted, and, with a little recruiting, gained his point, and came off a conqueror. Christ, in his agonies, was strengthened by an angel. In spiritual conflicts, even strong saints sometimes wax faint; then Satan attacks them furiously, but those that stand their ground and resist him shall be relieved, and made more than conquerors.[9]

Though David was old, he did not desire to live out his final days in ease. Rather, he desired to do what he could to preserve and enhance the kingdom. God blessed him for his faithful diligence; consequently, despite some setbacks, David never lost a battle against his enemies. As he already had plenty of glory at his age, David's actions in this chapter were not for personal gain, but for the good of Israel. David had learned firsthand the repercussions of idleness and leisure when God still had a work for him to do. The king is determined not to repeat that mistake.

June 25 – The Bright and Mighty Messiah
2 Samuel 23

David, *the anointed of the God of Jacob*, wrote at least 73 of the 150 songs in Psalms. The first seven verses in this chapter contain the final inspired poem of *"the sweet psalmist of Israel"* (v. 1). In other words, David was the lovely one whom God enabled to sing Israel's songs of praise to Him. The Holy Spirit inspired David to write his songs, but verse 3 seems to indicate that the Rock of Israel spoke directly to David concerning the future of his family.

The Lord told David that the ideal king for His people would be perfectly just and would rule in utter awe and reverence for the Lord. When such a ruler reigned in Israel, it would be like a morning without clouds, such that the sun would reflect its radiance in every direction off the shimmering dew-soaked grass.

When the "Light of the World" does return to the earth, all will see the radiance of His divine beauty, His moral excellence, and His immense goodness. Christ's glory will shine out everywhere and will especially be reflected in His saints. Isaiah informs us that during the Kingdom Age a faithful remnant of the Jewish nation will be restored to Jehovah, and His light will reflect through Israel as a beacon to draw the nations to Jerusalem to worship: *Arise, shine; for your light has come! And the glory of the Lord is risen upon you. ... His glory will be seen upon you. The Gentiles shall come to your light, and kings to the brightness of your rising* (Isa. 60:1-3).

David realized that he was not the king God was speaking about, but rejoiced in God's eternal covenant that ensured that One of his descendants would be. He would properly order all things to make His people secure and to bless them with much increase. The coming Messiah would judge the sons of rebellion and would eliminate all unrighteousness from His glorious kingdom.

The king's "last [official] words" give us a delightful pattern to follow: David does not hide his shortcomings, error, and failures, or the painful consequences of such, but his heart is overcome with joyful thoughts of the coming kingdom. None of us is perfect in deed or thought, but the more our hearts are filled with the glory of Christ, the more our consciences will be unhindered to serve Him!

June 26 – David's Mighty Men
2 Samuel 23

At the end of his reign, David lists the men who had contributed most to his kingdom. In listing the names of his faithful warriors, David divided them into three classes. The three mightiest are listed first (Josheb-Basshebeth, Eleazar, and Shammah), then the second class (Abishai and Benaiah) and then the third class, "the thirty," over whom Asahel was chief. After addressing the feats of the first grouping of mighty men David tells a story of three of his mighty men who came to him while he was encamped in the cave of Adullam fighting the Philistines located in the Valley of Rephaim.

The Philistines either had control of David's hometown of Bethlehem or were well-positioned between David and Bethlehem. The king casually expressed his longing for a drink of water from the well in Bethlehem (i.e., he did not intend for anyone to take his request seriously).

Three men did hear David and desired to please their king. Without conferring with their commander, and at great risk to themselves, they broke through enemy lines, drew water from the well in Bethlehem and brought it to David. The king was so overcome by this gesture of loyalty that he poured the water out on the ground as a sacrifice to the Lord – it cost too much to drink and thus was deemed a worthy offering. Perhaps David also felt foolish for uttering vain words of an indulgent nature that risked the lives of his highly esteemed men. In either case, David would not gratify his palate knowing the peril that his soldiers had placed themselves in to retrieve the water. Yet, David was refreshed by their selfless gesture and thus he records their deed.

At the judgment seat of Christ, the Lord Jesus will likewise honor all who have honored Him with their lives (Rom. 14:10-12; 2 Cor. 5:10). Our wonderful Savior does not forget any act done in His name that is accomplished in His power! Then our faithfulness to Christ will be rewarded more than any honor that David could bestow on his devoted mighty men. Chapters 22 and 23 show us that David greatly appreciated two things at the end of his life: the faithfulness of God and the devotion of his faithful servants. Let us remember that the Lord Jesus, whom David often typifies, appreciates the same and will reward those who diligently seek Him (Heb. 11:6).

June 27 – David Numbers Israel
2 Samuel 24

The events of this chapter likely occur after David took Jerusalem from the Jebusites. David's kingdom was approaching its apex and would have been the most advantageous opportunity to arouse his pride. We learn in verse 1 that the Lord was already angry with His people (their sin is unknown) and would use David's foreknown sin of numbering Israel to reacquaint His people with His holy character.

David ordered Joab to conduct a nationwide census, but even carnal Joab rebuffed the idea as there was no good rationale for the effort, which meant it was motivated by the king's pride. Joab knew that David was to trust in the Lord not the numbers of his soldiers. God had prospered Israel as He deemed appropriate; hence, David could not boast in the size of his army. Gloating over God's blessings is not the same as resting in His sufficiency! Accordingly, may we all avoid the pitfall of numbering what we have in order to boast before others.

Nevertheless, David would not heed Joab's or his captains' objections in the matter and they departed to perform the census. It took Joab almost ten months to number the tribes, including those residing in the Transjordan. Joab returned to Jerusalem and reported the results to David: *"there were in Israel eight hundred thousand valiant men who drew the sword, and the men of Judah were five hundred thousand men"* (v. 9). 1 Chronicles 21 records a more exact tally which includes David's standing army of 288,000 men.

As soon as David heard the number, his conscience condemned him and he confessed his sin to the Lord. The Lord responded to this by sending the prophet Gad to him the next day with a choice of three disciplinary measures. Having already learned of God's mercy, David chooses to put the nation in the hands of the Lord and suffer His wrath – pestilence.

God's judgment from our standpoint seems extreme – 70,000 deaths because of the king's pride? But, let us remember that David is Israel's king, and that God absolutely hates pride (Prov. 6:17) and that a proud king stimulates the same in those he rules over. Moreover, the main emphasis at this juncture was God's anger already kindled against Israel. It was David's sin that opened the floodgates of wrath, but the people as a whole had added to the deluge.

June 28 – The Prayer of Jabez
1 Chronicles 6

Jabez's name means "sorrowful." Apparently, there was some adverse situation or hindering obstacle at the time of Jabez's birth that continued to afflict him afterwards. He desired the Lord to remove whatever it was:

> And Jabez called on the God of Israel saying, "Oh, that You would bless me indeed, and enlarge my territory, that Your hand would be with me, and that You would keep me from evil, that I may not cause pain!" So God granted him what he requested (1 Chron. 4:10).

Jabez petitioned the Lord for three things: enlargement of territory, closer intimacy with God, and preservation from evil. The land allotments bestowed on Israel's tribes in the book of Joshua were to pass down from generation to generation within the same tribe. This meant that an individual or clan could not increase their inheritance by buying or stealing from their brethren, but only by engaging and defeating the enemy. Accordingly, the Law prohibited Jabez from gaining land through financial acquisition; he could enlarge his territory through legal conquest (i.e., seizing land from those whom God said should be removed from the Promised Land).

To further advance the Kingdom of God today, believers must do more than entertain each other in conquered territories (i.e., their homes and church buildings). They must be willing to venture out beyond these safe havens and to storm the gates of Hell with the gospel message of Jesus Christ. The Lord is building His Church through the earnest efforts of His people to evangelize the lost. Let us never be satisfied with the status quo – may the Lord enlarge our capacity to serve Him as He enlarges His Church.

Jabez also asked the Lord, *"that Your hand might be with me."* Jabez wanted intimacy and close fellowship with God. And whenever there is someone who desires a closer fellowship with God, the Creator will be eager to reveal Himself in new and meaningful ways. As seen with Enoch years before Jabez, those who walk with God will benefit by God's companionship and protection from evil.

June 29 – The Sons of Korah
1 Chronicles 6

Most of us are not going to get too excited about reading a long list of names of people who died two to four thousand years ago. Yet, there are a number of applications embedded within Jewish genealogies which we can benefit from. The lineage of Levi's three sons Gershom, Kohath, and Merari is recorded in 1 Chronicles 6. The descendants of Korah are listed first (which includes the priestly line through Aaron).

Samuel's father, Elkanah, resided within the mountainous region of Ephraim in the town of Ramah (1 Sam. 1:1). Elkanah's genealogy (1 Chron. 6:22-37) indicates that he was the son of Jeroham, a descendant of the Levite Korah, who rebelled with others against the Aaronic priesthood in Numbers 16 (Jude 11). Though disengaged from active religious service, Elkanah's existence verifies the validity of Moses' statement after Korah and his household was judged: *"Nevertheless the children of Korah did not die"* (Num. 26:11).

Korah's sons were not self-assertive and chose to side with the Lord, rather than with their father when the call for separation came. This decision not only saved them from death, but is also honored in the Psalms. David wrote twenty of the psalms in Book 2 (Psalms 51-70), and seven of these are ascribed to or dedicated to "the sons of Korah" (Psalms 42, 44-49).

Understanding what happened in Numbers 16 gives much more meaning to Psalm 84:10: *"For a day in thy courts is better than a thousand. I would rather be a door keeper in the house of my God than to dwell in the tents of wickedness."* Indeed, descendants of Korah's sons Assir, Elkanah, and Ebiasaph went on to serve the Lord in the tabernacle and then at the temple in Jerusalem (1 Chron. 6:22-30). David actually appointed some of Korah's descendants as musicians to sing before the tabernacle once the Ark rested in (1 Chron. 6:37).

Paul instructs children to honor and obey their parents *"in the Lord"* (Eph. 6:1-4). The stipulation phrase, *"in the Lord,"* implies children are to serve their parents as unto the Lord in matters of righteousness, but not in matters of sin. The sons of Korah chose to stand with the Lord, rather than to side with their father who was rebelling against God, and, for that reason, they were spared judgment and then were honored by the Lord for generations to come.

June 30 – David's Farewell
1 Chronicles 28

The elderly king assembled Israel's various leaders at Jerusalem. David reminded them that he had wanted to build Jehovah a temple, but was prohibited from doing so because he had shed much blood over his lifetime. David reiterated that God had promised him an everlasting dynasty on the throne of Judah, and that the Lord had chosen his son Solomon to be Israel's next king and to build His temple. As long as Solomon was steadfast to observe God's Law, Jehovah promised to be a father to him and to establish and greatly bless his kingdom.

The king then charges his subjects to seek out and obey God's commandments so that they will be blessed in the land and have it for generations to come as a lasting inheritance. Likewise, David charged Solomon to remain loyal to God and faithful to the task that God had given him. If Solomon departed from the Lord, he would utterly fail to accomplish anything important for God, including the construction of the temple.

The charge is reminiscent of the Lord Jesus' parting charge to His disciples: *"I am the vine, you are the branches. He who abides in Me, and I in him, bears much fruit; for without Me you can do nothing"* (John 15:5). David then revealed the divinely inspired plans for the vestibule, the temple with its various chambers, and holy compartments, including the weights of gold and silver for the various holy articles. The king also confirmed the divisions of the priests and the Levites for all the work of the service of the house of the Lord, then added that all the information had come from the Lord.

David then issued a final charge to his son Solomon: *"Be strong and of good courage, and do it; do not fear nor be dismayed, for the Lord God – my God – will be with you. He will not leave you nor forsake you, until you have finished all the work..."* (v. 20). To assist Solomon in building God's house, David had secured peace throughout the region, had set aside a vast wealth of precious metals and building materials, had delivered God's specifications of all that was to be fashioned and built, plus he assembled a huge workforce and craftsmen to accomplish the task. Likewise, the Lord Jesus provides all we need to serve Him and He continues to labor with us from heaven to build up His spiritual temple on earth – the Church (Mark 16:20).

July 1 – The High Places
1 Kings 3

Before the judgeship of Samuel, the Ark had resided for about four centuries in the tabernacle pitched at Shiloh. Those loyal to Jehovah (e.g., Elkanah and Hannah) worshiped Him there (i.e., at the central sanctuary as decreed; Deut. 12:1-32). But this was not possible after the Ark had been captured by the Philistines, then relocated at Kiriath-Jearim after its return, and then taken to Jerusalem by David.

For over a century the Ark was separated from the tabernacle (i.e., its altars and other furnishings) so the Jews offered their sacrifices on high places throughout Israel. This was tolerated because technically there was no central sanctuary and the patriarchs had previously offered worship to the Lord in the high places. This explains why Solomon also offered sacrifices to Jehovah on the hills of Judah.

Obviously, without the Ark, some ceremonies, such as the Day of Atonement, could not be performed at all. Others, such as maintaining a lit Lampstand and presenting weekly showbread in the tabernacle at Nob and then later at Gibeon continued. By erecting the Lord's temple in Jerusalem, the central sanctuary would be again established as the only lawful place to offer the Levitical sacrifices (Lev. 17:3-4). Yet, offering sacrifices to God on high places remained a traditional practice in Israel until Hezekiah outlawed it almost three centuries later. In time, Israel began to adopt the pagan customs (often involving immorality) of the Canaanites who worshiped their gods and goddesses in the high places of Canaan and thereby angering the Lord (Isa. 57:4-5).

The Lord Jesus also commanded how and when His people are to gather to worship during the Church Age (Luke 22:19-20). The Corinthians learned this painful lesson in observing the Lord's Supper. The local church was obeying the Lord's command to break bread in remembrance of Him, but then changed the meeting into something it was not – a drunken and gluttonous love feast (1 Cor. 11:20-34).

While it may have been more convenient for the Jews to worship God at a nearby high place, the Lord cannot be honored by that which is rebellious to His expressed will. Believers should never adopt a the-end-justifies-the-means mentality in the work or worship of the Lord. It is God who sanctifies the means, or the end means nothing.

May We Serve Christ!

July 2 – The Queen of Sheba
1 Kings 10; 2 Chronicles 9

After hearing of Solomon's fame, the queen of Sheba (Yemen in Arabia) traveled nearly 1,200 miles to test his wisdom with hard questions. Solomon's mercantile navy operated along the Arabian coast and would have had contact with this influential Arabian kingdom. The queen's large caravan brought exceptional spices, gold in abundance, and precious stones as gifts for Solomon. Such spectacular presents corroborated her prestige and wealth.

The queen spoke with Solomon about all that was in her heart and he explicitly answered all of her questions expertly. Her interaction with Solomon was beyond anything she could have imagined. The king's incredible wisdom, immense wealth, enormous table provisions, and the incredible feats were all true. In fact, she concluded that the half had not been told to her.

One of the things that overwhelmed the Queen of Sheba was seeing Solomon's *"entryway by which he went up to the house of the Lord"* (2 Chron. 9:4). She was stunned to learn that the king had direct and private access to Jehovah's sanctuary. The king did not have to be concerned about his personal protection or public perception when coming before the Lord – he had the expedient opportunity to do so privately at any time. This access to God impressed the queen. The queen acknowledged that Israel was being blessed by God because He had put such a wise king on Israel's throne. This realization caused the queen of Sheba to extol Solomon's God.

Believers today also have a glorious and protected entrance before the Lord at any time; in fact, they are invited to come boldly to the throne of grace to receive mercy in time of need (Heb. 4:14-16). Christians do not have to travel to temples, shrines, mosques, synagogues, or even church buildings to have immediate access to God. May the lost be envious of the power and peace associated with such communion. Clearly, what believers have in Christ today transcends all Old Testament figures. Oh that the lost today might be in awe of our private and direct access to God through Christ (John 14:13-14). Our open access to God's throne should entice others, like the Queen of Sheba, to search out the truth for themselves and to want to know the God who has far more wealth, provisions, and wisdom than Solomon.

July 3 – Solomon Turns From the Lord
1 Kings 11

We are informed that Solomon had seven hundred wives and three hundred concubines, many of whom were foreign women from Moab, Ammon, Edom, Sidon, and included some Hittites and Pharaoh's daughter from Egypt. Regrettably, the next king of Judah, Solomon's son Rehoboam born to him by his Ammonite wife Naamah, would pursue wickedness (1 Kgs. 14:21-23). The writer then reiterates that Jewish men were forbidden to marry foreign women (1 Kgs. 11:2; Deut. 7:3-4). If Solomon knew that the Law of Moses prohibited Jews from marrying foreigners, why did he do it?

Many commentators believe that Solomon married foreign women to ensure peace with their nations and to obtain intelligence of the state of affairs in those countries. While this is possible, Matthew Henry suggests that the motive behind Solomon's marriages to foreigners was more likely lust: "I rather fear it was because the daughters of Israel were too grave and modest for him, and those foreigners pleased him with the looseness and wantonness of their dress, and air, and conversation."[10] Believers today fall into the same trap when they marry for sensual and not spiritual reasons.

Solomon should have heeded the warning he issued to his sons, that is, to keep away *"from the immoral woman, from the seductress who flatters with her words"* (Prov. 7:5); *"Do not let your heart turn aside to her ways, do not stray into her paths; for she has cast down many wounded, and all who were slain by her were strong men"* (Prov. 7:25-26). The king did not follow his own wisdom, but eventually fell prey to his own lusts. He also did not heed Moses' warning to future kings, *"neither shall he multiply wives for himself, lest his heart turn away"* (Deut. 17:17). The danger of many wives was in being emotionally drawn away from the Lord, who was to remain the king's first love.

In his autumn years, he trusted in his own strength and wealth and was led by unchecked lust, not by God's Word. Each of us has a free will to choose to follow God or not. Solomon's life illustrates that we are more inclined to rely on the Lord and obey Him when in lack or distress. It should be no surprise then that the Lord often uses various trials to both mature His people to Christ-likeness and to keep them near to Him.

July 4 – The Man of God Confronts the King
1 Kings 13

The Lord sent an unnamed prophet, a man of God from Judah, to Bethel to rebuke Jeroboam for his idolatry. The fact that his name is not recorded in Scripture suggests that his work for the Lord was more important than the recognition of men. Paul acknowledged that this is a good principle to govern how we serve the Lord: *"And whatever you do in word or deed, do all in the name of the Lord Jesus, giving thanks to God the Father through Him"* (Col. 3:17). Being heavenly-minded ensures our earthly good.

After arriving at Bethel, the man of God found Jeroboam standing by the pagan altar preparing to burn incense. The prophet delivered this message against him and his altar. There were both immediate and future aspects to the prophet's decree. He had foretold the name of a future king and what he would do nearly three centuries before it would happen! Godly Josiah, the king of Judah from 640 to 609 B.C., destroyed the altar at Bethel's shrine and slaughtered the pagan priests there to fulfill this prophecy (2 Kgs. 23:15-20).

This message infuriated the king, who stretched out his hand to point to the man he wanted his guards to arrest, but two things immediately occurred: First, Jeroboam's hand and perhaps his arm immediately withered and became fully paralyzed. Second, as the prophet had just proclaimed, the altar split apart and the ashes poured out of it – this sign from God validated the prophet's message. The king wisely chose not to resist the prophet further and asked him to petition the Lord to restore his hand. The prophet did so and the king's hand was fully restored.

In appreciation, Jeroboam requested that the man of God come to his home so that he could be refreshed and rewarded. Though a kind gesture, the prophet declined the invitation as he had been commanded by the Lord not to eat or drink during his mission into Israel. He was also to return to Judah a different way than he had arrived at Bethel. The prophet said it was better to obey the Lord even if the king offered him half of his kingdom, thus the prophet departed for home a different route. The scene shows us that the Lord has no tolerance for false religion, and the people of God are not to have any association with it, including all of its social traditions that Christians so readily embrace!

July 5 – A Lion Confronts the Man of God
1 Kings 13

So far, the man of God has completely obeyed the Lord and therefore his ministry has been fruitful, despite confronting the most powerful man in Israel. But there was an old prophet living in Bethel, who, through his sons, found out about the prophet's message and what happened at the altar that day. The old prophet went seeking the man and soon found him resting under the shade of an oak tree. The old prophet then invited the Judean prophet to come to his home and eat with him, but he refused, quoting again the instructions he had been given by the Lord. Eager to have such an esteemed guest in his home, the old prophet resorted to a falsehood; he stated that he was a prophet also and the God had told him to bring him back to his home for a meal. Regrettably, the faithful prophet believed the lie and returned to the old prophet's home and ate bread and drank water in his house.

All too often in Christendom today we hear the same kind of language, "I too am a prophet," being bantered about by those who want to justify their bad behavior. This lie might be spotted by statements such as: "Well, that is open to interpretation." "Everyone understands the Bible a little differently." "God will not judge me if I am wrong because He knows my heart." Scripture presents God's will in only one way and it is to be understood in only one way.

Although the old prophet had not spoken for the Lord earlier, God does use him to deliver a message of judgment against the Judean prophet now – because he had not obeyed God's Word, he would not be buried in the tomb of his fathers. This message implied that his death was imminent – he would not make it home. The old prophet then saddled his donkey for the Judean prophet and sent him on his way, but as he was journeying back to Judah, a lion slew him on the side of the road. A lion attacking a lone traveler was a real danger in those days, but to show that the death of the prophet was divine judgment instead of a naturally occurring event, both the lion and the donkey stood by the dead man's body.

Hearing of the uncanny scene, the old prophet searched for and found the body of his previous guest (with the lion and donkey still present). He then buried the corpse in his own tomb, thus fulfilling the prophecy he had uttered after having deceived the man of God to sin.

May We Serve Christ!

July 6 – Reviving Under King Asa
1 Kings 15; 2 Chronicles 14

Abijah's son Asa ruled Judah for forty-one years; he enjoyed peace for the first ten years of his reign. Evil Abijah had to die before revival could come under Asa. Likewise, believers must reckon, practically speaking, that the old man (who we were in Adam) was crucified with Christ. Only then can we live out the resurrection life of the Last Adam.

Both historians write favorably of Asa: *"Asa did what was right in the eyes of the Lord, as did his father David"* (1 Kgs. 15:11). *"Asa did what was good and right in the eyes of the Lord"* (2 Chron. 14:2). Although Asa was not a prophet, a psalmist, a writer, or a conqueror like David, his heart was right with the Lord and he consistently worshiped the Lord as the Law commanded. Asa is one of five Judean kings who stands out among the rest as being honorable. Judah had suffered three decades of wickedness under her last three kings, so Asa's godly character was a breath of fresh air for the Southern Kingdom. He was zealous for the Lord in his determination to spiritually purify Judah.

He removed the altars of foreign gods and their sacred pillars and images from Judah and banished the sodomites (i.e., paganized homosexuals). He removed his grandmother from being queen and destroyed her image of Asherah. The king's reforms were wide sweeping and his godliness caused his countrymen to follow after the Lord. Accordingly, the Lord blessed Judah with His peace which brought a deep serenity to the land. C. A. Coates comments on the recovery achieved during Asa's reign and what it would typify today:

> There was the unsparing judgment of evil and what was idolatrous. He did not follow his father or his grandmother but... David, so that we get dedicated things brought into the house of Jehovah, silver, gold and vessels. The silver speaks of redemption as that which is brought back to God in the value of the death of Christ. Gold expresses our new creation in Christ, and generally, all things of God. Vessels suggest persons dedicated so that God has His portion in them.[11]

Indeed, Christendom today must rediscover the value of Calvary, the necessity of becoming a new creation in Christ, and then a consecrated vessel for His honor and glory!

Daily Devotions

July 7 – Declining Under King Asa
1 Kings 15; 2 Chronicles 16

About twenty years into Asa's reign, Baasha king of Israel began fortifying the city of Ramah in Benjamin's territory as a staging area from which to attack Judah. After Asa became aware of Baasha's military buildup, he took silver and gold from the temple and the king's treasury and sent it to Ben-Hadad king of Syria. This bribe was to prompt Ben-Hadad to break his treaty with Israel, so that Baasha would withdraw from Judah's northern border. Asa did not call on the Lord for help; rather he relied on his own ingenuity to resolve the threat.

Asa did persuade Ben-Hadad to attack Israel's northern cities; this caused Baasha to withdraw from Ramah in the south to defend this new threat. Asa then dismantled Baasha's fortification in Ramah and used the materials to fortify Geba and Mizpah. These two strongholds just south of Israel's border would prevent any further military buildup on Judah's border. While Asa's plan did resolve the ominous situation, the Lord was not honored by it.

Defrauding God to enrich those who oppose Him will always earn God's rebuke. Nor should believers today use what the Lord has graciously given us (time, money, resources, spiritual gifts, intellect, etc.) to strengthen the devil's rebellion against the Lord. Asa had valued Syria's assistance above the Lord's help, so He sent the prophet Hanani to rebuke the king.

Hanani reminded Asa how the Lord had previously overcome the Ethiopians, a much greater threat to Judah than Israel had been. The prophet also reminded Asa that Syria was his true enemy, but through his manipulation of the circumstances, he had strengthened Syria. Finally, Hanani told Asa that because he had behaved foolishly, he would suffer wars during the remainder of his reign. Asa was enraged by Hanani's message and imprisoned the prophet.

Most of Asa's long reign was marked by faithfulness and devotion, and the Lord consequently prospered Judah under his leadership. However, in his final years, Asa became self-sufficient and the nation suffered. Asa became severely diseased in his feet in the thirty-ninth year of his reign, but he only sought his physicians for healing, not the Lord. Asa shows us that there is a difference between merely being devoted to the Lord and seeking His presence in all that we do.

July 8 – Elijah's Drought
1 Kings 17

We are now introduced to one of the premier prophets, Elijah the Tishbite from Gilead. He was called to the challenging ministry of upholding the name of Jehovah before an idolatrous people. There is no record of the Lord speaking to Elijah prior to his encounter with Ahab. But James tells us that Elijah spoke much with God before being used by Him in ministry: *"Elijah was a man with a nature like ours, and he prayed earnestly that it would not rain; and it did not rain on the land for three years and six months"* (Jas. 5:17). Elijah shows us that before believers can engage in effective public service, they first must have private exercise before God in prayer.

Ministry that profits others must commence in this fashion, otherwise we do not experience and learn from the Lord what is necessary to mature our faith. Ministry not fostered in prayer is merely an academic exercise which will lack God's power and will stymie our spiritual growth. Elijah first lamented Israel's state before the Lord; then he went to the palace of the wicked.

Elijah was a godly man who was emboldened to confront the king because he keenly felt the scorn Ahab had caused to Jehovah's name. But before he could exert a powerful influence on others, he first had to seek the Lord privately to escape himself, that is, his own expectations and fleshly devices. His time in God's presence purged whatever would hinder his zeal for God or would divert him from God's purposes.

Whether Elijah was called directly by God as a prophet, or brought into that office because of his zeal for God (like Phineas into the high priesthood) we are not told. Regardless, Elijah abruptly faced the king and announced: *"As the Lord God of Israel lives, before whom I stand, there shall not be dew nor rain these years, except at my word"* (v. 1). This was a bold move, which would normally have resulted in Elijah's arrest, but no doubt the court was somewhat stunned by his curt decree and by Elijah's prompt departure.

The long drought would be the first of seven miracles instigated by Elijah to declare the power of Jehovah's name to depraved Israel. The Lord then directed His brave prophet to retreat to the Brook Cherith on the east side of the Jordan River. This would be a safe location and the Lord would care for his needs.

July 9 – Elijah Drinks From His Own Ministry
1 Kings 17

Elijah obeyed the Lord and journeyed to Cherith. There the ravens brought him bread and meat morning and evening until the brook dried up because of the drought. As was often the case for prophets, Elijah drank from his own ministry and suffered with God's covenant people in their rebellion, though he was not personally a part of it.

After the brook dried up, *"the word of the Lord"* again came to Elijah. Elijah, who had no resources of his own, had to be completely reliant on the Lord's care and His word to carry him through the trial. Dependence and obedience mark the servants that God uses to exalt His name! How could Elijah later charge his countrymen at Carmel, *"If the Lord be God, follow Him,"* if he himself was defying God's Word?

The Lord commanded His prophet to travel about ninety miles north-northwest to the Phoenician town of Zarephath. The Lord had commanded a widow in that town to care for him. Luke 4:25 indicates that Elijah stayed in Israel (in Gilead) for the first six months of the drought and then remained at Zarephath for the next three years.

The Lord's instructions would have been distasteful to Elijah for several reasons. First, it was a long journey and he was without water. Second, the Lord was directing him to reside with unclean people (Gentiles) and in a pagan town. Third, his journey would take him through northern Israel, the jurisdiction of Ahab, who wanted to find and kill him. Fourth, living with a poor Sidonian widow did not sound very appealing; no doubt she was barely surviving the drought herself.

Despite all the reasonable objections Elijah might have had, he chose to obey the Lord. One of the lovely things about the providential care of the Lord is that He is quite able to chasten an entire nation for rebellion, while also benefitting and edifying individuals through the same experience. God was as concerned about refining His prophet as He was about dealing with idolatrous Israel. He also was concerned about a poor Gentile widow in Zarephath who also needed to experience His goodness and mercy. It is then no accident that Elijah's new home, Zarephath, means "refinement." The Lord would use the lowliest means, unclean birds and an unclean woman (a poor Gentile widow) to both provide for and teach His prophet important lessons. What a blessing to be in the care of an omniscient, gracious Teacher!

July 10 – God Claims Little to Give Much
1 Kings 17

When Elijah arrived at the gate of Zarephath, he found a widow gathering a few sticks with which to kindle a fire. He called her and asked, *"Please bring me a little water in a cup, that I may drink"* (v. 10). As she was departing to get the water, Elijah added, *"Please bring me a morsel of bread in your hand"* (v. 11). The harsh conditions of the drought are evident in Elijah's meager request for *a little* water and *a morsel* of bread. The woman's response to Elijah indicates discernment as to his identity: *"As the Lord your God lives"* (v. 12). Elijah's attire and facial hair would have identified him as a Jew.

The Lord had already told her he was coming and that she was to care for him, yet, she did not know how for the sum of her provisions included a handful of flour and a little oil. It was just enough to bake one cake. The widow believed that this would be her and her son's last meal. But the Lord had an entirely different plan for her future.

Elijah told her not to fear and then explained to her the solution. She was to use what she had to bake him a cake first and then she was to bake some for herself and son, for God would ensure that her jar of oil and bin of flour never went empty. Elijah demanded that her provisions be dispersed to him first; this meant that God was claiming the last of what she had. If she obeyed, then God would bless all of them! It was her choice: would she trust the word of a man she had just met whose God she did not know with all the food she had remaining in her house? The Lord had shown her that His word was reliable by foretelling her of Elijah's arrival. Despite his unreasonable request, she chose to obey the prophet's word and give up what little she had.

What a surprise it must have been to return to the barrel afterwards to find flour in it and also oil in the jar. She then made bread for herself and her son to eat. And such was her experience during the entire drought – she scraped the bottom of the barrel for their daily food and poured out the oil in the jar, but neither the barrel nor the jar remained empty. The Lord did not fill the barrel or the jar, for then she would not have had the daily thrill of discovering God's new and daily provision for them. Day by day she was learning about Elijah's God and His goodness. What a lovely way to journey through life! "He whose heart is kind beyond all measure gives each day what He deems best."

July 11 – The First Resurrection
1 Kings 17

After many days, the Lord permitted another challenge in the life of the widow; her son became ill and died. She charged Elijah harshly over the matter: *"What have I to do with you, O man of God? Have you come to me to bring my sin to remembrance, and to kill my son?"* (v. 18). Because she referred to a particular sin brought to memory by the death of her son, and not her sins in general, it is possible that she had committed a similar abhorrent sin previously (e.g., sacrificing a child to Baal in an attempt to resolve their difficulties).

Earlier the Lord had put His claim on all the remaining meal and oil she possessed. Now He lays claim to the most precious object of her affections – her only child. If God had merely provided for the widow's daily needs through the long famine, the widow would not have been prompted to consider her sin. The Lord knows how best to reach us where we are and to lay claim to what will make us aware of our need and His solution for it. Through her agony, the widow would learn what we also must realize to be most blessed: God alone is to be our first love and our only confidence in life. Those redeemed by Christ's blood are fully His (1 Cor. 6:19-20). As we observe the death of the widow's son, may we realize God's claim on us too and never permit our love for another to obstruct our obedience and devotion to Christ!

The widow had already experienced the painful loss of her husband and the deaths of one or more children. She might conclude that Jehovah was no better than the gods of her people and, therefore, there was no reason to continue living. Elijah told the widow to give him her son. He took him to an upper chamber and laid him on his own bed. He cried out to the Lord three times to revive the child while stretching his body out over the boy.

Elijah's faith is astounding in that he is requesting the Lord to do something never witnessed before – resurrection. The Lord had promised to sustain him through the widow's hand for the duration of the entire drought; therefore, she must have a reason to keep living. The Lord honored Elijah's request and the child revived. What a joy it was for the prophet to lead the child downstairs and give him to his grieving mother and say, *"See, your son lives!"* He was thus implying that nothing was too hard for his God.

July 12 – Obadiah Needs Direction
1 Kings 18

In the third year of the drought, the Lord directed Elijah to deliver a message to King Ahab – the drought was coming to an end. Previously, the Lord had commanded Elijah to go to the Brook Cherith and then to Zarephath; now he is to present himself before Ahab. Elijah's example is a good one to follow, whether going or coming, showing or hiding – the Lord should be obeyed no matter the cost. As a result, Elijah understands his course, while bewildered Obadiah must be pointed in the right way by the one openly walking with the Lord.

The famine was exceptionally severe in Samaria and threatened to wipe out all the livestock in the land. Ahab orders the steward of his household affairs, Obadiah, to search everywhere for brooks, springs, and any remaining grass that might preserve their livestock, horses, and mules. Though his master was entrenched in idolatry, Obadiah still feared the Lord greatly. He risked his life by secretly caring for and hiding one hundred of the Lord's prophets in two caves to protect them from Queen Jezebel's wrath. However, his close association with evil prevented him from seeing the spectacular in his life.

Believers are to remain in their callings and where God places them in the world (Matt. 13:36-43; 1 Cor. 7:20). Yet, the more believers openly associate with worldlings instead of with the Lord, their potential to represent Him and achieve great things in His name is also diminished. Hence, God used Obadiah to do some good, and Elijah to do much good.

Obadiah must have headed north from Samaria, because he suddenly met Elijah traveling southward from Zarephath. Obadiah recognized Elijah and fell on his face in disbelief. The prophet had a message for Obadiah's master; he was to return to Ahab and tell him that Elijah wanted to meet with him. Obadiah did not want to deliver this message to Ahab because the king had unsuccessfully searched Israel and the surrounding kingdoms to locate Elijah. Obadiah feared that if he delivered the message and the Lord directed Elijah elsewhere, that the king would kill him. Yet, Obadiah was a God-fearing man, so when Elijah vowed in the name of the Lord that he would present himself before Ahab that very day, Obadiah agreed to deliver Elijah's message. He now knew the right way to go!

July 13 – Who is the Troubler of Israel?
1 Kings 18

Ahab did come to meet Elijah and, when he saw him, said, *"Is that you, O troubler of Israel?"* (vv. 16-17). Ahab was distressed over the consequences of his sin, but not grieved because of it, so the prophet set the matter straight and challenged Ahab to a contest on Carmel:

> *I have not troubled Israel, but you ... in that you have forsaken the commandments of the Lord and have followed the Baals. Now therefore, send and gather all Israel to me on Mount Carmel, the four hundred and fifty prophets of Baal, and the four hundred prophets of Asherah, who eat at Jezebel's table* (vv. 18-19).

The nation could not continue much longer under the circumstances of the drought, so Ahab accepted Elijah's challenge. Elijah was not the troublemaker of Israel, but in faithful obedience to God's Word would stand against the one who was – Ahab. We see the same dynamic occurring today when a believer is willing to speak out against the life-strangling false doctrine and human traditions which have crept into the Church. The one causing the unrest is regarded by those settled in corrupt religion as a "troubler" of the Church. As we shall soon witness, fire fell from heaven on the water-soaked, sacrifice-laden altar on Carmel to prove God's authority and power to His covenant people. May the Holy Spirit raise up many more such *troublers* today that the power and authority of Jesus Christ might be known in His Church.

Ahab summoned Israel and the 450 prophets of Baal to come to Mount Carmel for the showdown; however, Jezebel's 400 prophets of Asherah remained in Jezreel. Elijah reproved the people, *"How long will you falter between two opinions? If the Lord is God, follow Him; but if Baal, follow him,"* but the people did not answer him (v. 21). Because he was outnumbered 450 to 1 by the prophets of Baal, Elijah was offering them more than a fair test to prove who ruled Israel – Baal or Jehovah. Baal's prophets were to prepare an altar, a bull for sacrifice, and then call on Baal to bring fire down from heaven to consume the sacrifice – no human was to put fire to the wood. Elijah would do the same in the name of Jehovah. The one who answered from heaven with fire would be proven to be the God of Israel.

May We Serve Christ!

July 14 – Victory on Mount Carmel
1 Kings 18

After confirming the rules of the challenge to the prophets of Baal, he gave them first choice of the two bulls to be offered. The prophets of Baal finished their altar, put their sacrifice on it and began calling on Baal to honor their request of sending fire down from heaven to consume their sacrifice. The prophets implored Baal all morning, but there was no answer, so they began leaping about their altar to entice Baal to respond. At noon Elijah mocked them, telling them they needed to cry louder for Baal might be meditating, or busy, or on a journey, or perhaps sleeping and needed to be awakened.

The ridicule of Elijah prompted the prophets of Baal to cry out all the louder as they cut themselves until the blood gushed out. Yet, after six hours of chanting, crying, and cutting, Baal had done nothing. So, at the time of the evening sacrifice Elijah called the people to come near. The people had probably moved away from the altar of Baal because of the bloody and grotesque scene. Elijah then repaired a broken down altar of the Lord that was there by putting in place twelve stones, thus showing the unity of Israel's twelve tribes in the matter of worship.

Elijah then carved a trench about the altar deep enough to hold two to four gallons. Next, Elijah put the wood in order, divided the bull, and put portions of it on the wood. He then instructed the people to fill four waterpots with water and pour each over the sacrifice on the wood and then to repeat the process two more times.

Though it was a huge effort to go down to the Brook Kishon to fetch the water the people obeyed Elijah. The water ran down the sacrifice and altar such that it filled the surrounding trench. It is not reasonable to soak a sacrifice for a burnt offering with water; this would further accentuate the miracle. What God was about to do would defy all physical laws of nature.

Unlike Baal who was unavailable, Jehovah heard his prophet and immediately responded to Elijah's prayer. Fire came down from heaven and consumed not just the sacrifice and wood, but also the stones, the dust, and the water in the trench. When the people saw this spectacular miracle, they immediately fell on their faces and declared, *"The Lord, He is God! The Lord, He is God!"* (v. 39). Likewise, it is impossible for us to serve a God that we do not know.

July 15 – Pagan Prophets and the Drought End Together
1 Kings 18

After hearing their profession of Jehovah as God, it was time to deal with the phony prophets. Elijah commanded that Baal's prophets be seized, taken down to the Brook Kishon and executed – all 450 prophets were killed. Just hours earlier the people would have been afraid to offend a prophet of Baal, but after realizing that Jehovah was God, they did not fear the one proven to be weaker than Jehovah.

Elijah then told Ahab to eat and drink without delay, for there was an abundance of rain coming. Ahab did so while Elijah journeyed to the top of Carmel. There he bowed down on his knees and put his face to the ground and asked his servant to look towards the sea to determine if there was a storm coming. The servant responded, *"There is nothing"* (v. 43). Elijah told his servant to look towards the sea six more times, and on the seventh time he said, *"There is a cloud, as small as a man's hand, rising out of the sea!"* Elijah told his servant to quickly go to Ahab and warn him to mount his chariot and get off the mountain before the rain prevented his return to Jezreel.

His servant departed and delivered this message to Ahab. In the meantime the sky blackened, the wind blew, and heavy rain began to pour down on the mount. Ahab heeded the prophet's warning and rode ahead of the storm back to Jezreel (almost 25 miles to the east-southeast of Mount Carmel; v. 45). The hand of the Lord came upon Elijah and he girded up his loins and ran to Jezreel, arriving at the city's entrance before Ahab did.

To demonstrate God's power, Elijah had commanded a long drought, foretold its end, called fire down from heaven to consume a sacrifice, and ran a marathon at a speed faster than a chariot drawn by horses. For three and a half years Elijah had suffered along with Israel because of their idolatry, but now, through awesome demonstrations of God's power, the people knew that Jehovah was the true God of Israel. He longed for the revival that started at Carmel to spread throughout Israel. Elijah sets a great example for us to follow: He is before the Lord, hears His word, obeys Him, lives in dependence on Him, and is not desirous of personal gain or fame and the Lord used him greatly!

July 16 – Elijah Despairs
1 Kings 19

Elijah yearned for spiritual revival to sweep through Israel. He waited at Jezreel's gate to see how evil Jezebel would respond to the news about what had happened at Carmel. Amazingly, even after all that he has witnessed, Ahab takes no leadership role whatsoever in the matter, but merely informs Jezebel about the death of Baal's prophets. He is concerned for temporal things only; true, his prophets were dead, but the drought was over and thus he was content. What was Jehovah or Baal to him, as long as he could eat, drink, and be merry?

Jezebel, on the other hand, was infuriated by the news, and vowed to take Elijah's life within the next day. Her response discouraged Elijah. He had already suffered much in fulfilling his prophetic ministry and now, instead of revival sweeping through Israel, there was to be persecution. The text reads, *"when he saw that"* (v. 3), meaning when he understood the hopeless situation in Israel was not changing, he fled.

Ahab had previously searched everywhere to find and arrest Elijah, so being a wanted man was no new thing for this prophet. In running away, Elijah seemed to be more motivated by discouragement than by fear for his personal well-being. Elijah surmised that his entire ministry had been a failure and that he was the only prophet of God remaining.

The situation seemed hopeless and he just wanted to run away and give up. Such a retreat occurs when believers get caught up with their circumstances instead of resting in God and His Word. Elijah had bravely withstood Ahab, his idolatrous countrymen, and 450 false prophets, but now the threat from one woman daunted him.

Any of God's people can suffer this type of despair – "spiritual depression." We all tend to have expectations for our ministries, and when these are not attained, we can become disheartened, even to the point of not wanting to go any further. We forget that God is sovereign and is working sextillions of situations all at once for His glory, meaning that we may be required to suffer so that God may accomplish the greater good of His foreordained design. God's timing, not ours, is always perfect.

It is natural for us to want to escape trials before God's best is achieved in us; however, it is spiritual to wait with God until He either removes the difficulty or removes us from it (Phil. 1:23-25).

July 17 – Elijah Bolts
1 Kings 19

The prophet hurried to the far southern border of Judah, Beersheba, and left his servant there. He then journeyed another day south into the Negev desert and, being exhausted and discouraged, rested under a broom tree and asked the Lord that he might die: *"It is enough! Now, Lord, take my life, for I am no better than my fathers!"* (v. 4). Although Elijah was not very rational at this point, he was correct on one point – he was no better than his fathers!

Though God's prophet, Elijah was flesh and blood, with the same nature as his fathers and, as James states, us too: *"Elijah was a man with a nature like ours"* (Jas. 5:1). Without experiencing the Lord's grace, we too are no different than our fathers. When ensnared by despair, we also will be prone to isolate ourselves from God's servants, to collapse under a tree in despondency, or try to hide in the dark cave of seclusion and self-pity.

The Lord chose to disregard Elijah's prayer because He was not finished with His servant. As the Lord's servants, we are permitted to remain on this earth for only one reason – to do God's bidding and make Him look good! All that we do must be for His glory: *"Whatever you do, do all to the glory of God"* (1 Cor. 10:31). *"For none of us lives to himself, and no one dies to himself. For if we live, we live to the Lord; and if we die, we die to the Lord. Therefore, whether we live or die, we are the Lord's"* (Rom. 14:7-8). Though Elijah was discouraged, it was not his time to die.

Accordingly, the Angel of the Lord ministered to him twice to strengthen him for the long journey down to Mount Horeb. William MacDonald observes that God's treatment for severe depression was *"rest; food and drink; more rest; more food and drink."* Of course, being soothed and encouraged by God's Word was mixed in with resting the mind and nourishing the body.

At Horeb (Sinai), God would restore His servant Elijah to fruitfulness again – His solution would be to yoke despondent Elijah with younger Elisha in a mentoring relationship. After Elijah ate and drank what was provided for him by the Lord, we read that *"he went in the strength of that food forty days and forty nights as far as Horeb, the mountain of God"* (v. 8).

May We Serve Christ!

July 18 – Elijah Alone
1 Kings 19

In the provision of the Lord's food, Elijah arrived at Mount Horeb and took up residence in a cave. The Lord spoke to Elijah while he was in the cave, *"What are you doing here, Elijah?"* (v. 9). In his depressed condition, Elijah responded to the Lord as a defeated and isolated warrior of Jehovah: *"I have been very zealous for the Lord God of hosts; for the children of Israel have forsaken Your covenant, torn down Your altars, and killed Your prophets with the sword. I alone am left; and they seek to take my life"* (v. 10). On Carmel, Elijah had vindicated Jehovah's name in an effort to convert his brethren; at Horeb, Elijah vindicates himself and accuses his brethren.

The same is true today. When a believer disregards his ministry calling and ceases to serve among his brethren, he will invariably exalt himself and accuse others of wrongdoing. It is natural for those who do the least to be critical of those doing the most, but thankfully the latter group has the least amount of time to worry about such criticism. While this situation is emotionally exhausting, it really pales in comparison to when those who have done much for the Lord justify their despondency by blaming everyone else (including the Lord) for their condition.

Before the Lord corrects Elijah's self-focus, He first will remind His prophet, to whom He spoke: *"Go out, and stand on the mountain before the Lord"* (v. 11). Elijah may have moved towards the entrance of the cave, but he clearly did not exit the cave as commanded. Regardless, the Lord passed by, and a powerful wind ripped rocks from the face of the mountain, but the Lord was not in the wind. Then there was an earthquake, but the Lord was also not in the earthquake. Next, fire roared across the mountainside, but the Lord was not in the fire either.

The wind, the earthquake, and the fire were awesome displays of God's power, but these were not His instruments of revelation to Elijah; rather, God spoke to His prophet in a still, quiet voice. Just as God was not confined to one agency in dealing with Elijah, neither was He limited to using one prophet to confront His wayward people. Elijah was just one of many agencies available to God; hence, Elijah should not think of himself as being the only tool in God's hand, but one of many. To think otherwise would be limiting God's omnipotence!

July 19 – Hiding One's Face Before the Lord
1 Kings 19

God had shown Elijah that He was not limited in the agencies available to Him – Elijah was not His only means of rebuking Israel. Furthermore, God was not limited in what He used. For example, He could use a still, quiet voice to accomplish more than an earthquake could, as in Elijah's case. In fact, God delights in using weak and foolish things to do His bidding, as there is obviously no question as to who was responsible for the feat (1 Cor. 1:27-29). Only the gentle voice of love could cause Elijah to realize what God wanted him to learn. George Williams explains: "He should have recognized that there was no difference between his heart and that of the nations; and, that as coercion failed to make him leave his cave, so it failed, and must fail, to compel men to leave their sins."[12] Truly, Elijah was not different than his fathers; indeed, all of us share the same rebellious nature!

Hearing God's soothing voice accomplished what the spectacular displays could not. When Elijah heard the Lord speaking in this fashion, *"he wrapped his face in his mantle and went out and stood in the entrance of the cave"* (v. 13). Having gained his attention, the Lord again asked His discouraged servant, *"What are you doing here, Elijah?"* Elijah repeats his earlier response of informing the Lord of Israel's desperate spiritual condition, and that he is the only one left in Israel loyal to Him.

Depressed people rarely think straight. Had Elijah forgotten about Obadiah and the one hundred prophets that he was secretly caring for? No servant of the Lord is excluded from suffering spiritual depression. It happens when we believe we have done our best for the Lord, but our expectations for our own ministry are not met. Thankfully, it was not the Lord's plan to take Elijah's life, nor to remove him from service; it was time for him to get back to work.

Elijah was finally moving in the right direction towards restoration – he came before the Lord. When we are before the Lord, it is hard to have high thoughts of ourselves or our ministries. Contact with God's majesty and greatness causes us to blush before our Creator, and like Elijah, we too want to hide our faces in our mantles. Every servant of the Lord must realize that He alone is to direct, to empower, and to be honored in what we do for Him.

July 20 – Time to Get Back to Work
1 Kings 19

The Lord's solution to Elijah's despondence was to get his focus off himself and his expectations and back on the Lord and doing His bidding. The Lord is responsible for the results of what His servants do; His servants are responsible to obey Him. The Lord then commanded Elijah to return by the way of the Wilderness of Damascus. He was to anoint Hazael to be king of Syria, Jehu to be king of Israel, and Elisha to be Elijah's replacement. In the future, God would be using these three men to chasten Israel for her idolatry and to purge Baal worship from the land. This exercise would teach Elijah that he was not indispensable; the Lord could use whomever He chose to do His work.

Lastly, the Lord informed Elijah that he was not the last Jehovah worshiper in Israel: *"Yet I have reserved seven thousand in Israel, all whose knees have not bowed to Baal, and every mouth that has not kissed him"* (v. 18). It was true; most of Israel had not responded properly to God's discipline, the vast majority remained rebellious. But, praise be to God; no matter how spiritually dark things appear, He always has a witness for Himself on the earth, including the Church Age (Acts 14:17; Rom. 11:5).

Yet, there have been few Elijah-like revivalists through the centuries. May God lift up more brave souls that have no ambition other than to do His will despite the personal cost. Until the Lord returns for His Church, there will always be a need to confront the sin of His people. Indeed, we cannot experience God and know what could be, until we have first come to Him in holiness.

The revelation of 7,000 fellow Jehovah-worshipers encouraged Elijah; things were not as bleak and hopeless as he thought – the Lord was completely aware of Israel's condition and was working to resolve it. And praise the Lord, we hear no more complaints from Elijah. This was all a humbling lesson for Elijah. On three previous occasions the prophet had obeyed the Lord's command to "go," but while suffering from depression he had failed to comply at Horeb. After being refreshed by the Lord, he promptly obeyed the Lord's fifth command to "go" and Elijah returned by the same way he had come to Horeb. Retracing our steps which led us into failure back to the place where we stepped out of God's will is always the safest route to restoration.

Daily Devotions

July 21 – Elisha Is Called – Part 1
1 Kings 19

Elijah had learned that he was one of many in the Lord's work of confronting Israel's apostasy. He would now largely withdraw from public ministry. As commanded at Mount Horeb, Elijah departed for Abel Meholah to find his successor, Elisha. Elijah found him plowing in a field with twelve yoke of oxen; he then passed by him and threw his mantle on the younger Elisha and departed. Elisha ran after Elijah and received permission to bid his parents farewell before following him. Elisha also slaughtered a yoke of oxen, boiled the meat using the oxen's equipment for fuel and gave to the people to eat.

Elijah was disheartened and no longer wanted to be a prophet; passing along his mantle and the responsibility that went with it suited him just fine. Notice that when Elijah found Elisha plowing in the field, he did not say anything to him, but literally threw the mantle on Elisha and quickly departed. Elisha actually had to run after Elijah in order to speak with him.

Elisha as a mentee demonstrates several admirable qualities, which we would do well to notice and ponder if we want to develop profitable mentor/mentee relationships with others. The following seven principles are drawn from the narrative relating to Elisha's calling, training, and commissioning as God's prophet:

1. God calls working people into His work. Elisha was plowing a field with twelve yoke of oxen – he was a working man. There is no example in the Bible of God calling a lazy or irresponsible person into ministry. Whether chores at home, classes at school, or tasks in the workplace, all that we do is a proving ground for what God wants to accomplish next in our lives (Luke 16:10-11). Those who are faithful to do what they are supposed to do are being prepared for greater responsibilities, challenges, and honor.

2. Elisha was in a right relationship with authority. Elisha requests that he be allowed to inform his parents of God's calling for his life. He was a young man still living under his father's authority. It is good to remain under authority in whatever station God has put us, until God clearly repositions us under new authority. One must be under authority to have authority (Luke 7:8).

May We Serve Christ!

July 22 – Elisha Is Called – Part 2
1 Kings 19

Continuing with the seven principles drawn from the narrative relating to Elisha's calling, training, and commissioning:

3. The mantle is to be handed over with care. The mantle represented the work of the Lord and is thus precious to God. Though it was a great privilege to wear this cloak, it also reminded the prophet of his responsibility to speak only the words of God and his accountability to God if he failed to do so. The Hebrew word *shalak* is translated "threw" in verse 19 and literally means "to throw" or "to hurl." Elijah was in such a poor emotional state when he found Elisha that he just threw his cloak on Elisha and left. Elisha, however, understood that having the mantle itself did not equip him to be a prophet; he needed instruction. The mantle cannot be thrown; the work of the Lord must be carefully committed to the next generation.

4. Elisha wanted the mantle. Elisha ran after Elijah. He appreciated the opportunity to serve with and learn from Elijah – it was a privilege to be mentored and he counted it a great blessing. It is especially important for young people to understand that it is a privilege to be mentored by others; it is not a right. Nor should the mentoring relationship be viewed as some program one finishes to achieve some church position or spiritual status. Close interaction with a mature believer, someone who genuinely cares about the mentee, is a wonderful provision from the Lord to promote spiritual growth. May God bless those who invest their time and resources to enhance others.

5. Elisha assisted Elijah in the Lord's work. Mentoring relationships are often thought to be unidirectional – the mentor serves the mentee, but that is not a correct understanding. Elisha ministered to Elijah (1 Kgs. 19:21). A few years later, it would be Elisha, on behalf of Elijah, who would anoint Jehu and Hazael, the tasks given Elijah at Mount Horeb. Long after Elijah had departed for heaven in a whirlwind, Elisha was still known as *"Elisha ... who used to pour water on the hands of Elijah"* (2 Kgs. 3:11). Certainly, Elijah taught Elisha much, but Elisha showed his appreciation for his mentor by selflessly serving him also.

July 23 – Elisha Is Called – Part 3
1 Kings 19

Continuing with the seven principles drawn from the narrative relating to Elisha's calling, training, and commissioning:

6. Elisha encouraged Elijah. Elijah's name means "God is my God." His name aligns with his ministry of calling an apostate nation back to the Lord. It was a hard and discouraging work. Elijah needed a friend, and who better than Elisha, whose name means "God is Salvation," to strengthen Elijah. Elisha was a companion of Elijah and helped him regain his zeal to serve the Lord again. Later, God would send Elijah to confront Ahab and Jezebel and pronounce judgment on them. Elijah and Elisha's rapport was mutually beneficial; they needed each other. Mentors need encouragement also; Elisha was a supportive mentee.

7. Elisha made a sacrifice to be mentored. After informing his parents that he would be departing with Elijah, Elisha slaughtered a yoke of oxen and burnt his implements in order to cook the meat for the people. More than being gracious to others, he was effectively closing the door on his former life. By removing the possibility of returning to farming, he was showing his dedication to Elijah and his commitment to learn from him. Likewise, mentees should understand that some activities will have to go by the wayside in order to have the time to be mentored properly. Mary had to say "no" to some legitimate activities in order to have time to sit at the Lord's feet and learn from Him (Luke 10:38-42). Although she was misunderstood by her sister Martha, the Lord complimented her in front of everyone for making the best choice. It is not just the mentor who sacrifices himself or herself; the mentee must also be committed to the mentoring process.

Elijah had a rough start in effectively passing the work of the Lord on to Elisha, but apparently he finished well. Elisha demonstrated many good attitudes in the mentoring relationship. Maturity in the mentee both endorses the mentor's ministry and prepares the mentee to be able to teach others in the future. Good mentoring relationships are active and will ultimately develop into a peer type of mentality as seen in 2 Kings 2: the mentor must go for the mentee to grow!

July 24 – Unnatural Unions
1 Kings 22; 2 Chronicles 19

King Jehoshaphat of Judah *"did what was right in the eyes of the Lord"* (1 Kgs. 22:43). Jehoshaphat bolstered Judah's fortifications and because he purified Judah of idols and pagan shrines, the Lord blessed him. He also ensured that the priests and Levites visited and taught God's law to the people throughout Judah. Despite the many positive things the king did, we also read that, *"Jehoshaphat made peace with the king of Israel"* (1 Kgs. 22:44), which had negative consequences to his kingdom.

To summarize, Ahab conned Jehoshaphat into forging an alliance with him in order to retake Ramoth, a City of Refuge in the Transjordan, which was under Syrian control. Ahab was an evil king and godly Jehoshaphat should have known better than to unite with Ahab, especially in a cause that God had not sanctioned. The king of Judah enjoyed prosperity and had fortified himself against military invasion, but not his heart against allurement. The result of this union nearly cost Jehoshaphat his life in a battle he should not have been fighting, but he cried out to the Lord and God saved him.

After the king returned to Jerusalem, the prophet Hanani rebuked him for his alliance with Ahab, *"Should you help the wicked, and love them who hate the Lord?"* (2 Chron. 19:2). Though Jehoshaphat had done many good things for the Lord, the king would suffer for affiliating with wicked Ahab. For example, Jehoshaphat's son Jehoram married Ahab's wicked daughter Athaliah, which later resulted in rampant idolatry in Judah.

Satan has used this tactic of *unnatural unions* on many throughout Biblical history. How many Christians today are reaping God's judgment for teaming up with the unregenerate to accomplish some religious cause or to support some charitable activity? If children of God and children of the devil are working together harmoniously, it is not God who is glorified in the endeavor, but the one who has wanted God's glory and station from the beginning (Isa. 14:12-15).

After rebuking the king for being involved with Ahab, Hanani ends with a consoling note: *"Nevertheless good things are found in you ..., in that you have prepared your heart to seek God"* Thankfully, failures are never final unless we make them so – God wants us to succeed.

July 25 – Our Eyes Are Upon You – Part 1
2 Chronicles 20

Not long after the failed attempt to secure Ramoth Gilead, the Moabites, the Ammonites, and the Meunites united against Jehoshaphat. They probably thought that since the Syrians had repelled the united armies of Israel and Judah that they could defeat Judah by working together. Jehoshaphat learned that this alliance had gathered at Hazazon Tamar (En Gedi) and would soon be assaulting Jerusalem.

Fearing this invasion, Jehoshaphat sought the Lord on the matter and proclaimed a fast throughout all Judah. Jews from across Judah poured into Jerusalem to seek the Lord with their king; it was an enormous congregation of men, women and children. Jehoshaphat led the standing congregation in prayer: the king first extols the immense power of their sovereign God. He then recalls God's past goodness shown to them as Abraham's descendants by giving them their homeland and also a central sanctuary to worship Him in.

Because of the Lord's command, the Israelites had spared the three nations now threatening them while journeying from Egypt to Canaan. So now they requested the Lord's help since they had honored His decree. Jehoshaphat then recalls God's friendship with Abraham, reminding the Lord that His people before Him now wanted to enjoy the same kind of communion with Him. Abraham enjoyed the Lord's fellowship and protection (Gen. 18). This was what the king desired for Judah at that present time and then concluded his prayer with this plea: *"For we have no power against this great multitude that is coming against us; nor do we know what to do, but our eyes are upon You"* (v. 12).

After the king finished praying, the Spirit of the Lord came upon Jahaziel, a Levite in the midst of the assembly. He told the king and his countrymen not to be afraid, for the battle with the approaching enemy was not theirs, but the Lord's. They were to go out the next day and take up a position opposite the enemy; they would find them coming from the Ascent of Ziz. Because the battle was the Lord's, they were to *"stand still and see the salvation of the Lord"* (v. 17). There was no need for them to fear the enemy because the Lord was with them and would protect them. After hearing this, everyone bowed their faces to the ground and worshiped the Lord and the Levites sang praises.

July 26 – Our Eyes Are Upon You – Part 2
2 Chronicles 20

The next morning, the people gathered to march out into the Wilderness of Tekoa to meet the enemy as God had commanded. The king charged the people, *"Believe in the Lord your God, and you shall be established; believe His prophets, and you shall prosper"* (v. 20). To express their faith in Jehovah, the king put the Levites in front of the army, so that they could "praise the beauty of holiness" as they moved forward. They sang, *"Praise the Lord, for His mercy endures forever."*

This sight may have stunned the enemy marching towards Jerusalem, as it was not a normal military strategy to post musicians and singers as your first wave of combatants in a military engagement. The Lord added to their confusion and set ambushes against the soldiers of Ammon, Moab, and Mount Seir by causing the Ammonites and Moabites to attack and utterly destroy those from Edom.

Afterwards, the Lord caused the Ammonites and Moabites to destroy each other. It was a total massacre, leaving the wilderness littered with innumerable dead bodies. Judah had fully trusted in the Lord and, as a result, not only was the threat totally removed, but the people were rewarded with the vast spoil of their enemy which took three days to gather. On the fourth day after their deliverance, Judah assembled in the Valley of Berachah to bless the Lord and then Jehoshaphat led his countrymen back to Jerusalem. They praised the Lord as they went. After returning to Jerusalem, praises to God continued to be offered by musicians and singers at the temple.

Not only did the Lord deliver His people from an enormous invading army and bless them with the spoils of His war, He also blessed them with peace by causing the surrounding countries to fear the God of the Jews, who fought for His people. Afterwards, *"the realm of Jehoshaphat was quiet, for his God gave him rest all around"* (v. 30).

The Lord longs to show Himself strong to those who are in a right relationship with Him and realize that He is their strength. The king conveyed this realization on behalf of the nation: *"we have no power ... nor do we know what to do, but our eyes are upon You."* God responded to their faith in Him by completely wiping out the advancing armies without one Jew lifting his sword. Dear believer, God is able!

July 27 – Contrasting Ministries
2 Kings 2

We have not heard anything about Elisha since he began serving Elijah in 1 Kings 19. The two men enjoyed about a ten-year mentor-mentee relationship. The lack of specifics would suggest that the nature of the mentoring ministry is a private and personal experience.

Elijah's prophetic ministry draws to a close in this chapter and Elisha will take his place as the premier prophet in Israel at this time. The prophets were similar in that both were appointed by the Lord and evidently both instructed the "sons of the prophets" as a leading teacher (4:38). Both men were empowered by God to do extraordinary miracles. The differences between Elijah and Elisha are more obvious. Elijah came from rustic Gilead beyond the Jordan River, and thus likely grew up in a poorer home. Elisha, on the other hand, came from Abel Meholah in Israel proper, and appears to have had a wealthy upbringing (i.e. plowing with twelve yoke of oxen). Elijah was prone to mood swings, but Elisha seems to be more even-tempered. Elijah was a hairy man, while Elisha was bald.

Elijah's ministry was to confront an apostate nation, whereas Elisha's ministry was more personal and compassionate; he labored to turn his countrymen from idolatry, as only Jehovah could meet their needs. Yet, Elisha's ministry superseded Elijah's in duration and in performed miracles. Elijah's miracles were dramatic (e.g. a severe drought and calling fire down from heaven three times). By contrast, Elisha's miracles were modest and personal – he was a champion of the people. In this sense, Elisha's ministry typifies that of the Lord Jesus, while Elijah's confrontational ministry represents the forerunning work of John to prepare wayward Israel for Messiah's coming.

Although Elisha did more miracles and showed compassion to individuals, it is Elijah, not Elisha, who is predominant in the New Testament. These men were vastly different in social upbringing, emotions, and ministries, but their mentor-mentee relationship enabled each one to powerfully serve the Lord.

This indicates that God may bring polar opposites together in such relationships, and also serves as a reminder that the goal of mentoring is not to recreate ourselves in those we mentor, but to enable the mentee to fulfill his or her divine calling.

July 28 – The Widow's Oil
2 Kings 4

A widow of one of the sons of the prophets informed Elisha that a creditor planned to take her two sons into slavery until her debt was paid off. She brought her dire situation to the attention of Elisha. It is likely that the widow lived in or near one of the cities associated with the schools of the prophets (i.e., Bethel, Gilgal, or Jericho).

The Lord's compassion on this woman, the former wife of one of His prophets, is touching. Elisha asked what she would like him to do about it and also what assets she still retained in the house. She told the prophet that all she had in the house was a jar of oil. Elisha told her to borrow as many empty vessels from her neighbors as she could and bring them into her house; then she was to shut the door behind her and her sons. The widow did what Elisha told her to do. After closing the door, she poured from her jar of oil and filled all the containers that she had brought into the house and then the supply of oil ceased. As instructed by Elisha, the widow then sold the oil and paid off the creditor who was threatening to enslave her sons.

The magnitude of this miracle depended on the widow's faithfulness to use what she had and to borrow vessels from others. The more she gathered, the greater God's blessing would be. Little in our hands is immeasurable in God's. If the widow chose to gather many common vessels, she would not only escape her debts, but also have adequate means to care for her sons afterwards. We often do not experience God's greatness because we think too little of Him; we decline to ask Him for great things.

Napoleon's army fought hard to secure a certain island in the Mediterranean Sea. During a victory celebration for his chief of staff a young lieutenant boldly approached the emperor and saluted him. Napoleon asked him what he wanted, and the lieutenant replied, "Give me this island; it is my boyhood home." This seemed to everyone else a ludicrous request, for many men had lost their lives in gaining the victory; yet, without hesitation Napoleon deeded the island to the lieutenant. When Napoleon was asked later why he had done such a thing, he replied, "He honored me by the magnitude of his request."[13] Likewise, the magnitude of our prayer requests indicate just how big we believe our God to be.

July 29 – Feeding a Hundred Men
2 Kings 4

A man from Baal Shalisha brought Elisha the firstfruits of his harvest – twenty loaves of barley bread and a sack of newly ripened grain. Elisha commanded that it be given to the people to eat, but his servant scoffed at the idea of placing such a small provision before a hundred hungry men. But Elisha insisted, saying that everyone would eat and there would be some food left over. So the bread was set before the people, they ate all they wanted, and there was bread remaining, just as the prophet had foretold. This was Elisha's eighth miracle.

The Lord Jesus did a similar miracle twice. First, He fed about 20,000 people by multiplying a boy's sack lunch of two fish and five loaves. Second, He likely fed over 15,000 people with a few small fishes and seven loaves, and yet there were many baskets of food remaining after both miracles (Matt. 14:17-21, 15:32-38).

There was both a physical and spiritual famine in Elisha's day – Israel was thoroughly starving. In his previous miracle of purifying a stew that was harmful to eat, Elisha had shown that swallowing a false religion would never satisfy their spiritual hunger. The stew looked harmless enough but proved disgusting and deadly. God's prophets helped counteract the deadly effects of Baalism in Israel – Elisha made the stew edible.

Elisha's miracles of multiplying resources showed that though Baal was supposedly "the lord of the earth," it was Jehovah alone who controlled earth's resources and could multiply such resources to bless His people. Likewise, when believers share with others and leave the implications with God, He is able to bless our generosity and cause us to flourish at the same time:

> *There is one who scatters, yet increases more; and there is one who withholds more than is right, but it leads to poverty. The generous soul will be made rich, and he who waters will also be watered himself* (Prov. 11:24-25). *Cast your bread upon the waters, for you will find it after many days* (Eccl. 11:1).

Because Jehovah controls all things, He alone is able to satisfy all our needs, even after we have been His instrument to bless others. The more God enables us to help others, the more we will be blessed.

July 30 – A Powerful Testimony
2 Kings 5

We are now introduced to Naaman, a powerful and honorable commander in the Syrian army who had an incurable case of leprosy. A young Israelite girl had been captured during a Syrian raid into Israel and was now serving Naaman's wife. The maiden must have been treated well, for she wanted to help her master.

She told her mistress that there was a great prophet in Samaria (Elisha) who could heal her husband's leprosy, that is, if he would seek his help. This was quite a statement of faith in Jehovah and His prophet, as there had never been a leper healed by any prophet previously – a fact that the Lord Jesus confirmed (Luke 4:27). D. L. Moody observes:

> A little maid said a few words that made a commotion in two kingdoms. God honored her faith by doing for Naaman, the idolater, what he had not done for any in Israel (Luke 4:27). How often has the finger of childhood pointed grown-up persons in the right direction. The maid boasted of God that He would do for Naaman what He had not done for any in Israel, and God honored her faith.[14]

The servant's girl's claim was reported to Naaman, who then received his king's permission to go to Samaria to see if it were true. The king of Syria wrote a letter to the king of Israel asking him to assist his trusted servant's quest for healing. Naaman left Syria with ten talents of silver, 6,000 shekels of gold, and ten changes of clothing. But he did not need to bring anything to Israel to be healed. If he exercised faith in Jehovah and obeyed Elisha's command to bathe seven times in the Jordan River, he would be healed. Although, initially irritated by the prophet's simple instructions and refusal to speak with him, Naaman did do as he was told and he was completely healed.

Naaman then returned and told Elisha that he would no longer offer personal burnt offerings and sacrifices to other gods, but only to the Lord. Next, Naaman returned home to tell the story of his healing that would spread Jehovah's fame throughout Syria. It all happened because of the testimony of a faithful little girl! May each of us follow her example and share what we know to be true – the gospel message, so that many can be cleansed and healed from the deadly disease of sin.

July 31 – Destructive Greed
2 Kings 5

Elisha's servant Gehazi did not understand why his master had not received anything from Naaman, who wanted to show his gratitude for being healed. Eager to profit from the situation before Naaman got too far away and the opportunity would be lost, Gehazi decided to run after him. Noticing Gehazi in pursuit, Naaman halted and got down from his chariot to ask Elisha's servant if all was well. Gehazi then spun his yarn, *"All is well. My master has sent me, saying, 'Indeed, just now two young men of the sons of the prophets have come to me from the mountains of Ephraim. Please give them a talent of silver and two changes of garments"* (v. 22). Naaman was more than happy to oblige, but pressed Gehazi to take two talents of silver and two changes of garments. This sounded good to Gehazi. Naaman then sent two of his servants to carry the silver and the garments to the citadel they had just departed. Gehazi then took the articles and hid them in the house.

Believing his entire enterprise had been covert, Gehazi went in feigning innocence and stood before his master. Elisha, who knew all about his offense, quizzed Gehazi who lied about his actions. Elisha then revealed the subterfuge and told Gehazi that Naaman's leprosy would cling to him and his descendants.

Interestingly, Elisha did not rebuke Gehazi for his falsehoods to Naaman or to himself; the weightier offense was of a spiritual nature, not a moral one. Elisha's rebuke centered in the question, "Is it time to receive money?" Since God had just taught Naaman about salvation being solely by His grace, was it the proper time to take his money and confuse God's message of obtaining life – that it was not freely received in grace?

Furthermore, many false prophets were fleecing their countrymen of their money with empty messages and under false pretenses, but a true servant of God should never be motivated by personal greed, but rather by God's glory. It is why Paul did not take anything from the Corinthians while he was sharing the gospel with them; he did not want them to question his motives or think that God's salvation in Christ could be purchased (2 Cor. 11:7-15). Those who honor the Lord will be cared for by the One who controls everyone's purse, but those, like Gehzai, who do not will be punished. Gehzai was a leper all his life.

August 1 – The Floating Ax Head
2 Kings 6

The living quarters for the sons of the prophets at Gilgal had become too small. It is quite understandable how this situation developed. Young men seeking to know God's Word better would have flocked to wherever the premier prophet of Israel was residing. After obtaining Elisha's approval, it was decided that each man should go to the Jordan and harvest timber for constructing a new residence large enough for their needs at that location. The men were not seeking cedar or stone for construction material, but, rather, each man was to hew his beam. This meant that they were erecting a simple, no-frills structure barely adequate for housing. Elisha accompanied the men.

While trees were being felled at the Jordan, an iron axe head flew off its handle into the river. The woodsman cried out to Elisha that the axe had been borrowed. This loss was doubly sorrowful, for not only was it needed for the construction project, but the poor prophet probably did not have the funds to replace it either. It is one thing to live in poverty with an honest mind, but quite another to be burdened with the guilt of debt towards those who have our affection.

Sympathizing with the loss, Elisha asked the man where the axe head had been lost. After the prophet was shown the place, he cut off a stick and threw it in the water, which caused the iron head to float upwards to the surface. Elisha then told the man to snatch it out of the water, which he did.

We might think of this incident as a little miracle in comparison to reviving the Shunammite's dead son, but that would be incorrect. We must remember that nothing in God's creation is harder for Him to control than anything else. Not only did the Lord create all things that exist, He also holds together all things (Col. 1:16-17). All that we observe consists only because God maintains it.

True miracles occur when God defies the natural order that He put in place to govern creation. So, it would be no less difficult for God to cause the molecular processes within a non-functioning body to begin again than to change the molecular status of iron to make it lighter than water. If there is nothing too hard for the Lord (Gen. 19:14), it stands to reason that there is nothing too easy for Him either, meaning He is not in any way challenged by or limited in managing His creation!

Daily Devotions

August 2 – More for Us Than Against Us
2 Kings 6

The king of Syria devised plans to covertly attack Israel, but Elisha repeatedly alerted Israel's king of the enemy's tactics, which thwarted the Syrian attacks. The Syrian king even suspected a traitor among his military staff. But then he was informed that this was not a matter of treachery, but, rather, there was a prophet in Israel named Elisha who was telling the king of Israel what they spoke about in secret.

The king then ordered a reconnaissance mission into Israel to determine Elisha's location, so that he could be captured. Elisha was in Dothan, so the king of Syria sent a great army, including cavalry and chariots, to surround the city during the night. Elisha's servant arose early and discovered that the city was surrounded by the enemy. He quickly informed his master, and then anxiously inquired as to what they should do.

Elisha responded by reassuring his servant, *"Do not fear, for those who are with us are more than those who are with them"* (v. 16). Elisha then prayed, *"Lord, I pray, open his eyes that he may see."* The Lord granted this prayer and the young man was enabled to see the host of angelic forces in fiery chariots that surrounded them (v. 17; Ps. 68:17). This was not a new sight for Elisha; he had witnessed his mentor being carried up into heaven by such a chariot drawn by horses of fire. Though normally invisible to the eye, Elisha knew by faith that God's angelic protectors were with him.

"Fear not" are often God's first words of comfort and reassurance to troubled believers in Scripture. Nearly everything we connect with in this sin-cursed world inspires some level of anxiety in feeble beings like ourselves. Who can answer these things and calm the agitation within the believer's heart? Only the Lord can – His grace is sufficient for every trial and every necessity in life! We find true, lasting peace and mental tranquility only in the Lord Jesus Christ! Hence, John's charge concerning the enemy lurking about to devour us is most encouraging, *"greater is He that is in you, than he that is in the world"* (1 Jn. 4:4; KJV). The Lord with anyone is a majority. Actually, the Lord alone is a majority! Elisha's servant discovered this truth. Elisha did not fear the enemy; his only concern was to do the will of God. May we follow his example, and not be anxious about anything else.

May We Serve Christ!

August 3 – Elisha Did Get a Double Portion
2 Kings 13

We are not told what Elisha had been doing since his last official act of anointing of Jehu four decades earlier (2 Kgs. 6). We learn in this chapter that Elisha had an illness that would result in his death. Jehoash (Joash) the king of Israel came down to visit the prophet. The king wept over Elisha, saying, *"O my father, my father, the chariots of Israel and their horsemen!"* (v. 14). This same expression was uttered by Elisha at Elijah's home-calling to show respect and fondness for the one departing. Although still embracing Jeroboam's paganism, Jehoash valued the prophet's presence in his kingdom. Elisha had been a loyal guardian of Israel and an honorable servant of the Lord, thus he would be missed. Elisha responded to the king's grief with a final prophecy.

He told the king to take his bow and some arrows. While the king held his bow, Elisha put his hand on the king's hand holding his bow, then Elisha told him to open the east window (towards Syria) and shoot an arrow through the open window, which the king did. The prophet then said that this represented the Lord's arrow of deliverance against Syria and that he must strike the enemy at Aphek until vanquished.

Elisha then told the king to take some arrows and strike the ground with them, which the king did three times. Elisha then reproved the king for striking the ground only three times, saying that he should have struck five or six times to symbolize a complete defeat of Syria. But since he struck the ground only three times, he would not completely overcome Israel's enemy. Even on his deathbed Elisha is declaring the word of God with boldness – he finished well!

Shortly after this, Elisha died and was buried in an unnamed location. Elisha's total ministry spanned about sixty years. The next spring, marauders from Moab raided Israel.

One such raid occurred while several men were carrying a man's body to a burial site. Not wanting to be caught by the Moabites, they hastily placed the dead man's body in Elisha's tomb, but when the corpse touched the bones of Elisha, the man revived and stood on his feet. This would be the fourteenth miracle associated with Elisha, which would be exactly twice the number of miracles performed by Elijah. Indeed, Elisha had received what he had requested – a double portion of Elijah's spirit.

August 4 – Uzziah's Pride
2 Chronicles 26

King Uzziah was better than many of Judah's kings: *"King Uzziah did what was right in the sight of the Lord, according to all that his father, Amaziah, did"* (v. 4). Sadly, neither man finished well. Like his father Amaziah, Uzziah was not a reformer; nor did he remove the high places of worship. He was, however, blessed for following the Lord, for *"as long as he sought the Lord, God made him prosper"* (v. 5).

Uzziah had many accomplishments, however, these caused him to think more highly of himself than he did of his God: *"But when he was strong his heart was lifted up, to his destruction, for he transgressed against the Lord his God by entering the temple of the Lord to burn incense on the altar of incense"* (v. 16). In arrogance he brought a censer into the temple to offer worship to Jehovah. This was strictly forbidden by God, only Levitical priests could perform such tasks. Eighty brave priests confronted the king in the temple. Uzziah became furious with them, but he was not able to argue his case for God had struck him in the head with leprosy (to symbolize the judgment of his pride). The priests quickly put him out of the sanctuary.

The Lord will not tolerate pride, especially in those ruling His people. God's judgment immediately fell on Uzziah while he was in God's house. This reminds us of Peter's exhortation: *"For the time has come for judgment to begin at the house of God; and if it begins with us first, what will be the end of those who do not obey the gospel of God?"* (1 Pet. 4:17). Today, the house of God is a spiritual temple that He is building one living stone (soul) at a time (1 Pet. 2:5). When the Church (composed of believer-priests) upholds the righteousness of God by judging sin within its members, the power of the gospel message is accurately conveyed in both word and deed. But a carnal and proud Church has no power to preach the gospel; rather, her hypocrisy numbs the consciences of the lost by endorsing their sin.

As a leper, Uzziah suffered from a pain-numbing disease; Israel's ongoing sin had made them numb to the pangs of their conscience, and they were further injuring their souls by idolatry. Pain is generally a good thing because it alerts us to what needs attention, but Israel was ignoring the prophetic warnings. May the Church heed God's warnings and judge itself!

May We Serve Christ!

August 5 – Keeping the Passover – Part 1
2 Kings 18; 2 Chronicles 30

The reign of Hezekiah was a fresh oasis for Judah after the long spiritually parched rule of Ahaz. Unlike his father, Hezekiah did what was right in the sight of the Lord. There had been several good kings of Judah since David, but none received such an outstanding commendation; Hezekiah held fast to the Lord and did not depart from the Lord's commandments. Because of his dedication, the Lord was with Hezekiah and prospered whatever he did.

Since his father Ahaz had shut down temple worship, there had been no opportunity to keep the Feasts of Jehovah for many years. But after Hezekiah became the sole ruler in Judah, he was exercised to keep the Passover. However, there were several difficulties to overcome. First, it was already the sixteenth day of the first month before the house of the Lord was cleansed and reopened and the Passover was to be kept on the fourteenth day of the first month. Second, the Passover lambs were to be set aside on the tenth day of the month to be observed and tested. Third, there was a lack of consecrated priests. Fourth, many of those he wanted to attend the Passover lived a considerable distance from Jerusalem. Since the Law contained a provision for those not able to keep the Passover in the first month to do so on the fourteenth day of the second month (Num. 9:10-11), Hezekiah decided to keep the Passover then, instead of waiting an entire year to keep the feast. Those residing in northern Israel would also be invited.

We pause to draw an important truth from the narrative that has a practical application for believers in the Church Age. The two reasons that God's covenant people could not offer acceptable worship to Him during the days of Ahaz were: the doors of the house of God were closed and there was no cleansed priesthood.

How lovely to realize that in the Church Age such obstacles have been eternally dealt with – worship can be offered by believer-priests any time. The Church is the spiritual house to God and the believers composing it are positionally holy in Christ (i.e., sanctified priests). This means that believers walking with the Lord can offer acceptable worship to Him at any time. We have an eternal privilege that we can actually enjoy right now!

August 6 – Keeping the Passover – Part 2
2 Chronicles 30

Messengers were sent from city to city throughout the northern tribes with a message to repent and be restored: *"Children of Israel, return to the Lord God of Abraham, Isaac, and Israel; then He will return to the remnant of you who have escaped from the hand of the kings of Assyria"* (v. 6). They were reminded that they had suffered God's displeasure because their forefathers had been stiff-necked and did not obey His Law and did not come to His sanctuary to worship (v. 8). The Israelites in the northern tribes were challenged not to continue in the rebellion of their fathers; rather, they had an opportunity to experience the Lord's mercy and compassion, instead of His wrath.

Many laughed at Hezekiah's messengers, but some from Ephraim, Asher, Manasseh, Issachar, and Zebulun humbled themselves and came to Jerusalem as requested. The mixed religion of the Samaritans scoffed at what God appreciated. Likewise today, humanized Christianity will always work to lead people away from Christ and into sin.

Because the hand of God was on them, those from Judah responded uniformly to the king's request and with singleness of heart obeyed the Lord. A great assembly gathered in Jerusalem to keep the Passover and the seven-day Feast of Unleavened Bread afterwards. After the Feast of Unleavened Bread ended, the people rose up and purged Jerusalem of its incense censers and altars and cast them in the Brook Kidron.

Ashamed over their past sins and their complacency in not being sanctified when the temple was first cleansed, more priests and Levites got right with the Lord and were sanctified. Because the feast day had come so soon, there were many in the assembly who were still ceremonially unclean per the Law, so sanctified Levites oversaw the slaughtering of the Passover Lambs for those who were unclean.

Given the unique revival from paganism, Hezekiah prayed that God would look favorably on all those who ate the Passover with a willing heart to honor Him, even though they were not ceremonially clean. The Lord honored Hezekiah's prayer and healed them. God did not want to judge those who had already benefitted from past chastening. Rather, His mercy would abound to cover their infraction: willful subjection was more important than the religious formality.

August 7 – Hezekiah's Humble Example
2 Kings 19

Sennacherib sent the Tartan, the Rabsaris, and the Rabshakeh from Lachish with a great army to besiege Jerusalem. Hezekiah sent three representatives, Eliakim, Shebna, and Joah, to speak with and hopefully to negotiate with Rabshakeh. Rabshakeh mocked the Jews, their army, and their God in the Hebrew tongue so all could hear. He concluded his blasphemous rant by instructing the Jews to surrender and not to listen to Hezekiah, nor to have confidence in their Jehovah, as no god had been able to stop the Assyrians previously.

After King Hezekiah heard the envoy's report, he also tore his clothes, put on sackcloth, and then went to the temple. Wearing sackcloth was an ongoing expression of brokenness until the distressing situation had passed. Any Jew seeing Hezekiah without his royal attire and earnestly praying in the temple would have been deeply moved. Rabshakeh had blasphemed God and threatened to destroy Judah. Hezekiah knew the situation was desperate and that there was only one remedy – the hand of God.

The king also requested Isaiah pray with them about this urgent matter. Speaking for the Lord, Isaiah assures Hezekiah that God heard every blasphemous word, and that Hezekiah was not to be fearful. God planned to put a rumor in the ear of Sennacherib which would cause him to return to his own land, and there he would be killed by the sword.

Rabshakeh had surrounded Jerusalem with a sizeable army, and Sennacherib had moved his remaining soldiers from Lachish to Libnah (about five miles north of Jerusalem). While there the king received a report that Tirhakah king of Ethiopia was moving north to war with him. Sennacherib withdrew from the region in order to properly array his troops for combat, but before doing so, he sent a parting message to Hezekiah: *"Do not let your god in whom you trust deceive you, saying, 'Jerusalem shall not be given into the hand of the king of Assyria'"* (v. 10). He then boasted that no god of any land that he had conquered had been able to deliver anyone from his hand and then listed several cities that had succumbed to Assyria's advance. Regardless, of the enemy's threats, Isaiah's prophecy was fulfilled and Jerusalem was safe because a godly king knew where to go for help.

August 8 – Hezekiah's Prayer
2 Kings 19

After Hezekiah received Sennacherib's parting message, he again went straight to the temple and laid the letter before the Lord and sought His help in prayer. This is a remarkable prayer of faith, a model prayer in many respects. First, notice that Hezekiah did not rush into God's presence frantic and fearful, but he commences his prayer with praise and worship. This is how the Lord Jesus taught His disciples to begin their prayers (Luke 11:2).

Hezekiah acknowledges that he is praying to the only true God, who dwells in heaven, who created all things, and who controls everything. To enter God's presence with accolades of praise and thanksgiving, and heartfelt worship shows God that we know Him and trust Him. If we believe that God truly controls all things according to His plan, then we must also believe that time is not a limiting factor for Him to work His best.

Second, Hezekiah asks God to take action against the Assyrians because of Sennacherib's blasphemous words. There was no need to repeat what was said, the king knew that an all-knowing, all-seeing, and all-wise God did not need the information. The Lord's people should not waste time supplying God with facts about situations that He knows much more about anyway. Rather, we should be in awe of Him, telling the Lord what we know about Him, giving thanks for what He has done, and expressing our confidence in His attributes and character to achieve the best outcome, even though we do not know what that might be. True faith wants what God wants.

Third, Hezekiah agrees with Sennacherib's claim that no people groups (with their gods) had been able to resist Assyrian aggression. The king was noting the incredible prospect that God had to glorify His name. The stage is set, so to speak, and Jehovah could prove to all Gentile nations that the God of the Jews is indeed Lord of all. The king did *"cast his care on the Lord,"* (1 Pet. 5:7) that is, he laid Sennacherib's letter before the Lord – a gesture meaning, "Lord, you handle this." Isaiah returns God's answer to Hezekiah, *"I will defend this city, to save it"* (v. 34). And He did. One angel was sent to the Assyrian camp and 185,000 soldiers died in one night. The Lord is able to defend those who are His – may we permit Him to do so!

May We Serve Christ!

August 9 – A Young Man Seeks the Lord
2 Kings 22; 2 Chronicles 34

Josiah was only eight years old when he sat on the throne of Judah; he reigned thirty-one years. Josiah *"did what was right in the sight of the Lord, and walked in all the ways of his father David; he did not turn aside to the right hand or to the left"* (2 Kgs. 22:2). The only other kings to receive such praise were Asa, Jehoshaphat, and Hezekiah, but only Hezekiah and Josiah removed the high places associated with Jehovah worship in Judah as required by the Law (Deut. 12:2-14).

The writer of Chronicles provides some specific details of Josiah's spiritual growth and zeal for the Lord: The young king began to seek the Lord in his eighth year of reign (i.e., Josiah would have then been fifteen years old). In the twelfth year of his reign he had matured sufficiently to begin purging Judah and Jerusalem of the high places, of wooden, carved, and molded images, and to break down the altars of Baal and destroy their associated images.

In the eighteenth year of his reign King Josiah sent Shaphan, the scribe, to the temple to make an accounting of freewill offerings received and to transfer that money to various faithful workers who needed it to repair the temple. While performing this task, the high priest Hilkiah found *"the Book of the Law in the house of the Lord"* (2 Kgs. 22:8). Hilkiah then gave the book to Shaphan, who read it.

Shaphan then reported to the king that funds to accomplish temple repair work had been transferred. Then Shaphan informed the king that the book of the Law had been found in the temple and had been given to him; the scribe then read the book to the king. Josiah was shocked at what he heard and tore his clothes to express remorse. Because Josiah loved the Lord, he keenly felt the sway of God's Word.

Unknown to God's people, the Word of God was in the same place that God's treasure was kept. How sad it is when God's people continue trudging through life ignorant of the great wealth of wisdom and guidance contained in Scripture. The Lord Jesus affirmed that failure is inevitable if we do not know God's Word (Matt. 22:29), and that true disciples long to know and abide in God's Word (John 5:38). May each believer agree with the psalmist, *"I rejoice at Your word as one who finds great treasure"* (Ps. 119:162). May we dig for treasure!

August 10 – A Godly Heritage
2 Kings 22

We will pause to consider the testimony of the scribe Shaphan, Josiah's trusted secretary, who is mentioned throughout the narrative of 2 Kings 22. Shaphan set a godly example for his children to follow, some of whom were used by the Lord in times of social and religious upheaval. Ahikam, the son of Shaphan, for example, was determined not to allow the people to murder Jeremiah and, though he risked a social backlash, used his political clout to gain Jeremiah's release (Jer. 26:24). It is also noted that Shaphan's son Gemariah, along with Elnathan, urged Jehoiakim not to burn Jeremiah's scroll (Jer. 36:12, 25). Shaphan's son Elasah hand-carried Jeremiah's letter to the exiled Jews in Babylon (Jer. 29:1-3).

Though his son Jaazaniah was a rebel, Shaphan reared up three fine sons who lived for God and, indeed, raised their sons to do the same. The grandson of Shaphan through Ahikam was Gedaliah, a just governor over Judah. Micaiah, the grandson of Shaphan through Gemariah, convinced the princes of the importance of Jeremiah's scroll after hearing it read (Jer. 36:11-26).

It has been observed that the value of parenting is witnessed in one's grandchildren. To this end, Shaphan was a father who obtained a good heritage from the Lord:

Children are a heritage from the Lord, the fruit of the womb is a reward. Like arrows in the hand of a warrior, so are the children of one's youth. Happy is the man who has his quiver full of them; they shall not be ashamed, but shall speak with their enemies in the gate" (Ps. 127:3-5).

The psalmist reminds us we are only stewards, not owners, of the children that God graciously entrusts to our care. If reared in the ways of the Lord, these skillfully sharpened and straight arrows become a rich blessing to all. In ancient days, older children ensured the defense of the family against the attacking enemy. Children must be trained up for the Lord to be a blessing to others and to further the kingdom of God. Untrained children, not surprisingly, remain foolish (Prov. 22:15) and predictably absorb what outside influences fill their void of understanding. God used Shaphan's heritage to confront evil and to preserve and to refresh His people. May God grant us the same legacy.

May We Serve Christ!

August 11 – Homeward Bound
Ezra 2

Almost two centuries before the events of this book, the Lord punished the unrelenting idolatry of the Northern Kingdom through Assyrian invasion and exile (2 Kgs. 17:23). A century later the Southern Kingdom was warned of military invasion, slaughter, and exile if they did not repent of their idolatry. Again these warnings were dismissed and God used the Babylonians to severely chasten His people. This explains why the first returning Jewish captives from Babylon were primarily from the tribes of Judah and Benjamin, and those descendants of the priests and Levites that had been in the Southern Kingdom at the time of its downfall. Yet, descendants of those exiled from the Northern Kingdom were permitted to return also.

Ezra supplies a roster of the Jews who were willing to take advantage of Cyrus' offer. He begins by listing the key civil and religious leaders. The appointed governor of the province of Judah, Zerubbabel and Jeshua (or Joshua; see Zech. 3:1) the High Priest are referenced first. After recognizing the tribal leaders, Ezra notes eighteen specific families and clans, inhabitants from twenty-one towns and villages, the priests and the Levites, which included singers and gatekeepers, the descendants of temple and royal servants, and, finally, 652 returnees who could not prove their ancestry. The total number of Jews (including women and children) returning home is stated to be 49,897.

Although the Jews were unified as a people and in purpose – to rebuild the temple, not all was festive; 652 returnees and three houses of priests could not verify their ancestry. This would be a hardship, for without genealogies, no legal claim to property previously held by clansmen could be verified.

Many professing Christ today suffer from a similar difficulty; though often having zeal, they are unable to provide a clear scriptural response to the hope that is supposedly within them. These Christ-namers praise Him with their lips on Sunday, but deny Him in word and deed the remainder of the week. Are these individuals really children of God? As shown in Ezra 2, we need to be careful in passing judgment, for only the Lord knows who are His and who are the counterfeits; His registry of holy priests is perfect (Rev. 20:15).

August 12 – They Found It Written
Ezra 3

The edict of Cyrus was issued in 538 BC and the Jews disembarked for Israel sometime afterwards in several groups, mostly arriving in their homeland during the first half of 536 BC. A few months after reoccupying various cities throughout Judah, the Jewish returnees *"gathered together as one man to Jerusalem"* to set up an altar on the first day of the seventh month of the same year (i.e., early September). The altar was erected among the remains of the previous temple.

Before the work on the temple could commence, God's sacrificial system for atoning for His people's sins had to be reinstated. The altar and its sacrifices at Jerusalem marked the Jews as a distinctive people among the nations. God's chastening had estranged them from their homeland, but now that they were back in Jerusalem, they were quite willing to identify with Jehovah, and none else. But how should they proceed in this matter? They simply searched the Scripture, and when *"they found it written,"* that was their answer. Scripture comes from God and *"is profitable for doctrine, for reproof, for correction, for instruction in righteousness, that the man of God may be complete, thoroughly equipped for every good work"* (2 Tim. 3:16-17). The Jews were unified in purpose and separated from defilement; they had the Word of God to guide them and the Spirit of God to enable them, which meant that the nation was primed to witness God's greatness!

What is the lesson for the Church? Unless what we say and do is true (scriptural), and Spirit-led, it does not honor God; it is mere religious form, without eternal value. This fact is in opposition to the thinking of some that doctrine should be compromised for the sake of unifying Christians together. In the practical sense, Christian fellowship (i.e. what we share together in the commonwealth of Christ), is dependent on how much we determine we have in common with other believers. While it is true that we will not be able to have the same degree of fellowship with all believers, we should strive to walk as far as we can with all those who have been redeemed by the precious blood of Christ.

In glory all true believers will come into the unity of the faith (Eph. 4:13), but until that time each believer is personally accountable to God to study His Word and establish his or her faith upon it.

August 13 – The Battle for Jerusalem Has Begun
Ezra 3

The Jews understood from the Law that they were required to offer morning and evening sacrifices on God's altar (Ex. 29:38-46) and to keep the Feasts of Jehovah. The first feast to be nationally commemorated after the return of the captives was the Feast of Tabernacles, which began on the 15th day of the seventh month of the Jewish calendar (Lev. 23:34).

The Jews did not have a temple, but they understood that it was through the daily offerings that God had been able to dwell in the midst of His people previously. Even if there was neither temple, nor mercy-seat for God to dwell above, the efficacy of the burnt offerings still remained as long the Jews continued to offer by faith as the Law demanded. As the Jews were surrounded by enemies in their own homeland, it took great courage to raise an altar and begin sacrificing on it after fifty years. Militarily speaking, they were unarmed and outnumbered; their only defense was Jehovah.

It is during this time frame (the third year of Cyrus) that Daniel is made aware of the intense angelic battle raging beyond what is seen, the outcome of which would determine the affairs of men (Dan. 10). Indeed, an intense battle for the control of Jerusalem, the place where Jehovah had chosen to place His name, commenced when the Jews began offering sacrifices to Him again. Edward Dennett observes:

> [They wanted] the protection of their God, and faith discerned that this protection would be ensured on the ground of the efficacy of the sacrifices. And what could be more beautiful than this exhibition of confidence in God? They were but a feeble remnant, having no outward means of defense, and surrounded by enemies of every kind; but their very weakness and peril had taught them the precious lesson, that God was their refuge and strength. The setting up of the altar was therefore their first object; and as soon as the sweet savor of the burnt offerings ascended up to God, all that He was, ... was engaged on their behalf.[15]

Indeed, the Jews were far safer with God and no army, than when Jerusalem was surrounded by her fortified walls, but God had departed from them. Likewise, may we remember that we have no power against wickedness in high places, unless we rest in Christ in the highest place!

August 14 – A More Glorious Temple
Ezra 3

Despite the hostile environment, many Jews offered freewill offerings in addition to the daily sacrifices. Having been purged of their idols, God's people were rejoicing in Him again and, thus, were generous in their giving. They donated funds to pay those working on the temple and to purchase the materials needed for its construction.

The Jews then paused from their labors to dedicate the temple foundation to the Lord. For most of the Jews this was a festive event, but for the ancients of the people, the smaller foundation before them was a bitter reminder of what had been lost fifty-two years earlier. So while the majority shouted for joy and praised God for this accomplishment, others wept with loud voices.

Solomon's temple was enormous and had stood for over four centuries. The temple to be erected on the new foundation was in its shadow; it would suffice as a place to worship Jehovah, but in their estimation the new temple would never hold the grandeur of Solomon's temple. But according to the prophet Haggai, the new temple, as yet unfinished, would have a glory beyond that of the previous temple: *"'The glory of this latter temple shall be greater than the former,' says the Lord of hosts. 'And in this place I will give peace,' says the Lord of hosts"* (Hag. 2:9).

What would make it great was that the Jewish Messiah, the Prince of Peace, would present Himself in the temple that the Jews had just begun to build. This prophecy was fulfilled 2000 years ago by the Lord Jesus Christ; then, about thirty-eight years after His coming, that temple was destroyed, meaning that no one else claiming to be Messiah could ever fulfill Haggai's prophecy. With surety, then, we can proclaim to every Jew, "Your Messiah has already been in Jerusalem."

In retrospect, it was probably best that the Jews did not think too highly of the temple they were erecting, for earlier generations of Jews had become "temple-worshipers," instead of honoring the One who resided there (Jer. 7:4, 14). The structure, having been disassociated from Jehovah, was itself regarded as a bastion of safety. This is a good reminder for Christians today not to worship their worship or to trust in humanly-devised organizations or institutions to support and to protect them against difficulties – our complete trust must be in the Lord too.

May We Serve Christ!

August 15 – Progress Invites Attack
Ezra 4

When God's people are working in unity and for His glory, the enemy of God is sure to take notice and oppose their efforts. This was apparent in Zerubbabel's day, as it was in New Testament times, for wherever the apostles went, laying the foundation of Church truth, the activity of the enemy was prompted.

This is evident in our times as well. Paul reminded the believers at Ephesus that their real battle was not with flesh and blood (i.e. people in the world), but rather *"against principalities, against powers, against the rulers of the darkness of this age, against spiritual hosts of wickedness in the heavenly places"* (Eph. 6:12-13). Satan consistently opposed the Lord Jesus Christ throughout His ministry on earth, and today he continues to oppose Jesus Christ, His gospel message, and those who would spread it. Satan despises Christ and those who identify with Him and works to manipulate various world systems of thinking to exclude Christ from consideration.

Ezra 4 contains two satanic attack strategies which have been repeatedly used in diverting God's people from accomplishing His revealed will. The first is to corrupt God's people through *unnatural unions* (i.e. through close associations with the children of the devil).

As soon as the local inhabitants (mainly Samaritans) heard about what the Jews were doing, they came to Zerubbabel and the other Jewish leaders with a request: *"Let us build with you; for we seek your God"* (v. 2). But they were not one with the Jews or with Jehovah; they were pagans, and their offer was flatly rejected. The enemy had hoped to infiltrate the work of God and cause it to collapse from within.

The second is to mentally fatigue God's people by *discouragement*. But believers are not be *"tossed to and fro, and carried about with every wind of doctrine, by the sleight of men, and cunning craftiness, whereby they lie in wait to deceive"* (Eph. 4:14). Through high-minded philosophies, crafty words, or unrelenting cynicism, Satan attempts to undermine God's work by deceiving or discouraging His laborers. The enemy hired counselors to harass the Jews in threatening or meaningless dialogue to cast doubt on the work's progress or success. Although this tactic by itself did not stop the work, it effectively slowed its progress. Mind-games and word-wars waste precious time.

August 16 – Comfort and Ease Please
Ezra 5

The temple foundation was completed and dedicated in 535 BC, but the building program ceased sometime after that due to the efforts of the enemy to discourage and break down the resolve of God's people. At the outset, the Jews rested solely on God's authority. The sufficiency of His Word was their battle-axe against opposition when they first arrived in Jerusalem; that focus needed to be regained. God called two prophets, Haggai and Zechariah, to reprove His people of sin and to motivate them to again begin the temple construction.

Haggai confronted his countrymen's spiritual complacency and their comfortable standard of living (Hag. 1:2-7). Apparently, materials earlier donated to build the temple had been used by the Jews to build themselves nice paneled houses, while God's house was in ruins.

The prophet went on to inform the Jews that they were being economically punished by God for their lethargic attitudes towards Him. After revealing this reality, he again appealed to them to consider their ways. The Lord's people responded well to Haggai's message. After 15 years of inactivity, the Jews began again to build God a house and they did not pause in their work until it was completed in 515 B.C.

The narrative reveals another satanic tactic used to confront the will of God: the promoting of ease and comfort among His people. Our flesh craves comfort and lusts for pleasure. Christians rarely fall into sin, but rather step down into it (1 Tim. 6:9-10). First, they enjoy *comfort*, an environment void of biblical exhortation and reproof. Over time they become *complacent* to the things of God. The next downward step is *compromise*, which finally leads to *carnality* – willful sin and an appetite for worldliness. Although in many parts of the world today the Church is vibrant and growing, often because of the purifying effect of persecution, this is generally not the case in the post-modern world.

The "pampered Church" today is weak and prone to worldliness. Why should the lost consider the claims of Christ when many Christians do not? Why should the unregenerate fear eternal judgment when the Christians they associate with are quite satisfied with the temporary thrills and the sensual trinkets? If the Church is to witness revival again, she must awaken from her spiritual slumber.

May We Serve Christ!

August 17 – A Prepared Heart
Ezra 7

In 458 BC, the scribe Ezra led a second group of Jews, numbering about 5,000 souls in all, from Babylon to Jerusalem. Under Zerubbabel's leadership a great post-exile revival had occurred among God's people – the *First Jewish Awakening*, per se. By God's help they had overcome immense opposition to erect His temple in Jerusalem. However, during the 57-year interim between Ezra 6 and 7 the Jews had become secular in thinking and worldly in practice. This can happen to God's people in any era when their love for the Lord wanes.

The Jews were no longer a consecrated people and they needed to be bluntly told so. This would be Ezra's calling as a teacher; he would use God's Word to confront, instruct, and encourage his fellow countrymen. The outcome of his ministry would be the *Second Jewish Awakening* (Ezra 7-10). Ezra was a priest with an authentic lineage to Aaron. He rejoiced in his priestly descent and longed to fulfill his calling to serve God by teaching others about Him and His Law. We too must be settled and committed to our calling in Christ if we are going to do anything meaningful for God. Each believer has been given some specific spiritual gift(s) and a calling within the body of Christ to accomplish (1 Cor. 14; Eph. 2:10).

Ezra's 900-mile trip from Babylon to Jerusalem would take four months. He would arrive in Jerusalem mid-summer of 487 BC. From the Jewish perspective, Ezra was a priest and a skilled scribe. He is referred to as a "teacher" four times in Ezra and as a "scribe" six times in Nehemiah.

But Ezra was not just a teacher of God's Word, he was a pursuer of truth and was committed to living out what he knew to be true: *"For Ezra had prepared his heart to seek the Law of the Lord, and to do it, and to teach statutes and ordinances in Israel"* (v. 7). Ezra studied God's Word and then practiced and taught what he knew to be true – these are exemplary marks of a good teacher. How did God respond to Ezra's prepared heart? We repeatedly read that *"God's hand was upon him"* (vv. 6, 9, 28, 8:18, 22, 31). When God empowers a believer who is earnestly determined to know, to do, and to teach others God's Word, great things are bound to happen for the glory of God. Ezra would be privileged to experience this honor.

August 18 – A Humble Prayer of Thanksgiving
Ezra 7

King Artaxerxes granted Ezra all that his heart desired. Ezra's prayer of thanksgiving in response to Artaxerxes' generous decree is admirable. First, he praises the Lord for what God was accomplishing through him, knowing the Lord had strengthened him. Second, he acknowledges that it was God who had put the matter into the king's heart to bless the Jews. It was not Ezra's political influence that moved Artaxerxes to be gracious, but God moving in the king's heart. Third, he states that God was acting to bring honor to Himself and glory to His house. Fourth, Ezra tells Artaxerxes' advisors and officials that his God had shown favor to him by the king's response to his request. Ezra's response to the goodness of God is indeed an honorable pattern for us to follow. Let us be careful not to steal from God what He alone deserves – the praise of men!

Ezra's humility keenly contrasts Artaxerxes' self-exalting pride; he refers to himself as *"the king of kings"* (v. 12). Ezra assumes no title other than what his Levitical heritage bestowed to him as a servant of God (i.e. "a priest"), and as a servant of the people (i.e. "a scribe"). Ezra functioned as a priest and a teacher, but had no formal title associated with those ministries.

Men covet titles so that they might be honored by others. But those who worship Christ must not dishonor Him by stealing His glory through ascribing titles of status to themselves (Matt. 23:8-12). Disciples of Christ seek neither the praise of men nor titles of position – all titles of status and all praise are reserved for the Lord Jesus Christ. Men love titles; yet, no disciple of Christ has any title of position before his or her name in Scripture.

In a spirit of humility, Ezra prepared his heart to follow God and God stirred Artaxerxes' heart and moved his tongue to ensure all that Ezra desired to do and more was made possible. *"The preparations of the heart belong to man, but the answer of the tongue is from the Lord"* (Prov. 16:1). Ezra understood this, but do we? Why do we fret and worry about what only God can control? Ezra sets forth a great example to follow; he declares God's goodness in all that has happened, he thanks the Lord for what He has done, and then he steps forward in faith anticipating what marvelous things God will yet do.

May We Serve Christ!

August 19 – Broken Before the Lord
Ezra 9

Having arrived in Jerusalem, Ezra delivered the king's decree to the governors. Shortly after this, some of the leaders from among the Jews paid a visit to Ezra, informing him that: *"The people of Israel and the priests and the Levites have not separated themselves from the peoples of the lands"* (v. 1). Even some of the Jewish leaders had married local pagans. This was forbidden, as it normally resulted in the corruption of idolatry, the very sin for which the nation had been exiled to Babylon.

The sin of spiritual adultery is hideous to God at any time, but it would be especially so when He had just purged it from His people through severe chastening. How could the people so quickly forget this painful lesson? This is a good example of just how powerful our lusting flesh can be. To willingly do what causes both us and God pain is not a rational or spiritual choice.

Thankfully, there were still some Jewish leaders who were keenly aware of the consequences of these *unnatural unions*, and were moved to help in order to deliver and to restore their brethren from what God abhors. We see that Ezra, having departed from the heart of the pagan world, and having just experienced four months of God's wherewithal through separation and faith, is exceedingly appalled at the pitiful condition of his brethren.

Ezra does not pull away from his spiritual moorings; rather, being immensely vexed, he tears his clothes, pulls hair from his head and beard, and sits down in the dirt. He remains in the dust of the earth until the evening sacrifice. What type of person bends the ear of God? Isaiah informs us: *"But on this one will I look: On him who is poor and of a contrite spirit, and who trembles at My word"* (Isa. 66:2). James puts the matter this way: *"The effective, fervent prayer of a righteous man avails much"* (Jas. 5:16). Thankfully, there were still such men among the remnant, and on them the Lord would bestow His blessing.

Most, if not all, of the great revivals of the Church Age have begun with the same two realities that we have before us. First, God's people were spiritually lethargic and pathetically settled in the world and a remnant of consecrated, God-fearing, Christ-loving, Bible-believing Christians earnestly sought the Lord for a miraculous solution – revival. With this being the case, the modern Church is ripe for revival.

August 20 – Give Us a Reviving
Ezra 9

The situation was bleak and swift action was required to avert God's judgment on them. Indeed, others *"who trembled at the words of the God of Israel"* gathered with Ezra to pray. At such desperate times as this, the words of the prophet Isaiah are worthy of meditation:

> *For thus says the High and Lofty One who inhabits eternity, whose name is Holy: "I dwell in the high and holy place, with him who has a contrite and humble spirit, **to revive** the spirit of the humble, and **to revive** the heart of the contrite ones"* (Isa. 57:15).

The remainder of Ezra 9 records the prayer of Ezra. With his companions, he bows before His Creator and, being fully identified with his countrymen, takes their place before God. He proceeds to confess the nation's past and present sins as his own. The Jews deserved instant reprisal for their offenses, but Jehovah again was demonstrating His long-suffering and forbearing nature to them.

Speaking to God, Ezra proclaims: *"You our God have punished us less than our iniquities deserve, and have given us such deliverance as this"* (v. 13). Ezra was affirming that all God's judgments were righteous and that He had extended to them much undeserved mercy. Even though His people were not faithful to Him, God was ever faithful to them, unchanging in mercy and grace.

The Lord's faithfulness is not dependent on the behavior of men: *"If we are faithless, He remains faithful; He cannot deny Himself"* (2 Tim. 2:13). God is a covenant-keeping God; His blessings and purposes are without repentance; and therein lies the reason for His patience and the fortitude of His people in the presence of their enemies. In confession to God, Ezra speaks as if he were among the guilty and pleads with God to revive them again. After declaring the sins of the nation, Ezra pleads for mercy, though they are undeserving of it.

Having completed the preparatory work of prayer with his companions and having completely entrusted God with the outcome, Ezra is now ready to gather the nation and declare God's Word. He is emboldened to confront sin without regard to religious or social rank.

August 21 – Confession
Ezra 10

In Ezra 9:5, we see Ezra fallen on his knees, spreading out his hands to God and praying as he sobbed aloud. But it is not until Ezra 10 that we discover the location of these exploits; Ezra cast himself down in front of the temple. This action showed everyone that, on behalf of the nation, he was throwing himself on the mercy of God. The entire scene, lasting for hours, was completely public. He was not telling the others what to do, but rather he was showing them the path of righteousness, the whereabouts of which they had long forgotten.

At first, those who feared the Word of God gathered with him, but as Ezra wept and confessed the sins of nations, a great congregation of men and women assembled about him. The Lord used the deep sorrow of His servant for the sins of his fellow countrymen to pierce through their dull consciences. Many of the Jewish leaders seemed to be aware of how far the people had slipped from holy ground.

The Jews did not feel the guilt of their own sin until they had witnessed how deeply it grieved a righteous man who, now prostrate before the Lord, openly mourned for them. The people also began to weep with Ezra, some for contrition and perhaps others in fear of the consequences of their crimes, for Ezra had the authority to judge them as he deemed proper.

It would have been far easier for Ezra to withdraw from those in sin and just let them go their own way, or perhaps preach against them from a lofty pulpit; instead, he personally identified himself with his brethren, demonstrated deep interest and concern for their sorry state, and through personal faithfulness to God lifted the entire company to a higher spiritual plane. God is glorified by the recovery of failing saints and Ezra wanted to reach more than the few who might have responded to direct reproof. Ezra wanted all to come to repentance, both those in sin and those who had winked at it.

Just as God had used one consecrated man, Ezra, to arouse the entire congregation to feel the guilt of breaking God's Law, He would use the zeal of one man, Shechaniah, to speak for the congregation and motivate them to confession and repentance.

August 22 – Separation
Ezra 10

Shechaniah is a man in touch with the character of His God. He boldly stands and speaks to the congregation about the mercy of God: *"Yet now there is hope in Israel in spite of this"* (v. 2). All was not lost – there was still a way of escape and recovery! He, like Ezra, owns the people's sins, and acknowledges their failures as a nation. Moses had commanded them not to marry outside of the Jewish community (Deut. 7:1-4). The taking of a foreign wife was forbidden because they were considered unclean, and their children were also regarded as unclean.

Shechaniah encourages the people to not only repent, but to take responsibility for their sin and put away their foreign wives and the children born to them. God wanted a holy nation, not a double-minded, semi-pagan people. Remember the command, *"Be ye holy; for I am holy"* (Lev. 11:44). This certainly was a difficult thing to do: families were divided and relationships severed, but the Mosaic Law demanded this action.

There would, however, be another set of laws, *the laws of the harvest*, which would dictate the consequences for their disobedience for what *"a man sows, that he will also reap; for he who sows to his flesh will of the flesh reap corruption"* (Gal. 6:7-8). The three laws of the harvest are as follows: You reap what you sow. You reap more than what you sow. You reap later than you sow. All the pain and suffering that they were now experiencing was the result of sinful behavior long ago. The consequences of their sin were much more than they could have ever imagined at the time of the initial sin.

After Shechaniah's confession on behalf of the people, and sensing God's work among His people, Ezra seizes the opportunity and he makes the leaders swear an oath to obey God's Word. The power of one consecrated person to God is thus witnessed – a huge crowd is propelled Godward in action. All Israel was called to assemble in Jerusalem and there Ezra rebuked the people and called them to consecration. The people were under conviction and said, *"Yes! As you have said, so we must do"* (v. 12). It took several months to investigate and take action, but in the end 114 families were impacted. The separations were distressing for all involved, but it is what God demanded – His people must be a holy people, for He is a holy God.

May We Serve Christ!

August 23 – The Cupbearer Mourns and Prays
Nehemiah 1

Nehemiah was the king's cupbearer at Shushan; he was to ensure that the king's wine and perhaps his food had not been poisoned. In the Persian court the cupbearer held a high position; Nehemiah may have been the chief treasurer and the keeper of the king's signet ring. His duties required frequent access to the king, which meant that Nehemiah enjoyed an influential relationship with Artaxerxes; it is doubtful that any Jew could have risen to a higher position than this.

A group of Jews, Nehemiah's brother Hanani being among them, had just returned from visiting Jerusalem. A concerned Nehemiah inquired about the welfare of God's people and the state of Jerusalem. The report was gloomy; the wall around Jerusalem and much of the city lay in ruins, and the burned gates had not been replaced. Though the temple had been built, and sacrifices were being offered to Jehovah, the people themselves were *"in great distress and reproach"* (v. 3).

We read of Nehemiah's response to this report: *"So it was, when I heard these words, that I sat down and wept, and mourned for many days; I was fasting and praying before the God of heaven"* (v. 4). Nehemiah was deeply affected by the dismal report and immediately petitioned the Lord for help while fasting *"day and night"* (v. 6). This does not mean Nehemiah prayed every moment of every day, but rather that he engaged in the type of prayer Paul exhorts the believers at Thessalonica to engage in: *"Pray without ceasing"* (1 Thess. 5:17).

The Greek word *adialeiptos*, which is rendered "without ceasing" implies that our prayers should be "constantly recurring" rather than "continuously occurring." To "pray without ceasing" means to stay in contact with God in such a way that our praying is like a long conversation with short pauses: we never sense a break in communion. The Lord should never be far from our thoughts, for He is always willing to bend His ear to the pangs of a humble heart (Ps. 10:17).

But do we have the same sense of desperation that Nehemiah felt long ago? Do we mourn over the Church's indifference, moral failures, and lack of commitment to Christ and His Word? What might God do today, if believers were broken over the Church's ruined testimony, and in prayer and fasting pleaded with the Lord for a reviving work?

August 24 – An Opportunity and a Quick Prayer
Nehemiah 2

Nehemiah did not know what to do about the situation in Jerusalem, so he committed himself to prayer and waited for the Lord to open the door of opportunity. In the meantime, he faithfully continued to fulfill his responsibilities to Artaxerxes. The king's court was to be a jovial oasis from personal threats and political criticism. Anyone with a downcast demeanor before the king was in danger of insulting him and reaping his wrath.

One day, while Nehemiah was performing his duty, the king noticed Nehemiah's glum disposition. The king knew Nehemiah well and rightly discerned that he was not ill, but rather heartsick with sorrow. The king inquired of Nehemiah what was bothering him, which caused him to become anxious for his life.

Rather than answering presumptuously, Nehemiah breathes out a quick prayer to heaven before making his bold request. These unuttered words from his heart resounded before the throne of grace and prompted an immediate response from heaven. As all believers today are indwelt with the Spirit of God (1 Cor. 6:19-20) direct access to God is available anytime. Through the intercession of the Holy Spirit (Rom. 8:26) and the mediation of God's Son (1 Tim. 2:5) our prayers are presented to God the Father. It is comforting to know that when we do not know what to pray, or are so downhearted we are unable of forming words in prayer, the Spirit of God intercedes perfectly on our behalf.

Nehemiah had been praying and fasting for four months while patiently waiting for God's answer. He had probably been pondering how he could approach the subject with the king, but God's solution was better: He moved the king to question Nehemiah about the matter. This situation teaches us how utterly defenseless the enemy is against the power of earnest praying. Nehemiah expresses the reason for his grief. Without hesitation the king responds, *"What do you request?"* Nehemiah asked the king to send him to Judah to oversee the rebuilding of Jerusalem. The king then gave Nehemiah leave for the time frame he had requested, but also provided building materials for the project and a military escort to ensure his cupbearer accomplished all that was on his heart! Nehemiah marveled at the hand of God upon him. May we experience the same wonder of effectual praying.

August 25 – Do Not Get Sidetracked
Nehemiah 2

Despite Nehemiah's great organizational skills, the work was hampered from the onset; this again reminds us that every true work of God will experience opposition of some sort. The enemy first attempted to *sidetrack* the Jews from commencing the rebuilding project. Sanballat, Tobiah, and Geshem laughed at the Jews for even thinking about undertaking such an immense project and insinuated that if they did fortify Jerusalem, that the king would consider them rebels.

Nehemiah's response was curt: *"The God of heaven Himself will prosper us; therefore we His servants will arise and build, but you have no heritage or right or memorial in Jerusalem"* (2:20). In short, Nehemiah was saying, "Butt out; this is none of your business; our God is with us, He has assigned us this task to do for Him, and that is all that matters." Thankfully, the Jews were not diverted from the mission by the challenge, but rather became a more invigorated workforce.

As in Nehemiah's day, the devil never bothers with halfhearted believers, but once they become desperate for God and burdened for the work of God, he will intensify his opposition against them. Satan hates that which is precious to the Lord; namely, a testimony of His greatness through His people. Jerusalem was and will be the center of God's earthly purposes for His covenant people. Thus, Satan opposed the building of the wall in Nehemiah's time as he had stood against the building of the temple in Zerubbabel's day.

Likewise, in the Church Age, Satan opposes any true testimony of God's character and nature as established in gatherings of His people (i.e. assemblies of Christians). Today, it is not a temple or a wall that manifests the manifold wisdom of God, but the Church: *"To the intent that now the manifold wisdom of God might be made known by the church to the principalities and powers in the heavenly places, according to the eternal purpose which He accomplished in Christ Jesus our Lord"* (Eph. 3:10-11). It should therefore be no surprise that when a local assembly becomes burdened to remove the debris of religious pride, carnality, and spiritual slothfulness from their midst in order to erect a true testimony for Christ, the enemy will intensely seek to thwart the rebuilding program.

August 26 – Ignore Ridicule
Nehemiah 4

In Nehemiah 3, we witnessed Nehemiah's ability to motivate the Jews to rise up and build, but the enemy quickly noticed and mobilized its forces to hinder them. Being unable to *sidetrack* the Jews with idle words and fanciful questions, the enemy resorted to a more brazen tactic – *mocking and ridicule* (vv. 1-3). Sanballat and Tobiah belittled the Jews in front of the Samaritan soldiers, calling them "feeble."

They further claimed that the task was too enormous to tackle and even if they did erect a wall around the city, it wouldn't be stable, saying that even a fox climbing on it would pull it down. The enemy wanted the work to fail in its infancy by insisting that the Jews did not know what they were doing and didn't have the means to accomplish the task. The devil labors to plant doubt where God's people are grounded in faith.

Sanballat asked five questions in an attempt to cause the Jews to conclude their situation was hopeless (v. 2). The implication of these questions was the Jews had no idea of the immensity of the work, nor did they have the proper resources to do the work, and thus there would be no celebratory offerings. Nothing has changed today; there are still people who want God-honoring ministries to fail and if they cannot stop the work of God, then they will ridicule the servants of God.

How did Nehemiah respond to the enemy's ridicule? He ignored what was said and resorted to prayer: *"Hear, O our God, for we are despised"* (v. 4). This was Nehemiah's pattern of service: he prays, he plans, he responds to attack with more prayer, and he keeps working. While this is a good example for us to follow, we realize that in the Church Age, we do not pray for God to directly judge our enemies, as Nehemiah prayed. Christians must (should) desire that their adversaries experience God's grace and be saved. The Lord instructed His disciples to pray for and show love to their enemies; perhaps some will repent and be saved (Luke 6:27-35). Such kindness demonstrates God's grace in action and can soften the hardest of rebel hearts. Thus, Christians are not to pray for the destruction of their persecutors, as Nehemiah prayed, but are rather to pray for their salvation and strive to overcome their evil deeds by good works (Rom. 12:19-21). Yet, the Jews' example of praying for God's protection as they continued His work is admirable.

August 27 – Be Watchful
Nehemiah 4

The Jews had a mind to work and the wall was raised to half of its final height fairly quickly. The enemy, aware of the Jews' persistence and their progress, countered them with more intense opposition. God's people are never more powerful than when they have a mind to work and a heart to pray! Seeing that the work was progressing quickly, the enemy gathered its forces and conspired together to fight against the Jews. Nehemiah knew how to organize the people and to agonize in prayer; he asked for God's protection and set a watch against the enemy day and night. He had a heart for the people, which inspired them to move beyond what they thought they could ever do.

Some Jews were taken from the rigors of building to the important task of watching and alerting others if the enemy attacked. Everyone was to be armed and in a state of readiness. If the alarm sounded, the Jews were to quickly depart from their designated work areas and engage their oppressors. This strategy would use the first line of defense to detain the enemy from penetrating into the ranks of God's people until reinforcements could arrive to drive off the attackers.

This scene reminds us of Peter's exhortation to Christians who were suffering Roman persecution: *"Be sober, be vigilant; because your adversary the devil walks about like a roaring lion, seeking whom he may devour. Resist him, steadfast in the faith, knowing that the same sufferings are experienced by your brotherhood in the world"* (1 Pet. 5:8-9). Watchfulness is an important feature of the Christian life; a matter the Lord stressed several times to His disciples in the final days of His ministry on earth.

Too often the enemy crouches in some unforeseen circumstance and then mercilessly pounces on unsuspecting believers who are caught completely off guard. The result can be personally devastating to the believer, but more importantly the name of the Lord Jesus is slandered by men. Believer, be blameless in your conduct and be alert for the enemy to strike at any time – when you least expect it, expect it. Rarely does the enemy attack where we anticipate. Consequently, we must be personally fortified with the whole armor of God at all times, otherwise Satan will eventually find out through observation where we are vulnerable and attack there.

Daily Devotions

August 28 – Remove the Rubbish
Nehemiah 4

Sanballat knew that the Jews were working with Artaxerxes' permission so a frontal assault by the Samaritan forces would not be a viable solution; however, guerilla warfare was. To engage in terrorist activities, especially if at night, would leave no credible evidence of the perpetrators, while it would incite fear in the Jewish workforce.

Besides the constant threat of violence, the resolve of the Jewish labor force was waning. As the enemy continued plotting without, the people grew faint within. There was a lot of debris from the previous wall that had to be cleared away before construction of the new wall could begin. Previously, Nehemiah was unable to navigate his horse through the debris field on the eastern side of the city during his nighttime inspection (2:14-15). Many of the stones from the previous wall had been exposed to intense heat, causing them to be brittle and thus unusable. It would have been easier to build upon the existing rubble, but the walls would have been less stable and durable.

The unprofitable debris had to be cleared away to build on a solid foundation – this was necessary for a lasting testimony. The application for us is this: before we build up for God, we first need to look down on ourselves. Religious smugness, careless attitudes, coldness of heart, and pride in any form must be removed before we can see clearly to erect a testimony for God. His Word alone is the Rock that we can build on. Foundations laid on personal glory, false doctrine, and humanism will crumble away (Luke 6:46-49; 1 Cor. 3:11-15).

It may seem like it would be easier to build on something that already exists, but ultimately only what is founded on Christ will stand the test of time and eternity. If your local church has been struggling to raise up a testimony for Christ, it is time to investigate the foundation you are building on; perhaps there is rubbish from the past which is hindering progress. We should not feel sentimental about that which is hampering the work of the Lord; it must be dealt with. We must look down before we can build up!

The Jews, despite the daunting task before them, were determined to clear away the debris first and build on a good foundation. They wanted a lasting testimony for Jehovah, not something that looked good at first and then crumbled away later.

May We Serve Christ!

August 29 – Fight for Your Brethren!
Nehemiah 4

Discouragement, the persistent foe of the soul, was gaining ground in the hearts of the Jews. The enemy was threatening, the work was immense, and God's people were weary – this is when the devil's tool of discouragement is most effective in neutralizing the zeal of God's people. Discouragement is like a stout airborne virus that rapidly infects others. As this emotional epidemic progressed, a defeatist mentality began to sweep through the Jewish community.

Today as then, if discouragement is not quickly treated, those rising to build a testimony for God will become self-focused and cease to be profitable in the work. Nehemiah knew this and furnished the Jews with a battle cry to help them overcome discouragement: *"Remember the Lord ... Fight for Your Brethren!"* (v. 14). In the midst of overwhelming circumstances, if believers keep their eyes focused on the Lord, they will find less opportunity to be occupied with self; despair cannot thrive in a selfless environment.

As a safeguard, he organized families and clans into work groups which would be responsible for protecting each other as they labored together. As a result, the enemy's counsel against them was defeated and the work continued. This panorama reflects how the Church should respond to attempts to hinder God's work today. God was *among* His covenant people in the days of Nehemiah and working with them to establish a vivid testimony of His prominence over the nations.

Today, God dwells *within* His people to accomplish the same purpose (Eph. 2:20-22). Through Nehemiah's leadership the wall was completed in fifty-two days and stood as a testimony of Jehovah's character and nature. This accomplishment proved to the opposition that the God of the Hebrews was most powerful and was with His people; this would serve as a warning to those who wanted to hurt them in the future.

Today, God declares His wisdom and power by confounding the opposition through the Church (Eph. 3:10-11). Through the Church, the unregenerate witness the awesome nature of God and His capacity to do the unbelievable in His people. May God's people today follow the example of the Jews with Nehemiah who, in the Lord's strength, live the theme: Remember the Lord – Fight for Your Brethren!

August 30 – The Need for Spiritual Revival
Nehemiah 8

King Artaxerxes commissioned Ezra to teach the Jews their own Law and to maintain order in the region by enforcing it. He initially arrived in Jerusalem some thirteen years before Nehemiah did. Ezra was appalled at the spiritual condition of his people; besides being ignorant of God's law, some, including Jewish leaders and priests, had intermarried with pagans. His anguish over the nation's sin led him to publicly fall prostrate before the Lord in front of the temple – his prayer moved the people to repentance and to separation (Ezra 9-10).

Under Nehemiah's leadership, the Jews unified and rebuilt the wall with its gates to secure Jerusalem from its enemies. In previous chapters, we witnessed Nehemiah's unwavering resolve to erect this spectacular testimony of God's greatness. Although the opposition continually sought to distract and demoralize the much smaller workforce, the Jews, sustained by divine grace, built the wall nonetheless.

Hopefully, every believer longs for such a working of God's grace within his or her life so that a lasting testimony of God's goodness will be recognized by others. We learn from Nehemiah that the key to triumphing over the enemy is to rely on the Lord for help and direction while at the same time refusing to be sidetracked from the objective, which is doing the will of God!

One of the greatest threats to the prosperity of the Jews was their poor spiritual condition – they were largely ignorant of the Law. Both Ezra and Nehemiah knew that they, as God's covenant people, were accountable to God to know the Law and obey it. God had already brought about the destruction of Jerusalem once because of willful sin, and certainly He could be provoked to do it again. Indeed, He did, in 70 AD after the Jews rejected His own Son as their Messiah.

The Jews had banded together to accomplish an incredible feat, but more than anything, they needed to draw near to God and experience ongoing spiritual revival. Without revival, their great accomplishments could easily be negated by moral decline; they must fully identify with Jehovah and live according to His Law. Thankfully, there was a second spiritual awakening among the people through the ministry of the scribe Ezra. We refer to this as the Water Gate Revival.

May We Serve Christ!

August 31 – The Water Gate Revival – Part 1
Nehemiah 8

A careful study of Nehemiah 8 and 9 will reveal several key characteristics of spiritual revival. These same attributes are associated with other revivals recorded in Scripture and in Church history. We will examine each of these eight characteristics and hopefully encourage ourselves to yearn for spiritual revival in our lives also.

1. Deplorable Spiritual Conditions

As was the case when Ezra first arrived in Jerusalem thirteen years earlier, even after the rebuilding of the wall the Jews were a spiritually destitute people (Ezra 9). They knew that they were God's covenant people, but the teaching of God's Word had been generally neglected since the fall of Jerusalem a century and a half earlier. Even two centuries prior to the Water Gate Revival, God's Word was not being publicly taught. The Book of the Law had been lost until priests in King Josiah's reign happened upon it (2 Kgs. 22). Because of neglect, the temple was in disrepair and the Word of God had been forgotten, though it resided right where it was supposed to be, in God's house.

Today, Christians are the temple of God (Eph. 2:19-22), and we too will fall into disrepair if we neglect God's Word which is to be hidden within our hearts (Ps. 119:11). If God's Word is merely in our Bibles and not hidden in the hearts, then we too, like the Jews before us, will experience spiritual decline. As in Ezra's day, declension results when believers neglect to read, to understand, and to obey God's Word.

2. Effectual and Fervent Prayer of the Righteous

Ezra's private and public prayers preceded the previous revival (Ezra 9:5-9). This pattern is also exhibited in Acts 1, where believers gathered for prayer while they waited for the coming of the Holy Spirit. When He did come, the Church was created and believers were empowered to preach the gospel message and 3,000 souls were saved that same day. These Christians obeyed the Lord's command to wait in Jerusalem until the Holy Spirit would take up residence within them (Acts 1:4-8). When God's people are revitalized by the Spirit of God, the lost are affected too – this is a true mark of spiritual revival.

September 1 – The Water Gate Revival – Part 2
Nehemiah 8

We are continuing to examine the eight key characteristics which marked the Water Gate Revival spawned by Ezra's teaching:

3. Renewed Reverence for God's Word

A large congregation of Jews gathered at the Water Gate and asked Ezra and the Levites to teach them the Law, which they were obliged to do. Unbeknown to the Jews, their assembling coincided with the Feast of Trumpets, which was to be held on the first day of the seventh month (Lev. 23:24). On this day, Ezra and thirteen fellow priests took to a wood platform. Besides creating an environment in which the preachers could be more easily heard, the entire scene shows the prominence the Word of God is to have in public meetings of His people.

Twice we read that *"all who could hear with understanding"* had gathered to listen; in other words, men, women, and children were together while Ezra was speaking. This was also the pattern of the early Church. Seven times in his first epistle to the Corinthians, Paul uses the expression "when you come together," or something similar, to speak of the entire assembly coming together for the meetings of the church (e.g., 1 Cor. 5:4, 7:5, 11:17, 14:23). This is not to say that believers should not come together privately throughout the week in order to encourage each other, but rather when the church gathers, it is for a common purpose as a unified body under its Head – Christ.

The Jews had all come together to hear the Law of Moses. Their respect for Scripture and their desire to understand it was demonstrated in that they stood for six hours while God's Word was being taught. The Jews were attentive as Ezra stood on a wooden platform in order to be heard by the large congregation. History has yet to record a revival among God's people in which the Word of God did not first have a prominent place in their hearts. Other biblical examples include the revivals under King Hezekiah and then later King Josiah. Church history also records that the Reformation in the 16th century, the Great Awakenings in the 17th and the 18th centuries, and the General Awakening and the Brethren Movement in the 19th century all began with a renewed passion for God's Word.

September 2 – The Water Gate Revival – Part 3
Nehemiah 8

We are continuing to examine the eight key characteristics which marked the Water Gate Revival spawned by Ezra's teaching:

4. The Worship of God
Prior to expounding Scripture, Ezra prayed. He praised the one and only great God. This action had a profound effect on the people. It was essential for them to be reminded of God's eminence and their own feebleness. They were in full agreement and responded with *"Amen, Amen,"* meaning, *"this is true, this is true."* As the Jews declared this, they lifted their hands and arms up above their heads, their palms held heavenward, and their faces downcast. Their posture silently proclaimed: "Lord, we are empty handed, we have nothing; all we need comes from You alone." Revival not only produces reverence for God's Word, but also deliberate recognition of the majesty of God.

5. Comprehension of Scripture
Ezra engaged in expository teaching of Scripture: *"So they read distinctly from the book, in the Law of God; and they gave the sense, and helped them to understand the reading"* (v. 8). After the Babylonian captivity, as a spoken language Hebrew had been largely displaced by Aramaic; therefore, the Hebrew words spoken to Ezra's audience required careful explanation. Scripture was read clearly, and then it was explained so all could both hear and understand it. It is quite doubtful that Ezra distracted the people with touching stories and funny jokes on this momentous occasion. Likewise, teachers today should be careful not to taint the teaching of divine truth with distracting fodder.

In order to help the people to understand, thirteen teachers, plus other Levites, were dispersed among the congregation to answer specific questions about what Ezra was teaching. Once the general populace understood what had been taught, Ezra continued by reading another portion of Scripture and explaining it. The Word of God had a wonderful effect on the people *"because they understood the words that were declared to them"* (v. 12). Ezra's teaching style was quite effective because he not only preached the Word, but also confirmed that his audience understood what was being taught.

Daily Devotions

September 3 – The Water Gate Revival – Part 4
Nehemiah 8

We are continuing to examine the eight key characteristics which marked the Water Gate Revival spawned by Ezra's teaching:

6. Remorse and Repentance of Sin

Comprehension of Scripture brought brokenness: *"the people wept bitterly"* (v. 9). This same contriteness was observed during the revival some thirteen years earlier, after Ezra's public prayer (Ezra 10:1). Now again, the people were grieved over their personal conduct, knowing that it was not what God expected and demanded of them. The people began confessing their sins, beginning with those in leadership, followed by the men, the women, and the children.

Although no public prayers are recorded in the narrative during Ezra's sermon, there can be no doubt that public prayers were uttered at this time. The earlier revival began when one brokenhearted man confessed the sins of the nation as his own; this in turn prompted the people to be grieved over their own sins as well (Ezra 10:1-2).

If Ezra were to visit our local churches today, he would have something to say to us about our spiritual adultery, cold hearts, materialism, and a lack of reverence for God and His Word. If we heard such a message, would it break our hearts that we too might be revived?

If we want to see revival in our lifetimes, we must step out of the darkness of sin and get real with God. Many who identify with Christ today are neither devoted to Him nor His Word, because of the blindness and despondency that sin causes. Godly sorrow is more than mere regret for our failures; it is a desire to get things right with God through repentance. If one only experiences the conviction of God's Word apart from repentance, he or she will be most miserable.

However, true repentance and divine forgiveness release all the sequestered guilt in one's soul. This is why Ezra, after the Word of God had accomplished its work in bringing about repentance, told the people, *"the joy of the Lord is your strength"* (v. 10). In fact, the Jews turned their day of reckoning with God into a day of feasting. Their mourning was displaced with joy.

September 4 – The Water Gate Revival – Part 5
Nehemiah 8

We are continuing to examine the eight key characteristics which marked the Water Gate Revival spawned by Ezra's teaching:

7. Obedience to God's Word

The crowd dispersed, but the next day, the leaders of the various clans and families returned to learn more from God's Word. These, the representatives of the nation, were taught about the Feasts of Jehovah, which they had neglected to keep for some time. They learned that the upcoming Feast of Tabernacles should be held on the fifteenth day of the seventh month (Lev. 23:34). Unlike the Feast of Atonement, which mainly involved the priests, the Feast of Tabernacles provided an opportunity for all Jews to participate and show devotion to God and His commands.

A proclamation was sent; the Jews were going to commemorate the Feast of Tabernacles. Instructions were also delivered to the people as to how to construct the booths associated with the feast. The Jews obeyed God's Word and constructed makeshift booths and then dwelt in them for eight days as required. The writer then notes that the Jews had not built and lived within booths for eight days since Joshua led them into Canaan.

8. Rejoicing With God

Although the chapter began with sorrow over sin, it ends with joy, for *"there was very great gladness"* among God's people (v. 17). The Levites had reminded the people that the joy of the Lord was their strength. Given the immensity of their failure, one might be tempted to think that the Jews should wallow in guilt and remorse for a while, but the instruction of the Levites to the Jews affirms that God wanted them to rejoice. Through the preaching of and submitting to God's Law the Jews experienced renewed fellowship with God. They were sensing God's presence and an atmosphere of joy pervaded Jerusalem. This is the outcome of revival – the Spirit of God filling His people with power and joy. God renews and revitalizes His people to experience the awe of His presence and to happily go on with Him. This is true spiritual fellowship which has the benefit of drawing lost souls to Christ!

September 5 – Fasting and Courage
Esther 4

The Jews, as an enslaved people in the Persian Empire, had no rights per se, thus they perceived the king's edict as a serious threat. Many, including Mordecai, tore their clothes, wore sackcloth, fasted, and mourned bitterly. Mordecai's example of publicly identifying with God's people and their unjust plight is one to follow. Civil laws that disdain the name of Christ and oppress His Church today should cause us to do more than to sorrow privately. We should be willing to expose corruption and ask the Lord to act against it (Eph. 5:11). Mordecai walked the streets weeping bitterly in response to Haman's unjust law.

After hearing of Mordecai's civil exhibition, Esther sent him proper attire, but Mordecai refused it; he would not discard his sackcloth. Esther then sent Hathach, one of the king's eunuchs, to inquire of Mordecai about the matter. Mordecai provided Hathach a copy of the deal Haman had struck with the king to destroy the Jewish people. Mordecai requested that Esther would petition the king on behalf of her people; Hathach then returned to Esther with the information.

After hearing her uncle and adopted father's message, Esther tells Hathach to inform Mordecai that no one can enter the king's inner court without being summoned and live, unless the king extends the golden scepter to him; she adds that the king has not requested her presence in thirty days. Esther believed that since a month had passed without her interacting with the king, a favorable response by the king towards her intrusion into his court was at best questionable.

Mordecai immediately answered Esther. He stated that the edict was against her as well as her family and therefore she could not keep silent. He then suggested that Esther may have been divinely chosen for this just cause: *"who knows whether you have come to the kingdom for such a time as this?* (v. 14).

Esther's reply to Mordecai conveyed her resolve to honor Mordecai's wishes and to seek the king's assistance no matter the personal cost to her. She also asked that he and other local Jews fast on her behalf; she and her maids would do the same. Then, she promises, *"I will go to the king, which is against the law; and if I perish, I perish!* (v. 16). Esther demonstrated selfless courage, an underlying hope in divine intervention. God will honor her bravery.

September 6 – Touching the Golden Scepter
Esther 4

Esther was true to her word, and after three days of fasting with her attendants, she put on her royal attire and stood at the entrance to the king's inner courtroom. Xerxes was sitting on his throne, which faced this entrance. At this moment Esther is completely helpless – she now has two death sentences against her, although Haman's law condemning her to death is still a secret matter.

The king looks up and notices his queen; no doubt there was an intense silence as everyone was wondering what Xerxes would do in response to this imposition. Given his favorable response, perhaps Xerxes even smiled at his queen as he held out his golden scepter to her. The only way for Esther to avoid execution was to acknowledge acceptance of the king's mercy. This she does by stepping forward and touching his scepter.

What a wonderful picture of God's mercy to us. Each of us was born into this world bearing two death sentences: an appointment with physical death, because we were born spiritually dead (i.e., separated from God; Rom. 5:12). Thankfully, the Lord Jesus nailed our death sentences to His cross (Col. 2:14) and bore the judgment for our sin. This one time act satisfied God's judicial anger concerning our offenses against Him. Hence, the solution to both calamities is found in the One who sits on God's throne in heaven and Who is quite willing to extend the scepter of mercy to those who request it by faith (John 14:6).

Xerxes knew that the Queen would not risk death to venture into his presence unrequested unless the matter was urgent, hence he addresses Esther kindly: *"What do you wish, Queen Esther? What is your request? It shall be given to you – up to half the kingdom!"* (v. 3). This meant that the king would grant any reasonable request. Here we are reminded that the Lord does not merely grant mercy to the undeserving but also abundant grace to satisfy all our legitimate needs. (Phil. 4:19).

What a relief to Esther's heart – the king favored her and encouraged her! Esther did not reveal the particular burden of her soul at this time, but merely requested the king and Haman attend a banquet that she had prepared for them. Haman was immediately summoned to attend. That very day, the two most powerful people in the Persian Empire privately dined with Esther as she had requested.

September 7 – Esther's Banquet
Esther 5

After the main meal was eaten, it was customary in Persia to continue the banquet with fruits and wine. It was at this time that Xerxes, sensing that Esther had much more on her mind than feasting with her king, again inquired of her request. Before she answered, he again affirmed his desire to grant her request if it was reasonable. Given Xerxes' readiness to oblige Esther, we might wonder why she only bid the king and Haman to return tomorrow for another banquet before informing the king of her dire appeal. William MacDonald suggests several reasons why Esther reacted this way:

1. She wanted time to ingratiate herself with the king, having apparently been out of favor with him (4:9-12).
2. Her courage failed her both times (i.e., in the throne room and at the first banquet).
3. She wanted to build up an element of suspense and impress upon the king that her business was vitally important and no mere whim.
4. She wanted to inflate Haman's pride and take him off guard before she exposed him as a vicious murderer.[16]

Perhaps elements of some or all the above entered into Esther's patient strategy, one that she had carefully thought through during the previous three days of fasting. She epitomizes the words of Isaiah: *"Whoever believes will not act hastily"* (Isa. 28:16). True faith is not easily rattled or fostered in rash behavior; it serenely rests in the providential care of an omnipotent and omniscient God. Regardless of what her reasoning, it becomes clear in chapter 6 that certain elements of God's sovereign plan had yet to be realized in order to achieve the greatest deliverance of His people – Esther's patience was rewarded.

A joyful Haman was puffed up more than ever after departing from Esther's banquet for home, that is, until he saw Mordecai in the king's gate. Mordecai did not even stand up, per Persian protocol, to acknowledge Haman's presence. Haman suppressed his indignation towards Mordecai and once home, called together his wife and his friends to boast of his wealth and political achievements, and his banquet with the queen and of another one to come. Life was good!

September 8 – The King's Insomnia
Esther 6

Xerxes had asked his queen twice as to the nature of her request, but she chose to delay answering him. The queen had risked her life to approach him, then twice denied his inquiries to know what the urgency was – that did not make sense to the king. There may have been other pressing matters, but certainly this domestic quandary was on the king's mind and sleep evaded him. What better way to try to fall asleep than to read something quite boring, so the king commanded that the court chronicles be read to him.

During this recitation, Xerxes learned that Mordecai had foiled a plot against his life by two doorkeepers (2:21-23), but nothing had been done to honor him. Note the improbability of all the following events occurring together: the king's insomnia, the decision to read the chronicles (with years of history), the reading of the exact portion about Mordecai's heroics, the king's inquiry as to how Mordecai was rewarded, the king's desire to immediately honor Mordecai, and Haman's planned visit the next morning to ask for Mordecai's life (the gallows were already built).

Clearly, God was exercising His sovereign control over the king's heart to ensure he would have a favorable opinion of Mordecai at the time of Esther's banquet the next day in order to react unfavorably against Haman. When Haman came to see the king the next morning, he had every intention of asking Xerxes for permission to hang Mordecai, but immediately after being admitted to the inner courtroom, the king interrupted Haman's intended request with a question: *"What shall be done for the man whom the king delights to honor?"* (v. 6).

Having ensured himself that the king could only be thinking of him, Haman suggested how to bestow high honor to such an individual: He should wear the royal crest and king's robe, and be placed on the king's horse and paraded through the streets by the most noble princes who will proclaim that "this is the man whom the king delights to honor." This all sounded good to the king, so he asked Haman to do all that he had suggested to Mordecai. Haman must have been speechless; the king delighted in the same man that he wanted to execute and worse, he was commanded to parade his chief antagonist through the streets and proclaim the king's esteem for him – indeed, pride goes before the fall!

Daily Devotions

September 9 – An Urgent Plea
Esther 6

King Xerxes had suffered a sleepless night and Haman had a busy morning parading Mordecai before the people, but both arrived at Esther's banquet at the appointed time. Xerxes asked his wife for a third time what her request was. The long suspense was over; The Queen revealed her petition: *"If I have found favor in your sight, O king, and if it pleases the king, let my life be given me at my petition, and my people at my request"* (v. 3). The king was stunned by this request, his beloved wife, the Queen of Persia, had become a beggar in his presence. Esther continued, *"For we have been sold, my people and I, to be destroyed, to be killed, and to be annihilated"* (v. 4). If the decree had pertained to slavery only and not the annihilation of her people, she would have remained silent. Having identified her ethnicity, Esther bravely takes her place with her condemned people.

Esther's passionate and articulate appeal struck the right chord with her husband. He immediately demands her to identify the person that wants to kill her. Having brought the dialog to its desired crescendo, Esther blurts out: *"The adversary and enemy is this wicked Haman!"* (v. 6) – strike one. This is one of the greatest moments of surprise recorded in Scripture; neither Xerxes nor Haman had a clue that Esther was a condemned Jew. Haman is instantly filled with terror – he knows his life is in jeopardy. The king never thought that Haman's plot would have such far-reaching implication to him personally. Enraged, Xerxes leaves the room to clear his head and think through the situation.

Haman felt no remorse for his actions; rather, he cast himself on the Queen's couch and pleads for his life. This behavior was a breach of proper etiquette and having found Haman in such a position next to Esther, the king accused Haman of wanting to assault the queen – strike two. Haman is arrested and a eunuch suggests that he be hanged on the gallows that Haman had built for Mordecai, the man the king desired to greatly honor – strike three. The King immediately approved this idea.

It is good for us to remember, that those who act in self-will sooner or later will suffer self-reproach. Although the initial Law could not be undone, a new one permitting the Jews to protect themselves was issued. God turned the entire matter around – the Jews won a great victory over their enemies and Mordecai was exalted in the kingdom.

September 10 – A Righteous Man
Job 1

We are now introduced to a wealthy man named Job. He dwelt in the arid land of Uz. Job was upright; honesty and integrity marked his relationship with others. He was a God-fearing man, which is the foundation of true wisdom. Job shunned evil; he genuinely hated what God detested and lived accordingly. God had immensely blessed Job and chosen to protect him, his house, and his affairs. Job was monogamous, and his wife bore him seven sons and three daughters. His laboring animals, herds and flocks were vast. Job and his family enjoyed a peaceful existence with frequent feasting. To atone for any sins committed, Job offered burnt offerings on behalf of his family.

In verse 6 we transition from this pleasant earthly scene to the throne room of heaven, where various angels are submitting reports and rendering homage to God. Satan is also present. God interrogates Satan, who relentlessly roves about the world causing havoc, about his doings. Satan cannot deceive God, so he answers Him truthfully.

Notice that it is the Lord who initiated the conversation with Satan concerning Job: *"Have you considered My servant Job, that there is none like him on the earth, a blameless and upright man, one who fears God and shuns evil?"* (v. 8). Satan could not contradict God's assessment of Job's godly behavior, but he could allege the man had wrong motives for worshipping God; Job was not serving God because he loved Him, but rather because of the prosperity he received from God. The Lord's response was concise: *"Behold, all that he has is in your power; only do not lay a hand on his person"* (v. 12). God willingly allows the devil to buffet Job, to test and refine him, for the honor of His own name.

Job was an upright man whose outward behavior showed immense reverence for the Lord. Yet, his heart was not perfect; there were secret attitudes that needed to be dealt with, which no one was aware of but the Lord. No matter how much we try to hide from God's penetrating scrutiny, He clearly sees into the deepest recesses of our hearts, into the undergirding of our souls (Heb. 4:13). Because God sees and knows what is best for us, He must act against that which is not pleasing to Him. As we will soon see, the process can be quite painful, but the end result is closer fellowship with God and Christ-likeness.

September 11 – A Righteous Man Tested
Job 1

Quite eager to commence mayhem in a Jehovah-worshipper's life, and now having divine permission to do so, *"Satan went out from the presence of the Lord"* (v. 12). He wastes no time in bereaving Job of his children and despoiling him of all his wealth. Demonic blow after blow fell in quick succession upon the devout head of Job. First, the Sabeans stole his oxen and donkeys, and slew his servants. Second, fire from heaven (possibly lightning strikes) consumed all his sheep and his servants watching over them. Third, a raid by the Chaldeans stripped him of all his camels, and they also slew his servants. Lastly, a messenger informed Job that all ten of his children had been killed when a great wind storm collapsed the house of his eldest son, where they had all gathered to feast.

In an instance of time, Job had been stripped of his commerce (oxen and donkeys), his comfort (his wool-producing sheep), his transportation (his camels), most of his labor force, and his posterity (his children). All that remained to Job was his health, his wife, a few servants, and a roof over his head; the posterity and prosperity of the richest man in the East had been swept away!

On hearing of the final catastrophe, an afflicted Job responded in a way few would. He tore his robe, shaved his head, and fell to the ground to worship: *"Naked I came from my mother's womb, and naked shall I return there. The Lord gave, and the Lord has taken away; blessed be the name of the Lord"* (vv. 20-21). By this amazing statement Job was affirming God's sovereign authority over himself and all that he had, thus transforming a most miserable situation into an occasion of adoration and praise. Job could say blessed be the name of the Lord, because he had been righteously wealthy and not filthy rich.

Though emotionally devastated by the entire ordeal, his faith was intact, *"Job did not sin nor charge God with wrong"* (v. 22). In other words, Job did not believe God was acting out of character in all that he had suffered. It is an astounding affirmation by one who honored God and outraged Satan. All the false accusations of the devil were now flung back in his face. Job had shown he was devoted to the Lord apart from receiving any gain for serving Him. May we remember that God is always good, but His goodness may not always be evident to us.

September 12 – A Righteous Man Tested Again
Job 2

We return again to the heavenly scene in Job 2. Satan returns to present himself before God as in Job 1. The Lord again raises the subject of His loyal servant Job: *"Have you considered My servant Job, that there is none like him on the earth, a blameless and upright man, one who fears God and shuns evil? And still he holds fast to his integrity, although you incited Me against him, to destroy him without cause"* (v. 3). In the throne room of heaven before all powers and principalities, the devil is reminded of his past failure. This must have been an infuriating discourse. Not only had he failed to entice Job to sin, but Job's allegiance despite immense hardship disproved his previous assertion against his motivation for honoring God. Indeed, Job had chosen to worship the Lord, even without receiving His good favor.

Yet, Satan is unabashed by his failure to rob God of glory and halt the worship of one of His servants. Satan levies a new accusation against Job: *"Skin for skin! Yes, all that a man has he will give for his life. But stretch out Your hand now, and touch his bone and his flesh, and he will surely curse You to Your face!"* (vv. 4-5). Satan suggests that Job would surrender everything, including his piety for God, in order to save his life. In response to this evil claim, the Lord gave Satan authority to physically afflict Job, but he could not take his life.

The enemy of God wasted no time; he promptly departed and *"struck Job with painful boils from the sole of his foot to the crown of his head"* (v. 7). So grievous was the affliction that Job took up residence on an ash heap and passed the days and hours by scraping himself with a potsherd.

Despite Job's debilitating condition, he held fast to his integrity, which was an affront to his grief-stricken wife. To this point, she had suffered with her husband in silence, but now her companion, provider, and protector had been attacked, meaning she was also helpless; for all her children are gone. In anguish of soul, she tells her husband: *"Curse God, and die"* (v. 9). Job knew that such talk was foolish so he asked her, *"Shall we indeed accept good from God, and shall we not accept adversity?"* (v. 10). In other words, if our God is good and does good, shall we not be willing to accept all that He has for us? May we all remember that the only answer to Job's question is an emphatic "yes."

September 13 – Three Miserable Friends
Job 2

Thankfully, God is more interested in bettering Job than just seeing him honored. He knows of something in Job which must be exposed and removed. Satan knows nothing of it; in fact, Job's response to his attacks has humiliated him and proven him once again to be a liar. Undoubtedly, Job was struggling with his thoughts, and wrestling with inner feelings and various questions. Yet, Scripture affords him a high accolade: *"In all this Job did not sin with his lips"* (v. 10).

Sadly, this remarkable testimony would be somewhat marred during Job's later discussions with his three friends: Eliphaz the Temanite, Bildad the Shuhite, and Zophar the Naamathite. Although they came to mourn with Job and comfort him in his distress, their influence on Job was not a good one. What Satan could not accomplish through direct attack, he was able to somewhat achieve through Job's friends. As the record shows, they did not speak for God and would be rebuked for that reason. This is a good reminder that we should be careful as to how we counsel and comfort those reeling in pain or grieving over the loss of a loved one. We do not want to find ourselves aiding the enemy in a cause that is contrary to God's will.

Eliphaz, Bildad, and Zophar were stunned when they saw Job. To see their friend in such agony caused them to weep and wail, to rend their clothes, and to put dust on their heads. For seven days they sat with Job on the ground and in complete silence. Job's grief became their grief and if they had only remained quiet, their efforts to comfort Job may have succeeded.

Indeed, these men showed much kindness to their bereaved and afflicted friend by leaving their homes and affairs to console him. However, their presence had the effect of stirring up thoughts and feelings in Job's heart which until their visit had not been outwardly expressed. In the next chapter, Job finally does speak to them, but it is to curse the day of his birth – he wanted to die (3:1).

But God was in full control of Job's circumstances. He would not permit the devil to do more than what was necessary to expose to Job the depths of his own heart. What will be revealed to Job about himself will lead to self-judgment and a deep mistrust of himself; only then can the servant of God rest in and fully delight in the mercies of God.

September 14 – The First Divine Interrogation
Job 38

The Lord Himself personally speaks to Job from a powerful whirlwind; such an ominous presentation signified divine judgment. God would now hold Job accountable for his arrogant, self-justifying accusations against Himself while speaking to his three friends. The scene before us is quite unusual; generally speaking, people do not continue to suffer in the Lord's presence without experiencing His healing or deliverance. But in keeping with the biblical precedent, Job will not be permitted to suffer much longer, for he is in God's presence.

We are most confident that it is God's utmost desire to refine and bless His upright servant Job. The windstorm of Job 1 brought ruin, death, and grief, but this tempest (Job 38-41) will result in Job's repentance, restoration, and abounding joy. Given the previous thirty-five chapters of strife, the Lord's words were welcome relief to Job, even if commencing with a rebuke, *"Who is this who darkens counsel by words without knowledge?"* (v. 2). The Lord then tells Job to brace himself like a man for His questions: *"Where were you when I laid the foundations of the earth? Tell Me, if you have understanding. Who determined its measurements? Surely you know!"* (vv. 4-5). These were not questions demanding answers, but to prompt reverent humility. For what man dare answer God anything about His wisdom or doings?

Job had accused God of being unjust (9:17, 32:2) and unwise (23:3-7, 31:35-37) in dealing with him, so God will now take the place of the inquisitive student and ask Job for instruction. This, of course, is the irony of the dialogue – an obvious scolding of Job's foolish claims. If Job, in his own wisdom, cannot fathom the creation of the world, what right does he have to accuse the One who does have such knowledge of being unwise? Job will not get his requested opportunity to cross-examine God; rather, it will be God that will demand answers from Job.

God's merciful rebuke of four chapters is further proof that Job is a true child of God in good standing with Him (Heb. 12:5-6). No true child of God should be a stranger to His chastening hand, for it is an expression of His eternal love for His children. But Job has not reached the spiritual apex of unspotted faith, yet. Hence, Jehovah stoops down to the earth to confront His beloved servant.

September 15 – The Lord: God's Sovereignty Confirmed
Job 39-40

God has quizzed Job about the dawning of creation and the order established then which continues to govern all things. The Lord has shown His rule over celestial bodies and terrestrial elements and in this chapter will address His providential care of living creatures. His questioning of Job affirms His perfect design for various creatures and His ability to sustain them in their diverse earthly habitats. God's majestic wisdom is obvious in all these matters of life – God's creation is well-ordered and cared for by its Designer and Sustainer. Job cannot answer the Lord's questions; he is speechless and rightly so!

The Lord finishes His first dialogue with Job with a rebuke and a challenge: *"Shall the one who contends with the Almighty correct Him? He who rebukes God, let him answer it"* (40:2). The "one who contends" refers to Job. He had previously said that God contended with him (10:1-2, 23:6), but paradoxically God turns Job's words around on him – in reality, he was the one contending with God. Since Job had charged God with wrongdoing, he should now answer God's questions, if he is so wise and awesome.

But after listening to the barrage of questions to challenge his bold assertion, Job utters a brief response: *"Behold, I am vile; what shall I answer You?"* (40:4). In his previous self-confidence, Job had invited God to summon him to His courtroom so he could defend himself and be acquitted (10:2, 13:22). However, after learning of his own insignificance before the Master of creation, a more contrite Job acknowledges that he is incapable of defending himself before God. He will go no further in doing so, but rather will place his hand over his mouth and remain silent.

Meekness and silence are not the same as repentance and restoration, so the Lord will fire another volley of questions at Job in a second speech. If the Lord is not satisfied with anything less than genuine repentance and repudiation of sin, then we should not be either. Remorseful crying or regretful outcome is not the same as accepting full responsibility for one's wrong behavior. If we neglect dealing with the true reality of sin, we diminish God's blessing on the outcome. But the Lord knew Job's heart and that there was more to be accomplished.

September 16 – The Second Divine Interrogation
Job 40-41

The Lord, again speaking from a whirlwind, repeated verbatim His former challenge to Job to brace himself like a man and to answer His questions. Having already dealt with Job's claim that He lacked wisdom, God now takes up Job's assertion of His injustice, even asking Job, *"Would you condemn Me that you may be justified?"* (40:8). The reality being that Job had carelessly accused God of acting imprudently to justify himself.

The Lord wondered if a mortal, like Job, had a strong enough arm to contend with Him. Was Job able to arm wrestle the Creator of the universe and win? Absolutely not! How reasonable then was it for Job to suggest that God had abused His power and authority? For someone to impose their way on another person, meant that they were at least equal or better than the other person. Job had no such equality and therefore could not do the great things that God does.

Job had questioned God's punishment of the wicked, so the Lord asks Job if he is able to properly punish the wicked. If he could, then Job could adorn himself with majesty and splendor, and should be able to take care of his own problems. The remainder of God's second message to Job centers in the discussion of two of His creatures: the behemoth (40:15-24) and the leviathan (Job 41). Rather than asking Job to play God and control all the planets and the stars, He greatly minimizes the assessment test: "Job, here is your opportunity to prove your power: just control these two animals, if you can!" Obviously, Job cannot, so the Lord asks: *"Who then is able to stand against Me? Who has preceded Me, that I should pay him? Everything under heaven is Mine"* (41:10-11). If Job is unable to vanquish even a fellow creature, how much more ludicrous is it for him to aspire to be wiser and more powerful than his Creator, who controls all His creatures?

Job obviously could not control the behemoth or the leviathan; thus, he had no righteous claim to challenge God's justice in ruling over His creation. Thankfully, Job's response to God's second interrogation is one of complete repentance; he acknowledges God's comprehensive sovereignty over everything (42:1-6). God had accomplished what He desired in Job's life and, thankfully, the trial was over. It was now time to restore, heal, refresh, and bless His upright servant Job.

Daily Devotions

September 17 – Job's Confession, Prayer, and Blessing
Job 42

Job is utterly overwhelmed by God's intense interrogation. He has had enough! He has come to the end of himself. After the Lord concluded His first discourse, Job confessed his own finiteness and agreed not to challenge the Lord further (40:3-5). But that was not far enough. Job was not yet repentant, so God continued to question him. In this chapter, Job confesses not only his low position before God, but also God's complete sovereignty: *"I know that You can do everything, and that no purpose of Yours can be withheld from You"* (v. 2).

The Lord had begun His dialogue by asking, *"Who is this who hides counsel without knowledge?"* Job then admits that he did not comprehend such wonderful things. God's appearances and words had overwhelmed Job and brought him to utter brokenness: *"Therefore I abhor myself, and repent in dust and ashes"* (vv. 5-6). Job now fully valued the greatness of God. God had shown how much He valued Job by visiting him and reproving him in holy love. The months of perceived futility produced its desired fruit of repentance (7:3). The fact that Job was willingly broken before the Lord – that his heart had the capacity to be penitent rather than bitter and resentful – proves that his standing with God was never in question. He was not a hardened sinner as his friends conjectured, but a pliable believer homeward bound.

Job's three friends were rebuked by God; they were to present their burnt offerings before Job, the one that they had brutally afflicted with their erroneous and self-exalting counsel. When Job prayed for his friends, the Lord restored Job himself. In the process of time he had twice as many sheep, camels, oxen, and donkeys as he previously possessed.

Job had lived an isolated and miserable existence without comforters; now all Job's kin and friends fellowshipped with him; each one brought gifts to Job to demonstrate their appreciation and love for him. The Lord gave Job seven additional sons and three beautiful daughters. God blessed His servant Job's latter years, more than his previous years. Job lived another 140 years after his restoration, and died a full man, having seen his posterity unto four generations. Job refined and blessed, Satan cast down, and God honored – this is the same outcome God desires for us in all of our long arduous trials!

September 18 – Job Epilogue

Scripture shows us that God permits both believers and non-believers to suffer the consequences and punitive reimbursement of their sins. However, this was not the case for Job; he was an upright man and his friends were rebuked by God for saying that Job was suffering because of his sin (Job 1:8, 42:8). Yet, God permitted an extreme trial in Job's life to reveal a proud superiority that resided deep in his own heart. Once Job understood that his self-justification and self-defense were at God's expense (i.e., he was defaming God's character), he repented and was blessed by God. God definitely judges sin, but that is not the key lesson from the book of Job. Rather, the child of God must trust in God's perfect character, sovereignty, and foreknowledge, and choose to worship Him in all circumstances, even when His ways make no sense at all to us.

Clearly, the upright are not exempt from suffering, but rather God manipulates the hardship of His people to better them. All that happened to Job was for his good; through suffering and God's rebuke, he became more aware of his own depravity and better acquainted with God's greatness. Through his sorrowful experiences he and others were refined and blessed, Satan was shamed, and the name of God glorified! This begs the question, What might God accomplish through our sufferings, if we humbly yield to Him?

The mystery of human suffering is not fully explained in the book of Job; however, we know that all suffering has its root in sin, the fall of man, and that God chooses to control the outcome of sin to accomplish His purposes. Satan is permitted to strike God's people with sickness and calamity, but only as God permits (Job 1-2; 2 Cor. 12:7). Thus, we may safely conclude that any beneficial outcome of human misery is evidence of God's merciful intervention in a sin-cursed world. Without God, suffering would be a most miserable and intolerable experience because there would be no purpose in it. With God, as He reckons eternal matters, only good can come from our adversity, though we often cannot comprehend this wonderful truth: *"And we know that all things work together for good to those who love God, to those who are the called according to His purpose"* (Rom. 8:28). God is good and does good.

September 19 – Oh, Foolish Atheist
Psalm 14

Only twice in the Bible are the thoughts of a fool recorded for us to consider, Psalm 14:1 and Psalm 53:1. Both Psalm 14 and Psalm 53 are essentially identical. Why does the atheist declare, *"There is no God"* (v. 1)? The real reason is so that he or she can willingly pursue a life of sin, that is, to live in such a way that shuns God's Word and authority. Because the atheist does not want there to be a God, he denies God's existence. In Romans 3, Paul refers to Psalm 14:2-3 in order to reinforce the conclusion that was carefully developed in Romans 1 and 2: *naturally speaking*, no one seeks after God, understands His righteousness, or can continue in well-doing (Rom. 3:10-12).

When the Lord peers down from His heavenly throne to examine humanity, He finds that there is no one who perfectly does what is right, and that most are unconcerned about their spiritual condition before God. Paul rightly concludes, *"We all have sinned and fallen short of the glory of God"* (Rom. 3:23). If man could keep God's Law, he would be justified before God (Rom. 2:11-13), but it is self-evident no one can approach God this way; rather, man must be justified through faith by the One who did meet all the demands of the Law – Christ (Rom. 3:26-28).

Having introduced the foolishness of atheism, David alludes to its outcome: divine retribution. The audacity of the atheist to think he could devour God's people (those justified in Christ) without invoking any consequences was astounding to David. The wicked did not realize the Lord was with His people in their sufferings and, thus, they would be totally surprised and filled with dread when their judgment did come.

While it is true the wicked may frustrate and inflict God's people for a time, they will learn one day that the Lord will vindicate all who seek Him for refuge. David closes the song by expressing his yearning for the Kingdom Age, when God's covenant people will be delivered from hostility, the wicked will be judged, and righteousness will reign in Zion.

Those who say there is no God may frustrate and inflict God's people for a season, but in a future day the Lord will righteously vindicate all who seek Him for refuge.

September 20 – Seeking and Waiting on the Lord
Psalm 13 and 27

When unjust suffering continues day after day without any sign that relief is forthcoming, the child of God is likely to cry out to the Lord, "How long, O God?" In Psalm 13, David does so four times in the first two verses through a series of rhetorical questions which seemingly are to motivate God to respond favorably.

David's heart was filled with sorrow as he wrestled inwardly with his thoughts and outwardly against his adversary. Had God forgotten him? Why was God ignoring him? David desired God to illuminate his mind with divine wisdom and insight concerning his situation, and to spare his life, lest his enemies gloat over his demise. Yet, David knew his enemies were fighting a losing battle, for they were challenging God's unfailing mercy. Having full assurance that God had heard his prayer, the song concludes with joyful praise to the Lord for the deliverance to come and for His abounding goodness.

Initially, in Psalm 27, David expresses a sincere confidence that the Lord will deliver him from his enemies. The Lord was his light (i.e. the One who illuminated the truth in his mind), his salvation from harm, and the strength of all his exploits. David yearned to commune with the Lord; in this composition, he conveys a desire to remain in God's earthly sanctuary (i.e., the tabernacle) at all times. Being in God's presence further ensured David's safety; thus, he assertively declares he will triumph over his enemies and will continue to sing joyful praises to God.

However, there is a mood change in verse 7 which introduces an anxious tone to David's petition; apparently, he did not feel the Lord's help was being provided in a timely manner. He pleads for the Lord not to forsake him and to continue to comfort and to assist him during perilous times. David was confident that though his own parents might forsake him, God never would. Hence, David wanted God to teach him the right way to go, so that his enemies would not be able to ambush and destroy him. The song concludes with an affirmation of confidence in God's protection and his resolve to wait for the Lord's deliverance.

Waiting on the Lord for relief often feels like a heavy weight. While David could not change his pressing circumstances, he found that a joyful, trusting heart cannot be crushed by them. Amen!

September 21 – Godly Sorrow Prompts Repentance
Psalm 38

Suffering severely under the chastening hand of the Lord, David petitions the Lord to temper His anger with mercy and to pardon him for his offense. David did not attempt to hide his sin, but readily confessed his foolishness; he was emotionally miserable night and day, and was also suffering from a debilitating illness because of his transgression. David's pitiful state, brokenness, and deep sighing were fully visible to the Lord.

In his distress, many of David's friends had abandoned him, and his enemies were speaking evil of him and plotting against him. Rather than listening to or speaking against his enemies, David acted like a deaf-mute; his trust was in the Lord alone to deliver him from his oppressors. The psalmist does not deny his sin, nor suggest his suffering is unjust; rather, he confesses the transgression before the Lord and pleads for God to rescue him from his vicious enemies who plan his destruction.

The situation was desperate, God's discipline had served its purpose, and David now entreats the Lord not to forsake him, but instead be his Savior. David teaches us to not ignore sin, but to confess it to God, and to not complain about His just recompense for our stupidity. Such repentance should never be repented of, for restored fellowship with God should be cherished (2 Cor. 7:10). May we all value God's abiding presence above anything else, but if not, may we then remember that the resulting calamity of our decision to walk alone was not worth it.

David had learned that man's moral integrity before God and genuine worship of God are integrally tied to the blessings of God. Having suffered the loss of the latter for a full year, David was determined not to repeat the painful consequences of gross sin again. Sin results in death (separation from God), but yielding to God's Word and His Spirit results in the abundant life (fellowship with God). What is David's message to us? Suffering the repercussions of moral failure is a tragic means of increasing one's resolve to stay intimate with God, yet, through sincere repentance and brokenness, communion with God may be enjoyed again despite our wayward choices.

May We Serve Christ!

September 22 – The Frailty of Man
Psalm 90

The Hebrew superscript accredits Moses with the authorship of this psalm. Given its tone, it was likely composed while the older generation slowly perished in the wilderness for doubting God's goodness at Kadesh-barnea. No doubt continuously burying friends and family members as the nation aimlessly trekked through the desert marking time weighed heavy on Moses' mind.

How did Moses find comfort while immersed in this scene of flickering human mortality? In the first six verses, he contrasted the everlasting nature of God with the finiteness of humanity. The everlasting and immutable God was present before anything was created; thus a thousand years to man is but as the passing of a day to God. Although man's existence on the earth is brief before he returns to the dust of the earth, all generations of the faithful have found God to be their eternal Refuge and safe dwelling place.

In comparison to the eternal God, man's earthly sojourn is like grass that withers in the heat of the day. Man's suffering and short lifespan (70 to 80 years), occurs because of God's judgment of his sin. Realizing that the reality of this pitiful, unchanging situation, Moses requested that the faithful would receive divine wisdom to behave properly during their limited time on the earth and that God would show mercy to those loyal to Him. This would turn their sorrowful existence into a joyful and satisfying one. If God granted his request then Moses knew that God's splendor would be displayed in His servants, and the next generation would witness the glory of the Lord.

This poem shows Moses understood the proper value of things in eternity, that is, in relationship to what we do in the will of God. He turned his back on the riches and fame Egypt offered in order to suffer the reproach of Christ (Heb. 11:24-26). After God called him forty years later, he proceeded towards Egypt with nothing but the rod of God – God was his full sufficiency. What motivated this dangerous pilgrimage to do God's will? Moses wanted to see the glory of God and wanted his children to know of God's majestic power also: *"Let Your work appear to Your servants, and Your glory to their children"* (v. 16). Similarly, if our children are to see the glory of God, we must surrender to the Lord what we have and number each day in wisdom.

Daily Devotions

September 23 – Worship in the Beauty of Holiness
Psalm 96

Three times in the first two verses the poet urges those who had experienced God's salvation to *"sing unto the Lord"* not by singing songs of dead rote, but new songs which reflect the soul's joy and enthusiasm over receiving fresh mercies from the Lord day after day. Those who have experienced God's salvation have the privilege of declaring His glory and His marvelous doings to the nations, so that they might revere and praise Him also. He is their Creator and the One who is above all false gods. The aura of God's presence saturated His temple with honor, majesty, strength, and beauty according to verse 6.

Such a great God should certainly be sought out by His people in the beauty of holiness (i.e., with sins confessed and cleansed) and He should receive from them offerings of praise and gifts befitting of His glory. In fact, everyone should praise the One who reigns over the world and will judge in righteousness all peoples and nations. Furthermore, all creation should honor the Lord and praise His holy name. The last verse previews the Second Advent of Christ to the earth when this reality will occur and the lament of the redeemed will abruptly cease, for the Lord shall rule in righteousness and peace over all nations, the curses on the earth shall be lifted (Gen. 3:17-19; Rom. 8:20-22), and the whole earth will be full of His glory (v. 13; Isa. 2:2).

As mentioned previously, Exodus 15 records the first occurrence of singing in the Bible as well as the lyrics of Scripture's first song. Euphoria swept through the Israelite ranks as they marched into the wilderness beyond the Red Sea as a redeemed people under the shadow of Jehovah's cloud. God's redemption of His people was complete; they had been purchased by blood in Egypt and had been powerfully delivered from Egypt through the sea.

As then, it is a great privilege for the redeemed to sing praises to the Lord, day after day through the generations. To do so powerfully reflects the believer's salvation (i.e., it demonstrates the Lord resides within him or her) to a lost world that desperately needs to see Christ. The redeemed must sing, come before the Lord with appropriate gifts (1 Cor. 16:2; Heb. 13:15-16), and worship Him in the beauty of holiness (1 Cor. 11:27-32)! God deserves what He has enabled each believer to give back to Him – worship!

September 24 – Commitment to Personal Holiness
Psalm 101

In the wilderness of Sinai, God conveyed His profound yearning for His people: *"Consecrate yourselves therefore, and be holy, for I am the Lord your God. And you shall keep My statutes, and perform them: I am the Lord who sanctifies you"* (Lev. 20:7-8). In the same vein, David was not content to merely praise God's rule of mercy and truth without any personal action on his part; rather, he wanted his own life and kingdom to be marked by wisdom, purity, and willing subjection to God.

Knowing "the eye gate" and friends are two things that often cause the righteous to fall away, David personally committed not to look on any wicked thing or to keep company with any vile person. Rather, he pledged to surround himself with faithful, blameless companions and servants, and not to tolerate slander, arrogance, lying, or deceitful behavior among his companions. Looking beyond the boundaries of the palace, David further promised to purge wickedness from the nation of Israel. A holy God deserves the service and worship of a holy people, who can have no expectation of His favor or communion if they are in sin. This is a timeless reality, one that John affirmed in the dawn of the Church Age:

> *God is light and in Him is no darkness at all. If we say that we have fellowship with Him, and walk in darkness, we lie and do not practice the truth. But if we walk in the light as He is in the light, we have fellowship with one another, and the blood of Jesus Christ His Son cleanses us from all sin* (1 Jn. 1:5-7).

King David knew God's blessing and fellowship were contingent on his personal commitment to holy living and therefore pledged to the Lord that he would remain pure. Peter puts the matter this way: *"He who called you is holy, you also be holy in all your conduct, because it is written, 'Be holy, for I am holy'"* (1 Pet. 15-16). God, His name, and His dwelling place transcend all that is common and earthly. God is holy; He is separate from all else! May each of us endeavor to daily follow the same resolve of David, John, and Peter – to be holy in order to experience the wonder of communing with a holy God!

September 25 – Sowing Tears – Reaping Joy
Psalm 126

The psalmist recounts the immense joy and jubilant singing of the Jewish captives returning to Jerusalem, perhaps from Babylon – this euphoric experience was like a hopeful dream that had finally come true. The writer accredits the Lord with ending their captivity and then prays that He would also bless and fully restore them in the land. Allen P. Ross explains:

> He [the psalmist] compared the returning exiles to streams in the Negev (the desert south of Judah), which in the dry season have little or no water but which in the rainy season overflow their banks. Under God's "showers of blessings" the highways from the east would be full of returning captives.[17]

The writer expands the illustration to include the agricultural principle of sowing and reaping. Presently, the land of Israel was barren, but as more captives returned in obedience to the Lord and sowed the land in tears (i.e., agonizing labor in God's work), this would return the land to productivity; they would eventually reap joy. Paul also discussed sowing and reaping, deriving a similar application:

> *Do not be deceived, God is not mocked; for whatever a man sows, that he will also reap. For he who sows to his flesh will of the flesh reap corruption, but he who sows to the Spirit will of the Spirit reap everlasting life. And let us not grow weary while doing good, for in due season we shall reap if we do not lose heart. Therefore, as we have opportunity, let us do good to all, especially to those who are of the household of faith* (Gal. 6:7-10).

Because the enemy will oppose any true work of God, the Lord's servants should expect to sow in tears (engage in arduous and often heart-breaking labor) to accomplish God's will; later, they will reap the full measure of blessing in joy.

Adoniram Judson, who served in Burma as a missionary for almost forty years, puts it this way:

> In spite of sorrow, loss, and pain, our course be onward still;
> We sow on Burma's barren plain, we will reap on Zion's hill.

September 26 – Children Are God's Heritage
Psalm 127

The opening line reflects Solomon's style of wisdom as expressed in Ecclesiastes: without the Lord's blessing, all that we do under the sun is vanity – it counts for nothing. Without the Lord's enablement all of our efforts are futile. This realization is similar to what the Lord taught in Matthew 7:24-27: if a man builds his life on the sand of humanism, he will certainly fall into chaos when the storms of life challenge him, but those who build their lives on God's bedrock of revealed truth will endure trials and have His praise.

This fact is perhaps no more evident than in family life. Are we truly counting on God to direct, endorse, and bless all the affairs of our homes? A Christian family is not a household of Christians, but a Christian household. It is more than Christ dwelling within the hearts of family members; it is a family that is pursuing the heart of God. If the Bible is not at the center of family life and all home affairs, that home cannot be called a true Christian home. The vital focus and end objective of every Christian household is the glory of God!

While in general it is God's plan for children to be born from the marriage union of a husband and a wife, Malachi reminds us God is not merely seeking offspring, but rather a "godly seed" who will live for Him (Mal. 2:15). The principle is that God is more interested in the quality than the quantity of children. To have more children than what parents can spiritually, emotionally, educationally, and economically care for is not wise. Hence, *"Children are a heritage from the Lord"* (v. 3) and for the Lord. The psalmist reminds us we are only stewards, not owners, of the children that God graciously entrusts to our care.

Children are *"Like arrows in the hand of a warrior, so are the children of one's youth. Happy is the man who has his quiver full of them; they shall not be ashamed, but shall speak with their enemies in the gate"* (vv. 4-5). If reared in the ways of the Lord, these skillfully sharpened and straight arrows become a rich blessing to all. In ancient days, older children ensured the defense of the family against the attacking enemy. Children must be trained up for the Lord to be a blessing to others and to further the kingdom of God. May we count on the Lord and His Word alone to build up our homes!

September 27 – The Blessed Home
Psalm 128

The Lord richly blesses those who fear and obey Him. As we learned from Psalm 127, working apart from the Lord is vanity, but working under His authority and in accordance with His ways prompts His blessing. To illustrate this concept, the writer shows how a man's home becomes a fruitful abode when those within it fear the Lord.

The poet likens a virtuous wife to a fruitful vine adorning the home with beauty: *"Your wife shall be like a fruitful vine in the very heart of your house"* (v. 3). In ancient times, fruit-bearing vines were often planted adjacent to the exterior walls of homes. Practically speaking, the custom optimized ground space, provided protection for the vine, and allowed easy access to the delicious fruit. From a cosmetic sense, cold barren walls were transformed into radiant color, for the fruitful vine was an ornament of beauty. Yet, neither the bountiful fruit nor the adorning aspects of the vine developed naturally – a labor of love was necessary to achieve both.

To become fruitful, the fragile vine required a *place* to be nurtured, a *purpose* to guide development, and specific *provisions* to ensure fruit-bearing. With these three key aspects in mind, the foliage illustration highlights God's general plan for a married woman: she is to be the keeper of the home (Tit. 2:5); there, she is to be a helper to her husband and to nurture her children (Tit. 2:4); but to do so, she requires stable direction and tender support, this love and care is to come from her husband (Eph. 5:25-29).

Likewise, the upright man in this psalm is blessed with olive plants around his table, speaking of children. Children, God's heritage to parents, also require special care to thrive in a world hostile to the things of God. Entire families normally traveled together to attend the Feasts of Jehovah, so this poem, when rehearsed during the pilgrimage, was a great encouragement to all. A virtuous wife and thriving olive plants are a tremendous blessing to a God-fearing man and to each other. After acknowledging one of God's chief blessings to the upright (i.e., family), the writer asked the Lord to further bless the God-fearing by securing Jerusalem with peace, which would permit parents longevity so that they would be able to enjoy their grandchildren. Thus, the blessings of a godly family could be enjoyed by generations!

May We Serve Christ!

September 28 – The Blessing of Unity
Psalm 133

The timeless benefit of blessed unity among God's people is introduced in verse 1 and then portrayed in two word pictures in verses 2-3. Unity and love among the brethren are likened to the fragrant anointing oil that flowed down Aaron's beard and priestly attire at His consecration as high priest, and as the dew that falls upon the mountains and flows downward to renew and sustain life below. The special anointing mixture used to consecrate priests and holy things for the Lord's service contained olive oil (Ex. 30:22-32). Oil is a fluid that is both active and enabling, as seen in the operation of a lamp where oil is drawn from a reservoir through a wick to produce light when burned.

The Holy Spirit is generally depicted as an active fluid in Scripture, such as blowing wind (John 3), seven flames of fire (Rev. 4), or rushing water from a rock (John 7). In one of Zechariah's visions, he saw two olive trees supplying oil to a lampstand. God used the expression *"Not by might nor by power, but by My Spirit"* (Zech. 4:6) in reference to the influence of the oil as a picture of the Spirit of God. The Holy Spirit enables and accomplishes the will of God through others in a powerful and unseen fashion. Only through the work of the Holy Spirit can unity be enjoyed among God's people; this is apparently what is symbolized by the oil and the dew in verses 2-3. Such an outworking of the Holy Spirit among God's people propagates the sweet aroma of Christ in the world and likewise refreshes our hearts (2 Cor. 2:14-16).

James ties strife and division with the work of the devil: *"For where envy and self-seeking exist, confusion and every evil thing are there"* (Jas. 3:16). Conversely, the unity of God's people is precious to Him: *"Behold, how good and how pleasant it is for brethren to dwell together in unity!"* (v. 1).

Believers must therefore labor to keep the unity that the Holy Spirit works to maintain within the Church (Eph. 4:3). This is accomplished by humbling ourselves and putting the interests of others ahead of our own (Phil. 2:2-4). A busybody inserts his or her interests into the affairs of others, but a Christ-minded believer puts the welfare of others above his or her own interests – this type of attitude ends strife. David desired the blessing of brotherly unity in his time, and we should likewise yearn for it in the Church today.

September 29 – Fatherly Wisdom
Proverbs 4

Child-rearing in Proverbs focuses mainly on the shaping and protecting of a child's heart. Unlike the mind, where reason is invoked and choices are made, the heart is "formed" and behaves as it has been conditioned. For example, exercising faith in the Lord is a decision of the heart; it is not an intellectual response. This is why it is easier for children to trust the Lord than well-educated or sin-hardened adults (Luke 18:17). Over time, godly training stimulates the mind to make proper choices, and the heart is formed emotionally in purity and godly values, though it is inherently defiled by a propensity to sin.

Solomon, the son of David and Bathsheba, was taught the commandments of God and the way of wisdom, which he had to actively keep seeking. By quoting his father David in verses 4-9, Solomon was passing down the instruction he had received from his father to his children.

Solomon is apparently pleading with a particular son to treasure in his heart the instruction that he had received, to pursue wisdom, and not to depart from the right path that had been set before him. Thus, Solomon implores his son, as David advised him, to go after wisdom and instruction, personified as a woman, and to never let her go (vv. 5, 7, 13). Coupled with these exhortations is the warning to not trod the treacherous wide path of wickedness, but rather remain on the straight and illuminated path of the just.

To consort with the wicked, that is, to speak their perverse words and to engage in their violence, is like running in the dark and unwittingly falling into destruction. What is in one's heart eventually passes over one's lips. In contrast, when one receives wise instruction and guards his or her heart from corruption, that person enjoys a full, healthy life and receives honor for their good conduct.

In verses 25-27, Solomon acknowledges, that one can avoid much trouble in life by looking straight ahead and focusing on the known path of righteousness. The glory of God is evident in the lives of all those who heed true wisdom, which is fostered in the fear of the Lord. Clearly it would be wise for us to heed Solomon's counsel as well; our hearts must be pliable to God's Word and protected from debasing influences – *"for out of it* [the heart] *are the issues of life"* (v. 23).

September 30 – The Foolishness of Adultery
Proverbs 4

How are we to understand Solomon's warning to his own son regarding not lusting after the immoral woman, when he himself had seven hundred wives and three hundred concubines, many of whom were foreign women (1 Kgs. 11:3)? Though Solomon did marry these women, clearly he did not exercise wisdom in this aspect of his life (Deut. 17:17). In time, his many wives turned his heart from the Lord (1 Kgs. 11:4-8). As in the Song of Solomon, here he apparently wants to set the matter straight; God's design for marriage is one man and one woman bound by a covenant for life (Matt. 19:5-6). The central message to his own son, then, is one that married men should heed today: do not lust for what is outside the will of God (i.e., the unchaste woman), but rather seek to be faithful and satisfied with your own wife!

Solomon begins by telling his son to "listen up" and gain vital wisdom and discretion on an important matter – avoiding immorality. The seductive words, attire, and body language of a strange woman are captivating, deceptive, and lead to one end: death! While one's unchecked lusting may be temporarily gratified through adultery, it is a terrible offense against one's own body (6:32; 1 Cor. 6:18), one's spouse (Mal. 2:13-15), and the Lord, which is why it was punishable by death (Lev. 20:10).

Adultery is an act of rebellion against God's regulations for marriage and family order. Hence, Solomon warns his son to avoid the seductive woman altogether; adultery has too high of a price tag associated with it. Besides invoking God's anger, suffering personal guilt, and losing the respect of others, immorality has long-term consequences such as the loss of wealth, health, and longevity.

In verses 15-20, Solomon explains the benefits of maintaining moral purity in marriage. When a man genuinely cherishes and cares for his wife and is faithful to her, the sexual interaction they share is enhanced and mutually gratifying. In this way the marriage covenant protects and enhances what is shared privately between a husband and wife. The wife is likened to a refreshing cistern which is abundantly satisfying. Solomon warns his son not to drink from another man's cistern, but rather to be satisfied with his own wife. All sexual energy and desires should be reserved and channeled into one's own marriage.

October 1 – The Foolishness of Fornication
Proverbs 7

Solomon solemnly warns his son of the consequences of being enticed by the immoral woman. He urges his son to obey his commandments and to embrace wisdom as a sister, rather than to foolishly consort with a strange woman. In Solomon's illustration, he pictures a naïve young man strolling down a dark street in which an immoral woman resides. Seeing her prey, this skillful seductress appeals to all five senses of her next victim: flattering speech and fair words – hearing (vv. 5, 18); spicy attire – sight (v. 10); a kiss – taste (v. 13); seductive gestures – touch (v. 13); and perfumed bed – smell (v. 17).

While women are generally excited by emotional interaction with the opposite sex, men are aroused through sensual stimulation. Consequently, with all five senses being stimulated, the inexperienced young man in this story does not resist seductress' temptation. She further affirms to her quarry that they will not be caught, for it is dark. She had a private location for them to enjoy each other all night; everyone else was away, including her husband. She is not only a married woman, but also a religious woman: *"I have peace offerings with me; today I have paid my vows"* (v. 14). Her proclaimed spirituality was an attempt to make her immoral conduct seem more acceptable. Many ignorant fools through the ages have fallen for this same ploy. Stirred up in his lusting, he casts reason aside and yields to her urging; he is like an ox being led to the slaughter. Indeed, she has led many strong men down into ruin.

The sexual sin of the woman is to lure (v. 21) and the sexual sin of the man is to follow (v. 22). His large harem had taught Solomon that unchecked gazing leads to more lusting and more lusting promotes immoral behavior. Our flesh nature is never gratified – it always wants more than what is reasonable and what God permits.

Practically speaking, a wife should appeal to her husband's senses to arouse him, while her husband should appeal to his wife's emotions to affirm security and his singular devotion. The goal is mutual satisfaction, so there will be no need to look elsewhere for sexual gratification. God created the sexual relationship as a means of strengthening the bond of marriage in such a way that permits a husband and wife to enjoy full disclosure and intimacy in a way sex outside marriage can never obtain.

October 2 – A Virtuous Wife Is a Blessing
Proverbs 31

The blessings of a virtuous wife are provided in verses 10-31. The word translated as "virtuous" in verse 10 is derived from the Hebrew word *chayil*, which means "she has a lot in her." Indeed, the text paints the portrait of a wholesome, industrious, efficient, and profoundly able wife. She is an incredible example of biblical femininity.

The wife in this chapter has won her husband's full confidence. In verse 11, we read *"the heart of her husband safely trusts her."* Verse 12 continues with *"She does him good and not evil all the days of her life."* She is the ultimate selfless companion who longs to serve her husband instead of placing expectations on him.

Verses 12-19 describe a woman who rises early in the morning to greet the day with hard work. The virtuous woman puts forth her best efforts in keeping the home and pleasing her husband. She is industrious and frugal. Neglect and ease are not words in her vocabulary. The woman in Proverbs 31 is industrious in the home and loyal to her husband; she is also compassionate. Verse 20 proclaims, *"She extends her hand to the poor, yes, she reaches out her hands to the needy."* One of the finest legacies a mother can impart to her children is an unselfish example. Children will pattern themselves after a recurring exhibition of selflessness.

Verse 23 reads: *"Her husband is known in the gates, when he sits among the elders of the land."* The gate of a city was commonly the location for business and the seat of government. Why can the husband be devoted to his business at the city gate? Because he had a wife who was totally devoted to her business at home. He was not concerned about the daily activities of the home. This sphere of responsibility was delegated to his wife in whom he had the utmost confidence.

Her speech is marked by wisdom and kindness. She is not prone to speaking evil of others or spreading gossip about them. Her tongue is a skilled instrument of instruction and healing. She knows that if she speaks foolishly, or is quick-tempered, or is prone to bitterness that her children will follow in her folly (Prov. 13:20; 22:24). But, if her speech is kind, discrete, and cheerful, her children will observe the power of life and peace as she interacts with others. Such a woman has the praise of her husband, her children, and all those looking on.

October 3 – The Meaning of Life
Ecclesiastes 12

In the opening verses of the book, Solomon conveys a bleak picture of man's existence: man's presence on the earth is transitory and meaningless – all is vanity. Now, the Preacher draws his ontological journey and literary work to a close; he sought to be a good shepherd of the people by sharing his wisdom in the form of well-tested proverbs. He readily admits that he has not exhausted the subject matter, but in his estimation, further examination of the meaning of life from an "under the sun" outlook would only yield the same conclusion. Solomon realized no human reckoning could adequately explain what God had purposefully arranged in obscurity (8:16-17). However, he did deduce that it is possible to experience a meaningful life, without fully comprehending the meaning of one's vain existence.

Our Creator has intentionally allowed us to perceive only a portion of absolute reality in order to prompt us to ponder the vast void beyond. God has constructed a cosmic stage, has put something bigger in motion than we can comprehend, and at the same time administers an unavoidable test for everyone to consider. Hence, Solomon concludes, all quandaries about our existence may be duly answered by seeking the Creator according to revealed truth.

Those who willfully close their eyes to what God has revealed will not see Him! Solomon wisely instructed his readers to *"Consider the work of God"* (7:13). Man is to ponder God's nature, character, word, and works, but not without including Him in the exercise, or else his humanly-derived conclusions will of necessity be lacking. We must reason together with God. Why? Because without God's help man cannot understand or reason out what God has purposefully concealed (Deut. 29:29). Because God alone holds absolute truth, He will always transcend human reasoning.

If we open our minds to God's calling and study Scripture to know His will, we find Christ the most wonderful answer to all our problems. By this I do not mean that our lives will be filled with prosperity and void of hardships, but rather that we will have joy beyond these things. Why is man on the earth? To *"fear God and keep His commandments, for this is the whole duty of man"* (12:13). Solomon knew that there was an inescapable judgment for those who rejected this conclusion.

October 4 – Doves' Eyes
Song of Solomon 1

The Shulamite maiden was enamored with a young shepherd (perhaps Solomon incognito). However, her brothers had forced their sister to work long, grueling hours tying up vines and setting traps for little foxes in their leased vineyard. She bemoaned the situation, as she could not take proper care of herself. For this reason, the Shulamite insisted her new admirer not gaze upon her sunbaked skin, blistered hands, and filthy attire. Yet, her diligent subjection to her family despite the personal hardship made her all the more attractive to him. He responded to her plea by affirming kind words, telling her she was *"fairest among women."* A friendship commenced that soon blossomed into mutual admiration and romantic expressions. He pledged to return someday and make her his wife. The Hebrew language conveys her acceptance of his love in verse 4: *"Take me away with you."*

The remainder of this first section records the mutual desire, praise, and assurance of these two lovers as their relationship progresses into maturity. Genuine love must be nurtured to grow; it cannot be forced (2:7). Principles for edifying conduct in our own marriages can be derived from the spectacular interaction of these two lovers. First, they had doves' eyes for each other. The bridegroom proclaims to his bride, *"You have doves' eyes"* (1:15, 4:1). In turn, the bride speaks of her beloved as having *"eyes like the eyes of doves"* (5:12).

These rock pigeons were normally seen in pairs. Doves cannot rotate their eyes to see; they must turn their necks to look elsewhere. By looking directly into each other's eyes, each would see the mirror image of themselves in their mate's eyes. Their fixed eyes convey single-hearted devotion to one another. Husband and wife are literally to have eyes only for each other. To look away from one's mate with wanton lust injures the one whose gaze has not altered; this damages marital companionship. Having doves' eyes for one another necessitates being with one another and spending time together to nurture one's marriage.

Second, the beloved accommodates the moods of his love. There are many factors, such as the need for security, emotional cares, and hormonal changes that can affect a woman's disposition. Husbands should be sensitive to their wives' mood changes and assist them.

October 5 – God Hates Sin
Isaiah 1

God had labored to create and build up a special people for His good pleasure, but the Jewish nation had rebelled against His intentions and care for them. Isaiah then describes the deplorable spiritual state of the Jewish nation as one of insensibility and indifference to the things of God. The Jewish nation did not even display the instinctive awareness and respect that an ox possesses for its owner, or a donkey (known proverbially as a stupid animal) for its master's crib.

Israel superficially identified with the Lord, but did not know Him, and worse, did not want to know Him, nor did they recognize the Lord's claims upon them; hence Isaiah's harsh indictment: *"Alas, sinful nation, a people laden with iniquity, a brood of evildoers, children who are corrupters! They have forsaken the Lord, they have provoked to anger the Holy One of Israel, they have turned away backward"* (v. 4).

Let us not pass over this injunction without challenging our own hearts. To what extent do we really know our Owner, the Lord Jesus Christ, and to what measure are we satisfied with Him? The crib speaks of where we rest and are fed – where we are refreshed. How well do we know God's Word and character? How willing are we to rest in Him, trust His promises, and honor His commands? The prophet's message is timeless: Those redeemed by the crucified One owe Him their full allegiance and devotion, not a superficial religious nod.

The title "the Holy One of Israel" is found twenty-five times in Isaiah and speaks of God's awesome purity in relationship to Israel. "The Holy One of Israel" was intimately aware that the spiritual disposition of His people was deplorable. Even with God-fearing kings ruling over them, they were full of iniquity, evil-doings, and corruption.

Then writing as if the future had already taken place, Isaiah said that Judah had experienced God's chastening hand through natural disasters and merciless invaders, but without a transforming effect. Their open sores and untreated wounds pictured their wretched spiritual condition, but though badly beaten and bruised, they were still oblivious as to why they were suffering. Militarily speaking, Judah was like a makeshift shelter for laborers in the melon patch – an easy target for conquest, but for the sake of His covenant, God protected His people from extinction.

October 6 – God Hates Religiosity
Isaiah 1

Having just spoken of the wicked cities God destroyed centuries earlier, Isaiah then likens the civil and religious leaders of his day to the rulers of Sodom and Gomorrah. Yet, Israel had greater guilt than the heathen, for Israel had more divine light to walk in. Hence, he calls Israel's vain religiosity an abomination to God and the Lord was fed up with Israel's vain religiosity: *"Wickedness and the solemn meeting I cannot bear"* (v. 13; JND). He unreservedly despised their sacrifices, offerings, prayers, and observances! The seriousness of Israel's offense is bluntly expressed by the phrase *"My soul hates"* in verse 14, which literally means, "I hate with all my heart!" The Jews were a morally corrupt and spiritually bankrupt people that were using religion as a cloak to cover their sin. The nation was superficially observing the Law without understanding the real purpose of what they were doing.

The Jews had religious movement, but no spiritual direction. The temple was bustling with pious activity, but true worshipers must approach God in revealed truth, and with pure hearts and clean hands to refresh His heart. To do otherwise, as Solomon proclaims, provokes the Lord to jealous anger: *"One who turns away his ear from hearing the law, even his prayer is an abomination"* (Prov. 28:9).

Though the Jews offered up *"many prayers"* to Jehovah, He ignored their irritating gestures of piety because of their deplorable spiritual and moral state. They lifted up their hands in prayer, but failed to notice that their hands were stained with innocent blood. Actions speak louder than words, especially when the One who is listening and watching is omniscient. Their hearts were far from the Lord; their actions were offending the Lord, and hence, their prayers were loathed by Him.

Much of the vain religiosity of Judaism is alive and well in Christendom today. Sadly, many professing Christians have become dull to the Word of God, deaf to the conviction of the Holy Spirit, and seared in their conscience such that they can mindlessly practice their religion while continuing in sin. Isaiah's rebuke of Judah is no less applicable today. Dear believer, are you appreciating the joyful presence of a holy God? Do you feel that the Lord is hearing and acting on your prayers? If not, it is time to take action.

Daily Devotions

October 7 – Does God Hear Your Prayers?
Isaiah 1

The prophet told his countrymen that because they were lifting up hands stained with blood God was not hearing their prayer. He loathed their vain religiosity. The following are several reasons why God may choose to ignore or not act on our prayers with favor:

1. Rejecting or not yielding to God's Word (Prov. 28:9; 1 Jn. 3:22).
2. Husbands not duly caring for and respecting their wives (1 Pet. 3:7).
3. Fostering selfish motives (Jas. 4:3).
4. Having an unforgiving heart (Mark 11:25).
5. Doubting God's faithfulness (Jas. 1:6-7; Mark 11:24).
6. Praying with unconfessed sin (Ps. 66:18).
7. Praying for what is contrary to God's will (1 Jn. 5:14-15).

The Church would do well to heed Isaiah's warning to Israel. It is human nature to traditionalize that which has no importance to God to displace what does. If Isaiah were before us today, he would affirm that the Lord hates check-the-box Christianity with the same fervor as He hates vain Judaism. That which displaces true devotion to and appreciation for Christ with meaningless religious trinkets and habitual routines is loathsome to God.

When our awe of God is supplanted by stained-glass windows, huge pipe organs, gold crucifixes, burning candles, smoking incense, fancifully robed clergymen; or when meetings of the church become social gatherings; or when the study of God's Word is replaced by friendly chit-chat, storytelling, and entertaining spoofs; or when praising God becomes the occupation of professionals instead of the delight of all God's people; or when family activities trump meetings of the church; or when the lack of creature comforts hinders us from engaging in worship, we are no less guilty of snubbing God than Israel was in Isaiah's day. Would not such behavior then provoke God's chastening hand?

Lord, we ask you to do whatever it takes to awaken the pampered Church from her lethargic, semi-comatose spiritual condition, for You must have the preeminence in all things, especially in Your Church (Col. 1:18)!

October 8 – Let Us Reason Together
Isaiah 1

The only solution to the spiritual travesty that Isaiah has just described is wholesale and heartfelt repentance. Israel needed to abandon the old life and to adopt new patterns of thinking which would prompt godly conduct. God's people must be washed through repentance, then cease from evil, seek justice, do what is good and proper, and assist those in need. One cannot pursue righteousness without first choosing to be cleansed of corruption. James affirms this to be the solution to spiritual lethargy in the Church Age (Jas. 1:25-27).

Christianity is not a religion, but Christian doctrine lived out produces the right kind of religion that pleases God. When one comes into a right relationship with God through the Lord Jesus Christ, then, and only then, is he or she able to please God by doing sincere and God-enabled deeds. World religion is an exhaustive system of *doings* apart from God's truth and God's enablement. The doing of good things does not define what true Christianity is, but Spirit-filled Christians do prove the reality of real Christianity. God is not impressed by religious ritual, developed church tradition, sanctimonious form, and denominational smugness, but rather with personal living that conforms to divine truth (Col. 2:20-23).

After confronting Israel about their vain religiosity and telling them what they needed to do to please God, Isaiah then informs them how to do it in verses 18-20. Truly seek the Lord and receive cleansing and forgiveness. The scene pictures a courtroom where two parties present their arguments in a particular case. Israel does not speak, but the Lord does: *"Come now, and let us reason together"* (v. 18). This statement cannot be separated from the previous rebuke: *"Wash yourselves, make yourselves clean; put away the evil of your doings from before My eyes. Cease to do evil, learn to do good"* (vv. 16-17).

Willful obedience verifies that the Word of God was effectual in changing the heart and conscience. This means that the hearer received and acted upon Scripture in genuine faith. God's grace is not contingent on doing good deeds or on self-advancement in righteousness; rather, His promises of blessings are received by those who trust and obey His Word. Divine blessing follows our repentance and cleansing. This is the type of reasoning which ultimately leads to receiving God's gift of salvation.

October 9 – Lucifer's Fall
Isaiah 14

Isaiah prophetically peers beyond Babylon's visible leader to the one who will prompt his brutality – Lucifer. Ezekiel refers to Lucifer as the anointed cherub that was created in perfection, sheathed with precious stones, and was in the Garden of Eden (Ezek. 28:13). Lucifer was created with a provision of timbrels and flutes to offer music before God (perhaps leading the angels in worship). In the celestial realms, worship (accompanied by music) was being offered by spiritual beings to their Creator, even before man was created (Job. 38:7).

As the anointed covering cherub, Lucifer may have had a view of God's majesty and glory that no other created being was afforded – he was with God on His holy mountain and enjoyed a state of perfection (Ezek. 28:14-15). Charles Ryrie writes that this is "evidently a reference to Satan, because of Christ's similar description (Luke 10:18) and because of the inappropriateness of the expression of Isaiah 14:13-14 on the lips of any but Satan (1 Tim. 3:6)."[18] Satan then became obsessed with his own beauty and wanted to be worshipped as God. In mutiny, the "light bearer" (Lucifer) became the ruler of darkness, and immersed the world in deceit, corruption, and violence. In depicting Satan's pride, Isaiah first recalls Lucifer's five "I will" decrees against God's rulership in verses 12-15, then details the consequences of his rebellion against God – to be cast into *"the lowest depths of the Pit."*

Lucifer was a spectacular creature that had been created to bring God glory; however, his prestigious position in creation and his unique vantage point of God's preeminence led him to be dissatisfied with God's creation order. Lucifer no longer desired to cover himself and protect the sanctity of God's glory; he wanted his glory to be visible above the stars of God and the heights of the clouds. He would no longer conceal his personal glory in God's presence, but being "lifted up" in pride sought to be like "the Most High" (v. 14).

God responded by casting him off the Holy Mount (Ezek. 28:16) and destining him to eternal judgment in the Lake of Fire (Matt. 25:41). Lucifer's rebellion in heaven also resulted in the fall of a third of all created angels (Rev. 12:3-4, 9). These fallen angels have various evil agencies: demons, spirits of divination, foul spirits, unclean spirits, and familiar spirits.

October 10 – All May Come
Isaiah 55

Having addressed, in the previous chapter, Israel's eternal salvation, Isaiah highlights the fact that God is merciful. He invites all in need to "come" to Him to be satisfied with provisions which cannot be bought with money. The invitation to "come" is repeated three times in the first verse: *"Everyone who thirsts, come to the waters; and you who have no money, come, buy and eat. Yes, come, buy wine and milk without money and without price"* (v. 1). While God does supply the physical needs of those who trust in Him, the primary focus of Isaiah's invitation is the spiritual satisfaction of individuals in Israel. Why spend money on bread which cannot satisfy one's true need? It would be wise to receive from God that which abundantly delights the soul forever.

God promises to satisfy our spirit's deepest need without any human compensation (i.e., no one can buy or earn His forgiveness through payment or doing "good works"). Peter reminds believers that their God counted only one thing precious enough to redeem their souls – the blood of Christ: *"Knowing that you were not redeemed with corruptible things, like silver or gold, from your aimless conduct received by tradition from your fathers, but with the precious blood of Christ"* (1 Pet. 1:18-19). Both Bible Testaments state that material wealth, regardless of its value, cannot redeem one sinner.

Gentiles who respond to God's invitation to come will be brought under His New Covenant with Israel, as a second benefactor. Gentiles who had not been God's people could become His, and receive His blessing which was previously promised only to Israel (Hos. 1:10, 2:23; Rom. 9:25-26). The New Covenant, sealed by Christ's blood, would accomplish what the Old Covenant could not – propitiation for sins (Heb. 8:8).

The Old Covenant with Israel was conditional in nature; the Jews had to keep God's Law to receive God's blessing (Heb. 8:9). The New Covenant would be unconditional in nature and would be the means by which God would honor His covenant with Abraham. The result of which meant that God could extend mercy to the Gentiles, as well as to Israel, through the work of His Son. Although individual Gentiles can be saved presently, this event speaks of when all Gentile nations will be blessed in the Kingdom Age after Israel's conversion.

October 11 – Called to Serve
Jeremiah 1

Jeremiah was called to rebuke a backslidden nation; his prophetic message would not be popular. His hometown was the priestly city of Anathoth, a small village located three miles northeast of Jerusalem. Jeremiah was a priest, the son of Hilkiah. Priests were esteemed among God's people, but prophets were often despised. As a young man, Jeremiah probably thought that being a priest would be a respectable profession; being a prophet could be an entirely different matter. The words the Lord Jesus spoke concerning a prophet being without honor in his own country were certainly proven true in Jeremiah's case (Luke 4:24). He was despised and generally hated by his own people. His ministry spanned the reigns of five Judean kings for a total of 40 years.

God divinely chose Jeremiah to be a prophet before he was conceived, before he was formed by God in his mother's womb. God thoroughly knew everything about Jeremiah. The phrase, *"I knew you,"* (v. 4) is derived from the Hebrew word *yada*, which means "to intimately know." In the process of creating Jeremiah, God intimately knew him inside and out. God, foreknowing Jeremiah, made a sovereign choice to use him as His representative to Judah and the nations. What God creates a man for is what He calls him to do; hence, Jeremiah was appointed to the work he had been designed to fulfill.

Initially, he excused himself from the appointment, pleading with the Lord that he was too young; this was probably to highlight his perceived inadequacy to speak for God. The humility of Jeremiah is noteworthy, but God does not summon those who cannot effectively serve His purposes. Jeremiah was likely in his late teens or early twenties.

The Lord told Jeremiah not think of himself as a child, for all that he spoke would be under His authority: *"For you shall go to all to whom I send you, and whatever I command you, you shall speak"* (v. 7). In response to Jeremiah's fear, God told him twice not to be afraid because He would be with Jeremiah every step of the way: *"'I am with you to deliver you,' says the Lord"* (v. 8). We are left to wonder why God chose a tender and compassionate man like Jeremiah to preach to a stiff-necked people engaged in gross sin, but the Lord's ways are best and we must simply rest in His sovereignty.

October 12 – I Remember You
Jeremiah 2

Chapter 2 begins the first of thirteen prophetic messages of judgment to be issued by Jeremiah and contains the first of the book's thirteen references to the Jews as God's "backsliding" people. When used metaphorically in Scripture, each of the numbers from one to forty holds a particular meaning. Throughout Scripture, the number thirteen is associated with rebellion, and this is likely the determining factor in the number of specific judgments that Jeremiah would speak to Judah.

The passage begins with God reminiscing about the early years with His people. He remembered the birth of the nation. Though at times they grumbled and complained against Him, overall He had their allegiance and devotion during their forty years in the wilderness. For this reason, Israel was holy to the Lord and His first fruits among the nations. But that had all changed – Israel's sin of idolatry had ruined the blessing of divine fellowship.

God's faithfulness to His covenant was unquestionable; there was no evil in Him that He should be abandoned by Israel. But like the Northern Kingdom, Judah was guilty of deserting Jehovah and His way. God had kept His word and greatly blessed the Jews. He had brought them from Egypt to a fruitful land, which was not theirs. But the Jews had defiled the land that God had given to them; they had polluted it with abominations and idolatries.

The Lord had provided Judah with priests, leaders, and prophets that they might have the means to know divine truth, experience His grace, and enjoy His communion. Yet, these human instruments were guilty of great offenses. God knew His people, but His people no longer knew Him or called upon Him. Instead, they prophesied in Baal's name and wasted time doing things which had no profit.

The Lord would severely judge those who had neglected to care for His people properly. Although God was grieved over the rejection of His people, He pled with them to return to Him and He would continue to do so. The longsuffering nature of God is a good reminder to us to continue to plead with those who have stumbled morally or who have displaced God with vain activities (Gal. 6:1). May we not allow fallen soldiers of the Cross to remain missing in action, but rather remind them of God's goodness and their need to be restored to Him.

October 13 – You Have Forsaken Me – Part 1
Jeremiah 2

Brilliant people sometimes forget elementary things. The famous physicist Albert Einstein once forgot his home address and the great inventor Thomas Edison once forgot his own name. Putting proper names and street addresses aside, how can a once God-fearing people forget their God? Jeremiah used the expression "you have forsaken" four times in the first two chapters of this book (1:19, 2:13, 17, 19) before switching to the phrase "you have forgotten," which he used twice (2:32, 3:21).

The progression is important to note – forsaking the Lord leads to forgetting Him. The Jews had not just recently deserted their God; the Lord bemoaned that He had been forgotten days without number. Jeremiah identified four forsaking activities which eventually resulted in the Jewish nation forgetting Him altogether.

The first action of forsaking was that the Jews gave their loyalty and devotion to false gods of wood and stone. They turned from Jehovah to worship the works of their own hands. The Jews created not just one or two false gods, but many; they were as numerous as the cities in Judah. It is one thing to be a pagan; it is an entirely different matter to be a pagan after having known the one true God, experienced His goodness, seen His glory, and received His promises.

The worst part of it was that the Jews did not even miss Jehovah's presence; it was an offense worthy of immense judgment. God loved His people too much to allow them to continue living a vain existence. In application, we recall that an idol is anything that draws us away from the Lord; believers should be wary of them, especially of those things which are associated with the doings of our own hands.

Israel's first error centered in misplaced affections; their second step in forsaking the Lord was to seek satisfaction from that which could never satisfy. Broken cisterns can neither hold water nor supply it when needed. The "broken cisterns" spoken of in this chapter refer to Judah's idolatry and to the foreign alliances they had established in an attempt to insure their protection. Idols would not provide Judah with spiritual power, and alliances with other nations would not protect them against God's judgment. Such behavior from His people always provokes God's chastening hand.

October 14 – You Have Forsaken Me – Part 2
Jeremiah 2

Not only had Judah forsaken God, *the fountain of living water* (v. 13); they now sought satisfaction from the Nile (i.e. an alliance and friendship with Egypt). At Calvary, Christ died, was buried and then was raised up out of this world to God's throne. The world crucified His Son, and thus Christ is no longer in the world – to enjoy spiritual life with Him we must by faith come along to where He is. Believers are privileged to sit at His table, and to receive from Him and commune with Him there (1 Cor. 10:16-21). How offensive it must be to the Lord Jesus to desert Him in order to party in the world with demons.

Paul warns, *"You cannot drink the cup of the Lord and the cup of demons; you cannot partake of the Lord's table and of the table of demons. Or do we provoke the Lord to jealousy? Are we stronger than He?"* (1 Cor. 10:21-22). In principle, the Jews had committed the same offense in Jeremiah's day. They had forgotten how Jehovah labored to deliver them from Egypt and how He had satisfied them at His table in the wilderness earlier. Throughout Scripture, Egypt is commonly used to symbolize the world; "the way of Egypt," then, denotes worldliness. Jehovah would not allow the solicitations from Egypt (i.e. the world) to interfere with His fellowship with His people.

In their unhappy downward progression of forsaking the Lord, the third slip the Jews had was that they rejected God's way of righteousness for the way of Egypt. The Jews had tasted of the Lord and His goodness, yet departed from Him to indulge in the filth of the world. They were no longer satisfied with God's provisions and divine communion, but rather lusted after what God had prohibited them from having.

The fourth and final indictment, *"you have forsaken the Lord"* (v. 19), is tied to Judah's lack of fear for Jehovah. The fear of the Lord involves a proper understanding of who God is and a proper reverence for Him. This was sorely lacking among the people, and was a matter that would presently be remedied by devastating judgments – God would soon have their respect again. To summarize these four "forsaking" sins, the Jews had misplaced affection, they were looking for satisfaction in other sources than God, they were misdirected from the way of righteousness, and displayed disrespect for God Himself.

October 15 – Roadside Lovers
Jeremiah 3

Jeremiah concluded his first message by acknowledging His people's obstinate persistence in sin and the gross nature of Judah's present harlotries. God's judgment was looming and Jeremiah was faithful to use both messages and prophetic illustrations to call the nation to repentance. Apparently, there was still time to return to the Lord. Yet, this opportunity seems to have been lost by Jeremiah's third message beginning in chapter 7. God instructs Jeremiah, *"Therefore do not pray for this people, nor lift up a cry or prayer for them, nor make intercession to Me; for I will not hear you"* (7:16). The people refused to receive divine correction and return to God (5:3), therefore, He was determined to punish them.

E. Paul Hovey once wrote that sin has four characteristics: "self-sufficiency instead of faith; self-will instead of submission; self-seeking instead of benevolence; self-righteousness instead of humility."[1] It is observed in Jeremiah 2 that the Jews exhibited each of these four qualities of sin. They were self-sufficient (2:31), self-willed (2:18), self-seeking (2:25), and self-righteous (2:23, 35).

In Jeremiah 3, the Jews are likened to a harlot who sits by the roadside eagerly waiting for anyone to venture by her. No questions were asked; any act of spiritual harlotry was acceptable, and repeated occurrences were customary. Spiritual union with any false god was the status quo. As a result, the land was full of spiritual uncleanness and immorality.

Judah was a married woman who shamelessly slept with anybody and then bragged about it without any regard for the hurt and disgrace she was causing her husband. The Law forbade a divorced wife from returning to her former husband after being joined to another man, but Judah had no remorse about being blatantly unfaithful to Jehovah and then returning to Him under false pretense (i.e. in religious rote). For this reason, Jehovah's judgment was imminent; He wanted a change of heart not hollow words. Love is motivated by what is best for another, and in this situation, love required stern measures, not pity. Wrongly applied pity endorses sin, and Jehovah is not a sin-enabling God. May we all stay near and dear to the Lover of our souls, this will keep us from being abused by roadside lovers too (i.e. idols in our hearts).

October 16 – Break Up Your Fallow Ground
Jeremiah 4

The phrase "fallow ground" is found only twice in the entire Bible (Jer. 4; Hos. 10). Both Jeremiah and Hosea had similar prophetic ministries, though Hosea preceded Jeremiah by a century and Hosea was sent to rebuke idolatrous Israel. God used Jeremiah to call both Judah and those remaining in Israel to forsake their idols and return to Him, for doing so would result in His blessing. Regrettably, the preaching of Jeremiah, Habakkuk, and Zephaniah was largely rejected; the result was that Judah suffered similar repercussions under the Babylonians as Israel had suffered earlier from the Assyrians. Like Israel, Judah had refused to break up their fallow ground as well.

Jeremiah pleads with those of the Southern Kingdom to *"Break up your fallow ground, and do not sow among thorns"* (v. 3). The Jews were a nation composed of shepherds and farmers. So when the prophet sternly warned them to plow up their fallow ground, they knew what he meant. Fallow ground is soil that was once cultivated, but now lies waste and is completely fruitless. The longer it remains uncultivated, the harder it becomes. In order for it to be made profitable again it must be broken up with a plow; only then can it be planted again and made fruitful. The purpose of the soil analogy was to call them to repentance.

Additionally, Jeremiah warned them against sowing among thorns. In Matthew 13, the Lord likened the ground in which seed (i.e., God's Word) is sown to the spiritual disposition of various human hearts. Then, the Lord used the imagery of thorny ground to describe how worldliness chokes out the impact of God's Word in a person's life (i.e. trusting the gospel message).

A similar spiritual consequence is true for believers also; lingering complacency to obey God's Word causes our hearts to become hard, cold, and dry; the only solution is to plow them up. Living under the shade of briars will block the light necessary for growth and fruit-bearing; it will amount to a wasted existence.

For revival to occur in the Church, we must be open to God's Word and shun worldliness. God's Word must penetrate our minds and take root before we can bear fruit. Revival must start in the Church before it can spill over and affect the lost. Much of the Church today has become unprofitable; we need reviving – Oh God, may it start with me!

October 17 – The Queen of Heaven – Part 1
Jeremiah 7

Jeremiah speaks of "the Queen of Heaven" in this chapter; a brief review will help us understand of whom he is speaking. The tenth chapter of Genesis identifies Babylon [Babel] as the fountainhead of all pagan worship. The human founder of this city was Nimrod, whose name means "rebel." Nimrod's quest for deity would hinge upon his success in constructing an enormous tower intended to bridge earth with heaven (The Lord brought the construction of Babel's tower to an abrupt halt by diversifying the language of the people.)

Babylonian history records that Nimrod met with a sudden and violent death. After this, his beautiful wife, Semiramis, gave birth to what she claimed was the essence of Nimrod. The developed Chaldean story states that Nimrod willingly gave us his life in order to further bless the Babylonian kingdom. In any case, Semiramis' son, Bacchus was said to be her deified husband. Classical history refers to the deified son as Nimus (or Yule), meaning "the son," while Scripture calls him "Tammuz" in Ezekiel 8:14.

Semiramis was licentious and gave birth to several children, though she had no husband. The story concocted around Nimus' birth not only secured her throne, but in time the people reverenced her as *Rhea*, "the great goddess Mother" or *Beltis*, "the Queen of Heaven." She derived all her glory and claim to deity through the son. Ancient art of the mother and son has the glow of the sun positioned behind each of their heads to indicate sun divinity, but the glory of Semiramis was accentuated above that of her son.

The Roman Catholic Church refers to Mary as "the Queen of Heaven" and the "Mother of God." Many have ascribed glory to Mary in the same way Semiramis was deified in the eyes of her people – through the glory of her son. The veneration of Mary has its roots in Babylon; indeed, it is simply a repackaged pagan lie. When the people dispersed from Babel, they carried their pagan traditions with them; this explains why many ancient cultures tell of a goddess giving birth to a deified son, the essence of her dead husband. This brief history highlights the main rudiments of paganism, which were eventually incorporated into the Roman papal system and, thus, infiltrated and adversely influenced much of the professing Church today.

October 18 – The Queen of Heaven – Part 2
Jeremiah 7

God told Jeremiah not to intercede for Judah any further; then He explained the reasons for His "prayer ban" – two forms of dreadful idolatry. First, families throughout Judah were uniting for a festive celebration in honor of the goddess Ishtar, the so-called "Queen of Heaven" (her identity is explained in Part 1). The event included preparing special cakes that bore her image and were offered to her in a sacrificial rite. Second, these same families were pouring out drink offerings, probably wine, before various idols. The Jews did not seem to care who they honored through these casual social traditions; as they did not consider these celebrations idolatrous, but just an opportunity for families to enjoy doing something together.

These false gods were not a threat to Jehovah; human imaginations cannot hurt Him or diminish His glory. However, God's anger was provoked by the confusion of truth among His people; they had *"confused faces"* (v. 19). Though the truth was before them, the Jews no longer had clear distinctions between what was right and what was wrong, between what was holy and what was unholy.

The same confusion of face is common today among those who associate themselves with the name of Jesus Christ. It is caused by a blurring of what is righteous and what is not. For example, many families gather to commemorate various "Christian" holidays which have pagan origins. Over time, various traditions have developed around these celebrations, which sound very similar to the practices of the Jews in Jeremiah's day. In these supposed Christian holidays, cookies, cakes, breads, chocolate figurines, etc. are often shaped after ancient pagan images. Fictitious personalities are honored through various traditions and gift-giving practices. A brief review of the holidays of Easter and Christmas will suffice to show their pagan roots.

We begin with Easter. Bunnies and decorated (or stained) eggs were symbols the ancient Babylonians used to honor their fertility goddess *Astarte*, also called *Eastre*. In 325 AD, the Roman Catholic Church (under Constantine) created a yearly religious holiday to commemorate the resurrection of Christ, setting it for the first Sunday after the first full moon on or after the vernal equinox. This was to align the new holiday with the ancient spring celebration of *Eastre* (i.e.

Easter). Although the word "Easter" appears in the King James Version of the Bible (Acts 12:4), it is an inaccurate translation, no doubt due to centuries of Roman Catholic influence. But the correct rendition of the Greek word *pascha* is "Passover," as it is translated elsewhere in the New Testament.

There is absolutely no trace of the Easter celebration in the New Testament. The early Church did not hold a yearly remembrance of the Lord's resurrection; rather, they kept the Lord's Supper weekly (Acts 20:7) in obedience to the Lord's command to regularly remember Him in that way (Luke 22:19-20). Today, much of Christendom is ignoring the commands and patterns of Scripture to practice social traditions which actually honor pagan deities.

Although the Christmas holiday has become something entirely different than what it was when first instituted by the Roman Catholic Church in 350 AD (by Julius I), its tie with Easter is unmistakable. There is no biblical or extra-biblical evidence that points to December as being the date for the birth of Jesus Christ. Rather, the date was chosen to honor the ancient Egyptian sun-god *Mithras* (or *Horus*). The son of Egyptian goddess *Isis* – *Mithras* was claimed to have been born on December 25th, which is nine months (human gestation period) after the spring equinox in late March – the time of the pagan fertility celebrations.

The pagan tie between the dates of Easter and Christmas is unmistakable. Neither observance was commanded in Scripture, but was developed by the Roman Catholic Church in association with existing Anglo-Saxon pagan rituals, derived from still more ancient cultures. In fact, nearly all the developed Christmas traditions practiced today have pagan roots (e.g., burning of the Yule log, lights/candles, decorating evergreen trees, gift-giving, baked images, etc.).

Today, these have become mere social events in which Christians, professing Christians, and non-Christians alike participate. Although traditions vary widely, one aspect that has never changed is the fact that these man-made traditions draw attention away from the Lord and how He wants to be revered. Idolatry, in any form, draws people away from the truth and causes them to engage in activities that God does not commend. This fact is affirmed to us in the life of the first pagan named in Scripture, Nimrod. What started with Nimrod long ago affected the Jews during Jeremiah's day and still influences the Church presently.

October 19 – The Suffering Prophet
Jeremiah 11

Jeremiah's messages of rebuke and judgment were not popular. The men of Anathoth, Jeremiah's hometown, offered him an ultimatum: "Jeremiah, shut up or die." Apparently, these rebels had already devised a plan to murder Jeremiah, but God revealed the entire matter to His faithful prophet. Without God's help, Jeremiah said he would have been like a lamb or an ox brought to the slaughter.

Besides the plot of the citizens of Anathoth (11:18-13), Jeremiah would suffer much verbal abuse by the people (18:18), he would be assaulted and chained by the priest Pashhur (20:1-3), the priests and prophets would seek to kill him (26:7-24), King Jehoiakim would burn Jeremiah's scroll and then order him to be arrested (36:22-26), Jeremiah would be struck by the priests and then imprisoned (37:15), and in a final attempt on his life, the princes would drop Jeremiah down into a deep pit where he would sink into the mire (37:11-38:13). But though they left him there to die, God had other plans. In each of these threatening situations, Jeremiah would be miraculously sustained and delivered by the Lord. Why? He was God's man doing God's will and was thus invincible until God's will for his life was complete.

God had promised Jeremiah His protection when He summoned him to be His prophet and the Lord's faithfulness to this pledge would be shown repeatedly. David, who also knew what it was like to suffer wrongfully, wrote, *"Many are the afflictions of the righteous, but the Lord delivers him out of them all"* (Ps. 34:19). Certainly, Jeremiah would suffer because of his ministry, but God would be faithful to preserve his life and deliver him from jeopardy. Until Jeremiah's ministry was complete, he was immortal. This truth is an immense comfort for those who drink from the bitter cup of their own ministry. Those who live godly lives will suffer in a wicked world (2 Tim. 3:12), but they cannot be overcome by the enemy until their work is done.

The Lord promised His prophet to severely judge Anathoth during the Babylonian invasion. God's dealings with the inhabitants of Anathoth would be a warning to all Jews that opposing God's Word and those delivering it had severe consequences. May this truth encourage every believer who has suffered for the cause of Christ.

October 20 – Restrictions for Life
Jeremiah 16

The Lord's next message to Jeremiah was of a personal nature; He was placing three restrictions on His prophet. First, he was not to take a wife. Certainly, this must have been a difficult thing for Jeremiah to concede, as no wife meant no lifelong companion and no children of his own. Yet, God reminded Jeremiah that, in the coming days, not only would death (and widowers) be common among the inhabitants of Judah, but the Jews would suffer grievously before dying. This was no place for a new bride, and it was certainly a poor time to raise a family. The request was not to punish Jeremiah in any way, but rather to save him grief later. His singleness would serve as a sign to the people that the future would be devastating to family life; many fathers, mothers, daughters, and sons would die by the sword, famine, or disease.

The second restriction levied on Jeremiah was that he was not to attend any funerals, meaning he was not to console the family of the deceased. He was also forbidden to show sorrow by cutting himself or shaving his head – there was to be no demonstration of sympathy or mourning.

This directive may at first glance seem unnecessary. The Law prohibited the cutting and tattooing of oneself during times of mourning because these acts were pagan in origin (Lev. 19:28), and it is not likely that Jeremiah would have done these actions which were expressly forbidden in the Law; however, the prohibition may have been mentioned to show that the Jews of Jeremiah's day were ignoring it and indeed cutting themselves. Jeremiah's lack of attendance of funerals or public display of grief was to illustrate that the Lord had withdrawn His love, pity, and blessings from His people.

Not only was Jeremiah not to mourn with his people, but the third restriction prevented him from feasting and making merry with them as well. Jeremiah could not attend any parties or festive occasions; this was to demonstrate that Jehovah would remove all joy and happiness from Judah. These three limitations again confirm that Jeremiah drank from his own ministry. Like Hosea before Jeremiah and Ezekiel after him, the daily affairs of God's prophets were themselves a message to the people. Similarly, the unregenerate watch all the holy peculiarities of God's people today – our lives are to proclaim the gospel message.

October 21 – The Deceitful Heart
Jeremiah 17

Jeremiah was perplexed: with the respective pathways to cursing and blessing so clearly revealed, why would anyone depart from the Lord and have their names erased from the earth? Yet, there were many that were ignoring his warning, saying that such talk of accountability and retribution was foolishness. They asked him how they could be assured of such things: *"Indeed they say to me, 'Where is the word of the Lord? Let it come now'"* (v. 15)! "Let it come now!" What prompted the Jews to be so arrogant and foolish? Jeremiah could not explain the reason for their insurrection, but he did understand the source of the problem – the human heart: *"The heart is deceitful above all things, and desperately wicked; who can know it?"* (v. 9).

The Lord declares that He knows all about the human heart: *"I, the Lord, search the heart, I test the mind, even to give every man according to his ways, according to the fruit of his doings"* (v. 10). David understood that the Lord knew his thoughts afar off (Ps. 139:2). The writer of Hebrews puts the matter this way: *"And there is no creature hidden from His sight, but all things are naked and open to the eyes of Him to whom we must give account"* (Heb. 4:13). We cannot hide from God; He intimately knows what motivates our behavior, the strongholds in our minds, and the mental gymnastics we perform to justify sin. God knows the human heart and just how wicked it is.

Jeremiah speaks of the "heart" nearly sixty times in his book. Usually these references do not speak of the heart organ, but of an invisible part of the human soul relating to emotions, desires, moral inclinations, and cognitive abilities. Figuratively, the heart is the hidden spring of the inward life. Interestingly, the bulk of biblical exhortation is not focused upon the soul or the heart, but on the mind. Thus, the mind must be *"transformed"* (Rom. 12:2) before a pure heart can be *"formed"* (Ps. 51:10). A pure heart serves to *"conform"* (Eph. 6:5-8) one's will to God's will.

The mind is the area between the physical and spiritual realms where spiritual battles are won or lost. Does the Lord have your whole mind, which is at the core of your heart? If you love the Lord with your entire mind, your heart and body will be constrained to do the same, which is what He desires (Mark 12:30).

October 22 – The Potter's Wheel
Jeremiah 18

The next message to the Jews came in the form of an illustration. Jeremiah was instructed to journey to the potter's house; there, as he observed the potter's skill in action, God would speak to him. Jeremiah did as requested and watched the potter work with a lump of clay on his wheel. In ancient times, potters' wheels were normally spun by a mechanical apparatus that had to be pedaled by the operator, which meant to form pottery was quite a laborious task. The potter had to use both feet to pedal the wheel and both hands to form the clay.

The first lump of clay was marred in the potter's hands, that is, it was not pliable. The potter tossed it aside and began to work with another lump of clay which he fashioned into a beautiful vessel. Then the Lord explained the illustration to Jeremiah: Israel was like the unworkable clay which God, the Potter, wanted to shape into a special vessel that all nations would admire. The second lump of clay shaped by the potter, after the first was discarded, is likely a reference to the Church. After God fashions it, He then will return to work with the first lump, the Jewish nation. During the Tribulation Period, the divine Potter will put that which was discarded back on His wheel and form it into a useful vessel; then Israel will be restored to Him forever.

One cannot read this text without pondering God's mysterious ways in each of our lives. When an individual, a lump of clay, so to speak, yields to the gospel message, the molding process begins; until then the clay is marred by sin and cannot be fashioned into a vessel of honor. When a potter sets a lump of softened clay upon the wheel in order to make something of it, the first thing he or she does is to poke into the center of the clay with his or her hand or some other instrument.

This reminds us that God molds us from the inside out; He starts by cleansing and shaping the heart. Circumstances in this life then supply the Potter's wheel with the turning motion to assist the Master's hand in molding our hearts to the pattern of Christ-likeness. Sometimes the wheel seems to be spinning so fast we may fear we will fly apart, but God promises us sustaining grace so we will bear up during the forming process (1 Cor. 10:13). May the divine Potter have His way with each of us while He fashions vessels glistening with His grace!

October 23 – The Broken Vessel
Jeremiah 19

In the arrangement of the book, Jeremiah placed the message of the broken vessel directly after that of the marred clay (Jer. 18); the potter connects both sermons. The one who creates also has the right to destroy what he has made. God had fashioned the Jewish nation in righteousness, but now that vessel was full of corruption; it needed to be shattered and scattered. Jeremiah purchased a flask used for carrying water from the potter; this bottle would be used as a prop to illustrate his next message. After gathering a group of Jewish leaders, Jeremiah walked through the East (or Potshard) Gate to the Valley of Hinnom located south of Jerusalem. The people used this gate to enter the valley to discard their refuse, such as broken pots (thus, the gate's name). The message was delivered at a place in the valley called Topheth.

The Valley of Hinnom was Jerusalem's garbage dump and piles of burning rubbish smoldered there incessantly. The Jews likely thought of this place when the Lord Jesus spoke of hell as a place of eternal judgment where fire burns continually (Mark 9:43-47). The summits surrounding the valley had become the high places of Baal, the scene of intense idolatry. This was where Jewish children were being sacrificed on pagan altars. With these altars as a backdrop, Jeremiah spoke the message first and then dramatized it before his elite audience.

Because of Jewish paganism, God would rename the Hinnom Valley to the "Valley of Slaughter." The Babylonians would use the valley as a killing ground for Jerusalem's inhabitants and leave the carcasses of the slain lying on the ground to rot and be devoured by beasts – there would not be sufficient tombs and graves to bury the dead. The siege of Jerusalem would be so severe that hunger would cause parents to eat the flesh of their own children. Then Jeremiah shattered the vase and said, *"Even so I will break this people and this city, as one breaks a potter's vessel, which cannot be made whole again"* (v. 11).

After pronouncing judgment on Jerusalem, Jeremiah departed and spoke the same message to the general populace at the temple. A useless vessel must be broken before God in order to be recreated by Him into a useful form; the process is painful, but profitable in the end. Brokenness is still the pathway to fruitfulness today.

Daily Devotions

October 24 – Brokenness
Jeremiah 19

Normally, when something breaks, it loses value. For example, a shattered keepsake is remorsefully discarded as a total loss. Within the physical realm the laws of nature work to depreciate the value of our possessions, but this is not so in the spiritual realm – in fact, the opposite is true. Scripture poses a number of metaphoric examples to show that in God's reckoning, things and especially people become more valuable for service after being broken. Here are some examples:

To Know Meaning in Life. The donkey's colt, which had never been saddled, became instantly broken in the presence of the Lord Jesus (Luke 19:30). Through brokenness, the colt learned God's purpose for its life and fulfilled it; he was to carry Messiah down the Mount of Olives into Jerusalem before a cheering crowd. It is when we are broken before God that we will be able to learn of Him and, like the colt, find true meaning in life.

To Offer Acceptable Worship. A few days before the Lord would be crucified, Mary took a stone flask of spikenard, broke it open, and anointed the Lord Jesus with its precious contents (John 12:1-11). As the ointment was very costly, some criticized the action as being wasteful, but the Lord was refreshed by her expression of devotion, and said, *"Let her alone; for the day of My burial has she kept this"* (John 12:7). The vessel which contained the spikenard had to be broken for her worship to be appreciated by the Lord and others, and the same is true for the believer (Ps. 51:17).

To Be Fruitful. Under his ephod, the high priest wore a blue sleeveless robe which hung down below his knees. Pomegranates, which rattle when dried, and golden bells were to be attached to the bottom hem (Ex. 28:33). The rattling of pomegranates and the tinkling of bells spoke of Christ's continual intercessory work before the throne of grace on the behalf of His people. Yet, for the pomegranate to be fruitful, its hard shell must be broken in order to release its seeds; if no seeds are planted, there will not be any fruit to come. What it was previously had to radically change in order for it to become fruitful – the same principle is true in the life of the believer.

To Have a Bright Testimony. Gideon was to assault a vast Midianite army with merely 300 men armed only with trumpets and torches (Judg. 7:9-22). The torches were hidden in jars that were to be broken on command to let their lights shine out. When the trumpets were blown and 300 torches were seen on the hillside, mass confusion ensued and Gideon was victorious. Likewise, we gain brighter testimonies for Christ through brokenness.

May We Serve Christ!

October 25 – Beware of Self-Seeking
Jeremiah 45

It was the fourth year of King Jehoiakim's reign and Jeremiah was busy dictating God's Word to Baruch who was recording it on a scroll. Jehoiakim would later burn this scroll, which caused the two men to repeat the tedious process of writing God's message on a second scroll. Apparently, Baruch was greatly discouraged by the contents of the scroll. God's severe punishment of His people was cause enough for grief, but he had been faithful to serve the Lord and it seemed unfair to him that God was adding sorrow to his life. He had hoped to be rewarded for his faithfulness, but instead there was to be punishment.

Baruch's high expectations of reward and greatness clearly clashed with God's national plan *"to overthrow and build,"* and *"to uproot and plant"* (v. 4). God admonished Baruch to trust Him in the matter of dealing with backsliding Judah and not to be self-focused. He was told that, while most Jews would die or become enslaved by Babylon, he would be rewarded with his life.

William Kelly identifies the valuable lesson for Baruch, which is indeed a lesson that all believers should understand: "Lowliness of mind always becomes the saint, but in an evil day, it is the only safety. Humility is always morally right, but it is also the only thing that preserves from judgment … which is executed in this world."[19] The low road is the pathway to divine blessing. God honors those who humble themselves and put their trust in Him, especially when it seems most sensible to invoke our personal rights.

Certainly the placement of this account here is out of place chronologically; we may wonder, then, why Jeremiah placed it at the end of his prophecies to Judah. It would seem that the message God delivered to Baruch some time prior to this is included here because it was the one God wanted the Jews to heed at the present time.

Jeremiah 45 forms the capstone over all that God has decreed to His people and desires of them. His call can be summarized as, "Cling to My Word by faith and hope in Me alone for future blessing." This was the response that God wanted from His covenant people whether they were captives in Babylon, sojourners in Egypt, survivors in Israel, or servants of the Lord, such as this prophet and scribe, and of us also (Rev. 14:13).

Daily Devotions

October 26 – His Compassions Fail Not
Lamentations 3

Jeremiah had experienced much affliction in the execution of his prophetic office. Though he had suffered much hardship, Jeremiah used metaphoric language in this chapter to express this fact rather than mentioning specific details. His allegorical explanations show that he has no desire to glory in His afflictions; instead, he wanted to highlight the joyous outcome of what God accomplished through them.

Because Jeremiah's sufferings were directly connected with Judah's chastening, he was able both to sympathize with his people and to inspire them to seek after the same solace he had found during arduous circumstances – trusting in God alone. Difficult trials often cause God's people to suffer spiritual despondency.

Even Jeremiah, during a moment of despair said, *"my strength and my hope have perished from the Lord"* (v. 18). But then, after calling on God to remember his past afflictions, Jeremiah also recalled God's past faithfulness to enable him to persevere through adversity. He had learned through experience that God's children should never feel hopeless, for they were always established in God's eternal love and His promises:

> *Through the Lord's mercies we are not consumed, because His compassions fail not. They are new every morning; great is Your faithfulness. "The Lord is my portion," says my soul, "therefore I hope in Him!" The Lord is good to those who wait for Him, to the soul who seeks Him. It is good that one should hope and wait quietly for the salvation of the Lord* (vv. 22-26).

The phrase "His compassions" (v. 22) in derived from the Hebrew word *racham*, which relates to the cherishing impulses that a woman has for the fetus in her womb. This is the type of divine tenderness that Jeremiah had consistently experienced. What Jeremiah is teaching us is that the work of God and His association with it is more important than the personal consequences received for being obedient to God's will. It had cost Jeremiah much to go on with God, but he deemed the entire ordeal as profitable given what he had gained – greater understanding of the sovereignty and faithfulness of God. This should be the response of God's people in any age and in all circumstances.

October 27 – The Son of Man
Ezekiel 2

Overwhelmed by the fantastic vision of the Lord that he had seen (Ezek. 1), Ezekiel fell prostrate on the ground. The Lord spoke to him, *"Son of man, stand on your feet, and I will speak to you"* (v. 1). God's initial address to Ezekiel is in keeping with the awesome vision of God's glory that he, a mere man, had just been permitted to see. The expression "son of man" is also used in reference to Daniel (8:17), the other major post-exiled prophet. "Son of man" is found ninety-three times in Ezekiel's book and affirms his scant human essence before the almighty Creator.

After pondering God's greatness and humanity's insignificance, David was prompted to inquire of God, *"What is man that You are mindful of him, And the son of man that You visit him?"* (Ps. 8:4). Yet, God is mindful of mankind and of His covenant people; He has plans for both that center in the work of Christ. Hence, Ezekiel's lowly title is fitting for his book, says J. N. Darby:

> God speaks to Ezekiel as to a "son of man" – a title that suited the testimony of a God who spoke outside of His people, as being no longer in their midst, but on the contrary was judging them from the throne of His sovereignty. It is Christ's own title, looked at as rejected and outside of Israel, although He never ceases to think of the blessing of the people in grace. This puts the prophet in connection with the position of Christ Himself. He would not, thus rejected, allow His disciples to announce Him as the Christ (Luke 9), for the Son of Man was to suffer.[20]

The tenor of Ezekiel's entire ministry would be characterized by this humble title – a title that expressed God's displeasure with Israel at that time. After the Lord commanded his prophet to stand, the Holy Spirit promptly entered Ezekiel and enabled him to obey the Lord, and also to hear and understand God's Words to him. In Old Testament days, the Holy Spirit did not regenerate and eternally indwell believers as in the Church Age, for Christ had not yet died and been resurrected. Believers today are baptized into Christ's resurrection life by the Holy Spirit and are thereby empowered to obey the Lord and to discern God's Word accurately. If God is directing and enabling our service, we never need to worry about being able to stand on our own two feet!

October 28 – Internalizing God's Word
Ezekiel 3

The Jewish nation had been like an obstinate horse rejecting the bit and bridle of its master. Ezekiel, however, was to willingly open his mouth and eat (i.e., receive) from the Lord whatever He put there (2:8). Chapter 3 commences with the Lord repeating the command: His prophet was to eat the scroll that was in His hand. By doing so, Ezekiel was internalizing the divine message he was to passionately communicate to God's rebellious people. This scene is a good reminder to us that before we can convey truth to others, we first must know it and live it ourselves. This will require us to read, to meditate on, to rightly divide, and to memorize Scripture (2 Tim. 2:15). By comparing Scripture with Scripture, the Holy Spirit enables us to understand the mind of God and to get right with God.

Ezekiel did eat the scroll and it tasted as sweet as honey in his mouth. Though the message pertained to devastating judgment, it nonetheless was God's Word, and Ezekiel was reminded that its source (God) was sweet, though the content of His message was bitter.

A few centuries later, John would also eat a scroll containing God's Word, which then equipped him to reveal the deep things of God to the Church of Jesus Christ (Rev. 10:8-10). Likewise, a few years before Ezekiel's commissioning, the prophet Jeremiah had also joyfully eaten God's Word, which sustained and delighted his soul (Jer. 15:16). This divine provision empowered him to shun the company of evildoers and fools in order to sit alone with the Lord and be guided by Him.

Because Jeremiah was in such close communion with God, he too felt indignation against Judah (i.e., he could identify with God's righteous anger over their sin). These benefits are available to all those who joyfully internalize God's Word and willingly submit to it.

Preachers today cannot expect to have any divine power unless they have first fed upon God's Word and permitted the Spirit of God to have His way. What God reveals must be lived out before it can be spoken out in power. God's Word and His work are a direct reflection of His character; that is, they are what He is: perfect, sure, right, pure, clean, true, and righteous. God's Word is more precious than gold, sweeter than honey, and ensures a prodigious reward if obeyed (Ps. 19:9-10).

October 29 – God's Watchman
Ezekiel 3

Ezekiel was less startled by the Lord's second appearance seven days later. This encounter was a natural development in his commissioning as God's watchman. Ezekiel had already been made aware of his calling, but was not too motivated to fulfill it. We are not told what the source of Ezekiel's bitterness was. Perhaps it related to being called to proclaim a message of judgment against his own people, whom he loved, but who had exasperated him by their conduct. Yet, after being permitted to observe their poor spiritual condition for seven days, Ezekiel's calling as God's watchman on their behalf seems to have more importance.

Beside spending time with those God had called him to serve, spending quiet time before the Lord provided Ezekiel the opportunity to better align his own emotions with God's own hurt concerning Israel's sin. He found that he now possessed a fierce indignation towards the sin of his countrymen. Likewise, as we commune with the Lord in prayer and meditate on His Word, we learn to think as He does about the necessity of holy living. Real fellowship with the Lord compels us to feel the abhorrence of sin as He does and to love the sinner as only He can.

After days of sitting in silence, Ezekiel had a fresh, less self-focused motivation for ministry, the holiness of God. He also acknowledges the source of power and direction for his prophetic ministry, *"the hand of the Lord"* (v. 14). These two complementary aspects of service cannot be separated. Our zeal for holiness and truth must be accompanied by God's authority and power or we will not be able to serve Him, and worse, we will likely bring disdain upon His name.

Each believer must submit to God's ongoing work of sanctification to be led by the hand of the Lord into His purposes. Without the work of sanctification, ministry for God is impossible. Fancy words and good intentions do not define a missionary. His or her character is the message and without Christ-likeness, he or she will fail miserably in representing Christ to the lost.

In personal holiness and in the power of the Holy Spirit, Ezekiel was to steadfastly rebuke Israel for what God hated – their deep-seated idolatry and their stubborn, rebellious nature. God's watchman was responsible only to deliver God's warning; he was not accountable for the response of those hearing it. The same is true today!

October 30 – Search Our Thoughts
Ezekiel 11

The Spirit of God then lifted Ezekiel up and brought him to the East Gate of the temple which overlooked the Kidron Valley below and the Mount of Olives eastward. From this location he saw twenty-five elders. Since Jaazaniah was among them, these men were likely a part of Israel's corrupt political leadership identified earlier (8:11). These men devise iniquity and render perverse counsel to the people: *"The time is not near to build houses; this city is the caldron, and we are the meat"* (vv. 2-3). In other words, they were encouraging the people to ignore Ezekiel's prophecies of doom; they were as safe in Jerusalem as meat was in a cooking pot. These wicked leaders proposed that they should be building up the city, not waiting for its destruction.

However, God informed Ezekiel that He knew what they were really thinking; they feared a Babylonian invasion and wanted to bolster their defenses against such an attack by building up Jerusalem. For rejecting God's Word and trying to strengthen themselves against His chastening rod, Ezekiel was commanded to prophesy against them. Verse 5 affirms that our omniscient Lord knows all our thoughts, the quality of our thoughts, whether conscious or unconscious, and He does not forget them, though we usually do in time.

David fully understood this attribute of God and welcomed His examination: *"O Lord, You have searched me and known me. You know my sitting down and my rising up; You understand my thought afar off"* (Ps. 139:1-2). Because David realized every aspect of his life was searched out, planned, and meticulously controlled by the Lord, he could praise the Lord for His wondrous works and invite further inspection and refinement of his inner man (Ps. 139:23-24).

Divine inspection of David's heart would both prove his loyal devotion to the Lord and permit God to further test and enrich David's character. He knew he could not hide his thoughts and doings from the Lord, so he desired to transform all his contemplations and deeds to those that would please Him. This is the proper response to the omnipresent, omniscient, omnipotent God. Concerning one's devotion to the Lord, David shows us that there is no middle ground, for neither the wicked or the righteous can escape His scrutiny or judgment.

October 31 – The Sins of the People
Ezekiel 22

God calls on Ezekiel to be His prosecuting attorney and to review the evidence so that Israel will understand their guilt and why their abominations demanded severe reprisal. The two chief sins imputed to Jerusalem were murdering innocent people and creating idols to worship. Hence, Jerusalem's days as Israel's capital city were drawing to an end; God was going to vanquish their pride and make them a reproach to all nations. The Law shows sin (Rom. 3:20), but it also reveals how to show love to God (worship Him alone in holiness) and love to others (not stealing from others, but rather meeting their needs).

However, the Jews did not love God, or others, or His Law in general (Ex. 20:1-17). Rather, they flagrantly rebelled against it. Ezekiel then lists the social and moral sins demanding judgment: abusing civil authority in order to murder; dishonoring parents, mistreating strangers, neglecting widows and orphans; despising God's holy things and His Sabbaths; idolatry; gross immorality (often associated with idolatry); taking bribes, charging exorbitant interest, and extortion. Then, the prophet named their greatest offense – they, as a nation, had forgotten the Lord.

God would strike His hands together and smite Jerusalem for disregarding Him and His Law. Verse 14 serves as a potent warning to all those who would willfully disregard God's Word: *"Can your heart endure, or can your hands remain strong, in the days when I shall deal with you?"* Paul similarly challenges believers, *"Do we provoke the Lord to jealousy? Are we stronger than He?"* (1 Cor. 10:22). After Israel was defiled before the nations, the Jews would learn that it was unwise to provoke the Lord to jealousy and that they could not stand against His righteous indignation. They had forgotten the Lord, but He had not forgotten them, and God was determined not to rest until they identified with Him again in purity.

When God's Word is of little importance to those who identify with Christ, an immoral, lethargic, carnal Church is the result. As the Jews would learn, there are stringent consequences for forsaking the Lord. Regrettably, it is only those who are near to the Lord who dread this condition; the others need extreme measures to be awakened from their spiritual slumber.

November 1 – Pride and Beauty Denounced
Ezekiel 28

Ezekiel turns his attention from pronouncing judgment on Tyre and lamenting her destruction to condemning Tyre's proud ruler, *"the Prince of Tyre"* (vv. 1-10). However, there was an evil spiritual power behind this wicked prince that was opposing God's authority in Tyre. Ezekiel refers to him as *"the King of Tyre"* (vv. 11-19). Isaiah calls him by name, *"Lucifer"* (Isa. 14:12). The prophet first rebukes the prince, a man who wanted to be a god (vv. 1-2), and then rebukes the king, the beautiful cherub who wanted to be God (vv. 16-18).

Like the prince, the King of Tyre was also wise and beautiful, but far more exceedingly so. Ezekiel refers to him as the anointed cherub that was created in perfection, sheathed with precious stones and equipped inherently to worship God through music and was in the Garden of Eden. Lucifer was created with the provision of timbrels and flutes to offer music before God (v. 13). Perhaps, Lucifer led the angels in worship through initiating music. Regardless, worship (accompanied by music) was being offered by spiritual beings to their Creator, even before man was created. As the anointed covering cherub, Lucifer may have had a view of God's majesty and glory that no other created being was afforded – in perfection, he was with God on His holy mountain.

Yet, Satan became obsessed with his own beauty and wanted to be worshipped as God. In mutiny, the "light bearer," (Lucifer), became the ruler of darkness and immersed the world in deceit, corruption, and violence. Lucifer was a spectacular creature that had been created to bring God glory; however, his prestigious position in creation and unique vantage point of God's preeminence led him to be dissatisfied with God's creation order. Lucifer no longer desired to cover himself and protect the sanctity of God's glory. He would no longer conceal his personal glory in God's presence.

His insubordination was energized by his pride to be "lifted up" and to be like "the Most High" (Isa. 14:14). Lucifer wanted the supremacy in heaven and led a rebellion against Almighty God (Rev. 12:4), who responded by casting him off the Holy Mount and destining him to the Lake of Fire (Matt. 25:41). God will not permit competing glories in His presence, a matter that the Church is to constantly remember (1 Cor. 11:3-16).

May We Serve Christ!

November 2 – The Reappointed Watchman
Ezekiel 33

Previously, Ezekiel had been appointed as God's watchman to first warn Judah and then the surrounding Gentile nations of divine retribution for their wickedness. Now, Ezekiel is again appointed as a watchman for the Jewish nation, but with a different focus. While still upholding a message of divine accountability, he is to inspire the Jews concerning their future. Jehovah will restore His adulterous wife once she has been cleansed of her filthiness and sanctified for God alone.

The opening verses affirm the duties of a watchman to warn those in his care of threatening situations (e.g., the approach of an invading army). If the watchman faithfully sounds the alarm when appropriate, he is not responsible for how people respond to it. However, if the watchman chooses to save his own life and does not warn those in his care, God holds him responsible for all those slaughtered in the attack.

God had seen to it that His people were duly warned before the Babylonian invasion came; in fact, Jeremiah had been faithfully blowing the trumpet in Jerusalem for forty years. The prophet Ezekiel was chosen by God to be a watchman to the Jews in Babylon. God again warns him to be faithful to his calling or He will hold Ezekiel personally accountable for the deaths of the wicked. Ezekiel was not responsible for how his audience responded to his proclamation of the truth; God promised to hold each one responsible for their own choices.

The Jewish captives now knew that their temple, capital city, and entire homeland had been destroyed by Babylon. All that Ezekiel had been proclaiming for the past seven years had come to pass, clearly he was a true prophet of God. The fact that God was still speaking to them through Ezekiel meant that all was not lost, but rather that He had a plan for their future.

Ezekiel exhorted his countrymen not think that the Lord derived pleasure in being wrathful, but rather He longs to joyfully interact with those who will honor Him through obedience: *"I have no pleasure in the death of the wicked, but that the wicked turn from his way and live"* (v. 11). This is an ageless truth: no one should think that he or she has ventured so far down the wide path to destruction that he or she cannot be rescued – no one is hopelessly lost unless he or she chooses not to repent and turn to the Lord for forgiveness and mercy.

November 3 – Woe to Bad Shepherds
Ezekiel 34

Ezekiel was to sharply rebuke Israel's spiritual leaders who cared for themselves and neglected God's sheep: *"Woe be to the shepherds of Israel that do feed themselves! Should not the shepherds feed the flocks?"* (vv. 1-2). God had entrusted His sheep (His people) into their care, but they had failed to fulfill that responsibility. Before passing judgment, Ezekiel notes the offenses of Israel's rulers: They did not serve the people, but rather their own interest and often for profit. They did not care for the lost, injured and suffering. They were often heavy-handed and brutal and permitted the Lord's people to be scattered and be devoured. As a result, God was furious with these slothful men who called themselves shepherds, but were not.

If these delinquent shepherds had been God-fearing spiritual leaders, there would have been no need for God to chasten Israel by the Assyrians and then Judah by the Babylonians. For their profiteering and neglect of duty, Israel's shepherds would be removed from their positions and severely punished by the Lord.

The writer of Hebrews reminds both sheep to be obedient to their shepherds and shepherds (i.e., church elders) to be faithful to the Lord, for they shall give an account to Him in a future day (Heb. 13:17). Sheep are to follow their God-given shepherds, as the shepherds follow the Lord. If shepherds deviate from the teaching of Scripture or fail to live it out, they will forfeit God's blessing and their flocks will suffer, and experience God's displeasure. Whenever God's leadership is in clear violation of Scripture, those whom God has placed in their care are in no way liable to follow them, but should rather submit to the Lord (Acts 4:15, 5:19).

We understand from Acts 20:28 that the Holy Spirit appoints elders in the local church from among that gathering; elders do not come in from outside the local church in question. Hence, Peter exhorts church elders to willingly remain among those God has entrusted into their care and to maintain an exemplary life fostered in humility before them (1 Pet. 5:2-3). Pastoral care of God's people cannot be accomplished from a distance. This is a good reminder for all those engaged in mentoring others; mentors must be available to spend time with those being mentored and also they must be living what they are teaching.

May We Serve Christ!

November 4 – Don't Muddy the Water
Ezekiel 34

Unlike Israel's shepherds, the Lord would feed, protect, heal, console, and lead His sheep in Israel. The Lord promises: *"I will feed My flock, and I will make them lie down"* (v. 15). Sadly, there are many starving and restless sheep in the world, but none such in the Lord's pasture. He knows how to care for His own much better than we ever could. We venture where we should not, we do not rest where and when we should, and we do not feed on what we should and then we wonder why we are so weak – we need the Great Shepherd to rule and care for us! All those who know Him will agree with David: *"The Lord is my shepherd; I shall not want"* (Ps. 23:1).

When the True Shepherd does return to establish His kingdom, He will *"judge between sheep and sheep, between rams and goats"* (v. 17). The former phrase speaks of rewards and punishment for His people, while the latter relates to Him separating true believers from the lost; the goats will not be permitted into His kingdom. This verdict is referred to as the Judgment of Nations. At Christ's Second Advent, He will punish all those who followed the Antichrist and persecuted the Jews during the Tribulation Period (Matt. 13:47-50, 25:31-33). This judgment is effected suddenly and those unfit for Christ's kingdom will be abruptly removed from the earth (Matt. 24:36-44; Rev. 19:21).

When Israel's rams (older male leaders) stand before God's Shepherd, they will regret drinking first from the stream and muddying the waters so that younger sheep could not drink fresh water. They will be sorry that they ate the best pasture first and trampled it down before others could feed. Then they will wish that they had taken the low place and served others, instead of putting their interests before the needs of God's people.

Because Israel's tyrants had brutalized the weak lambs by butting them away with their horns, God promised to rescue the oppressed and sternly punish the aggressors. The Lord would save His sheep from the false shepherds by sending the true Shepherd to them, speaking of the glorious Kingdom Age.

If you are an older believer serving younger saints, remember that God notices when we trample the green grass and muddy the drinking water of His lambs. Let us mimic the True Shepherd in all that we do.

November 5 – Full Consecration
Daniel 1

Daniel begins by informing us of the tragic invasion of Judah by Nebuchadnezzar in 605 B.C. In the aftermath, many choice Jews were enslaved, and with the holy articles of the temple, brought to Babylon. Although there were many captives, four are specifically named in verse 6 because of their impact on the Babylonian society and their testimony for Jehovah: Daniel, Hananiah, Mishael, and Azariah. (They were probably between twelve and fourteen years of age.) Sadly, because each of their names honored Jehovah, they were renamed by their captors with Babylonian names which did not.

For three years they were to reside in the king's palace, eat the king's food, and learn the customs, literature, and language of Babylon. At the end of this training period, each pupil would be examined personally by the king. The king was likely grooming these astute captives to be his future counselors or for administrative positions in his kingdom. Slaves without families, and having no political ambitions, could be trusted.

These four consecrated young men were now unwilling subjects of a hostile pagan culture bent on driving all remembrance of their God from their existence. Four satanic strategies were used on Daniel and his friends to accomplish this corrupt agenda: First, the devil wanted their natural abilities and talents for his own wicked purposes. Second, the devil desired to control their speech; he did not want them speaking Hebrew, the language of Jehovah for His people. Third, he wanted them to compromise their dietary convictions as based on God's Law; they were to eat all that the world had to offer them. Fourth, the devil attempted to strip them of their identity as a Jehovah worshipper by giving them pagan names. Satan continues this same agenda in an attempt to conform Christians to the policies and philosophies of the evil world he has manufactured through sin and rebellion.

The highest calling of a believer is to be a living sacrifice for Christ, which means separation from worldliness and full consecration to Christ. This means that believers must reject the world's values and attractions by renewing our minds on what is true and spiritual (Rom. 12:1-2). Daniel and his friends did so (they were uncompromising), and the Lord greatly honored and rewarded them in the king's court.

May We Serve Christ!

November 6 – Seeking Mercy Together
Daniel 2

Daniel and his friends were in their second year of intense training, when the king began having a recurring dream that haunted his mind and deprived him of sleep. This was no normal dream, but rather a vision from God, planted in the king's mind while he slept. Being anxious to know the dream, Nebuchadnezzar summoned all his wise men to tell him what his dream was and also its meaning. The king suspected that his wise men had conjured up erroneous interpretations of dreams previously, and as the dream was so vivid and troubling, he wanted to know its true meaning.

Although his counselors felt that the king's request was absurd, the decision was final. Anyone who could accomplish this feat would be greatly rewarded and honored, but those who could not would be cut to pieces. Knowing that their lives were in danger, the Chaldeans voiced their complaint and admission: *"There is no other who can tell it to the king except the gods"* (v. 11).

The king was furious at their response and commanded that all the wise men of Babylon be slaughtered. Several Chaldeans had already died when Arioch, arrived to execute Daniel and his companions. After learning of the situation, Daniel bravely approached the king and requested time that he might tell the king his dream and its interpretation. Daniel's request was granted. Daniel informed his three companions of the king's decision and they all gathered at Daniel's home to *"seek mercies from the God of heaven concerning this secret"* (vv. 17-18). To earnestly pray with likeminded believers having pure hearts and clean hands is one of the most enjoyable and powerful endeavors that mere humans on earth can ever engage in. Daniel and his friends had cast themselves upon a sovereign God and fully rested in whatever outcome He deemed would bring Him the most glory.

Daniel received the revelation that would preserve their lives. Before revealing it to the king, he gave God thanks for answering their collective prayers, *"What we asked for."* The king was ecstatic to learn the meaning of his dream. He responded by honoring Daniel and more importantly Daniel's God throughout the kingdom. To be anxious for nothing, but be given to prayer is the epitome of identification with Christ and of devotion and faith in Him (Phil. 4:6).

November 7 – Another Satanic Attack
Daniel 3

According to the Septuagint, Daniel and his Jewish friends would be in their mid-thirties when the events in this chapter occurred. Nebuchadnezzar had a ninety-foot tall gold image of himself erected in the plain of Dura. The king commanded his provincial governors to summon all government officials to come to the image dedication ceremony. Officials throughout the empire (excluding Daniel for an unknown reason) gathered for the image dedication. A herald explained that when the people heard the Babylonian orchestra playing that they were to fall down and worship the idol in the king's likeness. Anyone not doing so would be immediately thrown into a burning fiery furnace.

We pause to consider four tactics that the devil employed against Shadrach, Meshach, and Abed-Nego in an attempt to cause them to compromise what they knew to be true. First, surprise is used to stun believers and hopefully cause them to render a quick decision which they do not have time to think through. It is important for believers to remember that God is patient and wants us to understand and to confirm in our minds what is wise before acting in questionable matters (Rom. 14:23). Satan is a high-pressure salesman! Second, an enormous group of influential people in Babylon had gathered for the dedication of the image. Peer pressure is often an effective method to cause God's people to compromise the truth.

Third, Satan used the emotional effect of music in an attempt to make the situation more favorable to those whose consciences were unsettled. This is a tactic often employed in the entertain industry: a sensational song or humor is used to make some biblical heresy more palatable to unsuspecting viewers. The fourth strategy employed against the three Hebrews was the threat of death through political authority. We should expect that governments, under the control of *the god of this age*, will constantly approve statutes that contradict God's Laws and thereby threaten His people.

This is the situation before us and Shadrach, Meshach, and Abed-Nego did not compromise the truth; rather, they were willing to suffer the fiery furnace of civil dissidence, even if the Lord decided not to deliver them. But God miraculously saved them, the outcome of which brought honor to the three Jewish men, and much fame to their God.

November 8 – An Open-Window Relationship
Daniel 6

We come to one of the most popular stories in Scripture: Daniel safely spends a night with hungry lions because he would not compromise his faith – a faith that God would wonderfully honor. King Darius (under Cyrus' authority) reorganized the new empire into 120 districts, each having its own district leader reporting to one of three governors.

Daniel, now in his eighties, was known for his wisdom and intellect and was one of the three governors. However, Darius was so impressed with Daniel that he thought to make him the leading governor in the kingdom. This created a conspiracy against Daniel by the other officials, but because Daniel was a man of high morals and blameless in his conduct, his jealous enemies could not find any wrongdoing to accuse him of before the king.

These evil men then surmised that the only way to bring Daniel down was to devise a civil law that would be contrary to Daniel's religious convictions. A plan was devised that would cater to the king's pride, would promote unity throughout the kingdom, and would also condemn Daniel as a lawbreaker: for thirty days no one in the empire was to petition any man or god for anything, except the king; anyone found guilty of violating this law would be thrown into a den of lions and devoured. The law appealed to the king's ego and he overstepped his God-given authority by signing the statute into law.

After hearing of the edict, Daniel was determined to turn the matter over to his God. He would not abandon his normal practice of kneeling three times a day while facing Jerusalem to offer thanksgiving, praise, and supplications to his God (Ps. 55:17 and 138:2). Daniel continued his custom of praying in front of an open west-facing window, that is, towards Jerusalem. His adversaries must have been surprised that Daniel did not even try to hide his praying. His window was already open and it would have been cowardice to close it in this situation; likewise, if it had been closed, it would have been courting needless persecution to open it. But Daniel was a praying man; thus, his window was still open which illustrates his unbroken communion with God! All believers should desire this type of continuing fellowship with God, for He invites us to come to Him anytime we find ourselves in need.

Daily Devotions

November 9 – Giving Thanks In Adversity
Daniel 6

Not only did Daniel not shortchange his normal praying routine before an open window, but despite the threatening circumstances, he was determined to give God thanks. Verse 10 reads:

Now when Daniel knew that the writing was signed, he went home. And in his upper room, with his windows open toward Jerusalem, he knelt down on his knees three times that day, and prayed and gave thanks before his God, as was his custom since early days.

We do not know if Daniel even mentioned the plot against him in his prayers, obviously the Lord knew about it anyway. We do know that Daniel was careful to praise the Lord and give Him thanks. How often the Lord's people become rattled by circumstances and rush into the throne room of grace in a state of hopeless panic, as if God is unaware of what is happening in our lives or is somehow not in control. We must remember that God's peace resides within His sovereign control over all things. From Daniel's heavenly perspective, nothing has changed but a few details pertaining to his earthly supplications. When Christians can look heavenward during arduous times and give God thanks "in everything" (1 Thess. 5:18) and "for all things" (Eph. 5:20) it proves that we really trust Him with the situation. God is above all and controls all; there is nothing too hard for Him to deal with.

For their devious plot to succeed, Daniel's enemies had counted on both the vanity of the king and Daniel's conviction to hold to his habit of prayer with unwavering devotion, even if it cost him his life. Their character assessment of both men was correct. A bit of flattery promptly elevated the king's pride and upright Daniel would not compromise.

After witnessing Daniel's repeated resolve to pray (apparently watching him pray more than once; v. 13), the jealous constituents immediately sought an audience with the king: First, they confirmed the edict that he had signed into law. Second, they affirmed that it could not be changed. Third, they accused Daniel of showing contempt for the king by willfully breaking it, for he had been observed praying to his God. What a testimony: Daniel never went to the king to argue his case, rather his enemies watched him consult his God!

November 10 – No Compromise, No Matter What
Daniel 6

Darius was displeased with himself after hearing the indictment against Daniel; he knew that he had been tricked by a ploy that appealed to his ego. The king sought to release Daniel, but apparently there were no loopholes in the statute and Daniel's accusers were insistent that Darius uphold the law. Having exhausted his options, the king regretfully commanded that Daniel be cast in the den of lions as his edict demanded. Nevertheless, this pagan king encouraged Daniel that "his" God whom he served continually would deliver him. William MacDonald comments on the effect that the life and convictions of a dedicated believer like Daniel have on an unregenerate soul:

> It is beautiful to see how even unbelievers will sometimes pick up on the faith and morals of consistent believers whom they observe at close hand. Only too often Christians fail their unsaved friends and relatives by not having as high standards of faith and practice as the world expects from God's people.[21]

Daniel was not such a person; he was willing to suffer loss, even to die, rather than to compromise his God-honoring convictions, and that testimony spoke volumes to the king. Religious hypocrites uttering "sweet Jesus" endearments do more harm to the cause of Christ than anything else; the lost need to witness men and women with unwavering devotion to the Lord Jesus as shown by obedience to His expressed will without reservation. The Lord Jesus said, *"But why do you call Me 'Lord, Lord,' and not do the things which I say?"* (Luke 6:46).

Dear reader, do not call Jesus Christ "Lord" if you are not going to do what He says. Obedience to the Lord Jesus proves our love for Him (John 14:15, 21). A lack of love for the Lord will be shown through an unyielding spirit and through disobedience. There is such an intimate tie between genuine love for the Lord and obedience to the Lord that Paul bluntly states, *"If any man love not the Lord Jesus Christ, let him be anathema* [eternally condemned]" (1 Cor. 16:22). Daniel loved the Lord and was willing to demonstrate his love through conviction and consecration to God. His God was the one true God, and he had now been given an opportunity to publicly testify to that fact!

November 11 – Lions Judge Properly
Daniel 6

The entire language of the narrative paints a picture of the den of lions as being a cave-like enclosure with a single entrance, a hole in the ground, over the top of the cave or crevice. It was deep enough that no lions could jump or climb out, and the entrance was small enough that a rock could be pulled over the opening to secure it. It had to grieve the king to see a righteous man in his eighties being thrown down into a cold, dark enclosure with hungry lions – the fall alone could have easily killed Daniel. The king and his lords sealed the stone that secured the mouth of the den with their own signets ensuring that no person, including the king, could tamper with the stone until morning.

Being troubled by the affair, the king suffered a sleepless night. He was back at the den at first light. After the stone was removed, Darius cried out with a lamenting voice, *"Daniel, servant of the living God, has your God, whom you serve continually, been able to deliver you from the lions?"* (v. 20). The eerie silence was broken by Daniel's replied, *"O king, live forever! My God sent His angel and shut the lions' mouths, so that they have not hurt me, because I was found innocent before Him; and also, O king, I have done no wrong before you"* (vv. 21-22). The miracle proved his innocence; God had protected him from jealous men who contrived evil.

The king was ecstatic and commanded that Daniel be lifted up out of the den. He was examined and found to have no injuries; neither the lions, nor the fall, nor even the cold had harmed Daniel in any way. The very snare that Daniel's conspirators had set to extinguish his life ultimately proved his innocence; this meant that his accusers were the ones guilty of corruption. Darius commanded that they and their families be thrown into the den of lions. The wild beasts made mastery of them even before they reached the bottom of the den. Daniel's God did not protect them, which meant they were guilty. The story closes with Darius making a decree throughout the empire that exalted the God of the Jews as the living, eternal, and powerful God, who should be feared by all. Daniel also enjoyed stately honor and prosperity afterwards. *"Those who honor Me I will honor"* (1 Sam. 2:30) and through faithfulness and diligent prayer, Daniel experienced the full victory of God's promise!

November 12 – So He Went
Hosea 1

The prophet Hosea's marital crisis and restoration, recorded in the first three chapters, forms the thematic framework for the entire book. The unfaithfulness of Gomer, Hosea's wife, projects into the text the Lord's own heartache over Israel's idolatry. Such blatant infidelity resulted in harsh consequences for Israel and also, as we will see, for Gomer. But eventually redeeming love triumphs to restore Gomer to Hosea, just as it will in a future time to reestablish the Jewish nation with the Lord. Throughout the book, this theme is reinforced with two intertwining ideas: judgment for rebellion is inescapable and abounding mercy is available for deliverance.

Gomer's situation seems to picture the fidelity of Israel who began in holiness to the Lord, but then became adulterous (Ezek. 16). Accordingly, the Lord's statements to Hosea about Gomer were either predictive concerning her character or that He was referring to the land of harlotry from which Gomer had come.

Since the Lord ties the wife of harlotry with her offspring, He is anticipating what she will prove to be in time – a disloyal wife; He is not speaking of her sexual impurity at the time of marriage. This conclusion is confirmed when Hosea takes abandoned Gomer back to himself after previously rejecting her for her adulterous behavior (3:1-3). It seems doubtful therefore that he would have married her initially if she were actively fornicating with other married men, an offense punished by death under the Law.

Gomer may have been a lascivious woman before marriage, or she may have only participated in pagan sexual rites before marriage, or she may have been a virgin who, being adversely influenced by a pagan society, became adulterous after marriage. Regardless, Hosea did not question God's will, nor did he delay in doing what the Lord commanded; *"so he went"* (v. 3) reflects the faithful attitude servants of God should have in fulfilling their callings. This is a good example for us to follow – obey the Lord even when it seems unreasonable to do so. Hosea married Gomer even though he foreknew that she would be unfaithful to him and would bear children of infidelity. Their first child was apparently Hosea's son; yet, there is no masculine pronoun in the text to confirm that he fathered Gomer's next two children.

November 13 – Seeking to Repair My Marriage
Hosea 2

Ezekiel explicitly describes Israel's treachery against Jehovah, her Husband, as allegorically displayed in this narrative by Gomer's marital betrayal (Ezek. 16). Despite all of God's sacrificial love, Israel developed an ever-deepening lust for secular thrills and sensual pleasures and the gods associated with such things. In time, she forsook the Lord and embraced these false gods, even giving to them in worship the abundance that God in His love had provided her (Ezek. 16:15-19).

This wicked behavior caused God to summon Israel to appear before witnesses to publicly accuse her: *"Bring charges against your mother, bring charges; for she is not My wife, nor am I her Husband"* (v. 2)! Israel, as the children's mother, was no longer united to Jehovah by faith and love, nor did He any longer identify with her in a marital relationship. Hence, her orphaned children who had lost the protection of their Father were to earnestly plead with their mother in respect to her sinful disposition.

This public decree is followed by a passionate call to repentance: *"Let her put away her harlotries from her sight, and her adulteries from between her breasts"* (v. 2). *"Between her breasts"* is not a sexual statement, but rather an expression associated with profound marital communion, which Gomer had perverted through disorderly passion. Unfortunately, Israel's yearning for false gods and the wickedness they promoted demonstrated that she no longer valued her purity – a requirement for unhindered companionship with Jehovah.

Israel is charged with pervasive idolatrous infidelity by Jeremiah: *"Lift up your eyes to the desolate heights and see: Where have you not lain with men?"* (Jer. 3:2). What faithful husband would not weep when speaking of such lascivious conduct by the one he loves? The prophets labor to convey to us both God's profound pain over His people's abandonment and His yearning heart to have them back.

The Lord's plea for Israel to repent of her harlotries affirms that He has not divorced Israel yet, but is trying to repair the relationship. This is a good reminder that adultery does not demand divorce, which God hates, but divorce is permissible for ongoing marital infidelity (Mal. 2:16; Matt. 19:8-9). God is honored when the marital relationship can be repaired and His design for marriage is yielded to (1 Cor. 7:10-11).

May We Serve Christ!

November 14 – Breaking God's Heart
Hosea 2

Jehovah's fervent appeal for Israel to repent and return to Him is immediately followed with the threat of punitive measures: *"Lest I strip her naked and expose her, as in the day she was born, and make her like a wilderness, and set her like a dry land, and slay her with thirst"* (v. 3). Because an adulteress secretly exposed her nakedness to her lovers, she was publicly stripped naked for all to see; this was a punishment suitable for such criminal disloyalty (Ezek. 16:38-40). This meant that God would utterly humiliate Israel among the nations, if she continued embracing false gods. He promised to smite Israel with drought – there would be no agricultural reproduction in the land, again a fitting punishment for illicit sexual behavior – no procreation.

To heighten Israel's awareness of God's own heartache over her betrayal, the prophet Hosea is permitted to suffer an additional hurt by his lascivious wife Gomer: *For their mother has played the harlot; she who conceived them has behaved shamefully. For she said, "I will go after my lovers, who give me my bread and my water, my wool and my linen, my oil and my drink"* (v. 5). Hosea watched Gomer bless her lovers for the very provisions (bread, wool, linen, oil, etc.) that he had sent to her to sustain her. To be abandoned was hurtful to God, but then for Israel to praise false gods for what He had provided them in mercy was an even worse insult. God's goodness had been used to fuel their rebellion; therefore He was withdrawing His blessing from them.

Similarly, Paul warns believers in Galatia who were leaving their simplicity and joy in Christ for the cold, humanized legalism: *"But now after you have known God, or rather are known by God, how is it that you turn again to the weak and beggarly elements, to which you desire again to be in bondage?"* (Gal. 4:9). *"What then was the blessing you enjoyed?"* (Gal. 4:15). Were they happier now that they were pursuing the mutable tenets of human tradition than they had been in intimately knowing and following Christ?

If in our Christian experience we are less content, less fruitful, or less joyful, it is not God's fault. We have moved away from Him, that is, from His Word, and His mind. God is most honored when we are satisfied with Him alone. *"Come, and let us return to the Lord"* (6:1) is a good charge for all generations!

November 15 – The Unworthy Is Redeemed
Hosea 3

This chapter opens with one of the most astounding commands in all of Scripture – God instructing a righteous man to again love his wife who had deserted him to be in the arms of other men: *"Then the Lord said to me, "Go again, love a woman who is loved by a lover and is committing adultery, just like the love of the Lord for the children of Israel, who look to other gods and love the raisin cakes of the pagans"* (v. 1). Israel was baking raisin cakes to honor false gods (e.g., honoring the goddess Ishtar, the so-called "Queen of Heaven", Jer. 7:18).

Hosea was allowed to experience the infidelity of his wife Gomer to illustrate not only the Lord's heartbreak over Israel's idolatry, but also His resolve to be reconciled to her. Even after Hosea had observed Gomer thanking her lovers for the provisions he had secretly provided for her, God commanded Hosea to redeem his now abandoned wife and take her back. The Lord does not call her, "Hosea's wife," but rather He refers to her as "a woman" – an adulteress – and thereby she had no claim on Hosea in respect to covenantal privileges. The command to "go again, love" signified that there had been no excuse for Gomer's infidelity; she had been previously and appropriately loved by Hosea.

In contrast to God's sacrificial love, Gomer's lovers exploited her, consumed her resources, and then forsook her. Though destitute, she would also experience the further humiliation of being stripped bare and sold as property to the highest bidder at a slave auction. Hosea was there and purchased his own adulterous wife for fifteen pieces of silver and a homer and a half of barley.

Both silver and barley are used to symbolize redemption throughout Scripture (Ex. 30:12-16; Lev. 23:9-14, 25:9). The Lord Jesus was betrayed for thirty pieces of silver, which was later referred to by the Pharisees as "blood money" and indeed it was (Matt. 26:15, 27:3-9). Additionally, the Lord most likely broke unleavened barley bread at the Passover Feast the night before His crucifixion (Luke 22:14-20). Both these symbols of redemption in Scripture are associated with the Lord's redemptive work at Calvary. The payment, the pain, and the shame Hosea suffered to redeem Gomer is incomparable to what the Lord Jesus suffered on our behalf at Calvary. May we never forget the redeeming love of God.

November 16 – All Adulterers!
Hosea 7

Despite His patient mercy, and endearing appeals from His prophets, God's people only waded deeper into sin, despite His expressions of love and goodness to them. The Jews were unconcerned that the omniscient God observed all their evil doings, or that the holy God would be offended by their sin, or that the just God might even invoke retribution. The Jews were so engulfed in shameless sinning that their consciences had become numb to guilt and to the fear of chastening. To willfully break a covenant with the one true God despite His faithfulness is alarming, but to not even care how He feels about it or how He might respond reveals the innermost depravity of man.

The indictment *"they are all adulterers"* in verse 4 is not explained. The charge was not explained. Was physical adultery rampant among the Jews, or was Hosea speaking of their spiritual desertion of Jehovah for idols? Both sins of infidelity were clearly prevalent in Israel. The nation had an unquenchable passion that was always ready to spread sinfulness throughout the society. Both spiritual and physical adultery commence when one's lusts for what is outside of God's will and unchecked passion leads to unrestrained behavior. God's passion for holy living is the same in all dispensations.

In the New Testament, believers are commanded to abstain from fornication, which is any sexual relationship outside the bounds of marriage: *"For this is the will of God, even your sanctification, that ye should abstain from fornication"* (1 Thess. 4:3, KJV). If married, a man is to have only his wife and the wife only her husband; there is to be no sexual lusting after, or "touching," of another person for sensual reasons (1 Cor. 7:1). God's judgment falls not only on fornicators, but also upon those who *"approve of those who practice"* fornication (Rom. 1:32). Believers are not to even look on those committing fornication with any sense of approval.

It is this *looking* upon sexual perversions to achieve pleasure that has become a scourge to our society and has led to many broken marriages and splintered families. Besides hurting others and offending the Lord, fornication is a grievous sin which afflicts one's own body (1 Cor. 6:18). May we remember that God is always deeply offended by both spiritual and physical adultery.

November 17 – Do Not Be Fruitless
Hosea 10

The Jewish nation bore some refreshing fruit for the Lord during those early years together in the wilderness, but that was not the situation now (9:10). Hosea rightly assesses: *"Israel empties his vine; he brings forth fruit for himself"* (v. 1). Centuries earlier, Asaph spoke of Israel as a vine brought out of Egypt that had once flourished because of God's care, but because of the nation's unfaithfulness had been repeatedly trampled on by invaders (Ps. 80). Hosea uses the same imagery and message for Israel now: the nation was a worthless vine/vineyard because of its fruitless disposition towards God.

Israel had lush foliage, but its fruit was worthless because it was self-produced for itself, and was not from God or for God. At a superficial glance, the vine appeared prosperous and healthy, which characterized Israel's economy during the reign of Jeroboam II. The more God blessed Israel materially, the more she became self-absorbed, yielding corruption. God's vine had produced nothing valuable to Him – it was empty from His perspective and should be uprooted.

James reminds us that *"a double-minded man* [is] *unstable in all his ways"* (Jas. 1:8): Jehovah would no longer tolerate the divided heart of His people. Their religious formalities towards Him (pictured in the altars) were as nauseating to Him as their sacred pagan pillars – He promised to tear down both. It is impossible to live a holy life for God's glory unless single-hearted devotion guides the way. From Israel's inception, the Lord desired communion with a holy nation, not a double-minded, mostly-pagan people: *"Be ye holy; for I am holy"* (Lev. 11:44). Israel had forgotten from where they came, hopeless slavery, and why God had delivered them from Egypt, to rescue them from Egypt's corruption to be His special redeemed possession.

Believers today can also forget from where they came, both dead in trespasses and sin and enslaved to sin. Likewise, the Lord Jesus wants a spotless bride for Himself (Eph. 5:27), one that does *"abstain from the appearance of evil"* (1 Thess. 5:22). This means fully consecrating one's spirit, soul and body for God's purposes by abhorring evil in thought and deed. The life of Christ within believers must be lived as He would live; hence, we cannot pursue our own ambitions or lusts.

May We Serve Christ!

November 18 – Break Up Your Fallow Ground
Hosea 10

Israel should have yielded to God's plan, which is likened to a trained heifer dragging a threshing board across grain. This was a relatively easy task, plus the heifer received the benefit of feeding on some of the grain that had been separated from the chaff. However, stubborn Israel sought the much harder work of plowing. She preferred the heavy yoke of sin and suffering, a hard life, rather than yielding to the Master's design for her and enjoying a less stressful life with His approval and blessing. God would honor her choice; indeed she would plow hard and to utter exhaustion. Verses 12-13 are a refreshing oasis of mercy in a wilderness of condemnation and despair. Despite Israel's clear guilt and God's anger towards His people, He was still willing to offer them restoration and blessing through genuine repentance:

> *Sow for yourselves righteousness; reap in mercy; break up your fallow ground, for it is time to seek the Lord, till He comes and rains righteousness on you. You have plowed wickedness; you have reaped iniquity. You have eaten the fruit of lies, because you trusted in your own way, in the multitude of your mighty men* (vv. 12-13).

Their pursuit of righteousness would result in experiencing God's overflowing mercy, but this could not occur until the sin encrusting their hearts was broken away. To stress this point, Hosea employs an agricultural analogy of a farmer plowing hardened fallow ground. The phrase "fallow ground" is found only twice in the Bible, here, and in Jeremiah 4:3. Fallow ground is soil that was once cultivated, but now lies waste and is completely fruitless. In order for it to be made profitable again, it must be broken up with a plow; only then can it be planted again and made fruitful.

The purpose of the soil analogy was to call Israel to repentance. It would be better for them to plow up their own fallow ground (hearts) in response to God's Word, than for God to enforce His word through the Assyrians without their cooperation.

Choosing to cultivate righteousness ensures the child of God will reap the unfailing love and favor of God. For revival to occur in the Church, we must be open to God's Word and shun worldliness. God's Word must penetrate our minds and take root before we can bear fruit.

November 19 – The Day of the Lord Is at Hand
Joel 1

Joel's messages coincided with a devastating locust plague that impoverished much of Judah (1:1-2:1). The prophet uses the plague to indict and warn the Jews of their apostasy and call them to repentance. The plague is then used as a backdrop to explain God's future prerogatives to be accomplished in the Day of the Lord: purifying and restoring the Jewish nation to Himself, judging of the wicked (including Israel's enemies), and establishing Messiah's kingdom.

Joel understood that the terrible locust plague was a precursor and sign of an even more horrific event that would devastate the entire world: *"Alas for the day!* **For the day of the Lord is at hand***; it shall come as destruction from the Almighty"* (v. 15). In the same way that the Church is to anticipate the Day of Christ (which speaks of the rapture of the Church and Judgment Seat of Christ), Israel was to live in respect to the Day of the Lord. To summarize, the Day of the Lord is an Old Testament term that speaks of those times when Jehovah intervened in a visible and powerful way to judge the wicked on earth. This meaning continues into the New Testament and is further clarified to speak of the Tribulation Period and Christ's Millennial Kingdom.

Peter tells us that *the Day of the Lord* and the Millennial Kingdom conclude with destruction of the earth (2 Pet. 3:10), and will be followed by *the Day of God*, often referred to as *the eternal state* (2 Pet. 3:12). Isaiah states that *"all the host of heaven shall be dissolved, and the heavens shall be rolled up like a scroll"* (Isa. 34:4). He later foretells that after the Millennial Kingdom, God will create a new heaven and new earth (Isa. 65:17) – a matter which John says occurs right after the 1000-year reign of Christ and the Great White Throne judgment of the wicked (Rev. 20:7-21:1).

During the Kingdom Age, Jerusalem will be the religious center of the world (Isa. 2:1-5). Christ will reign from there and all the nations will come there to praise, worship, and learn of Him. There will be no war or violence, only peace. All the earth will see the glory of the Lord Jesus (Isa. 60:18-20) and any nation opposing the Lord will be laid waste (Isa. 60:12). The Day of the Lord speaks of the era in which God will bring all this about. Ultimately, it will be Christ alone who will be exalted on earth.

May We Serve Christ!

November 20 – Restoring the Years of the Locust
Joel 2

Joel's call to repentance in verses 15-17 marks a dramatic shift in the book. Previously, he mentioned all that the locust had and would eat; now he promises divine restoration of all the locust did eat. Israel was to heed God's call of repentance after experiencing loss, so that they could experience His blessing again. The result would be that weeping will be replaced with gladness, shame with honor, drought with the abundance of water, invaders with no invaders, etc. Hosea promised that if his countrymen approached God in humble repentance, *"then the Lord will be zealous for His land, and pity His people"* (v. 18).

Furthermore, God would bless them by refreshing the land to satisfy all their needs; then they would no longer be a reproach among the nations. Beginning with verse 20, we gain a deeper sense that the events Joel is foretelling reach far beyond the locust plague in Joel's day to the time of Israel's final repentance and restoration in the Tribulation Period. Then, a refined Jewish remnant will turn to and receive the Lord Jesus Christ; these Jews will be kept safe and secure during the time of Jacob's Trouble (Rev. 12:13-17).

At that time, the Lord will intervene to wonderfully protect Israel against the invading northern army. *"Then you shall know that I am in the midst of Israel: I am the Lord your God and there is no other. My people shall never be put to shame"* (v. 27). After the Lord defeats the Antichrist at the Battle of Armageddon, the Jews will never need to fear foreign raiders again. The Lord will greatly bless His land (and their habitation) with rain and agricultural fruitfulness. In this fashion, the Lord will restore all that was lost through years of chastening, poetically expressed as *the years of the locust* (v. 25). God could not replace the years themselves, as if they never existed, but He will replace the lost productivity of the land. Israel will then be completely satisfied in the Lord and rejoice in the land's abundance. The Jews will gladly praise Jehovah, who will not permit them to suffer shame again.

Dear believer, if you, like Israel, have suffered some painful failure, please know that our merciful God wants you to know the wonder of His love. He wants you to learn from the experience and get up in grace and go on with Him – only He can restore what the locusts have eaten.

November 21 – I Will Pour Out My Spirit! – Part 1
Joel 2

God instituted a New Covenant with the Jews that would give them eternal salvation, a new and clean heart, and allow the Holy Spirit to indwell them forever (Isa. 45:17-19; Jer. 31:31-40; Ezek. 34:23-28). With His own blood, Christ sealed the New Covenant with the house of Judah and the house of Israel (Heb. 8:8). In anticipation of Calvary, God could promise Israel, *"A new heart also will I give you, and a new Spirit will I put within you"* (Ezek. 36:26). Joel also foretells that Israel will receive the Holy Spirit, and a new heart. He would enable the Jewish nation to both know and reveal the Lord to all nations:

And it shall come to pass afterward that I will pour out My Spirit on all flesh; your sons and your daughters shall prophesy, your old men shall dream dreams, your young men shall see visions. And also on My menservants and on My maidservants I will pour out My Spirit in those days (Joel 2:28-29).

Peter quoted this promise at Pentecost to show that Joel's prophecy had been partially fulfilled (Acts 2:17-21). Prophesying, dreaming dreams, seeing visions, speaking in tongues, etc., will be evidences that the Holy Spirit has been received by Israel. The Holy Spirit will enable direct communication with God and the ability to express His will to others. This was the day the Church Age began. The Holy Spirit came to the waiting believers as promised by the Lord Jesus, baptized them into the body of Christ, bestowed spiritual gifts on them, and enabled them to supernaturally serve the Lord and speak for the Lord.

Although a few Jews had turned from Judaism to Christ, Israel as a nation, rejected Him and will continue to do so until His second advent at the end of the Tribulation Period (2:18-3:21; Zech. 12:10). This explains why Peter exchanged "afterward" to "in the last days," when quoting Joel to his countrymen to denote a future time when Messiah would return to earth to reestablish Israel. Peter was affirming that Pentecost was only a foretaste of better things to come for the Jewish nation in the Kingdom age, when God pours out His Spirit on all flesh. Joel tells us that this event will be accompanied by supernatural signs in the heavens; that did not happen at Pentecost.

May We Serve Christ!

November 22 – I Will Pour Out My Spirit! – Part 2
Joel 2

Presently, the nation of Israel is still waiting for the fullness of God's chastening to be complete and for the coming of the Holy Spirit. However, believers in the Church Age have been baptized into the Body of Christ and are securely sealed by the Holy Spirit (Eph. 1:13). Unlike Israel, this means the Church is exempt from divine wrath. Those who responded to the gospel message during the Church Age will be removed from the earth before God begins to work with His covenant people again during the Tribulation Period. Thus, Christians are commanded to wait for Christ's imminent appearing in the clouds to translate them from the earth (1 Thess. 4:13-18), to receive glorified bodies (1 Cor. 15:51-51), to be escorted to heaven and to be examined by Christ at His Judgment Seat (Rom. 14:10-12). There they will be appropriately rewarded by Him (1 Cor. 3:11-15; 2 Cor. 5:10).

The Church will not suffer God's wrath during the Tribulation Period. Rather, Christ promised: *"I also will keep you from the hour of trial which shall come upon the whole world, to test those who dwell on the earth"* (Rev. 3:10). For this reason the Church is to expect the imminent return of Christ who will deliver from the wrath to come all those who have been born again:

> *Much more then, having now been justified by His blood, we shall be saved from wrath through Him* (Rom. 5:9).

> *And to wait for His Son from heaven, whom He raised from the dead, even Jesus who delivers us from the wrath to come* (1 Thess. 1:10).

> *For God did not appoint us to wrath, but to obtain salvation through our Lord Jesus Christ* (1 Thess. 5:9).

The Church will be in heaven before Christ opens the first seal on the scroll which begins the Tribulation Period (Rev. 6:1). Surviving Tribulation saints and those Jews of spiritual Israel will be spared death when God judges the nations at the end of the Tribulation Period. May we never forget that God's wrath is against wickedness, not against His redeemed (Zech. 12:8-9). The Church is to be watching and waiting for the sudden appearing of the Savior, not the revealing of the Antichrist!

November 23 – God Hates Religious Hypocrisy
Amos 5

The message Amos delivers to Israel in verses 21-27 is similar to what Isaiah will declare a few years later to Judah: the Lord was fed up with Israel's vain religiosity. He hated and despised their feasts and He would not accept their burnt, meal, or peace offerings. Through His prophets, God voices His utter disgust for Israel's religious hypocrisy. Through Isaiah, He said, *"Wickedness and the solemn meeting I cannot bear ... My soul hates"* (Isa. 1:13-14; JND). God hated Israel's devotionless sacrifices, offerings, feasts, prayers, and observances. The Jews were morally corrupt and spiritually bankrupt people that were using religion as a cloak to cover their sin. God had had enough – He wholly detested being associated with these phony doings of His people! Having censured Israel's religious fanfare, Amos appeals directly to individuals to repent and to seek the Lord.

The Lord was not interested in hearing any individual sing or play musical instruments before Him, unless they first were committed to following justice and righteousness inwardly. The Lord wanted to see compassion and devotion spring up out of a pure heart and then flow out as a mighty, ongoing stream of goodness to others. Israel's superficial piety and religious nonsense did not refresh Him or others.

Regrettably, much of the vain religiosity of Judaism is alive and well in Christendom today. Many professing Christians have become dull to the Word of God, deaf to the conviction of the Holy Spirit, and seared in their conscience such that they can mindlessly practice their religion while continuing in what God hates. The Church would do well to heed Amos' warning to Israel.

It is human nature to traditionalize that which has no importance to God to displace what does. If Amos or Isaiah were before us today, they would affirm that the Lord hates secularized Christianity with the same fervor that He hated vain Judaism. That which displaces true devotion to, and appreciation for, Christ with meaningless religious routines is loathsome to God. Beloved, He deserves much more than empty rote, fanciful productions, vain prayers, and weekly pew-warming exercises by holy misfits. The Lord wants the real thing from those who have received and experienced real life – His life.

November 24 – Fleeing God
Jonah 1

Jonah was already serving as God's prophet (2 Kgs. 14:23-25). One day the Lord told him to go to Nineveh, the capital city of Assyria. The Lord was mindful of Nineveh's wickedness and He was poised to judge that city, but not without first warning them and providing the city an opportunity to be delivered. Jonah was not at all sympathetic to God's compassion for Israel's enemy; he therefore went the opposite way to the seaport of Joppa and boarded a ship *"to Tarshish from the presence of the Lord"* (v. 3).

Jonah did not simply ignore God's command; he was resolved to get as far away from Nineveh as possible. A ship full of pagans was a strange place for a Jewish prophet. His dress and features must have aroused some suspicion. The fugitive quickly boarded the ship and withdrew from sight into the lowest level of the ship.

Jonah did not want the Ninevites to have an opportunity to receive God's forgiveness; he wanted God to wipe them out for their brutality to Israel. We are not told why Jonah acted against God, but racial hatred and the desire for revenge seem likely motives. All this to say that God's dealings in the book of Jonah are as much about God working to refine His prophet as averting judgment of sinners in Nineveh. The Lord's response to Jonah's rebellion was decisive: *"The Lord sent out a great wind on the sea, and there was a mighty tempest on the sea, so that the ship was about to be broken up"* (v. 4). The experienced mariners knew by its sudden development and swelling intensity that this was no natural storm. This realization caused each one to consult his god for answers and to throw the cargo overboard. Jonah, however, was in the lowest part of the ship fast asleep.

Jonah sought to escape the heavy burden of his guilty conscience through slumber. His sleep pictures his dull spiritual perception and ineptness, having willingly erred from the path of righteousness. Instead of being wearied in service for God, Jonah was exhausted by his own disobedience and slept on in self-complacency. He did not discern the peril that he was in and was insensible to the distress he was bringing on others who had no part in his evil. If God's prophet can behave as such, then so can we, dear believer. To be under the hand of God and be oblivious to it is the most dreaded place a believer can be.

November 25 – I Would Rather Die Than Obey
Jonah 1

In fear for the lives of his crew and himself, the captain woke Jonah from his sleep and begged him to consult his God also. No doubt the captain wondered how a non-seafaring man in his right mind could be peacefully asleep in a ship being pounded by a fearsome tempest. Jonah's slumber portrays his spiritually complacent, unperceptive, and powerless state. James tells us that there is only one remedy for believers locked into that sorrowful state of mind: *"Draw near to God and He will draw near to you. Cleanse your hands, you sinners; and purify your hearts, you double-minded"* (Jas. 4:8). So it should be no surprise, then, that the pagan captain of the ship had more sense than Jonah about their perilous situation. Indeed, there is an insanity to sin!

While others recognized their peril and were praying, Jonah was oblivious to the danger he was in. Then, after being awakened and learning of their situation, the prophet still had no mind to pray. In stubborn superiority he had set his course away from God, meaning that prayer was out of the question. This was no ordinary gale, so the sailors cast lots to identify the deity-offending culprit.

God permitted an accurate casting of lots and Jonah was rightly identified. The fearful mariners asked Jonah questions to ascertain the reason for the storm. Jonah honestly answered them, *"I am a Hebrew; and I fear the Lord, the God of heaven, who made the sea and the dry land"* (v. 9). Indeed, Jonah was a Hebrew and his God was the Creator of all things, but Jonah did not fear Him enough to obey His command. Reverential fear, devotional awe, and unwavering lordship all walk together.

While the pagan sailors would not understand what it meant to love and obey the true God, they did know that Jonah was wrong to flee from his God. The sailors then wanted to know how to remedy their grave situation. Jonah's answer was selfless, but not God-honoring, *"Pick me up and throw me into the sea; then the sea will become calm for you"* (v. 12). Jonah knew the storm was his fault and he was willing to suffer death to preserve those he put at risk. Jonah believed that death was preferable to preaching to Israel's bitter enemy and seeing God show mercy to them. But the Lord had a better plan; He did not want a dead prophet, but a yielded one to represent Him to Gentiles.

May We Serve Christ!

November 26 – God Saves a Boatload of Pagans
Jonah 1

The men, not willing to throw Jonah overboard, rowed hard towards the land, but the wind and likely the tide were against them, plus the tempest continued to gain strength. Finally, these desperate and exhausted seamen concluded that everyone would be lost if they did not do what Jonah had said. The sailors were gaining appreciation for Jonah's God, so they beseeched Him and God honored their prayer:

> *O Lord, please do not let us perish for this man's life, and do not charge us with innocent blood; for You, O Lord, have done as it pleased You." So they picked up Jonah and threw him into the sea, and the sea ceased from its raging. Then the men feared the Lord exceedingly, and offered a sacrifice to the Lord and took vows* (vv. 14-16).

Jonah's statement was correct, that the storm had resulted from his disobedience. The moment he was cast into the sea, it dissipated instantly. This unnatural event proved to the mariners that Jonah's testimony was correct – his God was *"the God of heaven, who made the sea and the dry land."* Not only is our amazing God able to correct His wayward prophet through a supernatural gale, but He does so in such a way to turn the heart of pagans towards Him in worship also. The sailors had petitioned their own false gods, but none of them could do what Jonah's God did in a moment.

The narrative shows God's compassion for His errant prophet, for the wicked people in Nineveh, and also for a few frightened pagans sailing on the Mediterranean Sea. Truly, as Paul proclaims, He is the God of the Gentiles also (Rom. 3:29). The entire incident shows how God can reach the most remote soul with the truth, and, through the most unusual means, see him or her saved. No one is beyond God's reach, and His mercy is abundant!

The Lord had no intention of permitting His prophet to drown in the sea: *"Now the Lord had prepared a great fish to swallow Jonah. And Jonah was in the belly of the fish three days and three nights"* (v. 17). Jonah had been preserved in the storm, and now he was spared from the sea. God had a purpose for his life – Jonah was going to Nineveh via a great fish! This is a good reminder for us not to give up praying for the wayward and the unregenerate – no one is out of God's reach!

November 27 – Going "Down"
Jonah 2

Notice that as Jonah tried to flee the will of God, he went "down": *"down to Joppa"* (1:3), *"down into the lowest parts of the ship,"* and had *"lain down, and was fast asleep"* (1:5). Later he was cast *down* into the sea by the sailors and the prophet acknowledges, *"I went down to the moorings of the mountain"* (v. 6). For the believer, pursuing things that are outside God's revealed purposes will always result in a downward out-of-control spiral into carnality and destruction. Sin is a product of unbelief; that is, choosing human reasoning over God's revealed Word, and that is exactly what Jonah did. He went his own way (away from the Lord) to resolve his perceived difficulty.

Warren Wiersbe comments on God's manifold wisdom and grace in working with His wayward and spiritually despondent prophet:

> Jonah lost God's voice, for now God had to speak to him in a storm. He lost his spiritual energy and went to sleep in the hold of the ship. He lost his power in prayer, and even his desire to pray. The heathen were praying, but Jonah was sleeping. He lost his testimony with the men on the ship, and he lost his influence for good, because he was the cause of the storm. He also almost lost his life. But how patient and long-suffering the Lord was with him.[22]

Each of us was born after the flesh, but those born of God need not live after the flesh any longer (Rom. 6:2). It is God the Father's earnest desire that His children live up to His Son's moral likeness; He pleads with us, *"Be ye holy; for I am holy"* (1 Pet. 1:16). He is jealous about our allegiances to other things, ideologies, and people (Ex. 34:14). Whatever prevents Him from being first place in our affections provokes Him to take corrective action (Rev. 2:4-5).

The prophet Jonah experienced this truth firsthand after acting in his flesh against the expressed will of God. In a practical sense, a believer who chooses to live after the flesh is daring God, "Do You still love me enough to correct me?" The answer is, "Yes, He does" (Heb. 12:6). May we glean from the lesson that Jonah learned the hard way – to trust in one's flesh always disappoints the Lord and leads us into a chastening storm. Let us move upward in God's purposes and not downward into trouble.

November 28 – Coming "Up"
Jonah 2

In Jonah 1, the Lord gained the *body* of his rebellious prophet – sequestered in a great fish. In this chapter, the Lord will labor to win over Jonah's *mind* as he meditates on the Psalms, on his situation, and on the cost of disobedience. In chapter 3, the Lord will have Jonah's *obedience*, and then the transforming work of the prophet's *heart* will commence in chapter 4. The entire book is a testimony of God's powerful work in transforming a rebel child of God into a fruit-bearing saint that exhibits God's character and is solely motivated for the glory of God. Jonah's story illustrates that God is as concerned about the character and disposition of His servants as He is for the nations.

Jonah began to pray from the stomach of the great fish. He does not ask the Lord to rescue him, but rather offers praise and thanksgiving for saving him from drowning. Jonah knew Scripture, as he quotes or alludes to about a dozen Psalms while praying. His prayer highlights the importance of committing Scripture to memory, for it is not always possible to pull out and read a pocket Bible during a temptation or trial. Jonah had no opportunity to read Scripture in his murky dismal setting, but he still could delight in God's Word and be sustained by it.

Obviously, Jonah recorded his prayer after being expelled from the fish, so his terrifying account is infused with praise and thanksgiving. Recalling the ordeal, Jonah recognized two important truths: First, it was God who cast him into the sea. Second, the sea's powerful billows and waves would have overcome him, if God had not prepared the great fish to swallow him. Thankfully, Jonah did not faint beneath the discipline of the Lord, but looked up to God and counted on His grace, and as a result was blessed. In faith, he knew that he would again be before God in His temple. Jonah understood that at that very moment he still had access to his omniscient, omnipotent God through prayer.

In his meditations, Jonah is being led along by the Lord into utter brokenness. The prophet prays and he vows sacrifices, but it is not until he comes to a complete end of himself and declares *"salvation is of the Lord"* (v. 9) that the Lord intervenes on his behalf. The offense and consequences of human sin cannot be remedied by human effort! God commands the great fish to vomit Jonah on dry land – Jonah comes up!

November 29 – Helping You Along In Your Calling
Jonah 2

Where did the great fish spit up Jonah? If Jonah's great fish was a sperm whale, how far could the whale have traveled in three days? Sperm whales can cruise over great distances at 3 knots, and can increase to 12 knots when chased.[23] This means Jonah could have traveled some 250 miles underwater via a whale! Jonah initially fled southwest to Joppa from Gath-Hepher in Galilee, a journey requiring three or four days on foot. In Joppa the prophet boarded a ship heading west to Tarshish. However, for two reasons it seems that the ship had not ventured but a few miles from shore when the storm struck: First, tired Jonah went directly down into the boat and fell asleep and then the captain woke him up shortly thereafter and the storm was already raging (1:6). Second, the men knew where the shoreline was and attempted to row back to it to escape the tempest (1:13).

If this assumption is correct, then the three-day journey in the fish must have been to carry Jonah northward to assist him in completing his mission at Nineveh. This means that Jonah could have been set ashore on the Phoenician coast near Tyre or as far north as Cyprus. If he was put ashore east of Cyprus, the prophet would have had a 45-mile walk to Hamath, requiring two or three days.

The distance from Jonah's hometown of Gath-Hepher to Hamath was 190 miles, and, given Sabbath rests, would have taken Jonah about two weeks to travel there, had he not rebelled. So the Lord, via whale, could have transported Jonah to Hamath (over one-third of the way to Nineveh) more quickly than if Jonah had walked there from Gath-Hepher.

If this hypothesis is accurate, the text bears out a lovely application to Jonah's deliverance and journey. While it is true that we choose our sin, God chooses the consequences of our sin; God does not want our failures to be final. Practically speaking, falling is not what makes one a failure, but wallowing in self-pity – choosing to stay down does. *"For a righteous man may fall seven times and rise again, but the wicked shall fall by calamity"* (Prov. 24:16). The Lord wants us to learn from our mistakes, to rise up in His grace and step forward with a revived tenacity to serve Him. Jonah indeed left the sea a chastened and humbled man and to encourage him, God helped him on his way.

May We Serve Christ!

November 30 – God Spares a Heathen City
Jonah 3

After being expelled on dry land, the word of the Lord came to Jonah a second time and Jonah obeyed God's command to go to Nineveh. The trek to Nineveh would have required several weeks on foot. As about an inch of Jonah's normal hair color would have been visible on his head and in his beard, he would have been bizarre-looking, no doubt a scary spectacle preaching in the streets of Nineveh.

After arriving in Nineveh, Jonah did not delay in preaching the simple message God had given him – it took three days to cover the city. The Ninevites now knew that God was aware of their wickedness and that He would destroy the city in forty days. Jonah's message spread through the city like wildfire; all social classes, including the king responded to it and put on sackcloth and fasted. The people *"believed God;"* this does not mean that they became worshipers of Jonah's God, but rather by faith they believed the message of Jonah's God.

Jonah's message contained no provision for escaping God's wrath, nor, given the prophet's disposition toward his enemies, did he likely imply one. However, the king believed that if God saw the city's contrition and repentance for their wicked behavior, perhaps He would change His mind. He therefore decreed that no man or beast eat or drink (likely during daytime hours) and that man and beast should be covered with sackcloth. No doubt the prophet looked on with amazement at more than a hundred thousand pagans responding to his simple message. It is a true work of God when *"the greatest to the least"* within an entire city cry out to God for mercy!

The Ninevites had obeyed Jonah's message and turned from their wickedness, which was the reason God told Jonah that He was going to judge them (1:2). Thankfully, God was more compassionate than His prophet towards this heathen city: *"Then God saw their works, that they turned from their evil way; and God relented from the disaster that He had said He would bring upon them, and He did not do it"* (v. 10). *"God saw their works,"* which as James tells us is evidence of true faith: *"Faith by itself, if it does not have works, is dead"* (Jas. 2:17). The Ninevites clearly had not gone as far as the mariners in worshiping Jehovah, but they had acted on what had been revealed to them.

Daily Devotions

December 1 – How Did God Do It?
Jonah 3

Given the time frame of Jonah's ministry, what factors may have contributed to the Ninevites' acceptance of Jonah's message? These were highly superstitious people and a rash of natural phenomena and calamities in the empire no doubt had raised their heathen anxiety:

- A solar eclipse (80% obscuration) in Nineveh on February 10, 765 B.C.
- A severe famine in 765 B.C.
- A total solar eclipse in Nineveh, June 15, 763 B.C.
- A massive regional earthquake in approximately 760 B.C.
- A severe famine in 759 B.C.
- Rebellions in various Assyrian cities in 758 B.C.[24]
- A Jewish man with bleached skin and hair, having been spewed out by a great fish, who came to warn them.

Dagon, the fish-god was widely revered in Mesopotamia and the eastern Mediterranean coast (1 Sam. 5:1-7). Archeologists have found several images of Dagon in Ninevite excavations, meaning that when Jonah arrived in Nineveh out of the sea via a great fish, he immediately had their attention. The point being, that God knows best how to get the attention of the most hardened sinner; His Spirit confronts, convicts, and points to the way of salvation, which is centered in Christ. May we be faithful to share the message of life that has been entrusted to us.

If the Ninevites, rattled by recent calamities and celestial signs, were responding to Jonah as an extension of Dagon, instead of as Jehovah's prophet, that would explain why there was no lasting revival in Nineveh. Simply fearing reprisal for doing what is against one's conscience, without revering the One who judges all wickedness, is not true repentance.

Genuine repentance fully agrees with God on the matter of sin and its just punishment, pleads for His forgiveness, and shows a change of heart by ceasing the evil and doing what God says is good. Trying not to sin is not the same as receiving light and life in Christ and following Him. The Ninevites turned from wickedness in fear, but they did not turn to Jehovah to receive forgiveness and more truth to walk in. Their humble response merely granted Nineveh more time before God's wrath would ultimately fall about 150 years later.

May We Serve Christ!

December 2 – A Sour Prayer
Jonah 4

Jonah became angry after he discerned that God had relented from punishing the Ninevites (probably because the forty days had passed) and he ventured eastward from the city. He built a temporary shelter, likely having a vantage point overlooking the city, and waited to see what the Lord would do. While he certainly did not want the Ninevites to live, he may have also felt that his integrity as a prophet had been tarnished because what he said would happen had not come about.

This is one of the most striking scenes in the book – God's prophet observing over 100,000 people who are more affected by God's Word than the messenger who delivered it. But, although Jonah was in a sour frame of mind, he did not lose sight of his relationship with God. He does pray, but only in grace can his statements be labeled a prayer:

Ah, Lord, was not this what I said when I was still in my country? Therefore I fled previously to Tarshish; for I know that You are a gracious and merciful God, slow to anger and abundant in lovingkindness, one who relents from doing harm. Therefore now, O Lord, please take my life from me, for it is better for me to die than to live (vv. 2-3)!

Jonah's four I's, two me's, and two my's in his prayer indicates that Jonah had withdrawn into himself for answers. He understood God's character (even quoting Ps. 48:14), but did not want to have His mind on the matter. Beloved, it is dangerous to quote Scripture in a way that spites God's goodness and ignores His will. The child of God should always want what God wants and then desire to know why He does what He does. Jonah confirms now, why he previously rebelled against his calling: he knew that Jehovah was a merciful God and he wanted the Ninevites punished, not forgiven. Now the worst possible thing had happened and Jonah keenly felt that this was his fault.

If we are honest, we all would have to admit that we have been frustrated that God did not punish someone who committed an injustice against us. We were more concerned with being vindicated than caring for the person's soul. Like Jonah, we did not want God to show them mercy. Gratefully, God's grace is beyond our mental grasp; He desires that the most people possible be redeemed by the blood of His Son.

Daily Devotions

December 3 – The Question
Jonah 4

Having betrayed his countrymen (from his point of view), Jonah requested that the Lord would take his life. Death would deliver him from bearing the shame of delivering Israel's nemesis. In the belly of the fish, he wanted to live despite what might happen in Nineveh, but somehow watching the Ninevites actually obey his message was a worse situation – now he just wanted to die. Sometimes a well-worded question appealing to the conscience is better than an explanation. The Lord responds to Jonah's prayer with such a question, *"Is it right for you to be angry?"* (v. 4). The implied answer was "no," but the Lord permitted Jonah to think it through. The Lord's entire message to Jonah consisted of three questions: with the first being posed twice.

In many respects, Jonah's attitude pictured the spiritual demeanor of the Jewish nation; they had forgotten that they were to be God's lampstand to the nations. Having experienced God's mercy and goodness, they should have wanted others to benefit from it also. Yet, at this juncture, Jonah is offended by God's mercy, even though he had earlier received God's unmerited forgiveness for blatant rebellion.

In his estimation, the Ninevites were so evil that they did not deserve God's clemency. But what Jonah had forgotten was that no one deserves God's mercy, nor is He obliged to forgive the guilty. The prophet's callous attitude is hence demeaning to God's character. Jonah apparently thought that he possessed a higher knowledge than God did, and had a better sense of justice and fairness than He did.

How long Jonah actually preached in Nineveh is unknown, but after he finished delivering God's message he probably left the city to see what would happen at the set time. Now that the forty days had passed and Nineveh was not destroyed we read, *"So Jonah went out of the city and sat on the east side of the city. There he made himself a shelter and sat under it in the shade, till he might see what would become of the city"* (v. 5). He probably erected a simple lean-to structure that was open on the east and west sides so that he could view the city and enjoy some cross ventilation and shade during the hottest part of the day. Even though he knows that God has granted mercy to Nineveh, he is determined to sulk for a while to see if the Lord will change His mind.

December 4 – The Plant and the Worm
Jonah 4

A sulking Jonah constructed a makeshift shelter east of Nineveh to see what would happen to the city. Besides a well-posed question, a good illustration is also an effective teaching technique to prompt reason. The Lord used an object that Jonah appreciated (because it brought him comfort) to rebuke his pitiless attitude toward lost souls. God caused a large, leafy plant to spring up overnight to shade Jonah's head from the sun the next day. Jonah was thankful for the plant, but then the Lord caused a worm to damage it the next morning and it quickly withered. The Lord then used a cloudless day and a hot east wind to buffet Jonah, so much so that he wished for his death.

The Lord asked Jonah a second time, *"Is it right for you to be angry,"* but then added *"about the plant?"* And Jonah quickly justified himself, *"It is right for me to be angry, even to death"* (v. 9)! The object lesson was to contrast Jonah's concern for his own creature comforts as compared to the spiritual welfare of all the souls of an enormous city. Because Jonah held selfish attitudes towards Nineveh and the plant, he became deeply frustrated that his expectations were not met. God's expectation for Nineveh had been accomplished, but that was of no interest to Jonah. In verses 10-11, the Lord explains with a parting question the illustration which has so angered his prophet: He was as angry (even unto death) over the loss of the plant that he did not labor for and was gone in a day, but yet had no pity on an entire condemned city of pagans. These were people that God had created, sustained for many years, and valued enough to speak to them about their miserable spiritual condition before Him.

How admirable is God's patience with his stiff-necked prophet! Jonah had not planted or cared for the plant, and yet he was angry over the absence of the shade it provided him for a few hours. In contrast, Jonah should consider how God felt over an entire city of lost souls that He had created and sustained for many years to bring Him pleasure, yet they were now so wicked that God contemplated destroying them. The hurt to God's own heart in the matter was not even comparable to Jonah's loss of the plant that he had not even labored for. Likewise, we should not be callous towards the lost. The gospel of Jesus Christ is the means for causing creatures whom God created, to love and adore Him.

December 5 – The Closing Question
Jonah 4

Jehovah has the last word, as indeed He always must have; hence, Jonah ends his book with God's question without recording his response to it. At that time the prophet was in no frame of mind to answer properly, but it is doubtful that he could have so vividly penned this testimony depicting his own wrong attitudes without having grasped the meaning of the Lord's lesson.

Jonah's disposition towards the Ninevites at this time reflected Israel's disaffection for God and for those things that mattered to Him. Instead of being a testimony of God's goodness and holiness to the nations, they were ensnared in vain religiosity. One purpose of Jonah's testimony was to awaken the Jewish people to their missionary calling.

No doubt Jonah was hoping that the final inquiry would assist his countrymen to learn what he had through the same probing question. Should not God have pity for the lost souls who will perish without His grace? And it is with that thought that the book abruptly closes; Jonah must answer God's challenge for himself, just as we also must answer it for ourselves. W. W. Fereday explains how this question applies to believers in the Church Age:

> When the Lord Jesus was on earth, there were two occasions when the compassion of His heart specially went forth. In Matthew 9:36, He felt for the people's spiritual need. The land was full of religious leaders, but the people were unfed. *"When He saw the multitudes, He was moved with compassion, because they fainted, and were scattered abroad, as sheep having no shepherd."* In Matthew 14:15, He was concerned about their temporal need. He *"saw a great multitude, and was moved with compassion toward them."* Thousands of hungry men, women, and children were around Him with nothing obtainable in the wilderness. But His disciples did not share the distress of their Lord. Indeed, they urged Him to send the multitudes away, regardless of consequences. The pressure of the people annoyed them, and interfered with their comfort! A great lesson is here! We live and serve in the midst of a suffering creation, and the suffering increases with the growing violence of men: but are our hearts really moved by the serious universal need? God's heart yearns over the masses, young and old, but do our hearts yearn in sympathy with Him?[25]

May We Serve Christ!

December 6 – Ruined, Beyond All Remedy
Micah 2

Micah utters the first of two "woes" in his book. A "woe," is a lament expressing despair, usually over guilt and imminent judgment. His woe is against those Jews who lay awake at night devising evil schemes and wicked acts to do the next day. Solomon contrasted the ways and demise of the wicked with the deeds and blessed life of the righteous: *The wicked man does deceptive work, but he who sows righteousness will have a sure reward. As righteousness leads to life, so he who pursues evil pursues it to his own death.* (Prov. 11:18-19). Micah's message was not negative; rather, it revealed how to enjoy a meaningful and joyful life. God longs to bless those who pursue Him.

Apart from God, man will always do that which displeases his Creator: *"the soul of the wicked desires evil"* (Prov. 21:10). Thankfully, those who delight in the Lord will also experience His delight: *"But mercy and truth belong to those who devise good"* (Prov. 14:22). Moral behavior where self is preeminent and the welfare of others is ignored will lead to the demise of a society, not to its beneficial development, for *"righteousness exalts a nation, but sin is a reproach to any people"* (Prov. 14:34).

Moral relativity devolves human society into chaos, while the pursuit of divine righteousness leads to prosperity – God's blessing. Ultimately, a society's conduct is a direct reflection of their attitude towards God, and where God is not revered, man will not prosper. Such was the state of Israel in Micah's day. Accordingly, Micah's woe is well placed on the wayward Jewish nation and on us too, if we defy God's rule and good intentions for us.

Besides crooked, self-promoting leaders, Micah also rebukes Judah's false teachers that were leading the people away from the Lord and into deeper sin: *"Do not My words do good to him who walks uprightly?"* (v. 7). These men prophesied to ensure their own welfare and reception; they conveniently told the people what they wanted to hear. Sadly, there are many preachers in Christendom today who engage in the same type of heresy to secure their own prosperity and fame. As a result, Judah had become so defiled by unrighteousness that she was *"ruined, beyond all remedy"* (v. 10). This can happen to any nation, who knows and then distorts or snubs God's Word.

December 7 – Hating Good and Loving Evil
Micah 3

The prophet's second oracle is in contrast with his first in that after listing the sins of Judah's leaders in chapter 3, the remainder of his message foretells Israel's future blessedness. Chapter 4 highlights the blessings of the coming Millennial Kingdom and chapter 5 introduces the magnificent King who will rule Israel at that time.

Addressing both the Northern and the Southern Kingdoms, Micah minces no words in his indictment of corrupt leaders who were perverting justice and ruining the people:

You who hate good and love evil; who strip the skin from My people, and the flesh from their bones; who also eat the flesh of My people, lay their skin from them, break their bones, and chop them in pieces like meat for the pot, like flesh in the caldron (vv. 2-3).

Because Jewish rulers hated good and loved evil, they failed to be good shepherds of God's sheep; rather, they were like hunters who kill and slaughter their prey. When spiritual leaders do not pursue the Lord, they not only betray the Lord, but also those in their care. The worst kind of pride is spiritual pride.

Whenever God's people settle into complacency and ease, there will always be an abundance of vain, self-confident men with high-sounding titles and ecclesiastical decrees. Such was the situation in Israel. But there was a calamity coming in which Israel's leaders would cry out to the Lord, but it would be too late; He would not answer them (v. 4). All Israel's leaders and false prophets who led God's people astray would be harshly punished.

In contrast to the fabricated message of peace by the false prophets, Micah was empowered by God's Spirit to deliver a message of power, truth, and justice to warn the people to repent before it was too late. Because their coffers were full, Israel's leaders spoke pleasantries such as, *"Is not the Lord among us? No harm can come upon us"* (v. 11). These so-called prophets were nothing more than con-artists and fortune-tellers. They spoke for profit, not for God. While it was true that the Lord was among them, He was not Israel's good luck charm protecting them from danger. Rather, He was a holy God burdened by His troublesome people; indeed, a great woe was coming to Israel.

May We Serve Christ!

December 8 – To Walk Humbly With Your God
Micah 6

In Micah's final message, the Lord summons Israel to stand before the mountains, depicting the various peoples of the world, so that God's case against her could be heard by all. The Lord prosecutes His people Himself and opens with a question: *"O My people, what have I done to you? And how have I wearied you? Testify against Me"* (v. 3). The rhetorical question was to affirm God's complete innocence – He had shown Israel tender care and faithfulness throughout their history.

To prove this assertion, the Lord rehearses examples of His authentic guardianship of Israel since the days of her conception. Throughout their long pilgrimage to Canaan, the Lord went before them every step of the way, even opening a way through the flooding Jordan River to conduct them safely to Gilgal. God's faithfulness is then contrasted with Israel's apostasy through a series of hyperbolic questions designed to awaken Israel to the gravity of her infidelity:

> *With what shall I come before the Lord, and bow myself before the High God? Shall I come before Him with burnt offerings, with calves a year old? Will the Lord be pleased with thousands of rams, ten thousand rivers of oil?* (vv. 6-7).

The prophet already knew that no sacrifice or offering would appease the Lord's anger over Israel's apostasy. The prophet then told the Jews ("O man" refers to anyone in Israel) what God did require of them: *"He has shown you, O man, what is good; and what does the Lord require of you but to do justly, to love mercy, and to walk humbly with your God?"* (v. 8). There need be no guesswork about it; God had revealed to them what would please Him. Only through repentance and conversion can an individual please the Lord.

The same reality is true in the Church Age – no one can walk with the Lord without exercising faith in the gospel of Jesus Christ and experiencing regeneration by the Holy Spirit. He then empowers believers to repudiate sin and not be mastered by it: *"Walk in the Spirit, and you shall not fulfill the lust of the flesh"* (Gal. 5:16). All this to say that believers in the Church Age can do what is good and just, can love mercy, and can humbly walk in the Spirit with their God!

December 9 – God Will Avenge His People
Nahum 1

The book commences with these words, *"the burden against Nineveh."* Jonah's preaching a century earlier had no lasting effect on Nineveh; God was now ready to render judgment against the wicked capital city of Assyria. In his message, Nahum prophesied that Nineveh, who had plotted against the Lord (vv. 9-11), would be destroyed (vv. 2-6, 8). Obviously, Nahum's message concerning the doom of Nineveh would delight Jewish readers who had suffered much under Assyrian rule. In this respect, the Lord remained a refuge for all those who would truly trust in Him.

The prophet commences his oracle by affirming that the omnipotent God of Israel was jealous for His people and would avenge those who had oppressed them beyond His intentions: *"God is jealous, and the Lord avenges; the Lord avenges and is furious. The Lord will take vengeance on His adversaries, and He reserves wrath for His enemies; the Lord is slow to anger and great in power, and will not at all acquit the wicked"* (vv. 2-3).

In referring to the majesty and power of God, Nahum conveys a message of confidence and hope to the Jews. God's vengeance flows from His holy and just character, meaning that all sin must be judged and crimes against those He loves must be avenged. Yet, such actions are fully orchestrated to accomplish His sovereign purposes and demonstrate the fullness of His holy character.

To ensure His audience understood why God must act against wicked Nineveh, Nahum first speaks of God's holy and just character, before stating what God would do. The prophet also reminds his audience that because God controls all things (e.g., the seas, the rivers, the hills, the mountains, and the earth's vegetation; vv. 4-5), there was nothing too hard for Him to accomplish. Since the earth convulses at His awesome presence, how could Assyria withstand His wrath?

Verse 6 then poses two rhetorical questions to emphasize this point: *"Who can stand before His indignation? And who can endure the fierceness of His anger?"* Obviously, no one nor anything can overpower God. All creation is subject to Him, including wicked Assyria who would soon experience His long-stored-up wrath.

May We Serve Christ!

December 10 – God Has His Way In The Storm
Nahum 1

In predicting God's vengeance on Assyria, the prophet says, *"The Lord has His way in the whirlwind and in the storm"* (v. 3). He was sending a Babylonian tempest to decimate Assyria. This was a storm of judicial wrath, but we should remember that not all of life's storms are expressions of divine wrath, but all are for God's glory. He sends challenging, refining, and chastening situations into our lives to accomplish His purposes not possible through direct blessings. While enduring a distressing situation David wrote, *"I would hasten my escape from the windy storm and tempest"* (Ps. 55:8). If given a choice between enduring hardship with the Lord or having a life of ease, the flesh will pick the latter. It is so easy to run from our difficulties, unless we understand that God has His way in the storms of life and that if we flee prematurely, we are actually withdrawing from God's presence.

Accordingly, every devoted Christian is destined for trouble, but not for despair. *"Yes, and all that will live godly in Christ Jesus shall suffer persecution"* (2 Tim. 3:12). The Lord Jesus explained to His disciples, *"In the world you shall have tribulation: but be of good cheer; I have overcome the world"* (John 16:33). Prepare your mind for the struggles ahead (1 Pet. 1:13), and don't get bogged down in self-pity, grappling with despair when those forecasted and necessary storms of life arrive.

The Lord Jesus suffered a divine tempest of indignation while being the Sin-bearer for humanity. He suffered His Father's full anger because of our sin, which necessitated His death. All God's anger to be released on Assyria was only a minute portion of the divine wrath poured out on Christ while He was nailed to a cross!

The Ninevites thought they were safe in their fortified capital city, but Nahum states that true security and protection are only found in the Lord: *The Lord is good, a stronghold in the day of trouble; and He knows those who trust in Him. But with an overflowing flood He will make an utter end of its place, and darkness will pursue His enemies* (vv. 7-8). Those who trust the Lord will find Him good, a bulwark of strength, and completely trustworthy; those who reject Him will also find Him decisively strong and utterly faithful to His Word, but sadly, too late for them to be saved.

December 11 – Lifting Up Our Burdens
Habakkuk 1

Habakkuk's prophecy was called a "burden," which is derived from the Hebrew word *massa* meaning "that which is being lifted up or carried" (v. 1). The burdened prophet lifted up weighty questions to the Lord for answers. Believers in the Church Age are also to lift up their burdens to the Lord as Habakkuk did: *"Therefore humble yourselves under the mighty hand of God, that He may exalt you in due time, casting all your care upon Him, for He cares for you"* (1 Pet. 5:6-7). Casting and lifting up in prayer those things pressing on our hearts is initially a laborious effort, but ultimately results in abiding peace.

Prayer is work, and the believer must always leave strength and time for prayer. The purpose of such praying is not to shift our loads so that we can better shoulder them (that is an exhausting waste of time), but rather to release them to the Lord to deal with as only He can. Hamilton Smith reminds us that lifting up our burdens to God is not the same as grumbling in prayer or complaining to others about them:

> In the presence of all these sorrows the prophet groans in spirit, for God's Word permits of a groan, but never a grumble (Rom. 8:22-27). Moreover, the prophet utters his groans to the Lord. Alas! Too often there is a tendency with us, as believers, to discuss among ourselves the failures of the people of God in such a spirit of bitterness that the groaning becomes mere grumbling, or complaining as to what God allows in His dealings with His people. Thus complaining words to one another may betray either a lurking spirit of rebellion against God, or an effort to exalt ourselves by belittling others. Good for us, if we escape these snares by pouring out the anguish of our spirits and the exercises of our souls before the Lord.[26]

The prophet was lifting up to heaven the burdens that were perplexing and grieving his soul: "Why was wickedness going unchecked?" "Why did God seem disinterested in punishing His people for their evil doings and in helping the righteous?" "Why was the Lord compelling him to observe unchecked evil day after day?" God's answer to Habakkuk's inquiries would enable the prophet to "see" and understand that God was very concerned with the welfare of the righteous and that He was going to punish the wayward.

December 12 – Why Lord?
Habakkuk 1

Habakkuk's petition, a sincere complaint of sorts, is framed by two inquires: First, "how long" refers to God's apparent lack of response to his prayers to judge the rampant plundering, violence, strife and contention that he was being forced to observe day after day. It is noteworthy that idolatry was not mentioned in the prophet's list, no doubt a lasting benefit of the great revival during the days of Josiah. But overall God's covenant people at this time were carnal and prone to violence and injustice. Why had not God brought relief to the righteous?

Second, "why" is used in connection to God's apparent indifference to ongoing wickedness in Judah. "Why, Lord, do you tolerate injustice and wrongdoing?" Habakkuk will repeat these same two questions during his second inquiry of the Lord (v. 13, 2:6). He saw that the Law had no power to maintain the morality of his countrymen, and justice was completely sidelined by crooked rulers.

Habakkuk probably felt as many Christians do today – it would be better to not see the deplorable state of the Church than to be constantly burdened by it and see no remedy for the worsening morality and lethargy. However, such an attitude merely contributes to the problem, for it reckons that God has not foreseen and provided for the situation.

Indeed, the Lord is building His Church and has wonderful plans for her. In a coming day, Christ shall present her to Himself as a pure, spotless bride and she will rule and reign with Him. Until then, may those who clearly see sin be burdened to pray for a reviving work of God that would invigorate the Church with holiness, devotion, and power. Let us not give up, nor think that God is not doing what we think He should. He will do all that He promises to do and all that will add honor and glory to His name.

Jehovah chose not to answer the prophet's inquiries in the manner posed to Him. Indeed, a sovereign God need not explain His actions, but in this case God wanted to reveal what He was doing and about to do, so that later His people would recognize His faithfulness in fulfilling His word. Throughout Scripture, the God of the Jews always keeps His promises! Likewise, Paul reminds Christians, *"If we are faithless, He remains faithful; He cannot deny Himself"* (2 Tim. 2:13).

December 13 – God's Answer
Habakkuk 1

It is not surprising that the Lord's response to Habakkuk and to others was not what they expected. The "you" in verse 5 is plural, meaning that the entire nation was to look, watch, and be utterly astounded: *"Look among the nations and watch – be utterly astounded! For I will work a work in your days which you would not believe, though it were told you"* (v. 5). The expression *"in your days"* indicates that what God was about to do would occur during the lifetime of the prophet and of those living with him in Judah.

The Lord's resolution to remedy the injustice that Habakkuk had been complaining about would be so shocking that it would seem unbelievable even after God told them in advance what He was about to do. Indeed, even godly Habakkuk was greatly perplexed that God would chasten Israel through wicked Babylon. Paul quotes verse 5 in the New Testament, but associates its baffling meaning to what God had accomplished through Christ at Calvary to resolve Israel's sin and rebellion: *Look among the nations and watch – be utterly astounded! For I will work a work in your days which you would not believe, though it were told you* (v. 5; Acts 13:41).

The Lord planned to use the Chaldeans (Babylonians), a ruthless and quick-acting people, to punish Israel for her idolatry and evildoings. In fact, God would use the Babylonians to sweep through the entire region to punish the wickedness of the nations (i.e., the known world at that time). God's chastening rod would be this terrible and dreadful people who, being a law and honor to themselves, were not obliged to abide by any recognized international authority or etiquette.

The Babylonians would be barbaric, high on themselves, and do whatever they pleased. Many today who deny their accountability to a sovereign Creator are marked by the same self-controlling, self-gratifying, and self-exalting disposition that marked the Babylonians.

However, their ignorant boasting was an offense against the One who had lifted them up as His instrument. He would soon use Babylon to chasten and refine His covenant people and also to punish adjoining nations for their wickedness. Yet, after His purposes were complete, God would then punish the entire nation for their vanity and brutality.

December 14 – More Questions
Habakkuk 1

Habakkuk was baffled by the Lord's initial response to his inquiry as to why He seemed indifferent to His people's sin. The prophet responds with a mixture of confidence and bewilderment:

> *Are You not from everlasting, O Lord my God, my Holy One? We shall not die. O Lord, You have appointed them for judgment; O Rock, You have marked them for correction. You are of purer eyes than to behold evil, and cannot look on wickedness. Why do You look on those who deal treacherously, and hold Your tongue when the wicked devours a person more righteous than he?* (vv. 12-14).

The gist of Habakkuk's response is: How can a God having *"purer eyes than to behold evil"* use a barbaric people, who are viler than His own people, to punish them. Habakkuk reasoned that even in their backsliding, the Jewish people were more righteous than the Babylonians.

However, the prophet was wrong in his assessment of the situation. True, the Babylonians were more pagan and more wicked than the Jewish nation, but God's people had much more revelation and were under a covenant to be a holy people. To have been given much more light and then to choose to walk in darkness is more offensive to God than to have had limited light and still be ensnared by darkness. More revelation means more divine accountability – unto whom much is given, much is required (Luke 12:48). The Jews had ignored Jehovah's Law and He was rightfully angry with His wayward people.

The prophet accepted God's Word and realized that the Jewish nation was on their own before their invaders. Yet, God would limit the severity of His judgment through the Babylonians to manifest His justice, but also to display His mercy. Accordingly, Habakkuk could rejoice in the reality that Jehovah was a covenant-keeping God and would be Israel's ultimate Rock of security and strength. God would not let Babylon bring an end to the Jewish nation – *"We shall not die"*! Clearly the prophet understood Jehovah intended to refine His people, yet, why would God use such a foul rod of correction to bring it about? God's response to Habakkuk's questions helps us to better understand how God works to accomplish His purposes and to better His people.

Daily Devotions

December 15 – Correct Me Lord
Habakkuk 2

The first chapter commenced with the prophet lifting his burdens to the Lord: Why was wickedness going unchecked? Why was the Lord not punishing evildoers and not upholding the righteous? The Lord responded by telling Habakkuk that He was aware of His people's sin and was about to severely punish them through a Babylonian invasion. Although delighted to know that God was not disinterested in Israel's doings, God's answer further perplexed Habakkuk. How could a holy God righteously use a people more wicked than the Jews to punish them? To Habakkuk it seemed wrong to permit the wicked to prosper at the expense of those more righteous (speaking of Judah).

Habakkuk did not have the answers, but knew the One who did. Like Habakkuk, we too must get alone with God to learn His mind and His ways. The Lord Jesus emphasized to His disciples the vital importance of watching and praying to accomplish the same outcome (Luke 21:36). Watching does not mean focusing on what men are doing or will do, but rather on how God will answer and direct our steps by faith. Waiting for answers is not wasted time; rather, intentional stillness before God leads us into deeper serenity and an understanding of God Himself (Ps. 46:10). This conveys our confidence in God.

In stillness and alertness Habakkuk prepared his heart to receive God's Word. While he waited anxiously for God's answer, he also thought about what his response might be, that is, *"what I will answer when I am corrected"* (v. 1). This statement indicates that although the prophet fully trusted the Lord, he was still wrestling with comprehending His ways. He longed for an answer that he knew would both correct his flawed human reasoning and enhance his appreciation for God. To pray, "Lord correct me when I am wrong and teach me what is lacking" indicates a faith that is settled in God's sovereignty.

Believers in love with the Lord Jesus do not want to err from God's best for them. Telling God that, though we do not understand what He is doing, we trust Him anyway because He is just, holy, and true is the essence of faith. If we ask the Lord to reveal the reasons for what He is doing, He may do so, but often the fullness of divine grace is revealed in time to give us a greater wonder and appreciation for what He does.

December 16 – The Just Shall Live by Faith
Habakkuk 2

Unlike the revelation posed by the phony gods of world religions in various holy books, Jehovah does not speak in poetic gibberish and vague ideas, but with clarity and directness. The Lord tells Habakkuk to write down the revelation on clay tablets to preserve it for others to read, to understand, and to herald throughout the land. Every prophecy issued by God has an appointed conclusion; some are immediate, some have a near-term fulfillment, while others will occur in the distant future. All prophecies of God are true, but some require more patience to be worked out according to God's timetable; such was the case with the prophecy that was to be written down. The fall of Babylon and the restoration of Judah would be yet future.

The wicked, like Nebuchadnezzar, naturally exalt themselves and pursue their own lusts whenever God in mercy delays their judgment (2 Pet. 3:3). In contrast to the condemned, the righteous seek to live humbly before God and to be guided by faith during such delays, *"for the just shall live by faith"* (v. 4). This verse is quoted three times in the New Testament to explain enjoying spiritual life in Christ through faith (Rom. 1:17; Gal. 3:11; Heb. 10:38). Romans emphasizes that those justified in Christ should be characterized by "just" behavior. The Galatian reference focuses on pleasing God by "living" in the resurrection power of Christ's life. The writer of Hebrews reminds us of the necessity of genuine "faith" to progress in the work of the Lord.

The message to Habakkuk (and to us too) is that trusting God and obeying His Word results in life (communion with Him), while pride and rebellion lead to death (separation from Him). Habakkuk was not to trust his feelings or emotions, but rather to have faith in God and His choices: God would chasten Judah, judge Babylon, and in the process exalt His great name in all the earth. The greatest good is accomplished when man lives by faith and trusts God with his fate.

True faith invigorates the soul with hope! Faith permits believers to discern and hold to the truth. Genuine faith enables God's people to humbly press on despite the toils of ministry and the contradiction of sinners in a sin-cursed world. "Faith is a deliberate confidence in the character of God whose ways you cannot understand at the time" (Oswald Chambers).

December 17 – Habakkuk's Doxology
Habakkuk 3

Habakkuk was burdened initially because God seemed to be unconcerned with Judah's unrestrained sin. The Lord graciously informed His prophet that He was not only aware of their wickedness, but also had been preparing an instrument to punish them – the Babylonians. When Habakkuk learned of God's plan to chasten His wayward people with the intention of restoring them and also of destroying Babylon in the process, he bowed his head in reverence. He poses no more quandaries or protests; rather, the prophet concludes his oracles with a hymn of mingled praise and thanksgiving.

After exalting the Lord, Habakkuk submits his only request in the entire prayer: *"O Lord, revive Your work in the midst of the years! In the midst of the years make it known; in wrath remember mercy"* (v. 2). This twofold petition expresses the deepest longings of the prophet. He yearned to witness the greatness of God's power in accomplishing what He had promised to do to Israel and the nations and also to see the full measure of God's mercy in pardoning Israel afterwards. Though the hour be late, may we still count on Christ to do a reviving work in the midst of His Church. Glorification of those composing the Church is assured, but a revived Church would bring glory to Christ now.

Physically, his personal encounter with God had caused his heart to pound in his chest, his lips to quiver, and his knees to knock together – he felt as if he were ready to collapse (v. 16). However, spiritually, the prophet had been revitalized to serve God with greater fervor. Peace resided in his soul and he was determined to wait patiently for the invasion of Babylon and also for the calamity that Babylon would suffer afterwards.

Even if all the fruit trees, vineyards, olive trees, croplands, flocks, and herds in Israel were confiscated or destroyed by Babylon, Habakkuk was determined to rejoice in his God despite catastrophic circumstances: *"Yet I will rejoice in the Lord, I will joy in the God of my salvation"* (v. 18). Satisfaction, full joy, and contentment are found only in the Lord – knowing and experiencing Him makes life worth living. Through this awareness, Habakkuk now felt that in faith he could rise victoriously above the hardship ahead, and hope in the promised blessings of his God for Israel.

December 18 – I Will Quiet You With My Love
Zephaniah 3

Having foretold God's judgment on nations to the west, east, south, and north of Judah, Zephaniah returns to predicting Judah's doom. The Jews had oppressed others through deceit and injustice; they had ignored God's Law, and were thoroughly polluted by paganism. God had been longsuffering with His people, but they had not received His word or His correction. Because they did not know or trust the Lord, they did not have any reason to draw near to Him.

It is absolutely important that believers continue exploring God's Word to learn more about Him and what He expects. Believers will not trust a God they do not know, let alone do what He says. Because the Jews had neglected God's Word, they had drifted into a superficial religiosity which did not value Jehovah or the things important to Him. Zephaniah then lists God's grievances against Jewish civil and religious leaders. Just as God had acted in righteousness to severely judge other wicked nations, He would also uphold His holy justice concerning those who had willfully transgressed His Law. Despite all of God's pleading through His prophets, the Jews continued in rebellion.

The "then" in verse 9 marks a major thematic change in Zephaniah's oracle – judicial wrath is replaced by immense grace. The remaining verses relate to the blessings of the Millennial Kingdom, when God will restore His covenant people to Himself and they in one accord will revere and serve Him. The Jews will be indwelt by the Holy Spirit and cleansed of all deceitful behavior and then they will enjoy the care of Israel's great Shepherd (v. 13).

With their sorrows behind them, Israel will respond with singing, shout praises, and by rejoicing in their God. But God's longings for Israel went well beyond just wanting to deliver her, care for her, and bless her; He wanted His people to know that He delighted in them: *"The Lord your God in your midst, the Mighty One, will save; He will rejoice over you with gladness, He will quiet you with His love, He will rejoice over you with singing* (v. 17). God, the Savior of Israel, will enthusiastically sing over His people to express His love and delight in them. Such is the tender affections of Christ to all the redeemed. What will it be like to be in His presence, with all sorrows past, and to be quieted by His love?

December 19 – Consider Your Ways
Haggai 1

The Jews returning from Babylon had laid the temple's foundation, but then, largely due to opposition, had decided that it was not time to rebuild God's temple. After fifteen years of inactivity, the Lord sent the prophet Haggai to ask His people a probing question and also to warn them: *"Is it time for you yourselves to dwell in your paneled houses, and this temple to lie in ruins?" Now therefore, thus says the Lord of hosts: "Consider your ways!"* (vv. 4-5). The prophet effectively confronts both the Jews' spiritual complacency and their pursuit of a comfortable standard of living in one statement. Apparently, materials earlier donated to build the temple had been used by the Jews to build themselves nice paneled houses, while God's house was in ruins. The prophet went on to inform the Jews that they were being economically penalized by God for their lethargic attitudes towards Him.

The Jews were laboring diligently and yet lacked because God was punishing them for disobedience. For example, God was withholding rain, which was limiting their agricultural prosperity. Sadly, they had drifted so far from the Lord that they had not even considered a spiritual reason for their shortages. So, Haggai appeals to them again: *"consider your ways"* (v. 7). The prophet's message was blunt: If you want God's blessing, you must obey His decree to rebuild His temple.

We in the Church Age do well to consider our ways also. For those of us who live in the affluent Western culture, the idea of trusting the Lord for our daily bread is a mostly untested theoretical concept. Little of our abundance is needed to supply our actual daily necessities and even less of it is used to feed and clothe the poor. Rather, our vast wealth is used to insulate ourselves against any conceivable mishap, to collect stuff we really don't need, and to indulge or pamper ourselves with thrills and creature comforts.

Few Christians in our post-modern society truly rely on God for their daily bread. We behave like the cosmopolitan man who has no need that he cannot provide for himself and hence surmises that he has no need for God. The prophet reminded the Jews that God could simply blow away everything they worked for with one puff of air. Their personal investments meant nothing to Him; He valued their obedience and commitment. The same is true today.

May We Serve Christ!

December 20 – By My Spirit
Zechariah 4

Zechariah was permitted to doze for a few minutes between the fourth and fifth visions, as the interpreting angel had to awaken him. The angel then asked Zechariah, *"What do you see?"* (v. 2). Zechariah said he saw two olive trees supplying oil through two receptacles and two pipes to a bowl reservoir sitting above a golden lampstand. The seven burning lamps received a constant oil supply from this bowl through seven tubes (one for each lamp). The pipes and bowl were made of gold. Zechariah asked the angel what the apparatus signified.

The angel explained that the gold lampstand symbolized the pure and faithful testimony of God to be displayed by Israel to the nations. The seven flames of the Lampstand show God's pure testimony of truth; its light is divine in origin because it is sourced by the pure oil – the Holy Spirit. As previously mentioned, the Holy Spirit is usually depicted as an active fluid in Scripture: blowing wind (John 3), seven flames (Rev. 4), rushing water (John 7), or, as witnessed in this chapter, flowing olive oil. The Holy Spirit, in these types, is not visibly doing the Father's will, but rather He is enabling it to be accomplished. Believers then, can do nothing for God without the Holy Spirit's help.

Zechariah asked what the olive trees represented, and the angel informed him that they represented Zerubbabel, Israel's governor, and Joshua, Israel's high priest, who were to lead their countrymen to complete God's House. The olive oil flowing from the trees to the bowl through gold pipes and to the lamps reflects the enabling power of the Holy Spirit to accomplish the construction task through them. Speaking of the oil, the Lord told Zechariah: *"Not by might nor by power, but by My Spirit"* (v. 6). Human wisdom, strength, and military might can never accomplish what only God's Spirit can! The bowl and conduits likely refer to the many means by which He accomplishes God's will.

By God's grace, Zerubbabel would finish building the temple, as symbolized by the expression *"he shall bring forth the capstone"* (v. 7). The outcome of this stupendous achievement would be a tremendous testimony of Jehovah's glory in Jerusalem, for Jehovah was *"jealous for Jerusalem"* (1:14). The Lord explains to His prophet that He would silence Zerubbabel's critics by completing the temple.

December 21 – The Day of Small Things
Zechariah 4

After the meaning of the golden lampstand was explained to Zechariah, the Lord then uses His prophet to rebuke those *"who despised the day of small things"* (v. 10). Who is the Lord speaking of, as those who despised the day of small things? Given verse 9, it seems likely that God is speaking to the returning remnant under Zerubbabel's leadership. Fifteen years earlier the work on the temple had stopped because the Jews were evaluating things with their own eyes instead of from God's viewpoint. Attaching smallness to those things that God greatly values leads to failure! However, Jehovah's sovereign purposes will be accomplished despite doubters and opposition, so the Jews were not to think God was not doing something great in their midst.

In verse 10, Zechariah refers to a portion of the prophet Hanani's message to King Asa: *"For the eyes of the Lord run to and fro throughout the whole earth, to show Himself strong on behalf of those whose heart is loyal to Him"* (2 Chron. 16:9). Both prophets rebuke those who thought too little of God's Word, wisdom, and His desire for their devotion. C. A. Coates suggests that verse 10 has a profound application for believers today:

> Those who despise "the day of small things" show that they ... have no idea of the greatness of what is before the mind of God ... "The eyes of Jehovah" rejoice when they see the plumb line in the hand of any builder today. Such a one has the thought of building according to the truth, of having things to correspond with the divine mind. We should bring everything to the test of the plummet. This will lead to the rejection of much that is commendable, and even imposing in the eyes of men, but there will be something which will cause the eyes of Jehovah to rejoice.[27]

When men say "not possible," God often does the impossible that He might be known. Human weakness provides a wonderful opportunity for God to add honor to His own name. Great things occur from God's point of view when small people faithfully do seemingly small things for God. Whether it is a boy taking down a giant with a stone and sling or a lad's lunch multiplied to feed thousands of hungry people, God specializes in using what is unfitting to do the incredible.

December 22 – Not My Fasts
Zechariah 7

A delegation of Jews from Bethel visited the temple (which was still under construction) about twenty-two months after Zechariah's eightfold night vision was received. The Bethel delegation inquired of the priests and prophets as to whether they should continue their mournful fasts to commemorate events related to Babylon's devastating invasion decades earlier.

Although at this time they asked about only one specific fast we later learn that for over seventy years the Jews had been observing four different self-initiated fasts (8:18). Since the Babylonian exile was over, the visiting Bethelites were wondering if they should continue recognizing the fasts associated with the siege, fall, and destruction of Jerusalem and also the death of godly Gedaliah.

The Lord bluntly informed the Jews through Zechariah that their self-concocted feasts were *their* feasts, not His; they were fasting and celebrating unto themselves. This meant that their motive and attitudes for what they were doing were flawed. Instead of wondering whether or not they had mourned sufficiently over their past calamity, they should have been inquiring into the cause of their sorrows and discerned whether or not they had truly humbled themselves before the God who had judged their rebellion. Edward Dennett suggests that Zechariah's response poses a sound principle for us to consider today also:

> In our sorrows, our weaknesses, and our chastisements under the Lord's hand, are we also not too often content with meetings for confession and humiliation, while we forget to enquire into the causes of our failures, and to ascertain what departures from the word of God may have brought us into our low condition? Let us be warned by the case before us ... the slightest departure from God's order, if known and allowed, is sufficient to grieve the Spirit of God, and to hinder blessing.[28]

Rather than self-imposed fasts, the Jews in Zechariah's day should have been concerned about honoring the Lord through obedience to His revealed Word. God was not in their fasts, because they were founded in the traditions of men. As the prophets had warned, the Lord desired true spiritual revival in His people, not their humanized rituals.

December 23 – Avoid Vain Religiosity
Zechariah 7

The spiritual problem addressed by Zechariah in chapters 7 and 8 was also addressed by Isaiah two centuries earlier: God's covenant people were engaged in religiosity in which He had no part (Isa. 58:2-5). God had only required Israel to fast one day per year (on the Day of Atonement), so why did they think fasting would somehow prompt God's favor? The answer is that they were engaged in mindless religious sacrifices, feasts, and vows, as an outward means to somehow leverage God to bless them.

The Jews in Isaiah's day even wondered if God was noticing how much they were fasting, and afflicting their souls through self-abasing religious activities. But it was obvious that their fasting was not motivated by genuine contrition because they showed no concern for the welfare of others. They were striving with each other, employers were exploiting their employees, and many were seeking their own pleasure instead of supplying the needs of others.

Because their motives for their humble religious expressions were corrupt, their prayers would not be heard and their worship would be rejected. They did not yearn to know God or to obey Him; hence there was no inward reality of faith in what they were doing – God was unimpressed. This sorrowful affliction infests much of the Church today – religious people, ignorant of who God is and what He says, are trying to impress Him through good deeds, instead of exhibiting a devotion settled in truth. Paul describes these as *"having a form of godliness but denying its power."* He then exhorts true believers, *"from such people turn away"* (2 Tim. 3:5). Believers should not be rubbing religious shoulders with those who are doing what God detests.

Believers will not value what we do not understand, nor will we sacrifice for what we do not appreciate. The entire focus of discipleship is summed up in "being," not "doing." The Lord Jesus did not say to His followers, "you cannot *become* My disciples…;" He stressed "you cannot *be* My disciples …." Discipleship is a lifelong pursuit of Christ; it is not something you suddenly arrive at one morning. A true disciple of Christ is compelled to learn of Christ (Matt. 11:29) and to be like Christ (Matt. 10:25). Before we can contemplate honoring the Lord, we must first know Him and what He desires of us.

May We Serve Christ!

December 24 – Honor Your Father
Malachi 1

In Malachi's second of six oracles (1:6-2:9), he will address how Israel has dishonored God's name and why the priests deserved God's discipline. In his rebuke, Malachi offers Israel a fourfold spiritual reality-check: The reality of their profession (v. 6), the reality of their gifts (vv. 7-8), the reality of their service (vv. 9-11), and the reality of their attitude (vv. 12-14). May we have the courage to honestly examine ourselves in each of these facets of spirituality also.

The Jews were offering polluted sacrifices, instead of giving their best to the Lord. Their sacrifices were an abomination to Jehovah because they reflected the low esteem His people had for Him and His covenant. The prophet begins his rebuke by invoking a rare title for Jehovah – *the one Father*, which Malachi uses again in the next chapter (2:10): *If then I am the Father, where is My honor? And if I am a Master, where is My reverence? Says the Lord of hosts* (v. 6). Most of the New Testament names for God are found in one form or another in the Old Testament, but one significant name – "Father" – is not, at least not in the same familiarity.

Old Testament saints did not refer in a familiar sense to God as "Father." But on resurrection day, the Lord said to Mary Magdalene, *"I ascend unto My Father, and your Father; and to My God, and your God"* (John 20:17). In the Old Testament we read of the "children of Israel" and the "people of God," but it is not until the New Testament that the intimate term "children of God" is found. By the gospel of Jesus Christ, we have *"received the Spirit of adoption by whom we cry out, 'Abba, Father'"* (Rom. 8:15).

Jehovah told Moses at Sinai that the nation of Israel was like a son to Him (Ex. 4:22). He also decreed later when Israel was at Sinai that children should honor their parents (Ex. 20:12). Thus, the title "Father" employed by Malachi is not meant to convey God's tenderness towards His wayward children, but rather to rebuke their lack of respect and obedience towards Him: *"A son honors his father, and a servant his master. If then I am the Father, where is My honor?"* (v. 6). Fathers were respected within their clans, but the Father of them all was scorned and insulted by their lip-service to His covenant and their superficial religiosity. The Jews did not truly fear Jehovah's name.

December 25 – Offering Polluted Sacrifices
Malachi 1

The priests, who were responsible for teaching the people God's commandments and prompting their devotion toward Him, had utterly failed in their primary duty. Rather than rendering sincere service to God, they had shown disdain for His name by their insensitivity to sin, by lackadaisically performing priestly duties, and by false piety (v. 6).

Malachi then puts these lethargic and ignorant priests in a defensive role by questioning God, *"In what way have we despised Your name?"* (v. 6). Malachi then answers their fictitious question: *"You offer defiled food on My altar"* (v. 7). By accepting blind, sick, and lame animals from the people and then offering them to God on His altar, the priests had broken Levitical Law and had offended the Lord (Lev. 22:18-25). From God's perspective, the priests had corrupted His table. *"The table of the Lord"* was His provision of food for the serving priests and God wanted to provide the best for those representing Him.

To prove how insulting to God such behavior was, Malachi tells the priests to offer such inferior animals to their governor and see if he would be pleased with them. This inferred that the governor would not be pleased, but rather affronted. How much more then should the Creator of all things be outraged by such offensive behavior. Malachi then wishes that someone would shut the doors of the temple to prevent the priests from kindling a fire on God's altar. It would be better to offer no sacrifices to God than to offer what was offensive to Him.

Malachi's rebuke of lethargic devotion towards the Lord is applicable for today. Although we are not under the edicts of the Law, we also offend the Lord by giving Him the "leftovers" of our time and resources in the Church Age. If we displace the meetings of the church with secular activities we teach our children what measly value the things of God have for us (Heb. 10:25).

If we give meagerly to the Lord's work, we show God how much we truly value His Son and what He accomplished at Calvary. If we neglect honoring the Lord's name in our speech and behavior through the week, why should He receive our praise and prayers on Sunday with any more legitimacy than He did of the Jewish nation in Malachi's day? Twice the prophet inquires of God's people, *"Is it not evil"* to do such things?

December 26 – The Lord's Table – Part 1
Malachi 1

When ordering the Levitical priesthood and sacrifices, God wonderfully provided for the needs of His priests, mainly through the peace offerings. God, the priests, and the common people all partook of this freewill offering, which symbolized the fellowship that God longs to enjoy with His people (Ex. 24:9-11). While atoning blood was being applied to the altar to sanctify it, the priest also appropriated the offering by eating it.

This is the pattern of Exodus 12 where the blood of a victim (the Passover lamb) was applied to sanctify the one who ate the victim's flesh. The themes of blood atonement, substitutional death, and sanctification to God are all interconnected in Scripture and, ultimately, have their typological fulfillment at Calvary. This is why the Lord Jesus instituted the Lord's Supper – He did not want believers to forget Him, nor the work that He completed to secure their salvation.

By offering substandard sacrifices, the Jews were tainting all that God was representing to them about the future work of Christ on their behalf. This weighty violation demanded God's chastening judgment instead of His blessing. Malachi informs his foolish and naive countrymen that their sacrificing behavior was provoking Jehovah to move against them; they had defiled the Lord's Table.

The Bronze Altar would be God's Table to supply His priests' needs, but the priests had to eat what was provided by the Lord before Him in the tabernacle. The New Testament equivalent of this privileged place of communion and blessing with the Lord is referred to as the "Lord's Table" (1 Cor. 10:16-22). The Lord's Table is an expression that is used in both the Old and New Testaments to convey the concept of divine provision and fellowship (Ps. 23:5, 78:19; Mal. 1:7, 12; 1 Cor. 9:13, 10:18). Both the Levitical priests under the old covenant of the Law (Lev. 6:16, 26) and believer priests under the new covenant of grace (1 Cor. 10:20-21) have been invited to abide at the Lord's Table.

The peace offering symbolizes God's fellowship with man through Christ; it was the only offering of which God, the offering priest, and the offerer all received a portion. As the believer's fellowship with God, provision from God, and ability to bless God are all pictured in the peace offering, there is much application for the Church to consider.

December 27 – The Lord's Table – Part 2
Malachi 1

Although once the enemies of God, through Christ, believers now have the opportunity to enjoy fellowship with Him and with other believers at His table and to receive daily wherewithal to serve Him. Often the biblical term "the Lord's Table" (which speaks of a spiritual table where believers receive blessings and enjoy fellowship in Christ – see 1 Corinthians 10) is confused with the biblical term "the Lord's Supper" (which refers to the remembrance meeting of the local church – see 1 Corinthians 11). Consequently, most of Christendom refers to the Lord's Supper with the non-scriptural term "the communion service." There is *communion with Christ* at the Lord's Table, but more specifically, there is a *remembrance of Christ* at every Lord's Supper – the value of His death is proclaimed afresh. The Lord's Table is spiritual and is set by Him, whereas the table at the Lord's Supper is physical and is set by us; at the former we receive provisions from the Lord, but at the latter we worship and remember Him.

To summarize, the Lord's Table speaks of the sum total of the spiritual blessings we have in Christ, while the Lord's Supper refers to the remembrance meeting of the Church. In the sense that the souls of believers are refreshed through Spirit-led worship, the Lord's Table likely includes the Lord's Supper, but the distinct terminology and significance of each should not be lost.

It is a great privilege to remember and refresh the Savior during the Lord's Supper, and it is a blessing to the heart of every believer to commune with and receive from the Savior at His table. Accordingly, Paul exhorts the believers at Corinth not to remove themselves from the Lord's Table to partake of the world's resources; to do so is to fellowship with demons: *I do not want you to have fellowship with demons. ... you cannot partake of the Lord's table and of the table of demons. Or do we provoke the Lord to jealousy? Are we stronger than He?* (1 Cor. 10:20-22).

May each believer realize the importance of eating at the Lord's Table and, accordingly, choose to abide with Him there. Failure to do so will provoke the Lord's jealousy and His chastening hand. Why would believers ever want to sever their communion with the Lord by longing for what He hates?

May We Serve Christ!

December 28 – God Deserves Our Best
Malachi 1

The prophet explains that the priests had committed two offenses against Jehovah. First, they had profaned His table by offering to Him stolen, lame, and sick animals. Because of their negligence, God bemoans, *"The table of the Lord is defiled; and its fruit, its food, is contemptible"* (v. 12). Second, the priests held God's provision for them at His table in contempt, *"'Oh, what a weariness!' and you sneer at it"* (v. 13).

Offering to God what He demanded had become burdensome and they now loathed the offerings. Although they knew what the Law demanded, they did not feel obliged to obey it – their awe of God and reverence for His ways had been supplanted by smug religious rote. Hamilton Smith suggests that the same disposition for the things of God can occur today also:

> Profession without practice, and service without devotedness, will lead to weariness in the things of the Lord, and what people are weary of they will end by despising. ... Alas, can we not see in our day this same weariness in the things of the Lord? Are there not many who were once active in the service of the Lord, but who have now grown weary? The hands hang down and the knees are feeble; the hands never lifted up in supplication, the knees never bent in prayer. They have grown weary – weary of prayer, weary of reading the Bible, weary of remembering the Lord, weary of preaching the gospel, and weary of hearing it, weary of the Lord's things, and weary of the Lord's people. And what we weary of we despise; little wonder, then, that they end by puffing at the Lord's things and the Lord's people. How deeply important to have Christ ever before us, the true motive for all service — to "consider Him," the Leader and Completer of faith, "that endured such contradiction of sinners against Himself, *lest ye be wearied and faint in your minds.*"[29]

The Law affirmed that it was both appropriate and expected that the Jews would, in thankful adoration, offer back to the Lord the best things they had received from Him. Malachi warned the Jews that offering anything less than their best to God was an insult to Him, not an act of worship! God gave us His best, His only Son, the Lord Jesus Christ; may we endeavor to give Him our best too!

December 29 – Honor the Lord's Name
Malachi 2

Having validated God's charge against His priests in the previous chapter, the prophet now admonishes them to honor the Lord or be cursed by God: *"If you will not hear, and if you will not take it to heart, to give glory to My name," says the Lord of hosts, "I will send a curse upon you, and I will curse your blessings. Yes, I have cursed them already, because you do not take it to heart"* (vv. 1-2). Under God's covenant with Israel, curses were promised for disobedience (Deut. 27:15-26, 28:15-68).

Through their blatant defiance, the priests had shown no appreciation for Jehovah's name nor had they attached proper significance to the place He had determined to set His name. God would not tolerate this transgression any longer; He was ready to invoke the judicial penalties of the Law if they did not repent.

Though the Church is not under the Law, believers today are also responsible to honor God's name by obedient conduct and to respect where He chooses to set His name. The name to be honored today is the Lord Jesus Christ – He is the head of the Church. And as P. Harding explains, those who gather in His name (speaking of the local church) have a vital obligation to honor Him through their collective testimony:

> To be gathered to the name of the Lord Jesus Christ surely means that He is the center of attraction, that His Lordship is owned and that His word is paramount. It means ... finding sufficiency in Him. His name is the sum of all that He is and involves His claims as absolute Lord. All must be in keeping with the loveliness, majesty, dignity, and holiness of His name. His name is all important and of necessity excludes all other names. It is the believers' privilege to exalt His name. Each local assembly has a responsibility to bear a faithful and harmonious testimony to all the truth of God in the locality, by complete obedience to His word and thus bring glory to His name. Those so gathered need to hear, take heed and honor God by obedience. The word of God is not given merely to increase head knowledge but to affect the heart and govern the life.[30]

Regrettably, the hearts of the Jewish priests were far from the Lord, so they did not feel the weight of disgracing the Lord's name as keenly as Malachi did. Those who stay near to the Lord will value His name.

May We Serve Christ!

December 30 – Treacherous Husbands
Malachi 2

Malachi's harsh rebuke of Jewish men divorcing their wives for carnal reasons demonstrates God's anger over unbiblical divorce. Plainly, *"God hates divorce"* and loathes the pain and violence it causes. The prophet likens such divorces to a covering garment, in that the terrible consequences of this sin are apparent for all to see. Hence, the prophet warns these Jewish men, *"Therefore take heed to your spirit, that you do not deal treacherously"* (v. 16).

God has a wonderful plan for marriage and family life, which, as Malachi tells us, necessitates a husband not forsaking the "companion" and wife of his youth (v. 14). God's aspiration for marriage was for a man and woman to enjoy intimate companionship (Gen. 2:18-20). By entering into a marriage covenant, a man and a woman become companions for life in God's best plan. The biblical meaning of marital companionship can be understood by evaluating the two Hebrew words used in the Old Testament to speak of the marriage partner.

First, the Hebrew word Malachi employs for "companion" in verse 14 is *chabereth*, which means "a wife." Its root word *chaber* means "to be united to" or "to be knit together." One aspect of companionship is a sense of duty and a commitment to stay knitted together. A marriage must be based on a forged commitment of both parties to stay together no matter what. Not only is the mindset of staying together a necessity for a marriage to thrive, but it is one of the greatest gifts to pass along to your children. Second, Solomon rebukes an adulterous wife in Proverbs 2:17, *"Who forsakes the companion of her youth, and forgets the covenant of her God."* The Hebrew word for "companion," *alluwph*, means "to be familiar and intimate, with a foremost friend." Besides commitment, another key aspect of marital companionship is intimacy, a deep desire to disclose and to be familiar with one another. God desires your spouse to be your best *earthly* friend!

Biblical companionship, therefore, consists of an unwavering duty of *commitment* and open disclosure that promotes *intimacy*. When will a marriage relationship be most satisfying? When total commitment leads to open disclosure. This type of full disclosure promotes exuberant passion being shared between a husband and wife.

December 31 – A Godly Seed
Malachi 2

Though the primary design for marriage is companionship, God also desires godly children through the marriage union of a man and a woman (v. 15). God does not desire merely morally-sound children; rather *"He seeks godly offspring."* God longs for spiritually-minded people in the world and He knows this training begins in the home (2 Cor. 12:14; Eph. 6:1-4). Parents have a God-given responsibility to train up their children for the One who gave them. C. H. Mackintosh explains why lackadaisical parenting produces unruly children:

> God has put into the parents' hand the reins of government and the rod of authority; but if parents through indolence [apathy] suffer the reins to drop from their hands, and if through false tenderness or moral weakness, the rod of authority is not applied, need we marvel if the children grow up in utter lawlessness? How could it be otherwise? Children are, as a rule, very much what we make them. If they are made to be obedient, they will be so, and if they are allowed to have their own way, the result will be accordingly.[31]

Christian parents cannot enjoy communion with God while at the same time allowing their children to be drawn into secular philosophies and to be controlled by the world's pleasures. Satan is craftily carrying away many young people into the darkness of a "teen culture" while those stronger in the faith calmly watch and do nothing. Let us be mindful of Satan's devices before he devours the next generation!

Let us remember that a Christian family is not a household of Christians, but a Christian household. It is more than Christ dwelling within the hearts of family members; it is a family that is pursuing the heart of God. If the Bible is not at the center of family life and all home affairs, that home cannot be called a true Christian home. The vital focus and objective of every Christian household is the glory of God! The Jews in Malachi's day had lost this important focus and were severely punished. May we both rely on the Lord and learn from their failures, and thus avoid the consequences of unbiblical marital life and family life. *"Unless the Lord builds the house, they labor in vain who build it"* (Ps. 127:1).

Endnotes

1. C. H. Mackintosh, *Genesis to Deuteronomy* (Loizeaux Brothers, Inc., Neptune, NJ; 1972), p. 122
2. Edythe Draper, *Draper's Quotations from the Christian World* (Tyndale House Pub. Inc., Wheaton, IL – electronic copy)
3. William MacDonald, *The Discipleship Manual* (Gospel Folio Press, Port Colborne, ON; 2004), p. 287
4. F. B. Hole, http://stempublishing.com/authors/hole/Pent/Exodus.html
5. John J. Stubbs, *What the Bible Teaches – Numbers* (John Ritchie LTD, Kilmarnock, Scotland; 2015), Num. 15:38
6. A. W. Pink, *Gleanings in Genesis* (Moody Press, Chicago: 1922), p. 187
7. William MacDonald, *Believer's Bible Commentary* (Thomas Nelson Pub., Nashville, TN; 1990), p. 240
8. C. H. Mackintosh, *The Mackintosh Treasury* (Believers Bookshelf Inc., Beamsville, ON; 1999), p. 228
9. Matthew Henry, *Matthew Henry's Concise Commentary on the Whole Bible* (e-Sword, electronic version), 2 Sam. 21:15-22
10. Ibid., 1 Kgs. 11:1-8
11. C. A. Coates, *C. A. Coates Commentary – An Outline of the First Book of Kings* (Kingston Bible Trust, West Sussex, UK), 1 Kgs. 15
12. George Williams, *The Student's Commentary on the Holy Scriptures* (Kregel Pub., Grand Rapids, MI; 1956), p. 196
13. Elmer L Towns and Charles Billingsley, *God Laughs* (Regal/Gospel Light, Ventura, CA; 2011), pp. 147-148
14. D. L. Moody, *Notes From My Bible: From Genesis to Revelation* (Fleming H. Revell, New York, NY; reprint from 1895), 2 Kgs. 5
15. Edward Dennett, *The Christian's Friend Magazine* (1885) http://stempublishing.com/magazines/cf/1885/Ezra.html
16. William MacDonald, *Believer's Bible Commentary*, op. cit., pp. 501-502
17. Allen Ross, *The Bible Knowledge Commentary*, edited by J. F. Walvoord and Roy Zuck (Victor Books, Wheaton, IL; 1986), p. 884-885
18. Ryrie, *Ryrie Study Bible* (NKJV), (Moody Press, Chicago, IL; 1986), p. 1054
19. William Kelly, *Notes on Jeremiah and Lamentations*, http://www.stempublishing.com/authors/kelly/1Oldtest/jeremiah.html
20. J. N. Darby, *Synopsis of the Books of the Bible Vol. 4* (Stow Hill Bible and Tract Depot, Kingston, ON: 1948), p. 279
21. William MacDonald, *Believer's Bible Commentary* (Thomas Nelson Publishers, Nashville, TN; 1989), p. 1082
22. Warren Wiersbe, *Wiersbe's Expository Outlines on the Old Testament* (Victor Books, Wheaton, IL; 1993), Jonah 1:1

[23] NOAA's National Marine Fisheries: The Kid's Times: The Spear Whale (Vol. 2 Issue) *www.nmfs.noaa.gov/pr/pdfs/education/kids_times_whale_sperm.pdf* [last accessed April 7, 2017]
[24] Donald J. Wiseman, *Jonah's Nineveh* (The Tyndale Biblical Archaeology Lecture, 1977), Tyndale Bulletin #30, p. 50
[25] W. W. Fereday, *Jonah*, STEM Publishing, The Compassionate Creator: http://stempublishing.com/authors/fereday/JONAH.html
[26] Hamilton Smith, *Habakkuk*, STEM Publishing, Hab. 1: http://stempublishing.com/authors/smith/HABAKKUK.html
[27] C. A. Coates, *C. A. Coates Commentary – Zechariah* (Kingston Bible Trust, West Sussex, UK), Zech. 4
[28] Edward Dennett, *Zechariah*, STEM Publishing, Zech. 7: http://stempublishing.com/authors/dennett/Zecharia.html
[29] Hamilton Smith, *Malachi*, STEM Publishing, Mal. 1: http://stempublishing.com/authors/smith/Malachi.html
[30] P. Harding, *What the Bible Teaches – Malachi* (John Ritchie LTD, Kilmarnock, Scotland; 2015), Mal. 2:2
[31] C. H. Mackintosh, *The Mackintosh Treasury* (Gute Botschaft, Dillenburg, Germany; reprinted by Loizeaux Brothers, Inc., Neptune, NJ; 1972), p. 500

OLD TESTAMENT
Devotional Commentary Series

- Christ-Centered Exposition
- Life-Changing Application
- Fourteen Volumes
- Over 5,400 Pages
- Nearly 200 Contributors

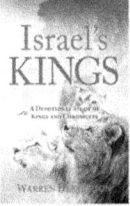

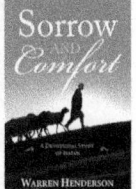

The primary purpose for studying God's Word is to know the Lord and learn how to please Him. The aim of a devotional commentary is to help the reader pause and consider the deeper, life-related implications of the portion being read. What is God telling us about His character, emotions and attributes? How is His plan of salvation being displayed? How should we respond to His Word? Today, the Christian community sits atop a vast array of written resources, many of which have been penned by those who have gone to be with Christ. Though some of these books are out of print, they still display a relevance to current issues while maintaining a deeply devotional viewpoint, sadly lacking in much of today's Christian literature. This *OT Devotional Commentary Series* captures some of the richest gleanings of nearly two hundred time-honored authors whose goal was sound biblical exposition that would magnify Christ and lead to godly living. Each volume contains dozens of brief devotions. This permits the reader to use the series as a daily devotional or as a reference source for deeper study.

— *Warren Henderson*

May We See Christ – An Old Testament Journey is a sequential study of Scripture containing 366 two-page devotions (758 pages). Besides the plain language of the Old Testament, God has employed a variety of types, symbols, and allegories in a complementary fashion to teach us about His Son. With the light of New Testament truth and the illuminating assistance of the Holy Spirit, we are able to understand and appreciate these fascinating Old Testament pictures. All of God's written Word speaks of Christ to some degree as He is the main emphasis of Scripture. Accordingly, the best reason to embark on this one-year journey is to more clearly see, know, and love Christ. May the Lord richly bless your daily contemplations of the Savior as you expectantly peer into God's oracles and witness the glory of His Son. — Warren Henderson

www.ingramcontent.com/pod-product-compliance
Lightning Source LLC
Chambersburg PA
CBHW060453090426
42735CB00011B/1971